TALK T·H·A·T TALK

An Anthology of African-American Storytelling

EDITED BY
LINDA GOSS & MARIAN E. BARNES

A TOUCHSTONE BOOK
Published by Simon & Schuster Inc.
New York   London   Toronto   Sydney   Tokyo

SIMON AND SCHUSTER/TOUCHSTONE
Simon & Schuster Building
Rockefeller Center
1230 Avenue of the Americas
New York, New York 10020

Designed by Sheree L. Goodman
Manufactured in the United States of America

Library of Congress Cataloging in Publication Data

Talk that talk : an anthology of African-American
storytelling /
edited by Linda Goss and Marian E. Barnes.
p.   cm.
"A Touchstone book."
1. Afro-Americans—Folklore.
2. Tales—United States.
3. Afro-Americans—History—Miscellanea.
I. Goss, Linda.
II. Barnes, Marian.
GR111.A47T35   1989
398.2'089'96073—dc20   89-10582
CIP

ISBN 0-671-67167-7
0-671-67168-5 Pbk.

1 3 5 7 9 10 8 6 4 2 Pbk.
1 3 5 7 9 10 8 6 4 2 Pbk.

Grateful acknowledgment is made for permission to reprint copyrighted material. Every reasonable effort has been made to trace the ownership of all copyrighted material included in this volume. Any errors that may have occurred are inadvertent and will be corrected in subsequent editions, provided notification is sent to the publisher. Permissions continue on pages 512–517.

PERMISSIONS

Achebe, Chinua—"Death of a Young Boy" by Chinua Achebe, from *Things Fall Apart* by Chinua Achebe. Copyright © 1959 by Chinua Achebe. Astor-Honor publishers, New York. Reprinted by permission of the author.

ACKNOWLEDGMENTS

T his project was a mammoth undertaking. I am deeply grateful to all of the friends, acquaintances, research assistants, typists, and scholars who helped me get through this. Storytelling is a shared experience. The storyteller calls out and the audience responds. I thank the following people for responding to my call:

Carole Weathers, Imani Lumumba, Carla Glasser, John Henrik Clarke, Maxine LeGall, Jermiah Nabawi, Geraldine Butler, Gerald Davis, Bill Wiggins, Larry Coleman, Joyce Wills, Tom McCabe, Jackie Trescott, Sonia Sanchez, Guy Carawan, LaWanda Randall, Reverend Caldwell, Rita Cox, Mary Carter Smith, Mary Umolu, Eleanor Tate, Constance Garcia-Barrio, Bill McNear, Martha Ruff, Ida Lewis, Amina Dickerson, Caroliese Fink Reed, Kofi Enini, Suzanne Hughes, Ardie Brown, Candece Tarpley, Yaa Asantewah, Ama Akumaaba, Leslie German, and Carole Hall.

Special thanks to the following organizations for allowing me to use their space and materials: The Association of Black Storytellers, Hola Kumbaya, My Solitude, Moonstone, Inc., the Charles Blockson Collection at Temple University.

—Linda Goss

DEDICATION

T o the Association of Black Storytellers who have perpetuated the African-American oral tradition by supporting "In the Tradition..." Festival of Black Storytelling.

To the Honored Ancestors such as Aesop, Sojourner Truth, Frederick Douglass, Charles Chestnutt, Ida B. Wells-Barnett, Carter G. Woodson, Edmonia Lewis, Arna Bontemps, Zora Neale Hurston, Langston Hughes, and Horace "Spoons" Williams, the pioneers of African and African-American storytelling who have shared with the world the beauty and power of our heritage.

To the Esteemed Elders such as Mary Carter Smith, Hugh Morgan Hill (Brother Blue), Maya Angelou, John Henrik Clarke, Mary Umolu, Vinnie Burrows, Jesse Jackson, and Rosa Parks who are the keepers of history and the weavers of dreams.

And to my family: my mother and father, Willie Louise McNear and Willie Murphy McNear; my husband Clay and our children, Aisha, Uhuru, and Jamaal; my mother-in-law and father-in-law, Alfreda and Douglas Jackson; and to the memory of my grandfather, Murphy McNear, on whose front porch I sat, forced to listen to his stories. So glad you made me listen, Grand-daddy.

—Linda Goss

CONTENTS

3

CONTENTS

PREFACE
ABOUT THE ART AND THE ARTISTS

O ur storytelling is in the midst of a sweeping renaissance. Brought into the Americas by African captives, the art form remained largely dormant among descendants of the original captives except in family and church meetings. Now, however, primarily through the work of pioneering giants in the profession such as Brother Blue (Hugh Morgan Hill, Ph.D.), Mary Carter Smith, and Jackie Torrence, the art is being resurrected.

The Black oral heritage is alive and growing among people of African blood, whose ancestors presumably originated storytelling with the creation of civilization in Africa, and among other ethnic groups as well. Calls for storytellers are crisscrossing the nation and much of the world. Audiences vary from intimate family gatherings to international storytelling festivals.

Who are these storytellers? What kinds of stories are they telling? Doubtless for the first time in history this book records in writing the answers to these and other questions about Black storytellers and their profession.

Masters of the spoken word in the true African tradition, Black storytellers are forming and adapting stories that reach and teach the hearts and minds of listeners in inimitable ways. It was sometimes frustrating for these contemporary artists to *write* the stories they tell. Typical comments: "It's not the same," "The writing falls flat," "How do I write to get the same effect I get from speaking?" Nevertheless, they persevered because although it is true that oral stories can lose some of their color and liveliness when put in writing, there is a gain that makes the change worthwhile. In the past, oral stories, and the identities of their tellers, were often lost to future generations because there were no written records. Now, storytellers yet unborn will be able to breathe new life into our tales and adapt them to the needs of listeners and readers of their time.

Meantime, present-day readers can enjoy meeting oral storytellers through this book, and, we hope, be enticed by it to experience the joys of attending their performances.

Since the beginning of time folks have always wanted to spread the word. The ones who can spread the word the most effectively have the ability to "talk dat talk" and "walk dat walk." In other words they can grab the imagination of the listener and hold on to it for as long as they like, conjuring up images of the good and the bad, the weak and the strong, and the trickster and the fool. They have the ability to make you laugh until you cry, cry until you laugh, stand up and shout, or stare in amazement at their gestures and characterizations.

In the African-American culture, past and present, these folks have gone by many names. Today they are called preachers, healers, teachers, comedians, blues singers, poets, dancers, rappers, liars, painters, and historians. In a performance, all storytellers will use whatever it takes to get the story across. To hear them is to hear the drum, the heartbeat of Africa. To see them tell the story is to experience highlights of African ritual, at its best, a total theatrical performance.

The storyteller, the story, and the audience are of equal importance. The drummers or musicians set the tone. The dancers or singers warm up the audience. The audience gives their approval by clapping their hands, swaying to the beat, and shouting comments or praises. The storyteller enters, dressed for the occasion in attire that may be colorful and exciting to arouse the curiosity or formal to create a serious mood. The storyteller senses the vibrations of the audience and begins to deliver the story, using his or her voice to mimic the characters. The storyteller may chant or scream. The storyteller may crawl around or jump up and down. The storyteller sweats, and the audience loves it, because this means that the storyteller is doing all that he or she possibly can to please them. The story is full of emotions, full of humor, full of rhythmic language, and full of wisdom.

The storyteller and the audience are flexible. No one worries about making a mistake. No mistakes are made. Something new is being

created. The story has fired up the audience. The storyteller has succeeded, and he or she exits in a fashion that will also be remembered.
The story has not ended. The audience has taken it home with them,
and the next day they spread the word to the ones who were not
there to witness the event.

As Dr. Pearl E. Primus reminds us, the African-American tradition
is rooted in Africa where there are many kinds of storytellers. She
explains:

There is the person who has exhibited the genius of tale telling from
childhood. The community enjoys and encourages that person. He is
given every conceivable opportunity while growing up to practice and
to polish the telling. While there are some fantastic female weavers of
tales, the vast majority of those who rise to tell the story in the evenings in the African compounds are males. They are usually of the
generation of the parents or grandparents. Such a person in Sanni-
quellie, Liberia, would dance and tell "Why Mr. Spider Has Such a
Small Waistline." Such a man would have his audiences laughing un-
controllably in Trinidad, West Indies, as he tells "How Baby Devils
Are Born."

There is the itinerant storyteller. This person is usually a professional artist traveling alone or with a very well-rehearsed troupe of
singers and dancer-actors. The community is informed ahead of time
when and where the event will take place. Sometimes it is the villagers
who send and invite the artist for a special occasion, which can be
accompanied by great feasting. Tremendous preparations are made for
the telling of the tales. The artists arrive and set up camps. The event
could last for days, with different stories dramatically told at different
times. In the hills of Makamba in Burundi, tale telling is the time for
the entire community to enjoy its own finest dancers, singers, and
musicians, as well as the magic of the visiting artists.

In the homes the basic culture values are subtly taught as the
mothers or big sisters prepare the evening meals or as the elders sit
around talking of events long past. A mother in Nigeria would often
amuse her children with "Why the Tortoise Has a Cracked Shell" or
"Why Turtle Lives in the Forest." Old men in Zimbabwe would
smoke their pipes and laugh aloud at the telling of "How Rabbit
Tricked Lion." Children sitting in the shadows of the house are learning that greed, laziness, dishonesty, arrogance, and theft are all negative values which their society will not tolerate. The tales fill in time,
teach, amuse, bring members of family close together.

Then there is one of the most important storytellers, the historian.

Among many people he is known as the *griot*. According to the Wolof people of the Senegal, West Africa, the true name is *gewel*. The term *griot* is a European adaptation. It also is used today by many groups of indigenous people. The *griot (gewel)* is that revered individual in the society who is entrusted with the exact cultural history. This exalted position is inherited. There are families in West Africa who have claimed this honor for many, many generations. The art of the griot requires music and song skill and also an unerring memory. The spiritual life of the citizens of the community, past, present, and future, rest in the virtuosity and unerring exactness of the griot. The songs of the griot are more precise than any history book. The writing of history books and the interpretation of the written words are not the valued duties of one special family spiritually endowed and given the sacred mandate by the Creator. The griot occupies a position of great historical importance not only in the cultural heritage of people of African ancestry but in the heritage of all peoples of the world.

Several African stories and storytellers are featured in this collection to illustrate the traditions from which our stories have grown.

Most of the contemporary African-American storytellers who have contributed stories for the anthology have been featured at "In the Tradition..." Festival of Black Storytelling. The purpose of this festival, founded by Linda Goss and Mary Carter Smith in 1982, was to show the rich diversity of African and African-American storytelling styles, to preserve these traditional stories and highlight contemporary stories, and to share their heritage with the world. The first festival was held in November 1983 in Baltimore, Maryland, on the campus of Morgan University. It was sponsored by Zeta Phi Beta Sorority through a grant from the Maryland Humanities Council. Over a thousand people attended.

Since that time the festival has been held in Philadelphia, Pennsylvania; Washington, D.C.; Chicago, Illinois; Berea, Kentucky; and Oakland, California. Medgar Evers College in Brooklyn, New York, is the host for the 1989 festival. New Orleans is the site for the 1990 festival.

The Association of Black Storytellers, formed in Philadelphia in 1984 to support the festival, finds future sites and publishes a newsletter that promotes African and African-American storytelling. What is unique and positive about the festival is that scholar embraces layperson, folklorist embraces folk artist, storyteller embraces historian, writer embraces preacher, and friend embraces friend. Everyone comes together in the name of storytelling and cultural pride.

Talk That Talk: An Anthology of African-American Storytelling attempts to embrace those same goals. We have included a variety of stories from a variety of storytellers who come from a variety of places. It is important for the reader to realize that animal tales and humorous tales are not the only kind of stories Black folks tell. It is important for the reader to understand that African-American storytelling does not begin and end with Uncle Remus, a character created by Joel Chandler Harris. It is crucial for the reader to feel the pain and suffering of slavery as well as the love Black folks have for each other.

This anthology is not solely a collection of folklore but a celebration of storytelling, including revivalist storytellers who tell stories they have learned through research and collecting, traditional storytellers who tell stories from their family and community backgrounds and experiences, and literary writers whose works reflect the language, rhythm, and other elements of African and African-American storytelling.

Talk That Talk contains commentaries by outstanding scholars and experts in the fields of folklore and storytelling. Now readers can share in the research that has been documented by African-American folklorists.

Zora Neale Hurston, J. Mason Brewer, Arthur Huff Fauset, Carter G. Woodson, Sterling Brown, Langston Hughes, and Arna Bontemps are all pioneers in collecting and preserving the African-American oral tradition. Contemporary folklorists such as Gerald Davis, Kathryn Morgan, Gladys Frye, William Wiggins, John Roberts, Daryl C. Dance, Beverly Robinson, Bernice Johnson Reagon, and Henry Louis Gates, Jr., to name a few, are some of the African-American scholars carrying on the tradition.

In the United States the African American has continually questioned his or her true identity. We have created new words and phrases to describe who we are and what we want. The stories in the anthology show that progression; therefore, the reader will see words such as, colored, Negro, Black, Afro-American, African-American, and African throughout the stories. Some of the stories are written in dialect to preserve their authenticity. Some of the stories are written in a poetic form to emphasize the phrasing of the teller. We hope while reading each story the reader will be able to hear the story-teller's voice and will be fascinated by it and will spread the word to others.

As an old man once said, I got a story in me and I aim to tell it as long and as loud as I please.

Introduction: Narration and Cultural Memory in the African-American Tradition

by Henry Louis Gates, Jr.

The encounter between African languages (Yoruba, Igbo, Twi, Ki-kongo, and many others) and Western languages (French, Spanish, Dutch, Portuguese, English) was perhaps the most subtle and most complex aspect of the cultural confrontation that the African slaves faced in the New World. Radically abstracted from their cultural communities, and broadly dispersed from plantation to plantation, state to state, and country to country, the African slaves in much of North America soon lost the capacity to speak their own African languages. Eager to "domesticate" the African slave by denying him and her their language, their religion, their values and belief systems, and indeed their entire sense of order, the slave owners, first, forbade the usage of African languages on their plantations. Soon after, the drum—through which those Africans speaking tonal languages (such as Yoruba) could communicate—was also prohibited. To facilitate this nefarious process of domestication, Africans from similar cultural regions were dispersed throughout various plantations, in an attempt to make communication in a language other than English virtually impossible. The strictest, most brutal forms of punishment were meted out to those Africans insistent upon retaining their own languages, calling themselves by their true names, or those intent upon continuing those cultural practices, such as religious ceremonies, that they had brought with them through the barbarous Middle Passage.

What we might usefully think of as the Americanization of the slave took place, most directly and forcibly, at the level of language.

For it is through our language that we know, and name, the world. True, the African slave—despite the horrors of the Middle Passage —did not sail to the New World alone. These African slaves brought with them their metaphysical systems, their languages, their terms for order, their expressive cultural practices which even the horrendous Middle Passage and the brutality of everyday life on the plantation could not effectively obliterate. What the planters sought to do—and what they failed to do—was to make of the African's consciousness of his or her cultural self a veritable *tabula rasa,* a blank slate, on which to build a new cultural and social order, and in which the very concept of "Africanness" was obliterated and erased, and the concepts of "slave," "absence," "evil"—and virtually every other negative connotation in the Western culture of "blackness" itself—would be reinscribed on this supposedly empty space.

But inscribed with what? Certainly the slaveholders did not want the slave to have access to the principles of individual liberty that would ultimately prevail in the United States. Learning to read and write, accordingly, were forbidden to the slaves by law. It is not an accident that those ex-slaves who managed to publish their autobiographical slave narratives almost always dramatized, early in their tales, the manner by which they learned to read and write. So important was this process to gaining their individual freedom that the relation between freedom and literacy became a motif in African-American literature, from ex-slaves such as Frederick Douglass and Harriet Jacobs to modern novelists such as Zora Neale Hurston and Ralph Ellison, or Ishmael Reed, Alice Walker, and Toni Morrison. For black people, learning to read and write, and simultaneously to tell their *own* stories, was as important to the gaining of freedom as was the Emancipation Proclamation, the Civil War, or even the Civil Rights movement.

But how would black people, no longer Africans but prevented from truly becoming "Americans," tell their own stories in their own culturally resonant voices? It is crucial to remember, first of all, that the space of black culture in the lives of the slaves was never—and could never possibly be—an empty one. Despite the severe restrictions against the preservation of indigenous African cultural forms, and the concomitant legal prohibitions against literacy mastery, black people *merged* what they could retain from their African heritage with forms that they could appropriate from the various New World cultures into which they had been flung. The blends that they forged, and which the horrible institution of slavery made possible, was a new culture, a culture at once "Pan-African" (composed as it was of several West African cultural strands) and Western. In the instance of the African in America, a truly African-American expressive culture emerged from deep inside of the bowels of enslavement.

This African-American culture was a veritable "underground" culture, shared surreptitiously, as it were, by word of mouth. African-Americans nurtured a private but collective oral culture, one they could not "write down," but one they created, crafted, shared with each other and preserved for subsequent generations out loud, but outside of the hearing of the white people who enslaved them, and, later, discriminated against them. It was in this isolated and protected black cultural space that African-American vernacular culture was born and thrived. Charting with any scholarly precision this complex and marvelous process of cultural formation and transformation is extraordinarily difficult to do, precisely because the process was surreptitious. Nevertheless, and quite uncannily, what was essentially an isolated, Southern, rural phenomenon migrated North and West with the ex-slaves, underwent various sets of transformations in urban settings, became transformed again and again as blacks continued to migrate throughout the country, and eventually emerged as a national black culture. And of the cultural forms that emerged from their complicated historical process, only black music-making was as important to the culture of African-Americans as has been the fine art of storytelling.

Telling ourselves our own stories—interpreting the nature of our world to ourselves, asking and answering epistemological and ontological questions in our own voices and on our own terms—has as much as any single factor been responsible for the survival of African-Americans and their culture. The stories that we tell ourselves and our children function to order our world, serving to create both a foundation upon which each of us constructs our sense of reality and a filter through which we process each event that confronts us every day. The values that we cherish and wish to preserve, the behavior that we wish to censure, the fears and dread that we can barely confess in ordinary language, the aspirations and goals that we most dearly prize—all of these things are encoded in the stories that each culture invents and preserves for the next generation, stories that, in effect, we live by and *through*. And the stories that survive, the stories that manage to resurface under different guises and with marvelous variations, these are a culture's *canonical* tales, the tales that contain the cultural codes that are *assumed* or internalized by members of that culture. For the African-American, deprived by law of the tools of literacy, the narration of these stories in black vernacular forms served to bring together the several colorful fragments of lost African cultures in a spectacularly blended weave that we call African-American culture.

Linda Goss and Marian E. Barnes have brought together these canonical narratives of the African-American experience in this country in all of their splendor. Never before has an entire anthology been devoted to collecting black canonical vernacular stories in such a wide variety. While drawing upon important precedents such as Langston Hughes and Arna Bontemps's *The Book of Negro Folklore* (and others), Goss and Barnes have managed to compile a collection of black stories unrivaled in its scope and breadth. Animal tales from slavery, historical narratives that recounted the achievements of great black women and men and of crucial historical events, classic sermons such as "The Prodigal Son" and "Ezekiel and the Vision of Dry Bones," maternal narratives told by black mothers to their daughters and sons, tales that perform the didactic function of conveying expectations about the institutions of marriage, the family, and parenthood, fantastic stories replete with ghosts and witches, mythic tales of duplicity, trickery, and the triumph of noble black figures over both natural and supernatural evil (such as the Devil himself), amusing tales that sketch the range of humor in the black tradition, short stories from the formal black literary tradition, even narratives ranging from the blues to rhythm and blues to rap—all of these types of tales are collected here. The book is divided into sections by genre, and each chapter is followed by a superb commentary by scholars *and* by those who perform the art of storytelling themselves. I find this interpretive frame one of the most attractive and useful innovations in an anthology that is innovative in so many ways. These interpretive essays will help both those deeply familiar with this material and those who are encountering it for the first time, to understand the nature and function of allegorical tales cast in a rich and densely figurative language, "adorned," as Zora Neale Hurston used to say, with the figures of speech of black culture. Each of these essays has been well chosen, and is especially informative.

Precisely when a debate is raging in this country over "multiculturalism," over the relation that the various American cultures bear to

Western culture, *Talk That Talk* has defined the history and contours of one salient aspect of African-American vernacular culture. This is the anthology of black vernacular culture that all of us who teach black literature have been waiting for. Every written literary tradition has been constructed upon a foundation of oral and performative culture. *Talk That Talk* will make it easier for scholars to document the fascinating relation between the culture that slaves, ex-slaves, and "the folk" made, and the written culture created by the creative author. But *Talk That Talk* is not only for scholars; it is a delightfully readable work that families can—and will—read aloud to each other in the evenings. Not only every African-American household, but every *American* household, should own a copy of this important book.

WHEN THE ANIMALS TALKED:
Animal Tales and Fables

No fish ever got caught with its mouth shut.

—*Curaçao proverb*

STORIES

BRER TIGER
AND THE BIG WIND

Retold by WILLIAM J. FAULKNER

Most of the stories William J. Faulkner tells were told to him by
Simon Brown, a former slave from Virginia who lived in Society Hill,
a section of Columbia, South Carolina, around 1900 and who for
years was employed by Faulkner's mother to work on their farm.

In olden days, the creatures used to plow in the fields and plant
their crops the same as menfolks. When the rains came, the crops
were good. But one year no rain came, and there was a famine in
the land. The sun boiled down like a red ball of fire. All the creeks
and ditches and springs dried up. All the fruit on the trees shriveled,
and there was no food and no drinking water for the creatures. It was
a terrible time.

But there was one place where there was plenty of food and a
spring that never ran dry. It was called the Clayton Field. And in the
field stood a big pear tree, just a-hanging down with juicy pears,
enough for everybody.

So the poor hungry creatures went over to the field to get something to eat and something to drink. But a great big Bengal tiger
lived under the pear tree, and when the creatures came nigh, he rose
up and said, "Wumpf! Wumpf! I'll eat you up. I'll eat you up if you
come here!" All the creatures backed off and crawled to the edge of
the woods and sat there with misery in their eyes, looking at the field.
They were so starved and so parched that their ribs showed through
their hides and their tongues hung out of their mouths.

Now, just about that time, along came Brer Rabbit, just a-hopping and a-skipping, as if he'd never been hungry or thirsty in his life.

"Say, what's the matter with you creatures?" asked Brer Rabbit.

"We're hungry and thirsty and can't find any food or water—that's what's the matter with us," answered the creatures. "And we can't get into the Clayton Field because Brer Tiger said he'd eat us up if we came over there."

"That's not right," said Brer Rabbit. "It's not right for one animal to have it all and the rest to have nothing. Come here. Come close. I'm going to tell you something." And Brer Rabbit jumped up on a stump so that all could see him as they crowded around. When Brer Rabbit had finished whispering his plan, he said, "Now, you-all be at your posts in the morning; everyone be there before sunup."

The first animal to get to his post was Brer Bear. Before daybreak, he came toting a big club on his shoulder and took his place alongside an old hollow log. The next creature to arrive was Brer Alligator Cooter, a snapping turtle, who crawled in the hollow log. Then Brer Turkey Buzzard and Brer Eagle and all the big fowls of the air came a-sailing in and roosted in the tops of the tall trees. Next to arrive were the tree-climbing animals, like Brer Raccoon and his family and Sis Possum and all her little ones. They climbed into the low trees. Then followed the littler creatures, like Brer Squirrel, Brer Muskrat, Brer Otter, and all kinds of birds. They all took their posts and waited for Brer Rabbit.

Pretty soon, when the sun was about a half hour high, along came Brer Rabbit down the big road with a long grass rope wrapped around his shoulder. And he was just a-singing. "Oh, Lord, oh, Lord, there's a great big wind that's a-coming through the woods, and it's going to blow *all* the people off the earth!" And while he was singing his song, a powerful noise broke out in the woods.

There was Brer Bear a-beating on the hollow log with all his might, bic-a-bam, bic-a-bam, bic-a-bam, bam, bam! Inside the log Brer Cooter was a-jumping, bic-a-boom, bic-a-boom, bic-a-boom, boom, boom. Brer Turkey Buzzard, Brer Eagle, and Brer Chicken Hawk were a-flapping their wings and a-shaking the big trees, and the trees were a-bending, and the leaves were a-flying. Brer Raccoon and Sis Possum were stirring up a fuss in the low trees, while the littler creatures were a-shaking all the bushes. And on the ground and amongst the leaves the teeny-weeny creatures were a-scrambling around. All in all it sounded like a cyclone was a-coming through the woods!

All this racket so early in the morning woke Brer Tiger out of a deep sleep, and he rushed to the big road to see what was going on. "What's going on out there, huh?" he growled. "What's going on out there?"

All of the creatures were too scared to say anything to Brer Tiger. They just looked at him and hollered for Brer Rabbit to "Tie me! Please, sir, tie me!"

Now, all this time Brer Rabbit just kept a-hollering, "There's a *great* big cyclone a-coming through the woods that's going to *blow* all the people off the earth!" And the animals just kept a-making their noise and a-hollering, "Tie me, Brer Rabbit. Tie me."

When Brer Rabbit came around by Brer Tiger, Brer Tiger roared out, "Brer Rabbit, I want you to tie me. I don't want the big wind to blow *me* off the earth!"

"I don't have time to tie you, Brer Tiger. I've got to go down the road to tie those other folks to keep the wind from blowing *them* off the earth. Because it sure looks to me like a *great big hurricane* is a-coming through these woods."

Brer Tiger looked toward the woods, where Brer Bear was a-beating and Brer Cooter was a-jumping and the birds were a-flapping and the trees were a-bending and the leaves were a-flying and the bushes were a-shaking and the wind was a-blowing, and it seemed to him as if Judgment Day had come.

Old Brer Tiger was so scared he couldn't move. And then he said to Brer Rabbit, "Look-a-here, I've got my head up against this pine tree. It won't take but a minute to tie me to it. Please tie me, Brer Rabbit. Tie me, because I don't want the wind to blow me off the face of the earth."

Brer Rabbit shook his head. "Brer Tiger, I don't have time to bother with you. I have to go tie those other folks; I told you."

"I don't care about those other folks," said Brer Tiger. "I want you to tie *me* so the wind won't blow *me* off the earth. Look, Brer Rabbit, I've got my head here against this tree. Please, sir, tie me."

"All right, Brer Tiger. Just hold still a minute, and I'll take out time to save your striped hide," said Brer Rabbit.

Now, while all this talking was going on, the noise kept getting louder and louder. Somewhere back yonder it sounded like thunder was a-rolling! Brer Bear was still a-beating on the log, bic-a-bam, bic-a-bam, bic-a-bam, bam, bam! Brer Cooter was still a-jumping in the log, bic-a-boom, bic-a-boom, bic-a-boom, boom, boom! And the birds were a-flapping and the trees were a-bending and the leaves were a-flying and the bushes were a-shaking and the creatures were a-crying—and Brer Rabbit was a-tying!

He wrapped the rope around Brer Tiger's neck, and he pulled it tight; he wrapped it around Brer Tiger's feet, and he pulled it tight. Then Brer Tiger tried to pitch and rear, and he asked Brer Rabbit to tie him a little tighter, "because I don't want the big wind to blow me off the earth." So Brer Rabbit wrapped him around and around so tight that even the biggest cyclone in the world couldn't blow him away. And then Brer Rabbit backed off and looked at Brer Tiger.

When he saw that Brer Tiger couldn't move, Brer Rabbit called out, "Hush your fuss, children. Stop all of your crying. Come down here. I want to show you something. Look, there's our great Brer Tiger. He had all the pears and all the drinking water and all of everything, enough for everybody. But he wouldn't give a bite of food or a drop of water to anybody, no matter how much they needed it. So now, Brer Tiger, you just stay there until those ropes drop off you. And you, children, gather up your crocus sacks and water buckets. Get all the pears and drinking water you want, because the Good Lord doesn't love a stingy man. He put the food and water here for all His creatures to enjoy."

After the animals had filled their sacks and buckets, they all joined in a song of thanks to the Lord for their leader, Brer Rabbit, who had shown them how to work together to defeat their enemy, Brer Tiger.

NO TRACKS COMING BACK

Collected by ARTHUR HUFF FAUSET

You know Brer Rabbit said to be the wisest animal in the forest. So Brer Rabbit was walkin' along one day when Brer Fox come along. "Say, Brer Rabbit," Brer Fox says, "ain't you goin' to de big meetin'? Everybody goin'." "Zat so," says Brer Rabbit, "sure I'm goin'." So Brer Fox went off an' Brer Rabbit he take an' look aroun'. Pretty soon he see hundreds o' footprints an' all goin' in de sam direction. Den he see dey all rabbit tracks. "Mmm," says Brer Rabbit, "all dem tracks goin' dat way, an' not a single one comin' dis way. Dat ain't no place fo' me."

BR'ER RABBIT
AND THE BRIAR PATCH

ANNIE REED

Way back in de old days, when de creatures was all people, Br'er Fox give a log-rollin' and invite all de neighborhood. Br'er Possum was dere, and Br'er Rabbit, and all de rest. Old Sis' Fox and some de neighbor women was fixin' de dinner. Dey done de churnin' too, and Sis' Fox go set de bucket of butter in de spring where it be good and cool for de big dinner.

Br'er Rabbit, he keep cuttin' he eye roun' all de time, and he see Sis' Fox put de butter in de spring. At dat, he grin to hisse'f and lick his mouf. When dey start rollin' de logs, Br'er Rabbit was right dar wid he shoulder down, jest a-gruntin'. But he ain't do no wuk.

'Long up in de mornin', when de sun get hot, Br'er Rabbit, he let out a big holler: "Hooee, Br'er Fox, got to run back home a li'l while!"

"What de matta now, Br'er Rabbit?"

"My wife gwine bring me a new heir."

Den, Br'er Rabbit, he run over in de woods like he takin' de shawtcut home. But he jest creep roun' to de spring and take up dat bucket of butter and eat it all. Den, he wipe he mouf and he hands and lay down in de shade to take a nap.

Jest 'fore dinner time, he git up and come out of de woods walkin' slow and proud.

Br'er Fox see him and holler, "Well, has you got de new heir, Br'er Rabbit?"

Br'er Rabbit say, "Uhuh, got a new heir."

Br'er Fox say, "What you name dis-un?"

Br'er Rabbit say, "He name 'Lickbottom.'" Br'er Rabbit tole dat 'cause he done lick de bottom of de butter bucket.

Br'er Fox say, "Well, dat sho' is fine; sho' hope he does well. And now, it's 'bout de middle of de day, so le's knock off and git dinner."

So dey all go up to de house, and Br'er Fox, he go down to de spring to git de butter. When he git dere, he find all de butter gone.

Br'er Fox, he go back to de house and he say, "Somebody done been to de spring and et all de butter. Any of you-all de one what done it?"

Dey all say dey ain't seen no butter. Den, Br'er Fox, he say, "Well, ain't nobody else been roun' heah, so somebody tole a lie. On'y way we kin find out is to hold ever'body up to de fiah and make de butter run out de one what done it."

Dey all 'greed to dat, and den dey start holdin' one 'nother up to de fiah, startin' off wid Br'er Possum. So dey keep on till dey git to Br'er Rabbit, and when dey hold him up, here come all de butter runnin' out.

Den, dey all say, "Uhuh, Br'er Rabbit got de butter. What us gwine do wid him?"

Some say to th'ow him in de fiah, and some say th'ow him in de brierpatch. Br'er Rabbit, he don't say nothin'.

Den, Br'er Fox say, "Br'er Rabbit, which one you ruther us do?"

Br'er Rabbit, he say, "Th'ow me in de fiah, please, Br'er Fox; dem ole briers jest tear my eyes out, if you th'ow me in de brierpatch."

So dey tuk him and th'owed him in de brierpatch. And Br'er Rabbit, he shook he'se'f and jump 'way up on de hill and laugh and say, "Thank you, Br'er Fox. I was bred and born in a brierpatch."

KING OF DE WORLD

ZORA NEALE HURSTON

"**Y**'all been tellin' and lyin' 'bout all dese varmints but you ain't yet spoke about de high chief boss of all de world which is de lion," Sack Daddy commented.

"He's de King of de Beasts, but he ain't no King of de World, now Sack," Dad Boykin spoke up. "He *thought* he was de King till John give him a straightenin'."

"Don't put dat lie out!" Sack Daddy contended. "De lion won't stand no straightenin'."

"Course I 'gree wid you dat everybody can't show de lion no deep point, but John showed it to him. Oh, yeah, John not only straightened him out, he showed dat ole lion where in."

"When did he do all of dis, Dad? Ah ain't never heard tell of it." Dad spoke up:

Oh, dis was way befo' yo' time. Ah don't recolleck myself. De old folks told me about John and de lion. Well, John was ridin' long one day straddle of his horse when de grizzly bear come pranchin' out in de middle of de road and hollered: "Hold on a minute! They tell me you goin' 'round strowin' it dat youse de King of de World."

John stopped his horse: "Whoa! Yeah, Ah'm de King of de World, don't you b'lieve it?" John told him.

"Naw, you ain't no King. Ah'm de King of de World. You can't be no King till you whip me. Git down and fight."

John hit de ground and de fight started. First, John grabbed him a

32

rough-dried brick and started to work de fat offa de bear's head. De bear just fumbled 'round till he got a good holt, then he begin to squeeze and squeeze. John knowed he couldn't stand dat much longer, do he'd be jus' another man wid his breath done give out. So he reached into his pocket and got out his razor and slipped it between dat bear's ribs. De bear turnt loose and reeled on over in de bushes to lay down. He had enough of dat fight.

John got back on his horse and rode on off.

De lion smelt de bear's blood and come runnin' to where de grizzly was layin' and started to lappin' his blood.

De bear was skeered de lion was gointer eat him while he was all cut and bleedin' nearly to death, so he hollered and said: *"Please* don't touch me, Brer Lion. Ah done met de King of de World and he done cut me all up."

De lion got his bristles all up and clashed down at de bear: "Don't you lay there and tell me you done met de King of de World and not be talkin' 'bout me! Ah'll tear you to pieces!"

"Oh, don't tetch me, Brer Lion! Please lemme alone so Ah kin git well."

"Well, don't you call nobody no King of de World but me."

"But Brer Lion, Ah done *met* de King sho' nuff. Wait till you see him and you'll say Ah'm right."

"Naw, Ah won't, neither. Show him to me and Ah'll show you how much King he is."

"All right, Brer Lion, you jus' have a seat right behind dese bushes. He'll be by here befo' long."

Lion squatted down by de bear and waited. Fust person he saw goin' up de road was a old man. Lion jumped up and ast de bear, "Is dat him?"

Bear say, "Naw, dat's Uncle Yistiddy, he's a useter-be!"

After while a li'l boy passed down de road. De lion seen him and jumped up agin. "Is dat him?" he ast de bear.

Bear told him, "Naw, dat's li'l tomorrow, he's a gointer-be, you jus' lay quiet. Ah'll let you know when he gits here."

Sho nuff after while here come John on his horse but he had done got his gun. Lion jumped up agin and ast, "Is dat him?"

Bear say: "Yeah, dat's him! Dat's de King of de World."

Lion reared up and cracked his tail back and forwards like a bull-whip. He 'lowed, "You wait till Ah git thru wid him and you won't be callin' him no King no mo'."

He took and galloped out in de middle of de road right in front of John's horse and laid his years back. His tail was crackin' like torpedoes.

"Stop!" de lion hollered at John. "They tell me you goes for de King of de World!"

John looked him dead in de ball of his eye and told him, "Yeah, Ah'm de King. Don't you like it, don't you take it. Here's mah collar, come and shake it!"

De lion and John eye-balled one another for a minute or two, den de lion sprung on John.

Talk about fightin'! Man, you ain't seen no sich fightin' and wrasslin' since de mornin' stars sung together. De lion clawed and bit John and John bit him right back.

Way after while John got to his rifle and he up wid de muzzle right in ole lion's face and pulled de trigger. Long, slim black feller, snatch 'er back and hear 'er beller! Dog damn! Dat was too much for de lion. He turnt go of John and wheeled to run to de woods. John levelled down on him agin and let him have another load, right in his hindquarters.

Dat ole lion give John de book; de bookity book.* He hauled de fast mail back into de woods where de bear was laid up.

"Move over," he told de bear. "Ah wants lay down too."

"How come?" de bear ast him.

"Ah done met de King of de World, and he done ruint me."

"Brer Lion, how you know you done met de King?"

" 'Cause he made lightnin' in my face and thunder in my hips. Ah know Ah done met de King, move over."

---

*Sound word meaning running.

WHY ANANSI HIDES IN CORNERS, A TALE FROM GHANA

Adapted and retold by
JERMIAH NABAWI

In Ghana both men and women tell the stories. Anyone who has the ability to make them up can tell stories. Most of the stories are about Anansi. When people are returning home to the village from a day's work and when the moon is shining down on them, one of the elders summons all of the children in the village. The children get excited because they are going to listen to "Ananse Sem." Ananse Sem means storytelling. Anansi stories are not just for children though. Many stories about him are for "adults only."

Anansi is a spider who can weave the most beautiful webs. He taught the people of Ghana, especially the Ashanti people, how to weave the intricate Kente cloth. Anansi can also be a devilish trickster who uses his wit and wisdom to get out of all kinds of sticky situations.

Anansi is everywhere, and his name is spelled many ways: Ananse, Anancy, Brer Nancy or Anansi. He has traveled throughout West Africa. He sailed on the slave ships to the Caribbean where to this day he is entertaining the people of Jamaica. Trinidad, and the Virgin Islands. Someone spotted him in Brixton, England, where he was trying to weave his web in the ear of a famous prince. He is currently sprinkling his magic dust into the eyes of schoolchildren in the United States. Long ago Anansi visited the Sky God and brought back the gift of storytelling and shared it with all the people. That is why we tell stories today.

ne day Anansi the Spider received a visit from his friend Rabbit. When Rabbit stepped inside Spider's house, he could not help but notice the beautiful goat skin hanging from Anansi's wall. On the floor stood a cooking pot. Anansi's wife Aso was stirring some peanut stew. Leaning against the pot was a big ax.

"Hello-ooo, Rabbit, my great friend! Come in! Come in! Welcome to our house." Since it was the custom to make all visitors feel welcome, Aso gave Rabbit some stew. Anansi poured Rabbit some palm wine. They chatted and chatted away about local issues and politics. But Rabbit wasn't really interested in politics. All he kept thinking about was the beautiful goat skin hanging on Anansi's wall.

"Anansi, Anansi, my great friend. Enough of politics. Listen to my idea. I've been noticing your beautiful goat skin. It could be used to make a fine drum."

"Yes, my great friend, Rabbit. You are correct. A fine drum indeed," said Anansi.

"Let us go into the forest," said Rabbit, "and chop down a big tree with your big ax to make the drum. We can have music and dancing."

"That would be nice," said Anansi, "but I don't know how to play the drum and, besides, I'm too tired."

"What? Can't play the drum? Too tired? What excuses! You are just being lazy!" said Rabbit.

"Lazy!" shouted Anansi. "How dare you call me lazy. I am not lazy, I am too sick." At that moment Anansi's two sons entered the house carrying fresh yams and plantains.

"Well then," said Rabbit, "if you are too sick, perhaps your oldest son can come and help me."

"Oh nooo," said Anansi. "My oldest son is sick, too."

"Then what about your other son?" said Rabbit.

"Oh no, he is also sick."

"You are impossible!" said Rabbit. "Then how about lending me your big ax so that I can go and chop down the tree."

"I'm so sorry. My big ax is sick, too!" said Spider.

"Then why don't you let me have that beautiful piece of goat skin doing nothing on your wall so that I can use it for a drum head?"

"Oh. Did I not tell you that my beautiful animal skin that is doing nothing on the wall is sick, too!"

"You are a terrible friend!" shouted Rabbit, and he furiously stomped out of Anansi's house.

Anansi laughed and forgot about the matter until late one afternoon he could hear drumming coming from the direction of Rabbit's farm:

DOON-DOON-DOC! DOON, DOC-DOC!
DOON-DOON-DOC! DOON, DOC-DOC!

"What beautiful drumming!" thought Anansi. The more Anansi heard the sounds of the drum, the more curious he became. Before long, Anansi, Aso, and their two sons were heading toward Rabbit's farm. But before they reached the farm, the drumming had stopped. Rabbit was nowhere to be found. However, there beside the drinking well was the drum that Rabbit had made without the help of his friend.

Anansi walked over to the drum, tapped it, and before long he was playing:

DOON-DOON-DOC! DOON, DOC-DOC!
DOON-DOON-DOC! DOON, DOC-DOC!

Aso began dancing—sahsh, sahsh, sahsh, sahsh—and their two sons began singing and clapping their hands. They were having a marvelous time. Meanwhile, Rabbit was in the forest chopping down a tree in order to make another drum. But Anansi and his family were playing so loudly and having so much fun that Rabbit could hear them way out in the forest.

"Somebody's playing my drum! Who's playing my drum?" Rabbit dropped his ax and ran so fast and so hard through the forest that Spider and his family could hear him coming. They immediately stopped the music making, and all ran around to the back of the house and hid from Rabbit.

"Hey! Who's been here playing my drum?" said Rabbit.

Rabbit looked around and around but he did not see anyone, so, he went back into the woods to finish chopping down the tree. Again, Anansi could not resist the sound of the drum and began playing:

DOON-DOON-DOC! DOON, DOC-DOC!
DOON-DOON-DOC! DOON, DOC-DOC!

And Aso started dancing—sahsh, sahsh, sahsh—and the children joined in.

This time, when Rabbit heard the drumming and merriment, he moved swiftly but he did not run as hard. And this time, when he got close to his farm, he began tiptoeing so that he could sneak up on whoever was playing his drum. He crept and he tiptoed....

"Ah-hah! So it is *you,* Spider! You hypocrite!" shouted Rabbit. "You who were too sick to come help me make a drum are now here beating the drum and singing and dancing and carrying on! You wouldn't even let me use your ax because *it* too was sick!" Rabbit was furious. He summoned the rest of the animals in the forest so that he could make a complaint and told them all that had happened. Anansi was so embarrassed and felt so guilty for not having helped his friend Rabbit that he and his family backed themselves into the corner of the house and hid their faces in shame. And to this day you can find Spider and his family hiding and spinning their webs in corners of houses.

We must be careful how we treat our friends.

ANANCY AN HIM STORY, A TALE FROM JAMAICA

LOUISE BENNETT

Anancy, the tricky little spider man who speaks with a lisp and lives by his wits, is both comic and sinister, both hero and villain of Jamaican folk stories. He points up human weaknesses and shows how easily we can be injured and destroyed by our greed or stupidity, or by confidence in the wrong people and things.

Anancy is an Ashanti Spider-god and has magical powers. He can change himself into whatever and whoever he wishes at certain times, and his stories make it quite plain that he is able to get away with tricks that ordinary mortals can't. He is a rascal but lovable, and every existing custom is said to have been started by Anancy. (Is Anancy meck it.)

Most Anancy stories have songs, and these have been the true lullabies to Jamaican children for generations. Each Anancy story ends with "Jack Mandora, me noh choose none," which means "I take no responsibility for the story I have told." (Jack Mandora—Keeper of Heaven's door. Me noh choose none—It is not of my choosing.)

Once upon a time Anancy wasa pass one oman yard, an him see her gran-pickney outa de doorway a read one storybook. Anancy go sidung side a de pickney an start look ina de book to. De pickney tun ovah one leaf, and Anancy see one big picture a Puss pose off ina de book.

Anancy gi out: "Bless me yeye-sight! Koo Bra Rat! Tun ovah leaf, pickney gal! For if Puss and Rat ina book, me mus een deh to!"

But all de tun de pickney tun, an all de look Anancy look, him nevah see himself.

Anancy get eena tempa en teck a oat seh him mus put himself ina storybook.

All dat time Puss an Rat was good, good frien an dem always play de debil ina people house wid tief. Anancy meck up him mine fi put a spokes to dem weel.

So one day him pass by a play grung an see Puss an Rat out deh a play game. Wen de game dun Anancy walk home wid Puss an seh: "Tap, Bra Puss, is how yuh dah play so nice wid Rat an noh eat him yet? Yuh noh know seh Rat is nice meat?"

Hear Puss wid him craven self: "True, Bra Nancy?"

Anancy seh: "True, yes. Nex time oonoo meet up yuh ketch him an tase him so see!"

Puss tank Anancy an lick him mout go home.

Anancy meck fi Rat yard.

Hear him to Rat: "Bredda Rat, me got bad news fi yuh. Lickle wiles as me dah pass Puss yard me hear Puss muma dah tell him seh dat anytime him meet up Rat again him fi ketch Rat an eat him for Rat a nice meat."

Rat start teck weh himself from Puss, an Puss start meck afta Rat, an de two a dem mine so deh pon one anada dat dem nevah got time fi tief.

One day one ole oman seh to Anancy: "Bra Nancy, me hear seh dat is yuh meck Puss an Rat fall out, an me haffi tank yuh."

Hear Anancy: "Is me, yes. De two a dem pose off ina storybook an me cyann go in deh."

De ole oman seh: "Cho, Anancy, dat shouldn't worry yuh. Me wi put yuh eena story."

Anancy seh: "How comes?"

De ole oman seh: "Me an all de odder ole oman dem wat yuh help wid Puss and Rat gwine tell yuh story to we gran-pickney dem a night time, an dem won't fegat it."

Hear Anancy: "Every night me wi come memba yuh someting bout meself fi talk."

So every night wen de ole oman dem a put dem gran-pickney to bed, Anancy come an show up himself pon de wall or de ceilin so dat de ole oman dem can memba fi talk bout him. Sometimes wen de ole oman dem sleepy Anancy tie up dem face wid him rope an wake dem up, meck dem talk bout him. So dem tell dem pickney Anancy story, de pickney dem tell smaddy else, dat smaddy else tell an tell, so till me an all dah tell Anancy story. Is Anancy meck it.

Jack Mandora, me noh choose none. Me did lef someting fi yuh, but storm-warnin blow it weh.

ANANSI'S RIDING HORSE, A JAMAICAN FOLKTALE

Adapted and retold by MARIAN E. BARNES

L inda was the most beautiful girl in ten villages. Brer Tiger and Anansi were both in love with her. For Linda there was nothing whatsoever to think about. Anansi was puny and weak, and not at all good looking. Nobody glanced around when he entered a room. His limbs were spidery, spindly, and colorless. They had no muscles or shape. His voice was thin and reedy. And who could even find his eyes? He was very stupid to think she would ever look his way. Linda laughed at him.

Brer Tiger was strong and handsome, with brilliant, burning eyes. His velvet black stripes looked bold and beautiful against his orange hide. When he loped through the fields, his great muscles bulged and rippled. Brer Tiger was powerful. When he roared, the ground shook and the trees trembled. When he came into a room, everybody noticed. Linda was in love with him.

But then the forest began to buzz with a most peculiar rumor: Anansi claimed for a fact that Brer Tiger was his riding horse. How Linda laughed when she heard the ridiculous story! But she kept hearing it and hearing it and hearing it again. Her friends repeated it over and over. They chuckled and giggled and said it was absurd, but it got harder and harder for Linda to laugh with them. It wasn't funny anymore. Indeed, it had become most annoying. It was all she could think about the day Tiger's eyes burned into hers and his mighty voice rumbled, "I love you, Linda. Let's we two get married."

"Well, I certainly will not marry Anansi's riding horse," Linda pouted. "That's what Anansi is telling everyone you are!" The sound of Brer Tiger's roar thundered for miles around. He raced toward Anansi's house, causing the earth to shake and send up swirling clouds of dust and clumps of dirt, smashing young trees and bushes in his way. Old trees trembled, animals scurried from his path in fright, and all the while the sound of Brer Tiger's thunderous, deafening roaring filled every glen and glade.

Stomping and spatting in front of Anansi's house, Brer Tiger shouted at the top of his lungs, "ANANSI, YOU'RE A DIRTY LIAR! COME ON OUT HERE!" Anansi's little house quaked and wobbled and seemed about to fall, but it didn't. The door opened slowly, and there stood Brer Rabbit. He pleaded with Tiger to be quiet. He said Anansi was near death.

"He *can't* die *now,*" Brer Tiger shrieked, and he bounded in the door. Sure enough there was Anansi covered up in bed, only his weak eyes showing. When Brer Tiger asked him about the dirty lie he had told, tears clouded Anansi's eyes.

"I never said that," he said weakly. "Please, Brer Tiger, let me die in peace."

"NO, SIREE," Brer Tiger roared. "You have to come with me to tell Linda the truth."

"I can't . . . I'm too weak to walk . . . I'm dying," Anansi gasped.

"Don't you dare die before you tell Linda 'bout that lie! If you're too weak to walk, climb up on my back. I'll carry you," Tiger said.

"Well, all right," Anansi said reluctantly. "Hand me my fly whisk." His voice was tired and thin.

"What do you want with a fly whisk?" Tiger asked in surprise.

"Those nasty insects in the forest will eat me alive if I don't have my fly whisk to chase them away," panted Anansi, pointing to his oxtail fly whisk, which Tiger then handed him. Anansi was struggling pitifully to come out of the bed. "Help me, please, Brer Rabbit," Anansi pleaded. "Put the blanket on Brer Tiger's back and help me up."

"How come you need a blanket?" Brer Tiger wondered irritably.

"My body is very sore. The ride would be too painful for me without the blanket," Anansi grunted softly between each phrase. "I couldn't stand it."

"All right. All right. Hurry up, Brer Rabbit," Tiger said. He was terribly afraid Anansi would die before they could get to Linda and clear his name.

After Brer Rabbit had saddled Brer Tiger and placed Anansi on the blanket, Anansi kept slipping down. "Oh, how weak and sick I feel!" Anansi said. "Everything is whirling around! Bring me a rope, Brer Rabbit. Please, bring me a rope."

"Why do you need a rope?" Brer Tiger groused, pawing the ground impatiently. Would they never get going!

"I must have a rope to hold on to, or else I shall fall off," Anansi replied, coming dangerously close to falling off as he spoke.

"Give Anansi a rope, Brer Rabbit!" Tiger roared. "For God's sake, why are you taking so long!" They were never going to make it to Linda in time, and it would be the fault of that slow, stupid rabbit!

But at last they moved off with such pleading from Anansi to Tiger to go slower because he couldn't stand the pace and was swooning. When they reached the clearing before Linda's cabin, she was standing on the porch with her friends. Her eyes grew wider and wider as Tiger approached, Anansi riding arrow straight on his back. Suddenly Anansi plunged his heels deep into Brer Tiger's sides and shouted, "Giddyap, Tiger! Giddyap!" He was whacking Brer Tiger with the fly whisk.

Tiger yelped with pain and leaped forward; Anansi jerked the rein back, shouting gleefully as he dismounted, "See, gal, didn't I tell ya he was my riding horse!"

Brer Tiger, embarrassed to his back teeth, dashed into the forest. He hasn't been seen in those parts from that day until this.

ROOSTER AND ROACH, A JAMAICAN FOLKTALE

Retold by RAMONA BASS

Rooster and Roach were fine friends and neighbors. So they decided to plant together. But just before starting work, Roach got so sick, sick, **sick!** He left the fields, and Rooster worked all day by himself.

Next day Rooster found Roach sick in bed. He said, "Don't worry, my friend. I'll take care of you!" Rooster served Roach camomile tea and toast, then left to work their fields. At once Roach danced out of bed, singing:

Cock-a-tee-hee! Cock-a-tee-hee!
Rooster sow and hoe the row.
Roach him reap a heap of crop.
Rooster him dumb, Roach him smart!
Cock-a-tee hee! Cock-a-tee hee? Cock-a-tee-hee!

Day after day Rooster visited Roach, saying, "Don't worry my friend. I'll take care of you." He served Roach breakfast in bed, then went to work their fields. Then Roach would dance and sing about how dumb Rooster was to do all the work.

Then word got out (audience repeats): "Roach isn't sick, he's not sick one bit." So Rooster determined to find out.

Next day, as usual, Rooster visited Roach and said, "Don't worry my friend. I'll take care of you." He served Roach tea to soothe his tummy and nerves, and left. Then Rooster crept back, and there Roach was, singing and dancing:

Cock-a-tee-hee! Cock-a-tee-hee!
Rooster sow and hoe the row.
Roach him reap a heap of crop.
Rooster him dumb, Roach him smart!
Cock-a-tee-hee! Cock-a-tee-hee!

Then Rooster marched up and took care of his friend Roach—in one gulp! Now anytime a Rooster sees a lazy Roach, he takes care of him (gulp)! Which goes to say, "When you work together, well, things can work out. But when you don't, you'd better watch out." (GULP!)

THE ANT STORY

CONSTANCE GARCÍA-BARRIO

One day an ant had a great stroke of luck. He found a huge crumb that even had a dab of grape jelly on it. He laughed out loud, knowing how happy everyone at the anthill would be with a taste of that crumb.

But when he started dragging the crumb toward the anthill, he realized he had a tough task ahead of him. His antennae quivered, his legs strained, and his jaw ached as he slowly dragged that crumb.

"This is too much for me," he moaned. "I can't do it alone. I can't. I can't!" When the bee came along, the ant yelled, "Stop and help me with this crumb!"

"Buzz," said the bee. "Sorry. I have all this pollen to carry back to my hive." And the bee flew off.

Soon the beetle, a practical joker, wandered by. When the ant asked him to help, the beetle said, "Sure!" and he took a big bite out of the crumb.

"I made it lighter for you, didn't I?" he hooted, walking away. The ant stood there fussing and fuming.

A spider had been watching the whole thing from her web up in a tree. She'd heard enough of the ant's "I can't! I can't!" She spun a thread down to where the ant was.

"I'm going to solve your problem," she said. "I'm going to wrap this crumb up and take it home to my children," she said, starting toward the crumb.

"You can't do that, not with my crumb," the ant yelled. Furious, the ant grabbed the crumb, pushed, pulled, shoved, and hauled. Be-

47

fore he knew it, he stood at the opening of the anthill with the crumb beside him.

When the spider saw him there, she winked at him and said, "See? I knew it. You can do a lot more than you think you can."

"And you know what?" says the storyteller, pointing at the audience, "I bet you can, too!"

WHY THE RABBIT IS ALERT

ARDIE STUART BROWN

Long ago Sungura* had a long, gorgeous tail and four long, graceful legs. But he couldn't decide where he wanted to live. He looked at the water and thought that might be nice. So he jumped in, but his legs got tired from trying to keep afloat. "No, no, too much!"

Then he looked at the earth. He dug a shallow hole and rested. Soon ants, gophers, and even a mole disturbed him, saying, "Dig a deeper hole, the earth must breathe."

"Too much work," said Sungura. So he looked up at the trees where the monkeys lived, and he climbed up there. He had food, he could rest, and he could see all around. Plus the monkeys did nothing to disturb him. So Sungura rested. Soon the wind began to blow, and the monkeys warned him that he should move to a stronger limb. But Sungura said, "Maybe tomorrow."

The monkeys warned him again as they climbed to stronger branches. "Move to a stronger limb, Sungura!" But the rabbit relaxed. Then a strong, howling wind broke the branch he was resting on, and Sungura fell to the ground. His lovely tail broke off, and his two hind legs were broken. Once more the monkeys warned him: "Go see the healer so she can set your legs properly."

But Sungura said, "Maybe tomorrow I will see the healer. Not today." He sat and relaxed. His hind legs healed just as they had broken. And ever since that time, all rabbits are born with crooked

---

*Swahili word for rabbit.

hind legs. But Sungura learned a lesson. Now rabbits are alert and quick. They hop very fast. They never wait. And you too can learn from the rabbit's mistake. If you have something to do, *do it now!*

BR'ER RABBIT AND BUH KING

MARY UMOLU

Br'er Rabbit wanted to get married. He went around telling all of the animals about his plans.

"I'm gonna get married. An' I'm gonna marry the finest women I can fin'," Br'er Rabbit bragged. Then he would proudly shake his tail.

But not one of the animals would allow him to marry his daughter because they all knew he was full of tricks. If Br'er Rabbit were to ask, each planned to claim that his daughter was elsewhere.

But Rabbit made it quite clear to them that he wasn't planning to marry any local or ordinary everyday girl. "The only girl I'll marry is Buh King's daughter."

All of the animals laughed because they thought that Br'er Rabbit was out of his mind.

But one day Br'er Rabbit went to Buh King and told him that he would like to marry his daughter.

Buh King asked him, "What gave you the right to feel worthy of my daughter?"

Br'er Rabbit began to tell Buh King of his cleverness. Then Buh King told him that he would have to prove himself first by bringing him a bag full of blackbirds and two teeth from a rattlesnake.

Br'er Rabbit began to plot. He went down the road singing: *"Ding, ding, ding, a-ding. . . ."* He went into the woods where black-birds were and began to talk to himself saying, "Which is heavier, a quail or a blackbird?"

Br'er Rabbit began to argue the point to himself out loud. The blackbirds began to argue, "Quails are all feathers and we are heavier."

"Let us not fuss about it. I'll just weigh you in this bag now. Then later I'll weigh the quails. Now you get into my bag."

The blackbirds got into the bag and Br'er Rabbit happily tied the bag. He went down the road smiling and singing: *"Ding, ding, ding, a-ding...."*

When he got to the rattlesnake's home, he found Mr. Rattlesnake fast asleep. Br'er Rabbit woke him up.

"Sorry to wake you up, Mr. Rattlesnake, but there is somethin' that you must know."

"That's all right, Br'er Rabbit. What is it?" the rattlesnake asked.

Br'er Rabbit cleared his throat and said, "I hate to be a bearer of bad news, but you have to know what they are saying. They are saying that your back is crooked."

"Crooked! My back crooked? Who could ever say such a thing?"

"Don't worry about it," Br'er Rabbit said. "I can take care of that. I can help you prove that you are straight."

Br'er Rabbit brought a stick and asked the rattlesnake to straighten himself beside it. He then tied the rattlesnake to the stick.

Br'er Rabbit jumped around Mr. Rattlesnake pinching him in several spots. Then he said, "It's not your back, it's your teeth." While Rattlesnake was trying to answer, Br'er Rabbit pulled out two of his teeth and was off to Buh King's singing: *"Ding, ding, ding, a-ding...."*

Buh King told Br'er Rabbit that there was just one more thing that he had to do. He gave Br'er Rabbit a bag and told him that there was a lot of money in it. He asked Br'er Rabbit to bury it.

On the way, Br'er Rabbit decided that he should remove a few dollars in order to buy himself a wedding suit. When he opened it, two of Buh King's big hunting dogs jumped out and began to chase Br'er Rabbit. They got so close that they bit off his tail. And from that day to this Br'er Rabbit has no tail.

THE FROG WHO WANTED TO BE A SINGER

LINDA GOSS

Well, friends, I got a question for you. Have you ever been frustrated? That's right, I said *frustrated*. Tell the truth now. Everybody in this room should be screaming, "Yeah, I've been frustrated," because you know you have, at least once in your lives. And some of us here are frustrated every single day.

How do you tell when you are frustrated? Do you feel angry? Do you feel depressed? Are you full of anxiety? Are you tense? Are you nervous? Confused? Sometimes you can't stop eating. Sometimes you don't want to eat at all. Sometimes you can't sleep. And sometimes you don't want to wake up. *You are frustrated!*

Well, friends, let's go back. Back to the forest. Back to the motherland. Back to the days when the animals talked and walked upon the earth as folks do now.

Let's examine a little creature who is feeling mighty bad, mighty sad, mighty mad, and mighty frustrated. We call him the frog. There's nothing wrong in being a frog. But this particular frog feels that he has talent. You see, he wants to be a singer. And there's nothing wrong in wanting to be a singer except that in this particular forest where this particular frog lives, frogs don't sing. Only the birds are allowed to sing. The birds are considered the most beautiful singers in the forest.

So, for a while, the frog is cool. He's quiet. He stays to himself and practices on his lily pad, jumping up and down, singing to himself. But one day all of this frustration begins to swell inside him. He becomes so swollen that frustration bubbles start popping from his

53

mouth, his ears, his nose, even from his eyes, and he says to himself (in a froglike voice): "You know, I'm tired of feeling this way. I'm tired of holding all this inside me. I've got talent. I want to be a singer."

The little frog decides to share his ambitions with his parents. His parents are somewhat worried about his desires, but since he is their son, they encourage him and say: "Son, we're behind you one hundred percent. If that's what you want to be, then go right ahead. You'll make us very proud."

This makes the frog feel better. It gives him some confidence, so much so that he decides to share the good news with his friends. He jumps over to the other side of the pond and says, "Fellows, I want to share something with you."

"Good!" they reply. "You got some flies we can eat."

"No, not flies. I got talent. I want to be a singer."

"Fool, are you crazy?" says one friend. "Frogs don't sing in this place. You'd better keep your big mouth shut."

They laugh at the frog, so he jumps back over to his lily pad.

He rocks back and forth, meditating and contemplating his situation, and begins to realize that perhaps he should go and talk with the birds. They seem reasonable enough; maybe they will allow him to join their singing group.

He gathers up his confidence, jumps over to their tree house, and knocks on their trunk. The head bird flies to the window, looks down on the frog's head, and says: "Oh, it's the frog. How may we help you?"

"Can I come up? I got something to ask you," says the frog.

"Very well, Frog. Do jump up."

Frog enters the tree house, and hundreds of birds begin fluttering around him.

"Come on in, Frog. Why don't you sit over there in the corner," says the head bird. Frog sits down but he feels a little shy. He begins to chew on his tongue.

"Frog, how may we help you?"

"Uh, well, uh, you see," says Frog, "I would like to become a part of your group."

"That's wonderful," says the head bird.

"Yes, wonderful," echo the other birds.

"Frog, you may help us carry our worms," said the head bird.

"That's not what I had in mind," says Frog.

"Well, what do you have in mind?"

Frog begins to stutter; "I-I-I-I-I want to-to-to sing wi-wi-with your group."

"What! You must be joking, of course. An ugly green frog who is full of warts sing with us delicate creatures. You would cause us great embarrassment."

"B-b-but . . ." Frog tries to plead his case, but the head bird becomes angry.

"Out! Out! Out of our house you go." He kicks the frog from the house. Frog rolls like a ball down the jungle path.

When he returns home, he feels very sad. The frog wants to cry but doesn't, even though he aches deep inside his gut. He wants to give up, but he doesn't. Instead he practices and practices and practices and practices.

Then he begins to think again and realizes that even though the birds sing every Friday night at the Big Time Weekly Concert, they don't control it. The fox is in charge. The frog jumps over to the fox's place and knocks on his cave.

"Brother Fox, Brother Fox, it's me, Frog. I want to talk to you."

The fox is a fast talker and a busy worker, and really doesn't want to be bothered with the frog.

"Quick, quick, quick, what do you want?" says the fox.

"I want to be in the concert this Friday night."

"Quick, quick, what do you want to do?"

"I want to sing," says the frog.

"Sing? Get out of here, quick, quick, quick!"

"Please, Brother Fox. Please give me a chance."

"Hmmm," says the fox, shifting his eyes. "Uh, you know something, Froggie? Maybe I could use you. Why don't you show up Friday, at eight o'clock sharp, okay?"

"You mean I can do it?"

"That's what I said. Now, get out of here. Quick, quick, quick!"

Oh, the frog is happy. He is going to "do his thing." He is going to present himself to the world.

Meanwhile, the fox goes around to the animals in the forest and tells them about the frog's plans. Each animal promises to be there and give the frog a "little present" for his singing debut.

And so Monday rolls around, Tuesday rolls around, Wednesday rolls around, Thursday rolls around, and it is Friday. The frog is so excited, he bathes all day. He combs his little green hair, parts it in the middle, and slicks down the sides. He scrubs his little green fingers and his little green toes. He looks at his little reflection in the pond, smiles, and says, "Um, um, um, I am *beauuuutiful!* And I am going to 'do my thing' tonight." And soon it is seven o'clock, and then it is seven thirty, and then it is seven forty-five, and there is the frog trembling, holding on to the edge of the curtain.

He looks out at the audience and sees all the animals gathering in their seats. The frog is scared, so scared that his legs won't stop trembling and his eyes won't stop twitching. Brother Fox strolls out on stage and the show begins.

"Thank you, thank you, thank you. Ladies and gentlemen, we have a wonderful show for you tonight. Presenting, for your entertainment, the frog who thinks he's a singer. Come on, let's clap. Come on out here, Frog, come on, come on. Let's give him a big hand." The animals clap and roar with laughter. The frog jumps out and slowly goes up to the microphone.

"For-for-for-for my first number, I-I-I-I—"

Now, before that frog can put the period at the end of that sentence, the elephant stands up, pulls down a pineapple, and throws it right at the frog's head.

"Ow!" cries the frog. And the lion pulls down a banana, throws it, and hits that frog right in the mouth. "Oh," gulps the frog. Other animals join in the act of throwing things at the frog. Some of them shout and yell at him, "Boo! Boo! Get off the stage. You stink! You're ugly. We don't want to hear a frog sing. Boo, you jive turkey!"

The poor little frog has to leap off the stage and run for his life. He hides underneath the stage. Brother Fox rushes back on the stage.

"Okay, okay, okay, calm down—just trying out our comic routine. We have some real talent for your enjoyment. Presenting the birds, who really can sing. Let's hear it for the birds." The audience claps loudly. The birds fly onto the stage, their heads held up high. Their wings slowly strike a stiff, hypnotic pose as if they are statues. Their stage presence demands great respect from the audience. They chirp, tweet, and whistle, causing the audience to fall into a soft, peaceful nod.

Everyone is resting quietly except the frog, who is tired of being pushed around. The frog is tired of feeling frustrated. He leaps over the fox. He grabs him, shakes him, puts his hands around the fox's throat, and says, "You tricked me. You tried to make a fool out of me."

"Leave me alone," says the fox. "If you want to go back out there and make a fool of yourself, go right ahead."

"Hmph," says the frog. "That's just what I'm going to do."

Now that little green frog hippity-hops back onto the stage. He is shaking but determined to sing his song.

"I don't care if you are asleep. I'm gonna wake you up. I came here to sing a song tonight, and that's what I'm going to do."

In the style of what we call boogie-woogie, the frog begins to "do his thing":

DOOBA DOOBA DOOBA DOOBA DOOBA DOOBA DOOBA DOOBA
DOOBA DOOBA DOOBA DOOBA DOOBA DOOBA DOOBA DOOBA

The frog bops his head about as though it were a jazzy saxophone. His fingers move as though they were playing a funky bass fiddle.

DOOBA DOOBA DOOBA DOOBA DOOBADEE DOOBADEE DOOBADEE DOO-
BADEE
DOOBA DOOBA DOOBA DOOBA DOOBADEE DOOBADEE DOOBADEE DOO-
BADEE
DOOBA DOOBA DOOBA DOOBA DOOBA DOOBA DOOBA DOOBA
DOOBA! DOOBA! DOOP-DEE-DOOP! . . . BLURRRRRRP!

The elephant opens one eye. He roars "Uuumphf!" He jumps from his seat. He flings his hips from side to side, doing a dance we now call the "bump." The lion is the next animal to jump up from his seat. He shouts: "I love it! I love it!" He shakes his body thisaway and thataway and every whichaway, doing a dance we now call the "twist." Soon the snakes are boogalooing and the giraffes are doing the jerk. The hyenas do the "slop" and the fox does the "mashed potato." The birds also want to join in: "We want to do Dooba Dooba, too." They chirp and sway through the trees.

Tweet Tweet Tweet Dooba
Tweet Tweet Tweet Dooba

The whole forest is rocking. The joint is jumping. The animals are snapping their fingers. They are *dancing,* doing something that they have never done before.

The fox runs back on the stage, grabs the mike, and shouts: "Wow,

Frog, you are a genius. You have given us something new."

From then on, the frog is allowed to sing every Friday night at the Big Time Weekly Concert.

And, as my granddaddy used to say, that is how Rhythm and Blues was born.

DOOBA DOOBA DOOBA DOOBA DOOBA DOOBA DOOBA DOOBA DOOBA! DOOBA! DOOP-DEE DOOP!...BLURRRRRP!

THE BUTTERFLY

HUGH MORGAN HILL (BROTHER BLUE)

When Brother Blue told this story to third grade students at the Haley School, Roslindale, Massachusetts, the children responded with rhythm and song. Brother Blue never tells this story the same way. He is a storyteller full of emotions, which he shares with his audience.

In the middle of you, in the middle of Blue, inside of everyone, there's something playing peekaboo. Something wonderful in you. You can't see it with your natural eye. There's something forever in us that can never die. It's the most wonderful secret; it's the true story inside of make believe. We are more than what we look like. We're many different colors. You see all these colors on my clothes? And this rainbow butterfly on my hat? It's for the whole human race. The human race is like a rainbow; you know, many different colors. Like right here. I call it the rainbow race, *[singing]* the rainbow race, so many colors on the human face *[end singing]*. Different color eyes, some brown, some gray, some green, some blue, we have rainbow eyes, rainbow skin, many colors. But past the colors you can see, there's something in you and me that the natural eye can't see. It's playing peekaboo. The skin is like the cocoon, you know. What's inside a cocoon, waiting to come out. [Children answer: Butterflies.] Shop-o-zee cop-o-zee, oh, cop-o-zee, cop-o-zee, cop-o-zee. There's something in me and you, like a butterfly, never dies. You can name it, if you want to. *[Singing]* Some call it the soul, some call it the spirit, it's something forever. *[Mouth harp]* "Somewhere over the rainbow, bluebirds fly." Past this rainbow of skin, all these colors we live in, there's something that's forever. Aaaahhh! *[Singing]* Some call it the spirit *[end singing]*. I call it aaaahhh. It's the story inside all the fairy tales they tell. It's the wonderful we wish for under every wishing well. In the ringing bell, in the ribbons, in the rainbows, in me and you, there's something that's forever. Here we go. Hey Sam, you're forever. There's something in you, I'll see it forever. As long as I live, I'll tell your story, my friend. Here we go.

Once upon a time ago.

Bop-i-dee, bop-i-dee, bip. Bopping, doo-wopping. A finger pop, a did-lee-bop, a doo-wop. A hop.

Ring around the rosie, tomorrow, now ago. Far away, cross the deep blue sea. No place away, right here away.

There was a little caterpillar. He was crawling around on the ground.

He was crying [sound on harmonica].

Poor caterpillar. He had never seen a butterfly. He didn't know what he was gonna be. But he wanted to fly. [Harmonica music.]

He said, [scream on harmonica].

People thought he was singing "Chicago Blues."

But he had never heard of Chicago. He was just paying dues, like you and me.

There's something he wants to do. There's something he wants to be.

[Children call out: butterfly!]

He had never seen a butterfly.

Poor orphan. No mother, no daddy, no sister, no brother.

A poor little caterpillar, crawling around.

He made a crying sound [harmonica cry].

He didn't know, he didn't know, he didn't know what he was gonna be.

He had that yearning.

He wanted to boogie up the sky.

He wanted to breakdance across the stars. To the sound of groovy guitars. Because he heard those guitars, you know, in heaven.

This caterpillar, who had never seen a butterfly, looked up in the sky. Guess what he saw?

[Children respond: a butterfly!]

Butterfly. He didn't know what to say. He went Aaaahhh!

It was so beautiful, it was so wonderful, it was so magicky. It was so musicky. It was so aaaahhh, aaaahhh, aaaahhh.

Then he thought of something. Guess what he said.

He said, "Wow! Far out! Wicked awesome!

"I could dig it! I could dig it!
"I could dig it, dig it, dig it!
"That's my thing. Far out!"
[Singing] *Poor caterpillar.* [End singing.]
Did you ever see a caterpillar try to fly before he's got the wings. Pitiful.
He couldn't get off the ground.
He took a running start. He was out of shape. He hadn't been jogging
   every day.
He couldn't get up in the sky.
Guess what he said.
He said, [SCREAM]. Made a lot of noise.
The tree said, "Don't cry."
"You are going to be a butterfly," said the sky, "that's your destiny."
He didn't know the word "destiny."
What does the word "destiny" mean? Tell me.
[A child answers: his goal. What you're looking for.]
It's more than what you're looking for. What is your destiny?
[Another child answers: Something that . . . I can't really explain it.]
[Another child: Something you always wanted to do, and you keep on
   trying until you finally do it.]
You finally do it. You gonna be that.
He didn't know that word destiny. He had never got to third grade. He
   had never been to school, he can't read and write. He doesn't have a
   dictionary to look stuff up in at night. [Cry.]
Pretty soon he made a little house. What do you call that house?
[A child calls out: cocoon!]
A little cocoon. He didn't call it cocoon. He just called it his bad pad.
   Little hip city, his tent city.
It wasn't that pretty, it was dark in there.
Hard to get any air, thought he was gonna die.
He began to cry. Guess what he said?
[Scream!]
What else?
Guess who heard him scream. What's that round thing in the sky at
   night?
[A child responds: the moon.]
The moon says, "Yo, what's happening, bro, que pasa, what it is. Cool it,
   bro."
The caterpillar said, "I don't want to die in the dark, I want to fly."
The moon said, "Cool it, baby. Cool it. Just hang. Be cool, be cool."

The moon said, "Don't you know, God is going to turn you into a
   beautiful butterfly?"
The caterpillar never heard of God.
He had never been to Sunday School, he had never been to Shabat.
Never sung those songs.
[Cry!]
Guess who heard him cry. The one that made the sky.
[Child says: God.]
The one that made the pretty green tree.
The one that made pretty you. The one that made raggedy me.
You know who that be.
The boss, the boss!
He said, "Cool it. I made everything.
"I made the sky. I made the river.
"I made the tree, I made the tiger.
"I make everything.
"Don't cry. Coochee coo, come on. Come on, don't cry, coochee coo. Don't
   cry, you pretty thing, you. Don't cry, come on. Oh, oh, oh.
"Don't you know you're gonna be my butterfly? 'Cause I make stuff.
"That's me crying in there.
"All you have to do is go for your cry, your dream. The dream is you.
"Try with all your might, and guess what, I'm gonna give you those
   wings. You're gonna be one of those things called butterfly."
The caterpillar said, "Far out, wicked awesome, I could dig it. Woo-ee,
   dynamite, outa sight, let's get tight, me and you. Woo-woo!"
So one morning, oh folks, it's so pretty, I can't tell you.
[Singing] It was early one morning, cop-a-zee, chuli-boo, cop-i-lee-a
   ee-ee, ooh, ow. [End singing.]
The sun is rising.
Did you ever watch the sun rise?
[Children shout: yes.]
The sun rose like this. I'm gonna show you.
The sun got up like this [demonstration with arms outstretched].
The sun rose high in the sky.
The sun was golden, bright, and the sun kissed that cocoon like this:
   [kissing sound].
Bright!
Were you ever kissed by the sun? Bright?
Well inside that cocoon, something felt that kiss. Guess what it was.
[Children shout: a butterfly!]

Something that was a butterfly is gonna come out.
Inside the cocoon, it said, "Woo-ee, dynamite," began to jump around,
to scream and shout. It began breakdancing.
Guess what happened.
It broke out.
Something came out of that cocoon, it came out backward, upside down,
breakdancing against the sky.
It rose high in the sky.
It was moonwalking on the sun.
Is that cool? [The children clap hands, sing and shout with joy.]
Guess what, when this thing rose, the stars said, "Wow, far out."
"Wicked awesome," said the morning lark. "What are you?"
And this thing said, "Dig it. I am a butterfly. I am my dream. I am
my cry. I am what I was dreaming about."
It began to shout, aaaahhh, far out.

All you children, this is about you. There's something in you dreaming, singing, winging. Guess what. You are more. Inside of you something's playing peekaboo, through your rainbow eyes, your rainbow skin. You are forever things. You can call it *soul*. You can call it *spirit*. You can call it *butterfly*. You come from heaven, you know. You heard this before you were born. You are *so* beautiful.

Remember that, as you go through this world. Remember that, if a friend dies, someone you love. There's something that never dies. It's forever. That's you.

The name of this story is "Aaaahhh!" It's too beautiful. I can't say it. Past all the oh-oh oh's of all the rainbows. Past all the aaaahhh-aaaahhh-aaaahhh's in the Land of Aaaahhh's. There's aaaahhh, and that's you. In the middle of you there's something that's sacred, it's holy. It's you! It's forever. Guess what, you heard this before you were born, you're from heaven's horn. Ah-aaaahhh. That's the true story inside the fairy tales we tell, under the wishing well. Cop-a-zee, bop-i-dee bop, ow, ow, ooohhh, aaaahhh.

Sam, my friend, you're always going to be in this world. Because I remember you, and I can tell your story.

DON'T PLAY WITH YOUR SUPPER, A TALE FROM GHANA

KWASI ASARE

Once upon a time a cat had some kittens running around, and the cat had to go out looking for food for her kittens. She went out, left the kittens in the house, oh, two, three, four hours; a long time passes, half the day, and she still has not come home. All day she was gone looking for food.

Finally, she came back empty handed—no food for the kittens, nothing at all. Well, when she got up to the village and the house, she realized that there had been some disturbance in the house; everything was in a mess: plates, pots and pans, and everything in the house. She asked her children what had happened while she had been away, and they told their mother, "We went out with some friends and invited them to our house for dinner. Our friends are mice."

"I beg your— What you say? Mice?" she asked. "Are you telling me that mice came to this house, had a party with you, and that is why this house is a mess?"

They answered, "Yes, Mother."

"Well, let me tell you something," she says. "Look. Don't you know that it is mice we eat? That is what I went hunting for. That is what I feed you. I feed you the mice. You mean to tell me the mice came here and you let them go?" she said. "My God."

The mother was upset, very upset. She said to the children, "Well, all right, don't worry. You know what I want you to do? I want you to go back and tell the mice that we are having another party."

They said, "Okay."

"So they will come to the house," their mother said.

But, mind you, while this was going on at the cats' house, the mother mouse had been out looking for her children. She came to her house, and the children were not there. She began to worry and started to look for them.

"Coome coome coome coom, where are you?"

While she was looking, the mice children came in.

"Where've you been?"

"Oh, Mommy," they said, "we have been out with some friends. We went out for a walk with some friends there. They invited us to their house."

"Well, well, what friends?"

"Oh, cats," they said.

"What!" "What's that you say? A cat's house! I don't believe it!"

They said, "Yes, Mommy. We went to a cat's house and had a nice party."

"And you mean to tell me you went to a cat's house?" she said. "Don't you ever go there again! Don't you know we are cat's food? If the mother cat had got you, she would have cut you and eaten you. Don't you ever go there again!" She was so upset. She was screaming and shouting and crying, "Don't you ever go there again!" She warned them and advised them what could happen, and she said, "Don't go there."

In other words, both sides are advised equally. The cat told the kittens what to do, "Go invite them to come back next time," and the mouse went out herself to hide her children, and they could not be found. Then the cat told her children to go out and call to the mice, and they did.

"Mousey, mousey . . . mousey, mousey." You could hear the echo down in the forest. The mice heard it say, "Mousey, mousey, come here, come here. You know the party that we had last week? Look! Now we are having a big one tomorrow. Better than the one we had before! Do come," they said, "it's going to be fantastic! You will enjoy yourself. Everything will be nice."

Well, the mouse children heard and went out and stood on the doorstep and they shouted back to the cat again, "Catty, catty!"

Catty can hear. They said, "Listen!"

"If your mother has advised you, so has our mother advised us, too."

BUSH GOT EARS,
A TALE FROM GUYANA

NAOMI CLARKE

T here is a story that I tell about a woman and her three daughters and a tiger. This story, passed down by the very old people and my great-great-grandparents, came from the African people who were slaves down there in Guyana.

I am of the Igbo tribe, which is in Nigeria. I do not know any of the Igbo language, but this is something I heard from one of my grandparents and from two other people as well. Neither my grandparents nor my great-grandparents had African names; they were given English names.

It was my grandmother, my mother's mother, who told me this story, and she said it was told to her by her grandmother. This story came up whenever children in the home spoke without thinking. They would say, "Bush gat ears," meaning that you never know who is listening to what you are saying; and then they would tell us about how this woman lost her two children because she never really thought that "bush gat ears" when she came home with food and things like that.

This is a woman who had three daughters, and she named them Tania and Salambi Tania; two pretty girls, and the last one had a funny face—she was not proud of that child, she was ashamed of her—so she called her Quacku Aja. It is a name that people use when they want to curse you and call you a name; they will say, "Your face is like Quacku Aja." Salambi Tania, that is one name.

The woman had no husband. She was the sole breadwinner for those three girls and she did farming. The farm was away from the home, so she would instruct them that when she left the home, they must stay in the house; she would lock the door, tell them to keep the doors locked, and when anybody came, no matter who, they must not answer.

She trained her voice in a way that she say only she, the mother, could call them this way. And she would sing this song:

Tania, come hyah.
Salambi Tania, come hyah.
Leh Quacku Aja, wan tan-deh.

You know? And she trained her voice and said,

Tania, come hyah.
Salambi Tania, come hyah.
Leh Quacku Aja, wan tan-deh.

Tan-deh means "stay there."

When she comes from work, she always prepared the food that was cooked fresh from the ground (because that was a real thing kids always look for; we call it "back dem food," which means food that is prepared from the farm, just take out from the ground). The parents would cook a pot of food that they reaped from fresh vegetables and cook it so delicious! There is always a pool that you can get fresh fish and things like that, everything fresh and nice. She would cook all this nice food and pack it in a nice basket that she weaved herself, and she would come home and as soon as she get into the yard, she would start to walk a fancy walk, like a dancing walk, you know, swaying on both sides, with her hand on one hip and her hand on the basket on her head, and she would be singing this song. She wore her head tied, and she would sing:

Tania, come hyah.
Salambi Tania, come hyah.
Leh Quacku Aja, wan tan-deh.

She would call them into the better part of the house, and in this other part, it was just like a dark room, she would tell them to leave the ugly face one there. And they would come, and she would feed them and see that they spread a nice cloth on the table and she would see that they eat, and she would feed them properly and so on. When they were finished, she told them to take all the scrapings, the bones, and everything to Quacku Aja. So Quacku Aja was very thin, very lean, very bony, skinny, and ugly because of malnutrition, no nourishment, and things like that.

But one day Buru Tiger (you call it Brer Tiger here, but the Guyanese Creolese say Buru Tiger) . . . so Buru Tiger was in the bush and, hearing what this woman was saying, he said, "Oh Lord, I always wanted to eat those three girls! And I have to learn this, because they do not open the door as soon as they hear; they wait and listen carefully, and when they are sure it is the mother's voice, then they open the door."

This particular time when Buru Tiger heard it, he go into the bush and he started to practice (in a tiger's voice),

TANIA, COME HYAH.
SALAMBI TANIA, COME HYAH.
LEH QUACKU AJA, WAN TAN-DEH.

They said to themselves, "That is not the mother's voice." And they know right away that it was Buru Tiger. So when she come home that afternoon, they say "Ma, you know, Buru Tiger has been here today, and he just singing, before we come outside, wait! wait!"

So she said,

Tania, come hyah.
Salambi Tania, come hyah.
Leh Quacku Aja, wan tan-deh.

"That is me voice. That me voice when you hear that. Buru Tiger can't sing like that."

The next day Buru Tiger listen to all this conversation between the mother and her daughters. They didn't believe he was in a little bush near the dwelling. He go back home and practice. The next day he is singing softer,

TANia, COme hyAH.
SALAMbi Tania, COME hyAH
LEH QUACKu Aja, wan TAN-DEH.

But the daughters know that it is Buru Tiger so they don't open the door. He realize he had to put some real practice and he took the time. He stay away because the girls had told the mother that he was back again, and she, well, she said not to open that door. He waited a few weeks in the bush, and he practice in the bush and pick up every tone from this woman's voice:

Tania, come hyah.
Salambi Tania, come hyah.
Leh Quacku Aja, wan tan-deh.

And this time Buru Tiger got the note so keen, and he began singing,

Tania, come hyah.
Salambi Tania, come hyah.
Leh Quacku Aja, wan tan-deh.

And they couldn't make out the man (didn't know it was him). He go a little earlier, it was minutes before the mother usually go. They wanted to say, "Ma don't come this time," but then they started to talk about Ma, and they said, "That is she voice, that is she voice!" and they opened the door, and he grabbed the two beautiful ones, and he took them in the bush, and only they bones were left and their clothes.

Quacku Aja knew what happened to them. She had that sense, she was a very sensitive child. When the mother come up just minutes after all this had passed and say:

Tania, come hyah.
Salambi Tania, come hyah.
Leh Quacku Aja, wan tan-deh.

And when she started to sing, Quacku Aja started to sing back,

Tania na dan hyah.
Salambi Tania na dan hyah.
Bu ony po me byah, Quacku Aja wan deyah.

She said, "Only poor me, only poor ugly me here." And the mother say,

Knock, knock, knock!
Open the door!
Open the door! Let me in!

Tania na dan hyah
Salambi Tania na dan hyah
Bu ony po me byah, Quacku Aja wan deyah.

And when she push the door open, she see that there is only the one that she didn't want, and so she say, "What happened to them?"

Quacku Aja say, "You just came and you called."

Then the mother said, "O God, Tiger gone with me pickney. Buru Tiger da gone with me pickney." (Pickney means children.) She started to run. And she run and run, and she go around the bush in places. When she go there, she found the bones—he had already eaten them—and their clothes, and she took up their clothes like a mother in grief and she go back to the house.

When she got back to the house, she say: "Quacku Aja, me love you." You know? She tell her, the child, that she love her.

Gone me daughda
Gone me lovely daughdas
Ony Quacku Aja

Come me, Muma
Me love you, me Muma,

Quacku Aja sang,

Me love you, me mother.

So she kept Quacku Aja, and started to feed her the same nice food and every day when she would come home she would feed her. Oh, she would bathe her and comb her hair. She would dress her with all the fancy dresses, and she would clean her. She made a clean bed and started to treat her right. And that was all Quacku Aja wanted. And now she was able to show her to the village people; she didn't have her hidden or locked up anymore. All that the child wanted was love and attention and care.

But there is a moral behind the story, for the old people always say:

Always listen.
Be careful when you speak because bush gat ears.

The song of Quacku Aja is in Creolese, and the song always goes with the story. Quacku Aja became the most beautiful girl in the village, the most beautiful child that ever walked through the village in that time. The villagers marveled because of her beauty. She became so beautiful that even the mother was surprised that this child was so beautiful. But she had to have that tragic lesson to realize what she had. And the child was kind, loving, and so good to her that she had no regrets.

HOW TROUBLE MADE THE MONKEY EAT PEPPER, A FOLKTALE FROM TRINIDAD

Retold by RITA COX

Crick! Crack!
Monkey break me back!

In a tiny village in Trinidad, Ma Minnie made her living by making the most delicious sweets. Oh! the smells that came from Ma Minnie's yard!

One day, returning from market, carrying on her head a gourd of molasses for making her coconut cakes, Ma stubbed her foot against a stone. The gourd crashed to the ground; the molasses spread all over.

Poor Ma Minnie! Scooping up the thick sweet syrup with a piece of the gourd, she wailed, "Ah me, look at my trouble." Sadly, she licked her fingers. "Now I shall have to go right back to market. Ah me!"

A monkey who was watching from a tree overhead scurried down after Ma Minnie left and tasted the molasses. "Mmm, if this is trouble, then trouble is sweet. I'll go and buy some for myself!"

Monkey dressed himself in his fine clothes and hurried to town. He entered a shop and said, "I've come to buy some trouble."

"Do you know what trouble is?"

"Yes, and I want to buy all you have!"

"All right, remember, you asked for it!" The other customer giggled; Monkey glared. Soon the shopkeeper brought him a bag from the back of the shop. Brer Monkey paid and left.

"This trouble is heavy," he thought, "and what strange sounds it

72

makes!" He came to a clearing, sat down to enjoy his trouble, licked his lips, and opened the bag. Out rushed three fierce dogs. Poor Brer Monkey! He dashed up a tree. The dogs stayed at the bottom barking and yelping.

All dressed in his fine clothes, Brer Monkey was hot and hungry. He had eaten nothing. In desperation he picked a fruit from an overhanging branch and stuffed it into his mouth. How could he know that it was from a pepper tree? Oh! did it burn! How Brer Monkey suffered! At last the dogs left. And that is how trouble made the monkey eat pepper.

I jumped on the wire and the wire bend,
And that's the way my story end.

UGLIER THAN
A GRINNING BUZZARD,
AN AFRO-AMERICAN
FOLKTALE

Retold by LOUISE ANDERSON

O nce upon a time, it was very hot in the jungle. The jungle was usually hot, but this day it was hotter than usual. Oh, the sun was beaming. And all of the animals were hidden behind the trees or they got beneath some leaves, just any place that was out of that sun because it was hot. Well, now, all of the animals were hidden except the old buzzard, and that old buzzard was flying through the air: flop flop, flop flop. He was trying to see what he could find to eat. Soon the little rabbit came out of the hole, trying to cool off. He was just sitting there, shaking and shaking, and old buzzard, lying there beside the rabbit, said, "Uh, good morning, Mr. Rabbit." Rabbit said, "Good morning, Buzzard." See, the rabbit didn't speak so politely because the rabbit knew all about that buzzard's reputation. Buzzard said, "Uh, Mr. Rabbit, how do you like this hot weather we're having?" Now, everybody wants to talk about the weather, so the rabbit said, "Oh, it's hot down in that hole, and it's hot up here. I can hardly breathe." Buzzard said, "Look at me. I'm just as cool as I can be. It's cold flying up there in that sky. Hey, Mr. Rabbit! Let's ride on the breeze and fly through the trees." The rabbit knew you weren't supposed to trust a buzzard. His mama always told him, "Whatever you do, don't trust a buzzard!" But it was so hot, and he looked down in the hole, and the hole looked hot. He decided to take a chance. He said, "Uh, uh, okay, Mr. Buzzard. I want to go for a ride." He got on the buzzard's back. Uh hah hah! Old Buzzard went flying through the air: flop flop, flop flop. And the rabbit sat up there cooling, because it was cooler up there on that buzzard's back. In a few minutes the buzzard said, "All right there, Mr. Rabbit, hold on tight. I'm going for a three-point landing." And then the old buzzard went into his power dive, wah hah! One hundred miles an hour straight down. He got almost to the ground, then swerved. He threw the rabbit off his back, broke the rabbit's back, then turned, ate the rabbit for breakfast. Hmph! The rabbit should have listened to his mama.

Later on the old buzzard was hungry again. He went flying through the air, flop flop, flop flop, and a little old squirrel went up a tree, de dedee dedee dedee. Cute little old squirrel (uh hah hah!). Old Buzzard landed on the limb. He said, "Good afternoon, Mr. Squirrel." Squirrel said, "Good afternoon, Buzzard." The squirrel didn't speak so politely either because the squirrel also knew about the buzzard. "Mr. Squirrel, you know it's so hot today that I thought I'd give all of my friends a nice little ride on the breeze. Would you like to go?" The squirrel said, "Uh, I don't know. It's, uh, I don't know." "Hold it right there now," the buzzard said, "I am not begging you to go. You don't have to go if you don't want to. I have folks lined up who want to go for a ride. I just came to you because you're a friend of mine and I thought you might like to cool off, but if you don't want to go, you just tell me."

Well, the squirrel knew that you weren't supposed to trust a buzzard, but he also knew that the farther you went up in that tree, the cooler it was, so he decided to take a chance. He said, "Uh, wait a minute, Mr. Buzzard. I want to go."

He got on the old buzzard's back! Old Buzzard went flying through the air: flop flop, flop flop. The squirrel sat there, cooling. Soon the old buzzard said, "All right there, now, Mr. Squirrel. Hold on tight. I'm going for a three-point landing." Again the old buzzard went into his power dive, wah, hah! One hundred miles an hour straight down. He got almost to the ground, then swerved. He threw the squirrel off his back, broke the squirrel's neck, then turned and ate the squirrel for dinner.

Well, sitting right there in a sycamore tree, swinging, tending to his own business was a monkey. The monkey saw how dirty the buzzard had treated the squirrel. The monkey had also seen what the buzzard had done to the rabbit, so he was just swinging and thinking, "Uh huh, um hum, right on, right on."

The next day it was hot again, and all of the animals were trying to hide from the sun, all of them except the monkey. The monkey was down there in the clearing, and the sun was beaming on that monkey. It was so hot, but the monkey, he just looked at the sky. He was out there so long till his friends began to peek from behind the trees and leaves—you know, the chipmunk and the other little animals that liked the monkey. They said, "What's the monkey doing out there in the sun? Oh, that monkey done lost his cool. The sun done burned that monkey's brains out." But the monkey was just sitting, looking and looking, and soon he saw a little speck in the sky. It was the buzzard coming. When the monkey saw that, he started dancing—a boop boopboop, a boop boopboop, a boop boopboop.

Old Buzzard landed and said, "Good morning, Mr. Monkey." "Good morning, Mr. Buzzard, good morning." The buzzard said, "Oh, what's that you're doing, Mr. Monkey?" "I'm doing my flying dance." "Why," the buzzard said, "Mr. Monkey, I've never seen anything like it." "Well," the monkey said, "I wish I could ride on the breeze and fly through the trees." And the old buzzard started grinning and said, "Ah! hah hah hah hah!" He had to turn his head. "You mean you want to go for a ride? There's nothing in this world I'd rather do than give my friends a ride in the sky. Come and get on my back." Ooh—all the monkey's friends just hid their faces. They said, "Oh, I know that monkey has better sense than that." Said, "That monkey's not going to get on that buzzard's back." But the monkey was cool. He strutted and got on the buzzard's back. "Hah hah hah hah hah"—the old buzzard was going off just a-grinning.

Now nothing in this world is as ugly as a grinning buzzard, and while a-grinning he said, "I'm going to eat some monkey meat! Now I'm not going too far, because this monkey asked for it." He said, "All right there, Mr. Monkey," he said. "Hold on. I'm going for a three-point landing." Monkey said, "You hold on, Mr. Buzzard. You ain't gon have no monkey dinner today." He took his tail, used it like a whip. Zzzp. He wrapped the tail around the old buzzard's neck and pulled on the tail, pulled it so tight that the old buzzard's tongue almost hung out of his mouth and his eyes almost popped out of his head. The monkey said, "All right there, Mr. Buzzard, now you straighten up and fly right!" Ah hah hah hah hah. The old buzzard had to go when the monkey wanted him to go. The monkey pulled on his tail. He made the buzzard fly by his friends, and the monkey waved at his friends: "Hey! Hey!" His friends, they just clapped; they clapped and started pointing at the old buzzard. Then the monkey pulled on his tail and made the buzzard fly in the air until he was ready to come down.

Then, in the cool of the evening, when the sun was going down, that old monkey pulled on his tail and made that old buzzard let him out just by his friends. The monkey strutted off like this, you know (finger popping). And the old buzzard had his head all down, looking all ugly. The monkey and his friends, they just pointed at him: "Ah hah hah hah!" From that day until this one, the buzzard can't kill anything else to eat—he has to wait until something dies. And the monkey and his friends started doing the flying dance.

THE STORY OF SKUNK AND WHY HE HAS SUCH A BAD SMELL

JERDINE NOLEN HAROLD

T his is the story of Skunk and why he has such a bad smell. Long before Skunk smelled as bad as he does now, he was just like all the other animals; he had his own smell, a scent. It wasn't good and it wasn't bad. He smelled like himself. Trouble was, though, since Skunk was with himself all the time, he couldn't tell that he had his very own scent. He just assumed he didn't have a smell, a scent at all. This made him very unhappy.

Wherever he went he admired every other animal for its scent. And wherever he walked he kept coming nose to nose with his problem. First, he went to Mountain Lion to pay his respects because the lion is the king of beasts and Skunk has never been disrespectful.

"Sniff, sniff," Skunk sniffed.

"Why are you sniffing around me?" the king roared.

"King," Skunk said trembling, "I am sorry to trouble you, but you have such a powerfully strong scent. I am just admiring you. I sure do wish I could be like you, smelling so strong and all."

"Roar, roar, roar," King Lion said with a new kind of self-importance. "You are right to admire me because I do admire myself. Now you can be dismissed because I have much more to do on account of who I am. You ought to be happy about having your own scent," he added.

But Skunk hadn't heard. He dismissed himself, walking away with his head low enough to touch the ground. Pitiful.

The king went back to his king-work, shaking his head all the time. "Poor Skunk," he thought. "I wonder if he ever admires his own skunk scent."

Skunk walked along until he caught a whiff of something on the breeze.

"Sniff, sniff, now that's a delicate fragrance." It was deer. "Your scent, your fragrance, it sure is something for me to admire," he told Deer.

"Well, I am flattered that you think so," she said. "I am quite pleased with it myself. No one smells quite like me."

As she was going on and on about how glad she was to have just the right fragrance for herself, Skunk turned and walked away from her in the middle of her sentence.

Tulie, his sister, came along the road. He sniffed the air around her: "Sniff, sniff, sniff," he sniffed. Nothing.

"What is wrong with you, Jamieson? Why are you smelling the air around me like that? If I didn't know your family, I would think you were ill-mannered."

Too ashamed to say anything, Jamieson walked away. He walked all the way down to For-to-Wish Pond. He liked to sit and watch the water so he could think.

It so happened that this was For-to-Wish-Day, and Jamieson had a wish coming. He decided he would use his wish to pick his very own scent. He was given the magic words to say in order to get the scent off the animal and another set of magic words to make the scent stick on him. He thought it was going to be easy! He got the three standard wishes.

First he wished he could smell better. Immediately, his nostrils cleared up: He could smell the dew waiting to be spread over the next day's morning, he could even smell what his momma was thinking of cooking in her cooking pot.

"That's pretty powerful smelling," Jamieson thought, "but that's not what I meant!"

He constructed wish number two: He wished he could pick and choose his very own scent.

Well, nothing happened at first, but soon he started to feel all jiggily inside. Then the sycamore tree shook its leaves and said, "In a cave at the other end of this pond you will find a scent jar. It will help you with what you wish."

Sure enough, there was a scent jar complete with instructions on a slip of paper on how to use it.

"Oh boy," thought Jamieson, "now I'm on my way!"

Jamieson saw buffalo grazing.

"The buffalo has a real tough hide," he thought. "If I wear a scent like that, nobody would bother me."

He took out his paper and said the magic take-the-scent-off words. No sooner said than done, the buffalo didn't know what happened.

But Jamieson did. He tried it on: "Interesting..." Before he could finish his thought, another buffalo came along. Thinking Jamieson was a buffalo, there was much confusion.

Jamieson didn't like buffalo scent after all. He took the scent off. "Until I decide which scent is definitely me," he thought. He put buffalo scent into the scent jar for safekeeping.

Next came pig, then goat, cow, horse, and crow. He was even able to magic-up whale scent. He tried them all, but nothing seemed exactly right because he wasn't exactly sure what he wanted to smell like. He knew he wanted to smell like... himself: skunk.

While he collected all the animal scents, he didn't realize the mess he was making in the world.

When Jamieson made his For-to-Wish, not only did he claim the animals' smell but their ability to smell as well. It's a sad thing to see animals such as the lion unable to smell to find his food or find his way home. And the wolf had the hardest time because most of the wolf's cunning is smell anyway.

Jamieson had collected about 4,392 smells in that scent jar, but he still wasn't satisfied. Not one was quite right. He had collected in his scent pot just about every scent of every animal for miles around. He was rather pleased with himself until he saw what a mess his friends were in and he realized he was to blame. He felt awful. He wanted to put everything back where it belonged. He had one more wish coming. He went back to the For-to-Wish Pond and made his final wish.

Now magic is magic, and it can sometimes lose a little of its power each time you use it. That's why wish givers give you only three wishes because they know magic's limitations. The point is that the magic words for calling out the scents didn't work too well. They needed a little coaxing to come out and return to where they were supposed to be.

Jamieson opened the lid the way he was told. He poked his face in and called out the scents one at a time.

"No!" they all screamed up at Jamieson. "No, we are not leaving this place until you climb down here and name us out." Jamieson would do anything to get things back to normal. He called out the scents one by one from the depths of the pot, and one by one the pot released them.

Jamieson was glad. He thought he was finished with the last of it, but not quite. While he was down in the pot a trace of each and every animal scent lingered. That is the way of a scent—it leaves a little of itself behind just to let you know it's been there—and all those scents mixed and mingled together.

Once Jamieson climbed out of the pot, it disappeared. "Whew," he thought, "my troubles are really over now!" But, standing out of the pot in the breeze, he caught a whiff of something that smelled really awful.

"What is that?" Jamieson wondered. "What is that awful odor?"

Turtle happened along. "Oooohhhhhhhh mmmmyyyyyy," Turtle said. "Jamieson, is that you? What have you been into? Boy oh boy, do you have a bad smell! When was the last time you bathed!"

"Bathed?" Jamieson said. He didn't really understand. "Well, I have worked hard today putting things back to normal," he thought.

He decided to go down to the pond to wash himself because it was getting to be supper time. But when he got down by the washing pond, the tide went out, as if running to about the middle of the pond bed, and yelled back, "Oh no, you don't. You smell much too bad. You're not going to give it to me."

And that's the way it was. Even the animals avoided Jamieson and his curious scent. The animals taught their children to stay away from his children. And from that day to this, all Jamieson's kinfolk carry the burden of that troubled time of long ago. Wherever he goes, all the creatures run and hide. Maybe they think he's hiding a scent jar, or maybe they're trying to stay away from his curious scent.

How Jamieson wished he could be his old self again.

But there is a happy ending in this sad one: Jamieson did keep that keen ability to smell, and he uses his powerful odor to protect him and keep him from harm.

HOW THE SNAKE
GOT HIS RATTLES

JULIUS LESTER

When the Lord made the snake, he made him all the pretty colors he could think of—reds and browns and oranges— and the Lord put the snake down here to decorate the ground and the bushes, to add a little color to everything.

Well, the snake didn't mind ornamenting the earth, but he wondered if the Lord knew what a hard life he had to lead. And it was hard! Wasn't no doubt about that. He didn't have wings like the birds, so he couldn't fly. He didn't have fins, so he couldn't go for a swim in the river. He didn't have feet, so he couldn't run fast. All he could do was crawl in the dust. He didn't even mind that so much, but he couldn't figure out why the Lord had given him such poor eyesight. Man, the snake was so blind he couldn't even see a flashlight if it was shining right in his eyes. He was so blind he couldn't see his hands in front of his face if he had had hands to put in front of his face. His eyesight was so bad he had to smell his way around. And to tell the truth, his nose was none too good, either.

Now you can imagine what it must've been like when the snake had to go to the store or down to the laundromat. Crawling around in the dust like that and being half blind, he was always getting stepped on. He couldn't see anybody coming, and since he was down on the ground, nobody could see him. The other animals didn't mean to step on him, but you know how it is sometimes. You're in a hurry trying to get somewhere, and you just ain't got the time to see whether there's a blind snake with a no-smelling nose in your path. Some days, the mere thought of going somewhere tired the snake out so much that he just didn't even bother getting up.

Mrs. Snake wasn't too happy about the situation, either. She couldn't even take the little snakes down to the playground anymore. The other children thought they were pretty jump ropes. So she was stuck in the house with the kids all day, and they were about to drive her out of her mind. "Why don't you do something?" she screamed at him one morning. "I went out to hang up the laundry this morning, and I almost got run down by two buffalo, three antelope, and a rabbit. I'm just sick and tired of this, and if you're half a snake at all, you'll do something about it."

Mr. Snake sighed. He'd heard it all so many times before. "Well, just what do you expect me to do? Grow arms? The Lord made us this way and ain't a thing we can do about it."

"Says who? You know as well as I do that God don't know what he's doing half the time. He just sits up there experimenting with this and that, and we were one of the experiments that didn't turn out well. You're going to do something or I'm going to know the reason why. You're triflin', lazy, and no 'count. My mama told me not to marry you, and I should've listened to her!" And Mrs. Snake proceeded to call him a whole bunch of dirty names. She even jumped on back in his family and started playing the Dozens. Said his mama was a lizard and his daddy was a fishing worm.

Well, Mr. Snake was trying to figure out what number he should play that day, and he couldn't half concentrate with all the yelling his wife was doing, so he decided to crawl off to Heaven and talk it over with the Lord. He figured that the Lord wouldn't be able to do anything, but at least it would shut his wife up if she got the word directly from God.

About two o'clock that afternoon, the snake got up to Heaven. The Lord was sitting back in his great rocking chair reading *TV Guide*. "Well, what's going on, Mr. Snake?"

"Ain't nothing happening, Lord. Same ol' same ol'. You know."

"Yeah, know what you mean. Pull up a chair. I was just sitting here seeing what was gon' be on television in 1970. Course, that's a long way off, but I figured I'd check it out now, just in case I wanted to take a vacation about then."

The snake curled up in a chair.

"Care for a cigar, Mr. Snake?"

"Thank you, Lord, but don't believe I do."

"I've been thinking about cutting down myself. Mrs. God tells me I smoke too much. She says it makes my breath smell bad."

"Is that so?"

"That's what she claims, Mr. Snake, and I just can't understand it. I brush after every meal. Well, that's neither here nor there. What's on your mind? You looking mighty well."

"Well, Lord, I ain't *doing* too well."

"You don't say."

"It's the truth. I hate to come up here bothering you and all, knowing how busy you are, but my wife just wouldn't let me rest until I did something."

"Well, why don't you tell me about it?"

"It's like this, Lord. You know my eyes are kinda bad. Seems to run in my family on both sides of the house. And me being low on the ground like I am, I can't tell when folks are coming down the road. As a result, me and my family are always getting stepped on. And Lord, I just ache all over, and you know I got a whole lot of muscles that can ache. The strain has made my nerves so bad that the rain beating on the leaves makes me jumpy."

"You in bad shape, Mr. Snake."

"I done tried Compoz and everything else you can think of for my nerves, Lord, but don't nothing help. Some days I think about going outside the house and getting stepped on, and I just don't get out of bed."

The Lord lit one of his big cigars and blew smoke rings for a few minutes. "Well, I didn't mean for nothing like that to happen to you." He reached in his pocket and pulled out a small bottle. "Here. This is poison. You put this in your mouth, and give the rest to all your kinfolks. This will be for you to use to protect yourself with. Anybody step on you, you can bite 'em and stick a little poison into 'em."

"Thank you, Lord. I sure thank you."

"Don't mention it, Mr. Snake. Glad to help out when I can. If you have any more problems, you just let me know."

The snake didn't waste a minute getting down the ladder and going home. When he told his wife about the poison, she was so happy she kissed him. He told her that she best be cool and went to bed.

• • •

Well, a few days later, the rabbit sent word through the forest that the animals had to send their union representative to a meeting. All the animals, that is, except the snake.

"The meeting will now come to order!" the rabbit announced. "Hey, Mr. Elephant! Can't you find a seat somewhere and stop blocking the sun? I don't know why the Lord made the dumbest thing in the forest the biggest."

The elephant sat down.

"You still blocking the sunlight, Mr. Elephant."

"I'm sorry, Mr. Rabbit."

"Well, I understand that it ain't all your fault. You think you can hold your head to one side so a little light can come through? That's good! Now, everybody know why I called this meeting. It's that snake! We got to do something, and do it quick, before he kills us all off. I've been to thirteen funerals this week, and today's only Tuesday."

"I know what you mean," the frog put in. "That snake killed three of my uncles, seven cousins, two aunts, and my brother-in-law. I have to admit, though, that getting rid of my brother-in-law was kind of a blessing."

"Well, blessing or no blessing, that snake has been a terror ever since the Lord gave him that poison. He's been biting everything that shakes the bush. He can't see, but ain't a thing wrong with his hearing. Why, if he just hear any little thing, he's dead on it."

"And he's got the best aim I've ever seen," the horse added.

"Who you telling?" exclaimed the rabbit. "I saw a leaf shake on a bush, and I guess you know that's one dead leaf now. Snake put all sorts of poison in that leaf."

"Well, what we gon' do about it?" the fox wanted to know.

"Tell him to move on over or we'll move on over him," said the panther. "Tell him the next time he lays his forked tongue on anybody, we're going to off him."

"And suppose he lays his forked tongue on somebody and you *don't* off him," said the rabbit.

"That's right," the owl put in. "Hustlers don't call showdowns."

The elephant said, "We could talk to him real nice-like and let him know that we don't mean him no harm, and all we want is our rights. He should be able to understand that."

"Like I said before, how come the Lord made you so big and gave you such a little brain? If your brain was magnified a hundred times, it would fit into the navel of a gnat and rattle around like a BB in a cornflakes box. Understand! He don't have to understand nothing he don't want to, as long as he's got so much power."

They talked and talked and talked and talked until the rabbit got so disgusted he just took off for Heaven by himself. They were going to do all that talking and end up saying they should send somebody to talk to the Lord. The rabbit wondered if he was the only one of the animals that had any sense.

The Lord was reading the newspaper when the rabbit came up on the porch. "Yeah, Mr. Rabbit. Just between you and me, I ain't gon' be nowhere to be found between 1960 and 1970. And if you take my word, you'll go somewhere and hide yourself. That's going to be a rough ten years. Yes, yes. I ain't answering no prayers during that time. No, indeed!"

"Lord! What're you talking about?"

"You just remember what I said, okay?" He folded the newspaper and put it beside his chair. "Now, what's on your mind?"

"It's that snake!"

"He was just up here a few days ago."

"Don't you think we know it. You gave him some poison, and he's bitten so many animals that a lot of them are packing up and going north. People are scared to let their wives and daughters go out alone at night. That's the truth! Lord, that snake has bitten three hundred and thirty-seven animals, five oak trees, seventeen palm trees, and one stickerbush. Ha! Ha! Ha! You should've seen him bite into that stickerbush. Ha! Ha! Ha! His wife was pulling stickers off his lips for two hours. Served him right, the low-down—"

"I get the point. You go on back and tell Mr. Snake to get himself up here in a hurry."

"Well, it kind of dangerous to get too close to him, Lord."

"You tell the elephant to yell the message in his general direction. Ain't a thing wrong with Mr. Snake's hearing."

A few hours later, the snake was curled up in a chair next to the Lord.

"Lord, I sure want to thank you for that poison you gave me a few days ago. I haven't gotten stepped on since."

"That's just what I wanted to talk to you about. What's this I hear about you using that poison for insurance instead of protection?"

"Well, Lord, you know my eyes ain't too good, and I can't see who's my friend and who come to do me harm. So I just bite everybody that come along, and that way I'm always on the safe side. I've been stepped on so much that I just can't take any chances."

"I can understand that, Mr. Snake. But now you just about terrorized everybody."

"I didn't mean to, Lord. I sure didn't intend to do that."

The Lord reached in his pocket. "Here. You take these rattles and put 'em on your tail. When you hear something, shake your tail. That'll be a warning. If it's your friend, he'll stop and pass the time of day with you. And if it's your enemy, he'll just keep coming, and after that, it's you and him. You understand?"

"Yes, Lord. I do. And I thank you. It was getting mighty tiresome biting everything that came along. Mighty tiresome."

And that's how the snake got his rattles. By that time, though, almost everybody was so afraid of him anyway that hardly anyone ever came around to see him. When they did, though, he shook his tail right hard, and it rattled through the forest, letting everybody know: this is Mr. Snake here. You can't step on me now.

A TUNNEL
TO OUR ANCESTORS

GERALD J. A. NWANKWO

The theme of "A Tunnel to Our Ancestors" thrust itself on me when the Nigerian military coup d'etat of January 1, 1984, revealed that the state governors and government officials, who cried to the gods to send manna from Heaven in order to raise the economy of the nation, had hoarded millions in Nigerian currency in their homes and foreign banks.

Many, many years before man learned to fight the forces of nature such as drought, cold, and heat, there was a terrible famine in the never-never land of the animals. It was so terrible that many animals starved to death, until Uncle Turtle, the oldest and wisest of the animals, came up with a plan that saved the day.

It happened when a fierce war broke out among the gods on Eligwe (Heaven). Each of the gods claimed that he did more in sustaining the world and its inhabitants than the others. All that one could hear in Eligwe (Heaven) was, "I'm the greatest, I'm the greatest." It was a fight of supremacy.

"If I fail, even for one day, to supply warmth to the world, everything will freeze up," said Anwu, the Sun god.

"But I think that my duties are more vital than that," replied Amadioha, the god of thunder. "It is my responsibility to cool off the earth after you've scorched it for a full day and sometimes for a full season. In addition, it is my responsibility to send out the bolts that crack the heavy stratus clouds so that the rains can fall and bring life to plants and animals. If I have to stop performing my duties for just a few days, the whole universe would grind to a halt, and life as we know it today would be a thing of the past."

Itiri, the ugly goddess of darkness, was becoming impatient with all this boasting of greatness.

"Let's see who's the greatest," she said to herself as she sneaked into Erebus, from where she prevented darkness from breaking up the monotony of daylight. There was no nightfall, and everyone worked without any rest. There arose an outcry among all creatures of the earth.

Anwu, the one-eyed Sun god, was the maddest. He did not get his daily sleep of twelve hours. He stayed there in the sky without darkness to relieve him. So he sent his dreaded son, Rana, to heat up every nook and crook to let the gods and the universe know that he was mad. Furthermore, he let his thirsty rays begin to drink up all the waters of the universe.

That did it. Life on earth became unbearable. There was no food to eat and no water to drink. Added to hunger and thirst, the air was too dry to breathe. Trees began to lose their leaves and grasses began to dry up. Starvation swept through the land.

But while most creatures on earth were making sacrifices to ask Amadioha, the god of thunder, to break the clouds so that rain could come to the world below, the wise Uncle Turtle was busy drawing a plan that could enable the animals to overcome. When he was through, he called an emergency meeting of the animals.

"If we sit here, scratching our heads and buttocks, and waiting for the gods to cool off the heat of their anger before they look down on Earth to answer our supplication, our lineage and possibly our race may be marching fast toward the narrow gate that leads to the land of our ancestors. And that could mean total extinction of what is now known as the animal kingdom. I know that none of you wants that to happen."

He waited to see their reaction, and they dutifully obliged him. They sighed and grumbled and chirped. He was delighted and proceeded to expose the lifesaving scheme.

"But if we stand up to what faces us," he asserted, "we may be taking in our hands not only our present but also our future."

Having ignited their spirits with this idea of running their own lives with or without the help of the gods, he told them that all they needed to do was build two gigantic silos—one to store water and the other to store food. He assured them that if they had both water and food to last them a full generation, they would have time to think of making Nature yield to their needs. The animals were crazy with excitement, and they wasted no time in building the silos at the center of the animal kingdom. It was necessary to build them at the center of the kingdom so that all eyes would be on them, and no one could rob them without their noticing.

After completing it, they worked endlessly to stock food and water to last the entire kingdom for a generation. The anxieties of hunger and starvation that drew deep lines on their faces were gone. They were surer of their daily ration of water and food than ever before. Each day they lined up in front of the silos for each family's dole. Uncle Turtle made sure that the rationing was fair and equitable, depending on family size and individual place in the society. No one thought of the famine anymore.

One day Uncle Turtle announced that he was making a long journey. The animals were shocked. They did not want him to travel now that they needed his presence most.

"Don't travel, most venerable messenger of Chineke, for some evil might befall us in your absence," cried the owl, the only animal who was more afraid of the day than the night.

"Fear not, my beloved one," replied Uncle Turtle. "Chineke, in his infinite mercy, will take care of all of you and this kingdom in my absence. Let me relieve your fears by telling you where I'm going and for what."

The curiosity of his audience was immense. Everyone wanted to know where he was going, and they all shouted in one voice: "Where are you going?"

"To the land of our ancestors," he announced proudly. "I would like to know why the gods are mad at us. I would also ask our ancestors to intercede with the gods for us. I'll be back in three moon cycles."

Although the animals were happy that Uncle Turtle was going to make a face-to-face intercession with their ancestors, they were apprehensive of the danger involved; something might go wrong and he would be dead, or his approach might make the gods angrier.

Uncle Turtle could see these concerns in their eyes and therefore allayed their fears by telling them how cautious he had been in making sure that no evil would befall him or his race.

"I asked the rabbit, the finest hole digger in the land, to make me a tunnel from one corner of my house to the outskirts of the land of our ancestors. He worked on it for six moon cycles. When it was completed, I made a sacrifice to Ogu, the god of peace. Ogu told me that there would be no danger if I traveled alone. Furthermore, he promised, if we would add two large huts beside mine where they could stay, he and his numerous messengers would keep an eye on the animal race."

The animals were satisfied. Nothing could have been as assuring as knowing that the god of peace, whose ever-reaching hand brought peace to many hearts, was in their midst every minute of the day. In a few days two new large huts stood beside Uncle Turtle's.

Two days after the completion of the new huts, Uncle Turtle was ready for the incredible journey that could change the history of the animal kingdom. All the animals came to bid him farewell. They danced and sang his glory until they had lost both their voices and the strength of their legs.

Life was pleasurable in Uncle Turtle's absence. It was even sweeter than *uvune*, the sweet fruit that the animals used instead of honey. No one had anything to complain about. There was no doubt that Ogu, the god of peace, and his messengers were in those huts beside Uncle Turtle's.

On the morning of the thirty-second day of the third moon cycle, the land was in an uproar. They were mourning. The silos were empty. There was no way to compare their sorrow, and there was no one to console them. They knew that they would starve to death, especially now that Uncle Turtle was away.

Out of desperation they braved the danger of going to their ancestors on foot. They stormed into Uncle Turtle's house, hoping to use the narrow tunnel he used to the land of their ancestors.

They were surprised. Uncle Turtle was home and enjoying a hot meal of foo-foo with the most delicious *egusi* soup.

THE STORY OF THE EAGLE, A WEST AFRICAN FOLKTALE

Retold by EDWARD ROBINSON

Once there was a chicken farmer who had a barnyard of white leghorn chickens. Hard times befell the farmer, and the chicken business wasn't doing too well. A friend of the farmer came to him one day and said, "I have an idea how you can make yourself some extra money."

Of course the farmer was all ears. The friend went on and said, "Up there in the mountains I spied an eagle last week. Now if you set a trap for her and capture her, you can bring her down, show her off, and charge admission to see her."

The farmer thought that that was a good idea. So he built a big trap, went up in the mountain, and finally caught the eagle. He brought her down and tried to transfer her from the trap to a big viewing cage he had built. But the eagle was too used to freedom, so she bit him, she clawed him, she fought him every time he tried to get near the trap. The farmer became so angry he got his gun and killed the poor eagle who only wanted her freedom.

The friend came again, saw what had happened, and said, "Look, brother farmer. I believe that eagle laid a couple of eggs. Go get those eggs from that eagle nest, bring them down, and put them under one of your setting hens. Then, when the eggs hatch those little eaglets, they won't know who they are. They will think they are chickens, so they won't fight back and bite you. They won't claw you. They will be peaceful and calm because they won't know who they are. Then you can show them off in that big viewing cage, charge admission to see them, and make yourself a whole lot of money."

The farmer got the eagle eggs and put them under one of his setting hens. In time one of the eggs hatched, and a little eaglet came out. He didn't know who he was. He thought he was a chicken. The farmer was happy. When he went near the little eaglet, the eaglet got frightened and ran away as fast as his little legs would carry him. The farmer called him Tom.

Tom ran around with the chickens and was very happy until one day he saw himself in the stream of water that ran through the barnyard. He saw that he was not white like the chickens. He saw that the feathers on his head did not lie down slick like the feathers on the chickens' heads. He became ashamed of his color and his head feathers, so he took some Porcellana and rubbed it over his feathers to lighten them up. Then he got some gheri curl* and put it on his head feathers. Now Tom felt happy that he was beginning to look more like a chicken.

By and by the other egg hatched. Now this eaglet broke bad when he came on the set. Somehow he got the nerve to stand his ground when the farmer stamped his foot. The farmer called him Turk. The other eagle, Tom, began coming over to give advice to Turk. First off he told Turk, "Now since I'm older than you, call me Uncle Tom. And here's some Porcellana to put on those feathers so you can lighten them like mine and the rest of our brother chickens. Then do something about that head. Do *something*."

When Turk refused and shied away, Tom whipped out a silk cloth. "Well at least put this silk rag on your head to do something to those feathers up there."

But Turk said, "I-I kinda like my color and my head the way they are."

Uncle Tom turned away in disgust and happily joined the chickens in play, leaving poor little Turk all by himself.

The only joy for poor little, lonely Turk was looking up into the sky for long periods of time, because somehow he felt that that was where he belonged.

One morning while he was looking up into the sky, a speck appeared. The speck got larger and larger until it became the largest bird he had ever seen. You and I know that it must have been an eagle. Well, the eagle saw little Turk on the ground and came in on a

---

*Gheri curl is a preparation which produces a greasy wet, curly hairstyle popularized by African Americans.

branch overhanging the barnyard. He looked down at young Turk and in a deep bass, eagle voice said, "What are you doing down there with those chickens?"

Turk, in his high eagle voice, said, "Why, I—I *am* a chicken."

The old eagle laughed in his deep eagle voice and said, "You're no chicken."

"Then what am I?" asked the young eagle.

"You're an eagle," bellowed the big eagle in his deep bass voice.

"An eagle?" asked Turk. "What's an eagle?"

"An eagle," bellowed the old eagle, "is the king of the skies. Spread your wings and fly up here on this branch so I can tell you who you are."

But poor little Turk, with tears in his eyes, said, "I can't. You know chickens can't fly that high."

The old eagle became very angry at Turk. "I told you that you aren't a chicken. You're an eagle. Now spread those wings."

Turk spread his wings out, as far as he could spread them.

"Now flap them," said the old eagle.

Turk began flapping them, faster and faster, and to his surprise he rose higher and higher—higher than he had ever risen in his life—and came in on the branch beside the old eagle.

"Now settle down," said the old eagle. "I will tell you your history. I will tell you who you are. Your father, as all eagles are, was the king of the skies. No bird was as strong. No bird could fly as high and as far as your father without rest. And your mother, as queen of the skies, ruled the skies alongside your father. And you are their son. That's who you are."

"But-but-but, what about my color?" asked Turk. "You see, the chickens are white, and I am a deep brown."

"Don't you know what that color represents?" asked the old eagle. "It represents royalty."

"That's heavy," cried Turk. "But what about the way the feathers are on my head? They don't lie down slick like the feathers on the chickens' heads."

"That's your crown. I told you that you are a king," said the old eagle.

"That's deep," said the young eagle. "Let's tell Uncle Tom." Spying Uncle Tom on the ground with the chickens, Turk shouted down, "Uncle Tom! Uncle Tom! This man up here is telling us about our history. It's so beautiful."

But Uncle Tom shouted back, "I don't want to learn anything

about our history. I'm too busy getting these crumbs off the ground. Anyway, you'd better come down out of that tree before you get us all in trouble."

The old eagle sadly shook his head. "He's too brainwashed. Uncle Tom doesn't want to learn about his history. Come, let us fly away to our destiny."

They took off. Pretty soon they flew over a deep valley. The young eagle got so frightened he screamed, "We'll fall."

But the old eagle smiled and said, "Don't be afraid. You won't fall. This is the Valley of Oppression. You will fly safely over the valley because you have the strength of kings in your wings. Fly on!" And they flew safely over the valley.

They came to a big desert. Again the young eagle screamed in fright, "I don't see any trees on which to rest." But the old eagle said, "This is the Desert of Mediocrity—the Desert of Don't Care—the Desert of Only a C Average. But you don't need to rest. You will fly safely over the desert because you have the strength of kings in your wings. Fly on!" And they flew safely over the Desert of Mediocrity.

But straight in front of them loomed a high mountain. Young Turk again screamed, "We'll crash into the mountain."

Again the old eagle smiled. "This is the Mountain of Injustice. But you won't crash. You will fly safely over the Mountain of Injustice because you have the strength of kings in your wings. Fly on!"

And the young eagle and the old eagle flew over the mountain.

I, the old eagle, say to you young Turks, learn the truths of our glorious age of Songhai West Africa, then you will be shielded from the darts and arrows of the falsehoods portrayed on television and the motion pictures about Africa and Africans. You will find that there is no subject you cannot master, that there is no profession that you cannot claim, that there is no height to which you cannot climb because you have the strength of kings in your wings. Fly on!

Some years ago I was having lunch with the director of the Philadelphia zoo, William Donaldson, when I told him the story of Turk the eagle. He almost choked on his food and sputtered, "We have an eagle here at the zoo that thinks he's a chicken. We got him from West Africa, just where you got your story. Come on. I'll show him to you."

On the way to the building where the bird was housed, he gave me some details: "His name is Mike, and the zoo got him about thirty-five years ago as a curiosity. In Africa some scientists put an eagle egg under a setting hen, and when Mike hatched, the first thing he saw was his foster mother, a chicken. His breed of eagle is called a battler eagle, one of the fiercest of all eagles. But Mike is afraid of everything, even chickens."

Well, Mike was everything Bill had told me and even more. When we entered the room where Mike was kept, this fierce-looking eagle fled in panic. Mike ducked around a corner of a box in the room and uttered sounds that sounded like a frightened hen clucking. Then he emitted a sound like a rooster crowing. "He can't make up his mind whether he's a hen or a rooster, so he tries clucking and crowing, like the sounds he first heard when he was hatched in the barnyard," Bill said.

Bill finally cornered and caught Mike. "Watch this," Bill said. He put Mike on a perch. Promptly Mike fell right off on his head.

"He tries to peck corn, but he really can't because his beak is not straight like a chicken's. But he tries and tries anyhow, so we have to make a special gruel for him. The reason he can't perch and balance himself and is totally opposite in his nature from an eagle is that he's brainwashed from birth. But the amazing thing is that he can't fly any higher than a chicken because he's brainwashed that he *is* a chicken. Yet his wing structure is precisely the same as other battler eagles who can fly higher and farther than any bird in the sky."

I was excited over this real-life enactment of my story of the eagle. I returned to the zoo with my wife and a few friends a few weeks later. This time Mike was in a yard with some chickens; the yard was enclosed by a four-foot wooden fence. We were invited to climb over the fence and pet Mike, which we did after some coaxing and patience. This was in the children's zoo, and he was a great favorite of the children. I took pictures of Mike—an eagle genetically destined to fly higher than the Empire State Building but who couldn't fly over a four-foot fence.

COMMENTARIES

ANIMAL TALES AND LORE

HOUSTON A. BAKER, JR.

One of the most widely known genres of black folklore is the animal tale. The earliest collector and popularizer of black animal tales was Joel Chandler Harris, whose first volume, *Uncle Remus: His Songs and His Sayings,* was published in 1881; subsequent volumes appeared for the rest of the author's life. His work and the work of his immediate followers, however, while it is of undoubted value, does not truly represent black folk values. Harris and his contemporaries adopted an antebellum perspective and put black animal tales in the mouth of a faithful black retainer —a simple, primitive child of nature. It is not surprising that Harris and others depicted white plantation children as this puerile narrator's audience.

In fact, black animal tales are similar in some respects to the animal tales of all other lores. That is to say, they began as etiological stories and accrued meaning as time passed.[1] From the earliest stages of his existence, man has had a keen interest in animals (if not out of intellectual curiosity, at least for self-interest), and his observations of their actions together with his lack of scientific knowledge has led him to evolve tales of explanation. The explanatory nature of the animal tale was ideally suited to the needs of the black folk in America, since the land and its fauna were alien to the founders of the black American race. Moreover, given the lack of sophistication of the black folk in relation to the advanced culture that surrounded them, one would expect to find a high incidence of animal tales in their folklore. The farther back we go in time, "the more conspicuous becomes the place taken by etiological animal tales."[2]

As time passed, however, black animal tales took on new meaning, moving closer to the fable. They lost part of their explanatory character and came to be employed more for entertainment and instruction. The chief character of the black animal tales, Brer Rabbit, is an entertaining figure who had much wisdom to impart to the black folk. J. Mason Brewer delineates the trickster rabbit as follows:

> The role of the rabbit in the tales of the American Negro is similar to that of the hare in African folk narratives—that of the trickster who shrewdly outwits and gains a victory over some physically stronger or more powerful adversary. The animal tales told by Negro slaves with Brer Rabbit as the hero had a meaning far deeper than mere entertainment. The rabbit actually symbolized the slave himself. Whenever the rabbit succeeded in proving himself smarter than another animal, the slave rejoiced secretly, imagining himself smarter than his master.[3]

Black animal tales, therefore, resemble the animal tales of other lores in their employment of the trickster, but the social condition of the folk producing them gives an added dimension, a certain psychical component which the slave narrator surely supplied and which his slave audience readily recognized.

The subliminal component of black animal tales is apparent in the delineation of the trickster as a cunning figure who tricks others into doing his work. The "avoidance of work" situation motivates the action of such tales as "Playing Godfather," "Tar Baby," and "Brer Fox and the Goobers."[4] In each of these tales Brer Rabbit sets out to evade work, and in the process tricks the larger animals, escapes punishment, and even comes away with certain material gains. Both "Playing Godfather" and "Tar Baby" have parallels in other lores,[5] but the very title of "Brer Fox and the Goobers" indicates its proximity to the black folk, since *goober* (peanut) is an African linguistic survival.

A second trait of the black animal tale—the hero's employment of disguises—reflects what must have been a familiar experience. In both "The Watcher Blinded" and "Why Brer Gator's Hide Is So Horny," Brer Rabbit shows his expertise in deception. After they had killed a stolen ox, "rabbit asked wolf what would he do if some ladies came and asked him for some meat." When the wolf answers that he would give it to them free of charge, the rabbit begins his performance. The stupidity of the wolf is emphasized by the fact that Brer Rabbit assumes four different feminine disguises and receives a portion of the wolf's meat each time. In "Why Brer Gator's Hide Is So Horny," the protagonist conceals his feelings about Brer Gator in order to trick the larger animal into a painful situation, one which alters the gator's perspective as well as his appearance.

A third trait of black animal tales—the ambivalent attitude toward the trickster—is shared by the animal tales of all lores. Brer Rabbit is not always the cunning and successful hero; he is often depicted as a coarse blunderer. "The Watcher Blinded" shows Brer Rabbit jeopardizing himself in an act of lyrical braggadocio; the "Tar Baby" story shows the trickster tricked; and in "Why Brer Rabbit Wears a 'Round-'Bout," the hero is brought to a painful end. In all lores these stories reflect the fact that while the narrator and the audience admire the trickster's cunning, they also envy his prowess and fear its possible ramifications.

Black animal tales thus contain both the universal aspects of the animal tale genre and certain characteristic aspects that mark them as the product of the black American folk experience. The common traits of the trickster are present, but his identification with the slave makes the tales unique. Like all animal tales, those in black folklore proceed out of a sylvan and agrarian environment, but they also proceed out of a slave experience in which the success or failure of the trickster had a singularly important didactic and wish-fulfillment value.

The agrarianism and didactism of black animal tales connect this genre with another genre of black folklore, the proverb.[6] Although they are not uniquely black in theme, black proverbs seem to come directly out of the agrarian soil that nourished the black American race, and the idiom in which they are expressed marks them as distinctively black. Proverbs like "Tarrypin walk fast 'nuff fer to go visitin'" or "Rooster makes mo racket dan de hin w'at lay de aig" or "Hongry rooster don't cackle w'en he fine a wum" are obviously close to the black animal tale in many respects, and the psychical element noted in the animal tales may have been present even in these terse reflections.

NOTES

1.   Alexander Haggerty Krappe, *The Science of Folklore*. New York: Methuen, 1930, pp. 60–63.

2.   *Ibid.*, p. 61.

3.   J. Mason Brewer, *American Negro Folklore*. Chicago: Quadrangle, 1968, pp. 3–4.

4.   The tales, sermons, testimonials, songs, and ballads used for illustrative purposes in my text may be found in Bontemps and Hughes, *The Book of Negro Folklore*. New York: Dodd, 1958.

5.   Cf. Aurelia Espinosa, "Notes on the Origin and History of the Tar-Baby Story," *Journal of American Folklore*, XLIII (1930), pp. 129–209.

6.   Brewer, *American Negro Folklore*, p. 28.

TRICKSTER, THE REVOLUTIONARY HERO

IVAN VAN SERTIMA

T he word *revolutionary* in my title is not lightly chosen. It has a double significance. The revolutionary role of the Trickster figure in the folk imagination is related in the first place to the longing of a powerless group, class, or race for social or political change, for transcendence over an oppressive order of relationships. This may be expressed in folktales by symbolic acts of sabotage or revenge by a weak or vulnerable or despised figure (Brer Rabbit, say) against an apparently stronger or more powerful opponent (Brer Wolf, Brer Bear, Brer Tiger, say). But I speak also of the revolutionary role of Trickster in a more radical and complex sense, a role Trickster played among aboriginal Africans and Americans, a role related to the profound and often obscure longing of the human psyche for freedom from fixed ways of seeing, feeling, thinking, acting; a revolt against a whole complex of "givens" coded into a society, a revolt which may affect not only an oppressed group, class, or race but a whole order—the settled institutions and repetitive rituals of a whole civilization. I will explain more clearly what I mean when I come to deal with Trickster in this complex role. All I want to point out at the beginning is that the purpose of my paper is to show how the Trickster functioned in the African folk imagination—the main roles he played—and how those roles were recast and redefined by Afro-Americans under the unique social and psychological pressures of the New World.

In their original African home and culture these figures took on other functions that are ignored, minimized, or forgotten among the

Blacks of the New World. Their functions in this hemisphere have become restricted to a treachery and guile aimed at transcendence over impotence and servility within a highly oppressive order of relationships. It would be interesting to look at some of those other functions and the reasons why they have been neglected or ignored in transplantation. The Trickster in Africa is not only involved in tricking the lords of the jungle—tiger, elephant, lion—which are symbolic of the class of the mighty and powerful but he also plays tricks on the rulers of Heaven itself, stealing fire or food for his fellows under the noses of the gods. We seldom find him in such a role in the New World.

Trickster is also in revolt against the mores of his own group—committing taboo acts, acts of outrage which release him from the confines and boundaries laid down and observed by his peers. We may find him, for example, on the eve of battle when the warriors have withdrawn from their families and are ritually forbidden to go unto their wives before the clash, slaking his lust to the full in a village of husbandless women. This is an imaginative way of escape from the collective pressure upon the instinctual life of individual man.

We also have Trickster as presocial man, that is, a figure which preshadows social man. *It* is man before the forms society made and dressed him in, man as free spirit, original energy, pure primal power before the limitation and rigidity of any social or ritual artifice. Such a form can imaginatively go back to beginnings, to the unstructured chaos of origins, in order to free the human psyche to explore new orders and forms.

Such functions of the Trickster were a luxury in a slave and colonial society. So deep, so intense, so total indeed was the negation of power in the real life of the Afro-American that the role of the Trickster in the life of dream was nearly always overpowering and triumphant, and never self-destructive, regressive, or anarchistic in a primal sense. Blacks, barracooned in the slave plantations and colonial ghettos of the Americas, could hardly afford this. They needed no vision of chaos to relieve their impatience with stable structures and immemorial orders. What they needed (at least in the past) was a new order through black lawlessness which would negate the old order of white lawlessness that had negated and outlawed them.

Thus, the role of Trickster as underdog, as representative of an oppressed group or class or race, became almost the only role or function transplanted here. I think the choice of animals for tricksters in Bantu culture (rabbit and tortoise) and in West African culture (Annancy, the Spider) is most revealing. Let us first observe the archetypal qualities of the Bantu pair.

Rabbit occupies a disadvantageous position in the animal world. Extremely vulnerable, without a heavy hide, claws, beak, or sting, his fragility is counterbalanced by an extraordinary sensitivity (huge antennae for ears) and a lightning nimbleness (fleetness of foot). Though he may seem an easy prey to the larger animals, the potential for outmaneuvering them belies his apparent fragility. In the body and spirit of rabbit, therefore, is crystallized a subtle and delicate radar for scanning the potential peril (which he averts) and the potential possibility (which he exploits) in a given situation—a situation usually (in those tales most native to the tradition) of menace from the Mighty. A typical tale told by Uncle Remus is that of Brer Rabbit and Brer Lion, in which Rabbit is invited to offer up his life for Lion's supper and is so adept in his survival strategy that Lion dies wrestling with his own shadow.

The tortoise is another symbol of the underdog in Bantu mythology. In fact he is more popular than the hare in some parts of East Africa. His main virtue is his capacity to endure, for he can live longer without food than any other animal. He moves with a painstaking slowness but with the sureness of the sun in motion across the streets of the world, and this impresses itself upon the Bantu mind as the unrelenting and invincible doggedness of an elemental force. The brooding silence and secrecy of the tortoise also invest him with a suggestion of craft and cunning and mystery. He hides his innards under a shell in the way the Black had to hide his true face and feelings in the Americas under shells and veils and masks of deception in order to carry and conceal the horror at the heart of his daily life.

Some interesting tales are told of Tortoise. Perhaps the best known is that of the Great Race, but to me the most significant is the tale of the Famine, of which there are innumerable versions. During the Famine the animals searching for food come across a tree, previously unknown, full of ripe fruit. They send messenger after messenger to the owner of the tree to ask its name. The name of the tree has a mystical significance (the fruit cannot be picked or made to fall without its precise utterance), but the messengers all forget it. Only the tortoise remembers, and he lifts the curse of hunger from the land by felling the fruit. But though he is the only one in the jungle who can summon a total awareness of origins (the name of the tree being the name of the tribal ancestress), the other animals turn on him and refuse him a share of the fruit. The tortoise in some versions is smashed to pieces and is put together again by the ants. On regaining his pristine strength he uproots the tree, with all the animals eating their fill in its branches, and they perish in the Fall.

The psychological value of this tale to Afro-Americans hardly needs to be underscored. The slave in the Americas may identify the smashing of the tortoise to pieces with his own dismemberment and fragmentation, the denial of its due share in the fruits of life with his own social deprivation, and its Samsonian uprootment of the tree on the recovery of its strength as a prophetic indication of his ultimate release in a cataclysmic act of vengeance and revolt.

It is strange that there are so many collections of Afro-American folktales and so few analyses of the significance of the animals in these tales. Grave misconceptions abound. One commentator sees the fairy tale as a flower of civilized societies and the animal tale as the relic of primitive tribes. Another finds it difficult to understand how the African can humanize animals in these tales and yet retain a clear distinction between the animal as creature and the animal as symbol of man. Yet others, close to our times, refuse to accept the obvious influence of African trickster figures upon the folk mythology of Afro-Americans. It is clear that this is a field as rich in its accumulations as it is poor in its theoretical premises.

An analysis in depth of the main elements in these African folktales will show that the animals are involved in a shadow drama of the human world. They are dream figures through which personality traits, values, or power relations of groups—commoner and king, slave and master, the weak and the strong, the powerful and the suppressed—may be reflected in a dreaming drama of the social world, within which dream and drama the figures are invested with a fluidity and metamorphic quality denied them in the more rigidly structured social world, so that they often seem to reverse and over-turn their given social role or condition. It is this capacity of the dream figure (animal archetype) to overleap and overturn an oppressive social condition that makes the personae of the tales (rabbit, tortoise in Black America, Annancy the Spider in the Caribbean) take on a heroic cast and revolutionary function.

This role reversal and revolutionary function of certain folk heroes account for their enormous popular appeal among the black communities of the New World. Like the Caribbean Annancy, the black American Brer Rabbit plays the role of outlaw and conman. Neither subscribes to the laws and moral values of their society. Secretive, elusive, cunning, deceptive, sometimes cruel and treacherous, they are in the role of the Transcendent Criminal, avoiding through their legendary agility of wit the onerous and unfair burdens imposed upon their fellows, always one step ahead of Brer Wolf and Brer Tiger, the predatory lords and overseers of the jungle.

The psychological value of the Trickster's role in the Caribbean slave society has not escaped all investigators, though they have been led into certain conclusions that are inconsistent with a full appreciation of Annancy's real function and meaning. Rex Nettleford, for example, in an introductory essay to *Jamaican Song and Story,* makes the following observations:

> In Jamaica this descendant of the West African semi-deity seems to take on special significance in a society which has its roots in a system of slavery—a system which pitted the weak against the strong in daily confrontations.... It is as though every slave strove to be Annancy and he who achieved the Spider form became a kind of hero.... This picaresque character misses no chance for chicanery...as though he lives in a world that offers him no other chance for survival...to cope with an unstraight and crooked world one needs unstraight and crooked paths.

It would seem clear from this passage that Nettleford understands the profound relationship between Annancy's *act* and the slave's *dream.*

Yet in the very same passage he commits the error of associating, in a very literal way, Annancy's characteristics with features of the Jamaican character:

> Annancy...expresses much of the Jamaican spirit in his ostentatious professions of love, in his wrong-and-strong, brave-but-cowardly professions of bluff, in his love for leisure and corresponding dislike for work, in his lovable rascality....

Here are echoes of the slaveowner's slander of the naturally resentful and reluctant slave: "dislike for work," "love for leisure," "cowardly," "lovable rascality." This patronizing attitude is unworthy of such an astute critic as Nettleford. The "black" character of Annancy does not represent the character of Jamaicans in that sense at all. Jamaican children, brought up within a puritan ethic, utter an oath of purification—*Jack Mandora me no choose none*—when they narrate Annancy stories, the oath being a plea to the doorman at Heaven's door to absolve them of responsibility for Annancy's wickedness. What we are really face to face with in Annancy is what I would call a black innocence. He is loved and lovable because his "evil" liberates rather than oppresses. He assumes aspects of evil in order to elude and conquer a condition of evil.

Finally, and most important, we must return to the function I highlighted at the beginning of this paper, the most complex and yet the most revolutionary function of the Trickster figure. In aboriginal African and American tales we sometimes find the Trickster emerging as a Fool or Idiot Extraordinary, functioning with the power and freedom of a god and yet displaying an astonishing innocence of its power and capacity, even of its fundamental nature, like a newborn babe. Paul Radin has cited tales in which this figure appears with its penis wrapped around its head, its right hand at war with its left, its proportions formless or undetermined. This incredibly vital and yet incredibly vulnerable creature demonstrates the godlike power to alter its amorphous shape as well as the babylike propensity to see itself, as for the very first time, with no given assumptions about its limitations, extensions, and capacities. What is the meaning of this? Why should the generative organ of this creature (symbol of creative power?) be so large that it cannot be comfortably coiled and contained within its accustomed lair? And why should it be so ignorant that it has to learn from scratch, like any creation at birth, to organize and utilize its power?

This power, I believe, is the pristine potential of the human before he is squared and squeezed, boxed and beaten, drummed and driven into a shape that would fit the patterns of a particular culture, time, or place. This innocence is the childlike nakedness of man before he is clothed and straitjacketed by the ritual fabric and collective costume of a particular society. This role of Trickster expresses the profound and obscure longing of the psyche to shed the familiar coat and dress of a particular order or civilization and return to an examination of origins so that it may rediscover the springs of original energy. That energy is the source of change. The need at times for such change underlines the psychic or psychological value of such tales.

I am highlighting this function for although it seems to have been lost in transplantation it may in fact have had no relevance to the Afro-American until now. He is no longer a separate, suppressed part of Western civilization but, in this latter half of the twentieth century, reenters the mainstream, no longer simply an underdog protesting the group or race or class in power, but becoming a power in his own right, sensitive to the fundamental malaise that afflicts the whole civilization. Thus it is that an Afro-American novelist, Wilson Harris, a writer of very complex and original fictions, has recently introduced this figure and function of the Trickster in a novel, *Companions of the Day and Night* (Faber and Faber, London 1975).

In that novel the Trickster functions as he does in the aboriginal African and American tales as a kind of god or superconscious Being. He is a god in the sense that all the creations of the world through which he moves seem also to move through him. They are not separate or divisible from him. They are extensions and complements of his own self, the limbs and organs of one body of which he is the heart and brain, the center of Consciousness. He is the Organic Creation before its separation and division into diminutive capsules of individual personalities, times, cultures. This is what Radin means when he speaks of "original energy." That is what I intend to imply when I speak of the freedom and power of a god. The object of this highly imaginative exercise is to demonstrate the capacity of the human spirit and substance to recreate itself, to feel its way toward a Consciousness that breaks down and breaks through apparently fixed and frozen, partial and polarized, states of being and belief. The revolution implied here is a revolution of the imagination, a revolution in consciousness, a fundamental revision and reassessment of static and ritualized modes of seeing, thinking, feeling, which may afflict a whole civilization, regardless of whether one is in the black or white race, the capitalist or communist camp, the group of the ruler or the ruled. This is, in effect, the ultimate conflict between man's *freedom* to remake himself and the world he has already made, which *imprisons* him in the tightly woven fabric of its ritualized reflexes, ideologies, and institutions.

It is not an easy concept to explain, but to simplify it further is to run the risk of misrepresenting the subtleties of the fable and its extraordinarily apt and skillful application to the American and global reality in the novel. What it demonstrates is that what often passes for arbitrary invention and imaginative sport or absurdity in these ancient tales contains the most explosive seeds of wisdom. It is like the dreams which rise with such apparent effortlessness from the depths of our daily lives as we are suspended in the flickering twilight of our sleep, watching the strange theater of the psyche unfold. The Trickster is one of the main characters on the stage of that theater.

In *Companions of the Day and Night,* this figure returns to a fiction of the Americas to illumine the danger of collapse in a social order or civilization. It is a signal of pressures in the human psyche for a new creature to evolve, powerful and yet babylike, original and yet formless (The Trickster God and Fool). It is the need for a revolutionary quality of the imagination to evolve among us, an imagination which seeks to rethread the basic fabric of the inner (and ultimately the outer) world, so much of which we take for granted. We are at a point where there are terrifying urges everywhere for change, but the impulse expresses itself more as a sentiment or protest reflex than as a genuine fundamental thrust for a revision of mental structures, a revision of the human itself. Both the rebel and establishment ideologies seem locked in the same fixed, programmed ways of seeing, feeling, thinking, and acting. The world has become a place where, in Matthew Arnold's phrase, "ignorant armies clash by night." The Trickster emerges as a counterbalance to that nightmare, an eye or light in the heart of a gathering but not implacable darkness. Fluid and free, a principle of revolutionary energy at war within forms that seek to contain it, it is able to see from within, act from within, move from within, the roots of its world, to *re-root* that world, so to speak, to point the way forward to a new course, a new possibility, a new human person.

SOURCES

Harris, Joel Chandler, *Nights with Uncle Remus: Myths and Legends.* Boston: Houghton Mifflin Company, 1911.

Harris, Wilson, *Companions of the Day and Night.* London: Faber and Faber, 1975.

Jekyll, Walter (ed.), *Jamaican Song and Story.* New York: Dover Publications, Inc., 1966. See introductory essays.

Radin, Paul. For this reference, see R. Abrahams, "Trickster, the Outrageous Hero" in T. Coffin (ed.), *Our Living Traditions.* New York: Basic Books, 1968, p. 171.

Van Sertima, Ivan, "African Linguistic and Mythological Structures in the New World" in Rhoda Goldstein (ed.), *Black Life and Culture in the U.S.* New York: Thomas Crowell & Sons, 1971, pp. 12–35.

———"My Gullah Brother and I: Exploration into a Community's Language and

Myth through its Oral Tradition," in T. Trabasso and D. Sears (eds.), *Black English: A Seminar.* New Jersey: Lawrence Erlbaum Assocs., 1976, pp. 123–146.

———"Into the Black Hole: A Study of Wilson Harris' Companions of the Day and Night," in *ACLALS,* Fourth Series, No. 4, Mysore, India, 1976, pp. 65–77.

SECTION II

LIKE IT WAS:
History
Remembered

Ananse sem kyiri kasa.
(Storytelling doesn't like idle talk.)

—*Ghanaian proverb*

STORIES

HOW WE GOT OVER

JACK AND ROSA MADDOX

Yes, I was born a slave and so was Rosa. We got out of the chattel slavery, and I was better for gettin' out, but Rosa don't think so. She says all we was freed for is to starve to death. I guess she's right 'bout that, too, for herself. She says her white folks were good to her. But don't you expect me to love my white folks. I love them like a dog loves hickory.

I was settin' here thinking the other night 'bout the talk of them kind of white folks going to Heaven. Lord God, they'd turn the Heaven wrong side out and have the angels working to make something they could take away from them. I can say these things now. I'd say them anywhere—in the courthouse, before the judges, before God. 'Cause they done done all to me that they can do. I'm done past everything but worryin' 'bout Rosa, 'cause she don't get 'nuf to eat and 'cause she feel bad all the time. But they ain't no complainin' in her. [To Rosa] Mama, how you feel in the sun?

Rosa Maddox: Best to be expected this time o' year.

Jack Maddox: I was born in Georgia on a farm. My mother's name was Lucindy. I heard other Negroes say she was a good woman, but she died when I was a little boy, not more than three or four. She left my little brother a crawlin' baby 'bout eleven months old. I can remember a little her dyin'. I can remember her rockin' me on the steps and singin', "Lord revive us. All our help must come from Thee." I can remember cryin' for my mama and bein' lonesome for her. They tried to tell me she was dead, but I couldn't get it through my little head. My little brother was pitiful, plumb pitiful. There was one between me and the baby and all of us was lonesome for Mama. I had a older brother and a older sister. My sister was so good. She wasn't nothing but a chap, but she did what she could for us.

Many times, when she wasn't but nine years old, I have held a pine torch for her to see how to wash our rags at night. Then Judge Maddox's cook was a good woman. She was half-sister to Judge Maddox and was a sister-in-law to my mama. For a long time she let the baby sleep with her in her bed.

But my other brothers and sisters had to sleep on the floor in the cabin, huddled together in cold weather so we wouldn't freeze to death. Our life was a misery. I hate the white man every time I think of us being no more than animals.

Judge Maddox moved into Buena Vista when I was real small. He had a big fine double-run frame house covering a large piece of ground. We used to wait outside the kitchen door of the master's big house. The baby would crawl up by the door and wait with us. The cook would give us what she could. Sometimes she would give us a teaspoon of syrup and we would mix it with water to make something sweet. I used to crave sweet. Or we would eat a biscuit with fried meat grease on it. We used to be too hungry to give the baby his rightful share. We would get the chicken feet where they threw them out and roast them in the ashes and gnaw the bone.

Judge Maddox had about fifty slaves, as I remember, when I was a little boy. Most of them stayed out on the farm and worked out there.

My father was a blacksmith. He could make everything from a horseshoe nail to a gooseneck. He was sold to Judge Maddox from the Burkhalters. My father said the Burkhalters were mean as they come. He said that his master, Mr. Burkhalter, had gone to a war when he was a young man and stayed six months. He told me that there had always been wars and there would always be wars and rumors of wars as long as the world stand.

Rosa never did know nothin' 'bout her father, eh Mama?

Rosa Maddox: That's right, I never did know nothing 'bout my paw, but I looked on my mama like a savior. Her name was Hannah Clemon, and Dr. Andrews, my master, had always owned her. Dr. Andrews was a good man and good liver. He was from Mississippi, but he moved to Union Parish, Louis'ana, when I was such a little girl I don't remember.

My mama said that she remembered when Dr. Andrews came from Louis'ana to Mississippi and got married. He brought her along and told her to piece quilts so much that she didn't have no time atall. But he moved back to Louis'ana.

Dr. Andrews had 'bout twelve slaves. I had all the time to play until I was 'bout nine years old. We made rag dolls and played dolls —that was me and the other little niggers. I was the baby of my mama. She had eight chillun besides me. We used to play "church." We would play "singin'" and "prayin'" and "dyin'."

We had good little cabins. There was four of them settin' out in the yard. And we had cotton mattresses and blankets. We had 'nuf to eat, too. They 'lowanced it out to us every two weeks. They'ud give us syrup, meal, flour and meat, potatoes, and plenty of milk. The madam, that's Mis' Fannie, Dr. Andrews' wife, had a garden, and she give us fresh greens and onions and things.

The neighbors used to say, "There goes Oat Andrews' free niggers." That's 'cause he never hardly whipped them and give them rest and play time. He doctored us when we was sick and took good care of us. I sho' thought a heap o' Dr. Andrews.

The Andrews had two boys and a girl. The girl died and they was awful cut up about it. The boys were good boys. It always seemed they thought a heap of me. 'Course, I thought a heap of them, too. They was smart boys with book learnin' and schoolin'. But they better not ketch any niggers with books. They say that was bad.

Jack Maddox: Now on Judge Maddox's place, if a nigger was caught with a book he got whipped like he was a thief. He had one man named Allen who went to work for a man whose boys taught him to read. When he came back to Judge Maddox's, he would slip off into the woods on Sunday and read a paper or a book. I 'member he told me, "It's a shame that a man couldn' read like he wanted to, cheap as paper is."

When I was about nine or ten years old—it was in 1853—Judge Maddox's family and the Blantons and the Wells and the widow Nutt 'lowed they would come to Texas. Judge Maddox sold off some of his slaves. He sold one man so he could stay with his wife that b'longed to another white man. But three men that I know of came to Texas with Judge Maddox and left wives behind them. One, I know, never saw his wife again. A man didn't have the freedom of a dog in them days. It was pretty good crowd came to Texas. Most of them rode in covered wagons, but 'course us niggers walked.

Judge Maddox settled near Mount Enterprise and built him a good frame house, and little double-room log houses for the niggers.

'Course, we got to go to church in fair weather. They used to fix up a brush arbor in back of the whitefolks' meetinghouse and let the niggers set out there. The white preacher would preach along and then he'ud say, "And you slaves out there, if you want to have the Kingdom Come you got to mind your masters, work hard, and don't steal your master's chickens."

After I was a plumb old man, I read in the papers that there was nine hundred preachers in the penitentiary and I said to myself, "There ought to be nine hundred more there, if they would just ketch them all"—them preachers and their left-handed fellowship.

Rosa Maddox: Now, me, I used to go to church. I used to ride on the horse behind Mis' Fannie. I went and set in the white folks' church. But later on I went to a colored church. I thought the singin' was just fine. I got religion when I was pretty little. I just remember that I felt the power of the Lord descend on me. But I was sinful for a long time. I kept on dancing and singin' reels and cotillion songs. But I ain't did that for a long time now. I wanted to do right, but I guess I had a lot of devil in me. One reason I guess was 'cause the Andrews were joyful folks. They just made me joyful.

The niggers on the Andrews place had clothes. The niggers was taught to sew and spin. They knitted socks. Mis' Fannie taught me how to knit and sew and spin. But she used to buy me good calico dresses and make them up for me. Shucks, I had good clothes as anybody. Maybe that was why I had lots of beaus.

Jack Maddox: Well now, Rosa, I believes you disremembers some of those good things. From what I seen, I didn't see much of goodness. I seen speculators coming by with womens and chilluns, as well as men. The older I got, the more I found the taste of they whips with my back layed open. And I seen niggers put in the stocks.

When I got big 'nuf to go fishing I'd go, and the old lady 'ud call me and take my fish away from me. I got tired of it and was hongry for fish. I cooked and ate them in the woods. They quit lettin' me go fishing on Sunday. They put a chain 'round my legs and on my arms. Then they put a stick under my knees and chained me down by the hands to it. I was hobbled worse than a animal.

One Sunday morning, I had on chains and I was mad. The judge had called me early that morning to go to a neighbor's house, and there was heavy frost on the ground. My feet were sore and scabbed over, and going on the frozen ground was worse than a misery, but I had to go. Later on I was building a fire in the fireplace and I kept lettin' the chains clank against the brass firedogs. I knew he didn't like it. But I thought as how I didn't like going in the frost with my sore feet, and I thought to give him a dose of something he don't like. I kept the chain clanking. He come in and got me, and he beat me half to death. Then he put a iron band and chain 'round my neck and it choked me terrible.

Yes, I'm a white folks' nigger. I loves them just like a dog loves a hickory switch.

Seems like there was a lot of speculators got to coming through Texas. Judge Maddox was buying a slave every now and then. One day he brought home a pretty mulatto gal. She was real bright and she had long black straight hair and was dressed neat and good. The old lady come out of the house and took a look and said, "What you bring that thing here for?" The judge said, "Honey, I brung her here for you. She going do your fine needlework." She said, "Fine needlework, your hind leg!"

Well, you know what that old lady done? When Judge Maddox was away from home she got the scissors and cropped that gal's head to the skull. I didn't know no more 'bout that case, but one thing I do know was that white men got plenty chilluns by the nigger women. They didn't ask them. They just took them. I heard plenty 'bout that.

Judge Maddox had three nigger boys run away to go to the free state all at one time. He got the dogs and trailed them, and they caught them, and it was a sorry day for them.

About that time the War come along. I can remember those days very plain. I used to see the men come by to talk it over about the War. When Judge Maddox's boys went, they didn't have time to get new clothes. They just went, and later on got their uniforms.

I was sent with my brother to haul salt from Grand Saline, Texas, 'cause the folks in our parts couldn't get the salt for their vittles. Then

I was sent with mules and more niggers to work on the government breastworks [temporary fortifications]. I didn't see it, but I sho' heard the Battle of Vicksburg. And that was something to hear, God knows.

Then I was right close to the Battle of Mansfield, in Louis'ana. I heard it and I got there and seen the dead laying round on the ground. I saw people I knew.

As I was going home, I stopped by a Mrs. Anderson's place and she had a boy named Bob who was a deserter and was hiding at home. When I was there, some Confederate soldiers came by and told his maw to tell where Bob Anderson was. She said she didn't know 'cause she hadn't seen him. The leader man told her, "You better go tell him that he will come out or we will burn him out." She went into the house and told that unless he give himself up they going to burn him out. So he came out.

They tied him with a rope and tied the other end to the saddle of one of the men. They went off with him trotting behind the horse. His maw sent me following along in the wagon. I followed thirteen miles. After a few miles I seen where he fell down and the drag signs on the groun'. Then, when I comes to Hornage Creek, I seen they had gone through the water. I went across and, after a while, I found him. But you couldn't tell any of the front side of him. They had drug the face off him. I took him home.

I hadn't been at Judge Maddox's very long when he got mad and tied up my shirt over my head and beat me bloody raw. I made up my mind to run away and join with the Federals. I told my brother just littler than me, and in the night we slipped away and went toward the east. We walked and ate and slep' in the woods. One place, we went into a blacksmith shop. We were awful hungry and wanted something to eat. The blacksmith asked us questions and told us to go home to our masters. We got so scared we ran out, and I left my walking stick. I think we walked over a hundred miles.

One night we were in the woods and I heard some men on horseback coming. I went to take a look on the road and I thought they was Federals. I went back to tell my brother. God knows why, but he got up and started running the other way. I had to go and ketch him. The fool ran a good half mile. After I caught him and talked to him, we set out to ketch up with the Federals. We came up to them the next day when they was resting.

That was just above Monticello, Arkansas. They was the kindest folks I ever saw. They gave us some hardtack—something like a hard old cracker—some sowbelly, and the first coffee I ever drank. They gave us blankets and let us rest. They let us lay right down by them. We didn't need no kivver-up. I will remember that day long as I live. It was June 25th. I stayed right 'round that bunch of Federals until December in the year '65. I seen the Federals heap corn in piles and burn it. Sure s'prised me to see folks burning good corn. I heard they did it all through lower Georgia.

I went with them to San Antonio. I got arrested there. I guess I got to feeling so good I wanted to make noise. I made noise on the street with a bunch of wild boys and they took me up. I'm proud to say that was the first and last time.

Rosa Maddox: But we had war where I lived, too. Dr. Andrews' niggers went off to work on the government breastworks. I didn't know what the War was 'bout, but I used to hear guns go off. Every gun goes "boom, boom," so I didn't know who was killing who. When the War was over, Mis' Fannie told me I was free, but she didn't tell me to go away. So I jest stayed, and for a long time I didn't see no difference in anything. Dr. Andrews just went on doctoring people, and folks 'ud say, "There goes Andrews' free niggers." I worked hard, but I got along all right, and I had good times and I had beaus.

Jack Maddox: Rosa didn't see no life like I did. I guess she didn't see no trouble till she saw me, but I'm going to get to that.

In '68 I went into Rusk County, Louis'ana, and worked for a man opening a new sawmill. In December of '69 I went to a party and that is where I met my wife. I had caught a little look at her before then, and I liked what I saw. I sho' loved her the first time I ever saw her. She was a good dresser, but not as fine a dresser as me.

Rosa was doing all them cotillions with her dress spreading out and some of these hug-up dances. A fiddle band was playing. I know they was playing that song about "Christmas time, Christmas time, almost day." I started right out to court Rosa then, but she told me I better go slow with her.

The next year I married Rosa. We decided to buy a farm and make a place for ourselves. We made a payment down on a piece of un-cleared land. We went into the woods and Rosa worked like a man. We sawed the trees and split the logs. Rosa cut shingles and together we roofed the house. We dug our own well and together we cleared the land and planted it. We had a baby after we was married 'bout ten months.

Everything went along for three years, and then the man we bought the place from died. We found out the place didn't b'long to us. The children of the first wife of the man who sold us the land took it away from us.

Then we went as tenants to a Louis'ana farmer. Every year, I come out with nothing but owing that man money. After three years he and his son fell out. The son came to me and told me that his paw was beating me on the books. He told me I was a fool not to learn to read and write and know somethin' 'bout figgers. I told Rosa, "I won't be going to bed so early these next nights." The boy helped me, and I got books and papers and, every night by the fire, I studied. When the time for the next agreement come, I told the man that we'd keep double books: he and I would both keep books. At the end of the year, he had me owing him money, but my books showed he owed me nearly a hundred dollars. I told him figgers don't lie, but the hand that made them sho' could. Well, I never got the money, but we parted our ways.

I farmed and did different things. I had five boys and two girls. They were good chillun. All of them dead now but one boy, and he is fifty-one year old.

Rosa and I been like sweethearts all the time. She has been the best woman I could ever have. I never wanted to make no swaps. It's never been too dark, never too cold, never too bad for her to do for me. She was never too tired to set with me at night if I was sick. She was gone from me visiting the chillun for two months once, and that is the only time we ever been separated. I wrote to her every day. I have courted Rosa ever since we been married. 'Course, I ain't always been so virtuous. I have stepped out of the middle of the road. But Rosa didn't take on none. She always caught on to me and womens and got on to me 'bout it a little.

Rosa Maddox: I guess it's a man's nature to do with women, and I guess they can't go agin' their nature. But I always been good. I always been good and religious. But Dada's been a right good man. He was good 'nuf to me.

Jack Maddox: Well, when we was pretty old we knew a woman had a baby. She treated that baby pitiful bad. She said he looked like he was a idiot. I remembered 'bout how miserable I was when I was a little boy, and I said to Rosa if she was willing we would take him. She was willing and the mother give him to us when he was twenty-two months old. He was covered with sores, but a little washing soon cleared it up, and he's been with us ever since, like our boy. He is a smart, nice boy. He is 'bout fifteen now. He knows all the names of the baseball players and the G-men. He knows how to read and gets his lessons fine. He plays baseball and marbles. He has thousands of marbles. I'm sho' proud of him to win the other chillun's marbles. I tole him, "If you don't grab for yourself then nothin' going to help you."

This is the first time I ever told my story.

HOW THE SLAVES HELPED EACH OTHER

Retold by WILLIAM J. FAULKNER
(collected from SIMON BROWN)

Sister Dicey was as good a soul as ever lived. She was the friend of all the folks, black and white. One day Sister Dicey passed away in her sleep. Now, the slaves had no undertakers, so the womenfolk came in and prepared her body for burial, which had to be done in twenty-four hours. After bathing her, they put on her the best dress they could find and laid her out in a homemade coffin, resting on two chairs. Somebody pinned a flower on her bosom.

Later that night slaves from all about came to the cabin and sat around while they sang and prayed. People kept coming and going all night long. The singing was mostly sad songs with happy endings, because the folks felt that now Sister Dicey was freed from all the trials and tribulations of slavery and was safe in Heaven, at rest and in peace forevermore. She wouldn't be a barefoot slave dressed in rags anymore. In God's Heaven, she'd have everything she needed to make her happy. The mourners at Sister Dicey's sitting up knew this and sang:

I got shoes, you got shoes —
All God's children got shoes.
When I get to Heaven
I'm going to put on my shoes
And walk all over God's Heaven.

I got a robe, you got a robe—
All God's children got a robe.
When I get to Heaven
I'm going to put on my robe
And shout all over God's Heaven.

I got wings, you got wings—
All God's children got wings.
When I get to Heaven
I'm going to put on my wings
And fly all over God's Heaven.

I got a crown, you got a crown—
All God's children got a crown.
When I get to Heaven
I'm going to put on my crown
And wear it all over God's Heaven.

I got a harp, you got a harp—
All God's children got a harp.
When I get to Heaven
I'm going to play on my harp
And play all over God's Heaven.

So, with this picture of Heaven in mind, the mourners weren't too sad at Sister Dicey's going away. They knew she was better off with a loving heavenly Father than she had ever been in this wicked world of slavery. Some of the people got so happy thinking about Heaven that they burst out crying and shouting for joy. And so the sitting up went on all night.

The next morning old Master John Brown came over to the cabin to pay his last respects to Sister Dicey, his faithful servant, and to tell the people that he would let them off from work to go to the funeral. They could use a pair of mules and his best farm wagon to carry the coffin through the woods to the graveyard.

The coffin was a plain pine box built by a good slave carpenter on the plantation who could make them to fit any size body—man, woman, or child. I didn't walk with the coffin and the mourners out to the graveyard because I was about thirteen years old and had been sent to help some of the men dig the grave. It was six feet long, three feet wide, and six feet deep. But I didn't help with the last of the digging. I was too scared to stay in the grave when it got down past my head.

When the family and mourners reached the burying grounds, six men carried the coffin to the grave and rested it on two long-handled shovels. Then they put plowlines under each end and let it down easy-like into the hole. A box lid was let down with the same ropes and fitted in place, and then a man climbed into the grave and screwed the lid on.

When this was done, the slave preacher said words of comfort over the body—something like this: "Sister Dicey, since God in His mercy has taken your soul from earth to Heaven and out of your misery, I commit your body to the ground, earth to earth, ashes to ashes, dust to dust, where it will rest in peace. But on that Great Getting Up Morning, when the trumpet of God shall sound to wake up all the dead, we will meet you in the skies and join the hosts of saints who will go marching in. Yes, we want to be in that number, Sister Dicey, when the saints go marching in."

Before the preacher could finish his benediction, some of the women got so happy that they drowned him out with their singing and handclapping and shouting. Then some men and boys began to fill up the grave. When it was full, they rounded it up real pretty-like and put one wood shingle at the head and another at the foot of the grave. The womenfolk laid some flowers and ribbon grass on top and put colored bottles, broken glass, and seashells all around the grave of Sister Dicey.

In that way, they showed their love for her. It was the best that slaves could do in those days, when everybody was poor and owned by their masters. But no man could own their souls or keep them from loving one another. These gifts came only from God.

HARRIET TUBMAN
IS IN MY BLOOD

MARILINE WILKINS

I am Mariline Wilkins, great-grandniece of Harriet Tubman. Most of the information that I have is information given to me by my mother when she would talk to people and answer questions about Harriet Tubman. My mother was raised by her, lived with her throughout her childhood and most of her young adult life. A lot of the things she told my mother were of her experiences during the Civil War, before the Civil War, and what went on prior to her wanting to free the slaves from bondage.

Harriet Tubman was the youngest of twelve children. She started out working when she was but five years old. She was small in stature. I always thought of her as big because of the things that she did; I just visualized her as being real tall and big, but this was not true. My mother was shorter than I am, and Harriet Tubman was about five feet one inch or five feet one and a half inches tall. She was small but she was strong physically.

Of course, you know that she did not read or write, but she had implicit confidence and trusted in God for everything that she did. She would pray to him for anything that she wanted to do, and she said He always answered her prayers. She conversed with Him on any item or anything that she wanted to do. Whatever she had in mind to do, she conversed with Him before she went through with it. She often had visions. This is the sort of thing that I think is most unusual. When you can't read or write, I think God gives you another group of senses to guide you. This is what happened with her.

The family had been bought by the Brodess family, which was

considered one of the wealthiest slaveowners on the Eastern Shore, and Harriet Tubman worked for them from the time she was five until she left to work for Mr. Cook, another slaveowner. Mr. Cook's wife was pregnant, and he wanted someone to come to his place to look after the baby when it was born and to help him with his muskrat trappings. So she was lent to Mr. Cook while still a child. Some of the stories say that she was sold to him, but she was not. She was lent to him, and Mr. Cook told Mr. Brodess that his wife would teach her how to weave cloth and this weaving would help clothe his family.

However, Harriet didn't like indoor work. She preferred to be outdoors. When the baby came, Harriet was so small that she would have to sit on the floor, and they would put the baby in her lap in order for her to take care of it. She also helped Mr. Cook with his muskrat trappings. While she was doing this, over two or three years, I think, she caught cold. When her mother heard about it, she asked Mr. Brodess to get her child and bring her back to her so she could nurse her back to health. She heard that she had been sick for a long time. This was because of this trapping through the swamp in the wintertime. Mr. Brodess did go and get her and, after she got better, she went back to the Cook house.

Eventually Harriet left the Cook household and returned to the Brodesses again, working in the fields. It was at that time, while working in the fields at the Brodesses, that a worker in the field left the field and one of the field supervisors followed him. Harriet decided, after the field supervisor had gone, to follow the worker in the field who had left; she would see what was going on. When she did, she went to the little store, and there the field supervisor was after the field hand who had gone away. When she appeared at the door, the field supervisor told her to stop him. She refused to stop him. When she refused to stop him, he picked up a tool, iron weights, threw it, and cut her. Some storybooks say she was hit in the back of the head, but the scar is on her forehead. She carried that until death, and she developed sleeping seizures.

They thought she was a nitwit after that. They said she wasn't capable of work and all that sort of thing, so she let them believe that because it was to her advantage. She continued to work wherever she was available, but she preferred working out of doors. And it was when she was working at the Cook house again that she heard them discussing, at one of the evening meals, that they were going to sell some of her family, her sisters and brothers, to another slaveowner farther south. She decided then that this business of slavery was terrible, and she didn't like it. She said, "Dear God, help me get rid of this terrible thing and these terrible people." She listened some more and heard some more information, and she decided that that was what she was going to do, try to free them. The first time she tried to go free or leave, she wanted her brothers to go with her, but they didn't want to go. They started out but got scared, so she decided not to continue because, if they didn't go, she was sure they would come back and tell what she was trying to do. For a long time, she told my mother, they thought that this person who was freeing the slaves was a man.

She did not dress like a man. When she started freeing the slaves, she would put on old clothes and act decrepit like an old woman. Because she was considered a nitwit, they never suspected her. They never suspected this little black woman, and it was to her advantage. She had many little tricks, and they never suspected this person who had gotten hit in the head and had these sleeping seizures.

She could be sitting here talking to you just like I am, and all of a sudden one of those spells would come over her and she'd go to sleep. And when she woke up, she would start right where she left off. I don't think you could consider her a nitwit, not in any way, shape, or form. Several times she would get caught in one of those things, and people would say, "Oh, just wake her up, wake her up." You couldn't wake her up, Mama said. She just had to sleep it off. Once she was lying on a park bench with her face to the back of the park bench, and somebody put this poster up offering a reward for her, dead or alive. When the man finished, she woke up and saw the poster, and she just looked at it and went on. She knew who it was, she recognized her face.

Before Cicely Tyson played in that story they had on television, she went up to Auburn and stayed for a while and visited with my cousin Gladys, so she could get the feel and go out to the home and all of that. Gladys can remember Harriet Tubman because Gladys was seven years old when she died. Cicely Tyson played in that scene where they made Harriet Tubman take the place of a horse pulling a cart. She was strong mentally and physically, by all accounts, and even though she couldn't read or write, she could think and had common sense. Why she let them do that I'll never understand, and when Gladys and I saw the premiere, we objected to it. This woman was a living legend; she wasn't a fictitious person. If she had been white, she would have been all over the history books, but because this little black lady was not considered knowledgeable and couldn't read or write, people thought, Why should we recognize her?

She married Tubman because he was a free man and could read and write; she thought he could help her, but he was not sympathetic to her cause. When she went back to get slaves, to free them, she would sometimes run across him. The last time this happened she tried to see whether he would be interested in helping, and he was not. So she just gave him up. Mama said she had other things to do. She didn't bother him. Next thing she knew he had been killed. That ended that. But in that television story they had her making money and saving it and counting it while he was looking in the window. She was not braggadocious or showoffish like that; she was quiet and reserved.

She was always looking for ways to make money. She worked to get money in various places because she knew she needed to have money to clothe and feed some of the slaves on the route. If she didn't get help from some of her white friends or the Quakers who were helping her, then she would work for a short while and get a certain amount of money to help them along the way. She never dressed flashy. The story showed her coming into town to see William Grant, wearing a little brown poplin suit and a little hat with fur around it. She never wore anything like that. She wore dark clothes, in the summertime white, navy blue, or black, and that was it. All during the time she was freeing the slaves and during her work in the Civil War, she wore navy blue and white. She would wear sunbonnets of different patterns. They might see her going down the street with a blue-and-white-checkered sunbonnet and then, when you looked again, she might have a plain blue one. And the bonnets covered part of her face so she wouldn't be visible. In the story they had her coming down the street with this little cocky hat on and her face was very visible. She would say she couldn't afford to be seen. Her face could not be viewed because she called herself the "ugly duckling." I thought all of that was wrong, to picture her in that vein.

When she was traveling, she wore several layers of clothing. She wore pantaloons on top of pantaloons and petticoats on top of petticoats. Why? She knew about the bloodhounds out for her, and if the bloodhounds got a taste of her blood, she would not be able to do the work any longer. So she had layers of clothing, and they would get the clothing instead of a taste of her blood. This was one reason why she kept layers and layers of clothing. What gave out, when she got older, were her limbs from all the water she had traveled through in the swamps and the cold winters and all of that. She did not get dressed up, and she didn't wear a man's hat while she was freeing the slaves during the Civil War. She wore bandannas or sunbonnets. I saw something where a family down in Maryland or Virginia had a reunion. One woman in the family was supposed to be dressed up like Harriet Tubman, and she wore this man's fedora. Mama used to say she wore bandannas and sunbonnets.

Harriet Tubman was born in Bucktown, Dorchester County, Maryland, near Cambridge. My mother, Eva S. Northrup, was born in Canada in St. Catherine. Her name was actually Evelyn Katherine Helena Harriet. The Harriet was from her father's side and the Helena was from her mother's side, but she cut the name in half. I was born in the States, in Auburn, New York, the same place as my cousin Gladys. Harriet Tubman raised most of her nieces and nephews, the children of her brothers and sisters who had passed on. My mother was the only one, I think, that lived with her for a long period of time. My mother's father, James Isaac, was Harriet Tubman's nephew. His father, James Henry, was her brother. There were William Henry's and James Henry's; they went down the line. Gladys's full name is Gladys Alidas Bryant, and William Henry was her grandfather.

Harriet Tubman had knowledge of many things, and this accounted for her success in bringing slaves to the North. For example, she knew about remedies, and this was how she helped the soldiers during the Civil War, knowing what herbs to pick and steep and how to help them with all the illnesses they had during the war. The family feels that she discovered penicillin. Whenever she did canning and air got into things that were canned, a mold formed on the top; she took that mold and didn't throw it away. She scooped the mold off and put it into another glass jar, and when that jar was about half full (and Mama did this in my lifetime because I had some of it for colds), she filled the rest of it with fresh lemon juice, honey, and some brandy or whatever she had. If she didn't have brandy, she used bourbon or something like that. She shook it and then let it set, and anybody who had a cold got a teaspoon of it. It did not taste good, but it was good for colds. And what was the green stuff? It was nothing else but penicillin. She would say, "This is good for colds."

My mother cut her hand once while she was living on the farm with her, and her thumb was cut so badly that her thumb was loose from her hand. Now the family refers to Harriet Tubman as "Grandma" because she was the oldest person and the one they looked up to. Mama said that Grandma took her and said, "Come on, Kit. Let's go to the barn." She got some white cloths that she had folded up and kept in a drawer in the kitchen, just torn from old sheets and stuff. Whenever they cleaned up the barn, she never wanted to take the cobwebs down that were up at the top; they stayed there. So she went up on the ladder and got the cobwebs, brought them down, and slapped them on Mama's hand and tied it up. In three days she took it off and put some more on. You couldn't see where my mother's hand, her thumb, had been cut. Mama said anytime you had a severe cut, that's what would happen. But I could never see where the thumb had been severed from her hand. Also, anybody who had the gout used to make poultices out of poke salad and put them on the feet to take the swelling down. These are greens, just like dandelion greens. She made poultices out of them as well as out of onions, camphorated oil, and a piece of flannel cut in a circle to fit front and back. Cut the onions up fine and add the camphorated oil. Mix them and lay those onions on, and then sew it and put it on your chest and lungs. Pin it up at the top and put you in bed. In the morning, if those onions were brown and you had no temperature, it meant that your fever had broken. Mama used to do that often with me because I had severe colds.

There were other herbs that she used to use, but I do not have that knowledge. Maybe I didn't take enough time or didn't think much of it at the time, but Mama used to take milkweed. She used to go out in the field and get a piece of milkweed, break it, and put the milk from the weed on the part of the body that needed it, and then throw it away. You were not to look where you had thrown it. She did that two or three times for a wart which I had on my hand, and the wart went away. Mama said that Grandma, Harriet Tubman, used to do that too because she had several of them.

She used to make soap; she taught Mother how to make soap. But I don't do it. I take pieces of soap and melt them up, but Mama knew how to do it from scratch because she had taught her. I admit I don't know. And I wouldn't try to do it. It was as easy for Mama as mixing up biscuits.

I wish now that I had taken time to put down a lot of things that she taught me over the years. Now I realize just what they meant. I would catch cold often, and I had whooping cough for a long time. That old-fashioned idea—they say that it's old-fashioned—of an asafetida bag. Mama once had one of those out—oh, that stuff smells! And there was something else, some nutmeg. I don't know what this nutmeg did, but she put a hole in the nutmeg and put a string around it and put it around my neck. Now I cannot tell you the significance of that nutmeg. Why I had to wear it I don't know because I don't think I ever remember asking my mother why.

I never heard my mother say that Harriet Tubman was superstitious. Maybe she believed in some things. If she did not have enough food (in the home that she lived in in Auburn) for the people staying with her, she would say, "Well, I have to get some more food in here," and she would take a basket and go out into the barn or near the barn and hold up the basket, and she'd start praying and ask the Lord to fill it. By nighttime, people would come out and bring her food so she would have enough to take care of all those people that were living with her. Her first thought was to have a home for the homeless and for orphan children and older people. She was always taking in somebody. That's why a lot of people who went to live with her claimed allegiance to her or claimed to be a relative of hers because everybody called her "Aunt Harriet" or "Grandma." They thought they were related to her, but many of them had no bloodline with her whatsoever because she never had a child.

In two marriages she never had any children. She never lived with John Tubman. She married Davis after the Civil War, and they never had any children. Her name was actually Harriet Tubman Davis, but the history books refer to her as Harriet Tubman; they don't add the Davis, and she herself held on to the name that was attached to her from the beginning.

She used to tell many stories of things that had happened to her and to other people. For example, there had been a man in Washington whose name was Eally, I think; she freed him. They were going to hang him up there in Albany. She heard about it and got the people in the community together, and she said, "When I give you the high sign, you holler 'Fire!'" They were having a meeting like a court, I guess, and she eased her way in like an old woman. By being small she was able to do a lot of this. That's why she wore dark clothes, so she wouldn't be conspicuous. She went in and stuck her head out of the window, and the people she had alerted started hollering "Fire!" When they brought Eally down the stairs, she wrestled him away from the guards. She had somebody waiting with a boat. She rushed him through the crowd and into the boat and pushed him off, and they were still trying to get him, but he went on to Canada. There is a school in Washington that is named after this man. They were going to kill him because he had escaped! They said he wasn't free, he was a slave and he had escaped.

As I said before, for years they thought this little black lady was a man. Before the Civil War, and after the Civil War had started, she had tried to get to Lincoln to tell him that in order for him to win the war, he was going to have to use the black soldiers. As you know they paid the white soldiers more; I think it was $15 a month, and the black soldiers got $7. She said that unless he used the black man, he was not going to win the war.

She met Lincoln and talked, but he never listened. She would get to some of her friends who were influential, such as Mr. Alcott and John Greenleaf Whittier. She talked to them and they listened. Sometimes up in Massachusetts she went to Mr. Alcott's house, and other men would be there. She talked to them and sometimes entertained them by telling stories and ideas. She asked Lincoln about doing something in that manner, but he didn't listen. She thought that by talking with these other men it would eventually get to him. She told them that she wanted to do something, and she felt that she could do it. The battle that changed the Civil War was the one that she designed and engineered herself. They do not give her credit, but she engineered the Combahee River battle; she was the one who carried it out. She asked for three gunboats and for General Montgomery who, she knew, was a guerrilla warfare man. She knew him well; she had had contact with him and worked with him. She told them to go down the Combahee River into Charleston, where over sixty cannons were planted. She planned to dismantle them and take the slaves that were along that river. It ended up that she did. She got about eight hundred of them and dismantled all the torpedoes. She didn't lose anybody and nobody got hurt, but she set fire to some of the plantations and this was the turning point in the Civil War. When it was found out that this little woman had shaken the Southern forces so badly, this little black lady who couldn't read or write had done all this on her own, then Lincoln began to listen.

She used to talk often to Mrs. Lincoln when Lincoln did not have time. He told her once, "When I get a chance, Harriet, to hit this thing, I'll hit it hard." But she thought he was taking a long time to hit. She believed in women's rights and said then that it was important, and black men's rights were just as important as women's rights.

She met with William Grant Still many times. She came here to Philadelphia as a stop for him to help her move on when transporting slaves. He wrote letters for her and gave her information where she could get certain things. You see, many times when she brought slaves out of the South, she had to go a good distance on foot. Sometimes she picked up a horse and buggy, and then she had to hide slaves in somebody's secret barn or house. She did most of her traveling on weekends, from Friday night until Sunday night, because the slaveowners could not arrest or take any of the fugitive slaves on weekends. She brought them to New Jersey and Pennsylvania before the Fugitive Slave Law, but after the Fugitive Slave Law she had to take them on to Canada. If she had brought them here after the Fugitive Slave Law, if they got caught, they would have to be returned. She never lost any passengers on the eastern route of the Underground Railroad, but Levi Coffin, who was a Quaker, was bold on the western route and even had stationery printed with "Underground Railroad" on it, which was wrong. They could track people easier that way. He suffered. They lost him, he got killed. Like John Brown, he was told and warned about what was going to happen. Harriet had a premonition, she said, but he was impatient. That's why he got killed. If he had just waited, he would not have gotten killed and massacred as he was. And, of course, she got help from Queen Victoria because she did not approve of slavery. That's why she went to Canada; she was safe there.

Mr. Brodess owned a lot of woodland in Maryland, and Harriet's father knew wood. Her father Benjamin had the right to supervise boat builders and lumber suppliers and teach them wood. Over the years he taught her. She had a good knowledge of which woods were for what use and could tell one kind from another. And she also followed tree signs. She tried to leave on moonlit nights, but the moon wasn't always bright, so she felt the trees for moss. The moss grew on the north side of trees, and she taught Mother that. People in the city don't have that advantage because there are no woods. At home, in the spring of the year and in the fall of the year, we would have trips through the woods.

You know these little black boys with the lanterns? They were used during the freeing of the slaves to let you know that this household was a place where you were welcome. That's what that was, a symbol to let you know that you were welcome. Harriet Tubman had boats that were taking slaves to Canada. They had two flags, a yellow and a blue. The blue one on top of the yellow one let you know that the boat had slaves on it. They used codes and symbols in their ranks, those she was freeing and those who were involved in the Underground Railroad. Her memory was keen, and when she went to someone's door and knocked and they asked who was there, she would say "a friend with friends." Sometimes the people said, "a friend of a friend"; she knew then that she was welcome. Once or twice, maybe three or four times, she knocked on a person's door and was not given the right signal; she then knew she was not welcome or some changes had been made. One time in particular, she had some slaves with her and these slaves had infants. When she knocked, thinking that it had been a place they stopped before, someone stuck his head out the window, and then she knew this was not the same. They didn't know the code when she knocked on the door but responded with, "What do you want?" She had to disperse everybody. They did not hide or keep on moving. She dispersed them. This particular time, she dispersed them and she took the children, the babies, and put them in a basket.

These are just some of the things that happened to her and to other people when she was bringing the slaves out of bondage. The history books say that she was 93 years old when she died. She told Mama that she had been born somewhere between 1810 and 1815. That would have made her 103, not 93. No records were kept, so there was no way of finding out. She and her family, her mother and father, should have been freed before they went to the Brodesses because Mrs. Patterson, who had owned them before, said that when she died they were to be freed. Harriet's mother told her about it. It wasn't until after the Civil War, when she went back to get a lawyer and dig it up, that she found out it was true. They should have been freed long before. This is what they did over the years, and they are still doing it. Mama said that Harriet used to say, "I feel that I have freed more than three hundred slaves," but no one kept records of the many slaves she helped escape.

THE IBO LANDING STORY

FRANKIE AND DOUG QUIMBY as told to
MARIAN E. BARNES

During the time of slavery they would load and unload slaves at Dunbar Creek, on the north end of St. Simon's Island on the east coast of Georgia. On one particular trip a ship went to Africa to get more people to bring them here to America to sell them for slaves.

While the slave traders were in Africa, they went by the Ibo tribe, and they found eighteen grown people. They fooled them. They told them, "We want you to go to America to work."

When these people got to St. Simon's Island, they found out that they had been tricked and they were going to be sold as slaves. Then all eighteen of these people agreed together. They all said, "No! Rather than be a slave here in America, we would rather be dead."

They linked themselves together with chains and they said a prayer. They said, "Water brought us here, and water is going to carry us away." Then they backed themselves out into Dunbar Creek and drowned themselves.

As they were going down, they were singing a song in their African language. We continue to sing that same song today using English words.

Today, Dunbar Creek on St. Simon's Island is a historical spot visited by throngs of people who have heard the story. Some visitors who have gone to Dunbar Creek on nights when the moon shines a certain way say they have heard the muffled sounds of voices talking, people wailing, and chains clinking.

"The Ibo Landing Song"

> *Oh freedom, oh freedom, oh freedom over me*
> *And before I'd be a slave I'll be buried in my grave*
> *And go home to my Lord and be free.*
>
> *No more crying, no more crying, no more crying will there be*
> *And before I'd be a slave I'll be buried in my grave*
> *And go home to my Lord and be free.*
> *No more groaning, no more dying will there be*
> *And before I'd be a slave I'll be buried in my grave*
> *And go home to my Lord and be free.*
> *Oh freedom, oh freedom, oh freedom over me*
> *And before I'd be a slave I'll be buried in my grave*
> *And go home to my Lord and be free.*

A PIONEER'S STORY OF LONG CREEK, GUYANA

NAOMI CLARKE

I was born in British Guiana, now called Guyana, on March 29, 1930, at Maryville Estate, on a small beautiful island called Leguan, in the county of the great Essequibo River.

The plantation bell was ringing, calling workers to be paid, as was the custom in those days. It was then that I sailed into this world on the raft of childhood, and landed on the reef of time, which now holds for me happy and sad memories from my tender childhood days that still linger on my mind. How dearly I cherish that place where I was born, those wonderful old folks who are now gone, my roots! I also cherish the beautiful sceneries I left behind. Way back there I became a storyteller, although I was only four years old, by telling stories in the new area where I moved about people and customs on the estate where I was born.

The morning after their father fell from a truck and died, our children covered his footprints with papaya and congopump leaves, making a trail from the farmhouse to the fields. They believed this would preserve his footprints forever. Those in the sun were soon gone. Deeper prints in soft soil under the papaya tree lasted about three months. One day they came home crying, "All Daddy's footprints are gone!" Grieved because even his footprints had been taken from them, they asked many questions. "Mammie, we have never seen the full moon so bright as the night after Daddy died, and when the moon passed, we had never seen such darkness; were the extra bright moon and the extra darkness real?"

One night I dreamt I was sitting on a takuba[1] thinking of my children. Then, I realized a man was beside me wearing work clothes and a red sallow.[2] "Me named Tad." He spoke the Creole of Guyana. "I was a child slave brought here in chains. On the ship I looked at the full moon, and I had never seen the moon so bright in Africa. Darkness came; I heard water lapping the side of the boat. But it was never so dark in Africa. That's why I know what you are thinking."

"Tell them pickney[3] to pray, go to school, and learn, that is the only way they will see that extra brightness of the moon in their lives. That's the only way we black men can take we-self out o' massa clutch.[4] Tell them the darkness will always be there, but they can use the light of the moon as hope."

Then Tad and I were walking through Guyanese fields, the scent of ripe pineapples and wiri wiri peppers in the air, the "who-you" bird asking in the night, "Who-you?" Suddenly Tad became a little boy and I a little girl minding goats in the green pastures of Africa. He disappeared, and I woke up with the feel of that land under my feet; and I said, "Oh, God! How can a dream be so real?"

---

1. Tabuka: core of a fallen, dead tree.
2. Sallow: Red waistband worn by Guyanese field workers.
3. Pickney: Creole term for children in Guyanese folklore.
4. The only way to become free of the bondage of white oppression.

AN OLD WOMAN REMEMBERS

STERLING BROWN

This poem tells a story of the 1906 Atlanta riots.

Her eyes were gentle, her voice was for soft singing
In the stiff-backed pew, or on the porch when evening
Comes slowly over Atlanta. But she remembered.
She said: "After they cleaned out the saloons and the dives
The drunks and the loafers, they thought that they had better
Clean out the rest of us. And it was awful.
They snatched men off of streetcars, beat up women.
Some of our men fought back and killed, too. Still
It wasn't their habit. And then the orders came
For the milishy, and the mob went home,
And dressed up in their soldiers' uniforms,
And rushed back shooting just as wild as ever.
Some leaders told us to keep faith in the law,
In the governor; some did not keep that faith,
Some never had it; he was white, too, and the time
Was near election, and the rebs were mad.
He wasn't stopping hornets with his head bare.
The white folks at the big houses, some of them
Kept all their servants home under protection
But that was all the trouble they could stand.
And some were put out when their cooks and yard-boys
Were thrown from cars and beaten, and came late or not at all.

And the police they helped the mob, and the milishy
They helped the police. And it got worse and worse.

"They broke into groceries, drugstores, barbershops,
It made no difference whether white or black.
They beat a lame bootblack until he died,
They cut an old man open with jackknives
The newspapers named us black brutes and mad dogs.
So they used a gun butt on the president
Of our seminary where a lot of folks
Had set up praying prayers the whole night through.
And then," she said, "our folks got sick and tired
Of being chased and beaten and shot down.
All of a sudden, one day, they all got sick and tired
The servants they put down their mops and pans
And brooms and hoes and rakes and coachman whips,
Bad niggers stopped their drinking Dago red,
Good Negroes figured they had prayed enough,
All came back home—they had been too long away—
A lot of visitors had been looking for them.
They sat on their front stoops and in their yards,
Not talking much, but ready; their welcome ready:
Their shotguns oiled and loaded on their knees.

"And then
There wasn't any riot anymore."

THE VIOLENCE OF DESPERATE MEN

MARTIN LUTHER KING, JR.

After the bombings, many of the officers of my church and other trusted friends urged me to hire a bodyguard and armed watchmen for my house. I tried to tell them that I had no fears now, and consequently needed no protection. But they were insistent, so I agreed to consider the question. I also went down to the sheriff's office and applied for a license to carry a gun in the car; but this was refused.

Meanwhile I reconsidered. How could I serve as one of the leaders of a nonviolent movement and at the same time use weapons of violence for my personal protection? Coretta and I talked the matter over for several days and finally agreed that arms were no solution. We decided then to get rid of the one weapon we owned. We tried to satisfy our friends by having floodlights mounted around the house, and hiring unarmed watchmen around the clock. I also promised that I would not travel around the city alone.

This was a comparatively easy promise to keep, thanks to our friend, Bob Williams, professor of music at Alabama State College and a former collegemate of mine at Morehouse. When I came to Montgomery, I had found him here, and from the moment the protest started he was seldom far from my side or Coretta's. He did most of my driving around Montgomery and accompanied me on several out-of-town trips. Whenever Coretta and "Yoki" went to Atlanta or Marion, he was always there to drive them down and to bring them back. Almost imperceptibly he had become my voluntary "bodyguard," though he carried no arms and could never have been as fierce as the name implied.

In this crisis the officers and members of my church were always nearby to lend their encouragement and active support. As I gradually lost my role as husband and father, having to be away from home for hours and sometimes days at a time, the women of the church came into the house to keep Coretta company. Often they volunteered to cook the meals and clean, or help with the baby. Many of the men took turns as watchmen, or drove me around when Bob Williams was not available. Nor did my congregation ever complain when the multiplicity of my new responsibilities caused me to lag in my pastoral duties. For months my day-to-day contact with my parishioners had almost ceased. I had become no more than a Sunday preacher. But my church willingly shared me with the community and threw their own considerable resources of time and money into the struggle.

Our local white friends, too, came forward with their support. Often they called Coretta to say an encouraging word, and when the house was bombed, several of them, known and unknown to us, came by to express their regret. Occasionally the mail would bring a letter from a white Montgomerian saying, "Carry on, we are with you a hundred per cent." Frequently these were simply signed "a white friend."

Interestingly enough, for some time after the bombings the threatening telephone calls slowed up. But this was only a lull; several months later they had begun again in full force. In order to sleep at night, it finally became necessary to apply for an unlisted number. This number was passed out to all the members of the church, the members of the MIA, and other friends across the country. And although it had sometimes been suggested that our own group was responsible for the threats, we never received another hostile call. Of course, the letters still came, but my secretaries were discreet enough to keep as many of them as possible from my attention.

When the opposition discovered that violence could not block the protest, they resorted to mass arrests. As early as January 9 (1956), a Montgomery attorney called the attention of the press to an old state law against boycotts. He referred to Title 14, Section

54, which provides that when two or more persons enter into a conspiracy to prevent the operation of a lawful business, without just cause or legal excuse, they shall be guilty of a misdemeanor. On February 13, the Montgomery County Grand Jury was called to determine whether Negroes who were boycotting the buses were violating this law. After about a week of deliberations, the jury, composed of seventeen whites and one Negro, found the boycott illegal and indicted more than one hundred persons. My name, of course, was on the list.

At the time of the indictments I was at Fisk University in Nashville, giving a series of lectures. During this period I was talking to Montgomery on the phone at least three times a day in order to keep abreast of developments. Thus I heard of the indictments first in a telephone call from Ralph Abernathy, late Tuesday night, February 21. He said that the arrests were scheduled to begin the following morning. Knowing that he would be one of the first to be arrested, I assured him that I would be with him and the others in my prayers. As usual he was unperturbed. I told him that I would cut my trip short in Nashville and come to Montgomery the next day.

I booked an early morning flight. All night long I thought of the people in Montgomery. Would these mass arrests so frighten them that they would urge us to call off the protest? I knew how hard-pressed they had been. For more than thirteen weeks they had walked, and sacrificed, and worn down their cars. They had been harassed and intimidated on every hand. And now they faced arrest on top of all this. Would they become battle-weary, I wondered. Would they give up in despair? Would this be the end of our movement?

I arose early Wednesday morning and notified the officials of Fisk that I had to leave ahead of time because of the situation in Montgomery. I flew to Atlanta to pick up my wife and daughter, whom I had left at my parents' home while I was in Nashville. My wife, my mother and father met me at the airport. I had told them about the indictments over the phone, and they had gotten additional information from a radio broadcast. Coretta showed her usual composure; but my parents' faces wore signs of deep perturbation.

My father, so unafraid for himself, had fallen into a constant state of terror for me and my family. Since the protest began he had beaten a path between Atlanta and Montgomery to be at our side. Many times he had sat in on our board meetings and never shown any doubt about the justice of our actions. Yet this stern and courageous man had reached the point where he could scarcely mention the protest without tears. My mother, too, had suffered. After the bombing she had had to take to bed under doctor's orders, and she was often ill later. Their expressions—even the way they walked, I realized as they came toward me at the airport—had begun to show the strain.

As we drove to their house, my father said that he thought it would be unwise for me to return to Montgomery now. "Although many others have been indicted," he said, "their main concern is to get you. They might even put you in jail without a bond." He went on to tell me that the law enforcement agencies in Montgomery had been trying to find something on my record in Atlanta which would make it possible to deport me from Alabama. They had gone to the Atlanta police department and were disappointed when Chief Jenkins informed them that I did not have even a minor police record. "All of this shows," my father concluded, "that they are out to get you."

I listened to him attentively, and yet I knew that I could not follow his suggestion and stay in Atlanta. I was profoundly concerned about my parents. I was worried about their worry. I knew that if I continued the struggle I would be plagued by the pain that I was inflicting on them. But if I eased out now I would be plagued by my own conscience, reminding me that I lacked the moral courage to stand by a cause to the end. No one can understand my conflict who has not looked into the eyes of those he loves, knowing that he has no alternative but to take a dangerous stand that leaves them tormented.

My father told me that he had asked several trusted friends to come to the house in the early afternoon to discuss the whole issue. Feeling that this exchange of ideas might help to relieve his worries, I readily agreed to stay over and talk to them. Among those who came were A. T. Walden, a distinguished attorney; C. R. Yates and T. M. Alexander, both prominent businessmen; C. A. Scott, editor of *Atlanta Daily World;* Bishop Sherman L. Green of A. M. E. Church; Benjamin E. Mays, president of Morehouse College; and Rufus E.

Clement, president of Atlanta University. Coretta and my mother joined us.

My father explained to the group that because of his respect for their judgment he was calling on them for advice on whether I should return to Montgomery. He gave them a brief history of the attempts that had been made to get me out of Montgomery. He admitted that the fear of what might happen to me had caused him and my mother many restless nights. He concluded by saying that he had talked to a liberal white attorney a few hours earlier, who had confirmed his feeling that I should not go back at this time.

There were murmurs of agreement in the room, and I listened as sympathetically and objectively as I could while two of the men gave their reasons for concurring. These were my elders, leaders among my people. Their words commanded respect. But soon I could not restrain myself any longer. "I must go back to Montgomery," I protested. "My friends and associates are being arrested. It would be the height of cowardice for me to stay away. I would rather be in jail ten years than desert my people now. I have begun the struggle, and I can't turn back. I have reached the point of no return." In the moment of silence that followed I heard my father break into tears. I looked at Dr. Mays, one of the great influences in my life. Perhaps he heard my unspoken plea. At any rate, he was soon defending my position strongly. Then others joined him in supporting me. They assured my father that things were not so bad as they seemed. Mr. Walden put through two calls on the spot to Thurgood Marshall, general counsel of the NAACP, and Arthur Shores, NAACP counsel in Alabama, both of whom assured him that I would have the best legal protection. In the face of all of these persuasions, my father began to be reconciled to my return to Montgomery.

After everybody had gone, Coretta and I went upstairs to our room and had a long talk. She, too, I was glad to find, had no doubt that I must go back immediately. With my own feelings reinforced by the opinions of others I trusted, and with my father's misgivings at rest, I felt better and more prepared to face the experience ahead.

Characteristically, my father, having withdrawn his objections to our return to Montgomery, decided to go along with us, unconcerned with any possible danger or unpleasantness to himself. He secured a driver and at six o'clock Thursday morning we were on the highway headed for Montgomery, arriving about nine. Before we could get out of the car, several television cameras were trained on us. The reporters had somehow discovered the time of our arrival. A few minutes later Ralph Abernathy, released on bail after his arrest the previous day, came to the house. With Ralph and my father, I set out for the county jail, several of my church members following after.

At the jail, an almost holiday atmosphere prevailed. On the way Ralph Abernathy told me how people had rushed down to get arrested the day before. No one, it seems, had been frightened. No one had tried to evade arrest. Many Negroes had gone voluntarily to the sheriff's office to see if their names were on the list, and were even disappointed when they were not. A once fear-ridden people had been transformed. Those who had previously trembled before the law were now proud to be arrested for the cause of freedom. With this feeling of solidarity around me, I walked with firm steps toward the rear of the jail. After I had received a number and had been photographed and fingerprinted, one of my church members paid my bond and I left for home.

The trial was set for March 19. Friends from all over the country came to Montgomery to be with us during the proceedings. Ministers from as far north as New York were present. Negro Congressman Charles C. Diggs (D.-Mich.) was on hand. Scores of reporters representing publications in the United States, India, France, and England were there to cover the trial. More than five hundred Negroes stood in the halls and the streets surrounding the small courthouse. Several of them wore crosses on their lapels reading, "Father, forgive them."

Judge Eugene Carter brought the court to order, and after the necessary preliminaries the state called me up as the first defendant. For four days I sat in court listening to arguments and waiting for a verdict. William F. Thetford, solicitor for the state, was attempting to prove that I had disobeyed a law by organizing an illegal boycott. The defense attorneys—Arthur Shores, Peter Hall, Ozell Billingsley, Fred Gray, Charles Langford, and Robert Carter—presented arguments to show that the prosecution's evidence was insufficient to prove that I had violated Alabama's anti-boycott law. Even if the state had proved such action, they asserted, no evidence was produced to show that the Negroes did not have just cause or legal excuse.

In all, twenty-eight witnesses were brought to the stand by the defense. I listened with a mixture of sadness and awe as these simple people—most of them unlettered—sat on the witness stand without fear and told their stories. They looked the solicitor and the judge in the eye with a courage and dignity to which there was no answer.

Perhaps the most touching testimony was that of Mrs. Stella Brooks. Her husband had climbed on a bus. After paying his fare he was ordered by the driver to get off and reboard by the back door. He looked through the crowded bus, and seeing that there was no room in back he said that he would get off and walk if the driver would return his dime. The driver refused; an argument ensued; and the driver called the police. The policeman arrived, abusing Brooks, who still refused to leave the bus unless his dime was returned. The policeman shot him. It happened so suddenly that everybody was dazed. Brooks died of his wounds.

Mrs. Martha Walker testified about the day when she was leading her blind husband from the bus. She had stepped down and as her husband was following the driver slammed the door and began to drive off. Walker's leg was caught. Although Mrs. Walker called out, the driver failed to stop, and her husband was dragged some distance before he could free himself. She reported the incident, but the bus company did nothing about it.

The stories continued. Mrs. Sadie Brooks testified that she heard a Negro passenger threatened because he did not have the correct change. "The driver whipped out a pistol and drove the man off the bus." Mrs. Della Perkins described being called an "ugly black ape" by a driver.

I will always remember my delight when Mrs. Georgia Gilmore —an unlettered woman of unusual intelligence—told how an operator demanded that she get off the bus after paying her fare and board it again by the back door, and then drove away before she could get there. She turned to Judge Carter and said: "When they count the money, they do not know Negro money from white money."

On Thursday afternoon, March 22, both sides rested. All eyes were turned toward Judge Carter, as with barely a pause he rendered his verdict: "I declare the defendant guilty of violating the state's anti-boycott law." The penalty was a fine of $500 and court costs, or 386 days at hard labor in the County of Montgomery. Then Judge

Carter announced that he was giving a minimum penalty because of what I had done to prevent violence. In the cases of the other Negroes charged with the same violation—the number had now boiled down to 89—Judge Carter entered a continuance until a final appeal was complete in my case.

In a few minutes several friends had come up to sign my bond, and the lawyers had notified the judge that the case would be appealed. Many people stood around the courtroom in tears. Others walked out with their heads bowed. I came to the end of my trial with a feeling of sympathy for Judge Carter in his dilemma. To convict me he had to face the condemnation of the nation and world opinion; to acquit me he had to face the condemnation of the local community and those voters who kept him in office. Throughout the proceedings he had treated me with great courtesy, and he had rendered a verdict which he probably thought was the best way out. After the trial he left town for a "welcomed rest."

I left the courtroom with my wife at my side and a host of friends following. In front of the courthouse hundreds of Negroes and whites, including television cameramen and photographers, were waiting. As I waved my hand, they shouted: "God bless you," and began to sing, "We ain't gonna ride the buses no more."

Ordinarily, a person leaving a courtroom with a conviction behind him would wear a somber face. But I left with a smile. I knew that I was a convicted criminal, but I was proud of my crime. It was the crime of joining my people in a nonviolent protest against injustice. It was the crime of seeking to instill within my people a sense of dignity and self-respect. It was the crime of desiring for my people the unalienable rights of life, liberty, and the pursuit of happiness. It was above all the crime of seeking to convince my people that non-cooperation with evil is just as much a moral duty as is cooperation with good.

So ended another effort to halt the protest. Instead of stopping the movement, the opposition's tactics had only served to give it greater momentum, and to draw us closer together. What the opposition failed to see was that our mutual sufferings had wrapped us all in a single garment of destiny. What happened to one happened to all.

On that cloudy afternoon in March, Judge Carter had convicted more than Martin Luther King, Jr., Case No. 7399; he had convicted every Negro in Montgomery. It is no wonder that the movement couldn't be stopped. It was too large to be stopped. Its links were too well bound together in a powerfully effective chain. There is amazing power in unity. Where there is true unity, every effort to disunite only serves to strengthen the unity. This is what the opposition failed to see.

The members of the opposition had also revealed that they did not know the Negroes with whom they were dealing. They thought they were dealing with a group who could be cajoled or forced to do whatever the white man wanted them to do. They were not aware that they were dealing with Negroes who had been freed from fear. And so every move they made proved to be a mistake. It could not be otherwise, because their methods were geared to the "old Negro," and they were dealing with a "new Negro."

BLOODY SUNDAY

AMELIA PLATTS BOYNTON ROBINSON

On February 1, 1965, Dr. Martin Luther King, Jr., was arrested in Selma and lodged in the county jail for leading the January 18 demonstration. This aroused people in all walks of life all over the country. They began to come to Selma to offer their services in whatever way was needed. The Reverend Andrew Young, Dr. King's aid, announced at a night meeting that a group of people from Washington, including congressmen, would visit Selma unofficially.

I was to drive to the Montgomery airport and lead the group back to Selma. The congressmen would ask at the city hall to see Dr. King. I was to sign his bond, and the entire group would come to my house for a meeting. I met the plane and found the fifteen congressmen, eight other friends, and a host of newsmen.

The whole group of about fifty persons tried to enter the side door of the city hall, but it was locked. I thought the front door would be open, but found that locked also, so we went to the prisoners' entrance, which was open. The day was cold and dismal with a drizzle of rain. The only bright spot of the day was the spirit of the congressmen.

The hall was clear of people except for one man who stood behind the entrance door with his hand on the doorknob. "Don't let them come in here," he said. He was a tall, frightened, unsteady, thin man —the mayor of one month of Selma, Alabama, a city of about twenty nine thousand in the Black Belt. "Don't let them come in here," he said again. Although all of the group was still outside the building except Congressman John Dow of New York, who was close behind me and halfway in the door, the mayor began to recite his canned speech.

"I am the mayor of the city of Selma," he began. I knew he meant to be heard so I said, "Mayor, these people cannot hear you. They will have to come in if you are talking to them." He took several steps backward, with both hands held up as though he were pushing something away from him, then said, "Well, let them come right in here" (motioning toward the small hall), "but don't let the newsman in."

The door was open now and the congressmen began to file into the hall, so it was natural that all the others would follow. The mayor was determined to get his speech out, so he started again. "I am the mayor of Selma and we have been getting along all right until outsiders came in. We don't need any outsiders." At this point Congressman William Fitts Ryan of New York and others said, "We want to see Dr. King."

The mayor said, "Gentlemen, you cannot see King unless you get him out on bond." One of the other congressmen answered, "We don't want to get him out. We just want to see him."

"Well, you just can't see him." The mayor was still nervous and did not realize that the worst was yet to come. When all the congressmen had entered the hall and the mayor gradually backed into the larger hall, one of the congressmen asked, "Why do you bar Negroes from registering and voting?" Another asked about the discriminating pattern practiced and another about the inhuman treatment of the demonstrators. The mayor having nothing to do with these atrocities tried very hard to answer these questions but often found himself getting so tangled up with the lawmakers of the nation that it was embarrassing.

Just then the city and county attorney came among the group and said, "Mayor, you don't have to answer their questions." But the attorney went away, leaving the mayor to continue the struggle. Later the attorney returned and took him by the elbow as one would a child in trouble and steered him away while he was yet talking, leaving the congressmen and the others, including newsmen, standing there amazed.

The spell was broken when Selma's safety director, Captain Wilson Baker, came and announced that Dr. King had been released. He was slipped through the front doors while the mayor was floundering with his hangups. When the group reached my house on Lapsley

Street, Dr. King was there waiting for us. Included in the conference, together with some of the local black leaders and SCLC people, were congressmen: Jonathan B. Bingham, James H. Scheuer, Ogden R. Reid, William Fitts Ryan, and Joseph Y. Resnick, all of New York; Jeffrey Cohelan, Kenneth W. Dyal, Augustus F. Hawkins, and Don Edwards, California; Weston E. Vivian, John Conyers, Jr., and Charles Mathias, Maryland. The son of Adam Clayton Powell of New York was there and others representing other congressmen.

Dr. King, SCLC representatives, and I answered questions as to what was going on in Selma, information that the congressmen could take back to Washington. The various congressmen later scattered and visited with other people, white and black, for further details. This groundwork led to their drafting of a right-to-vote bill, ratified by Congress the following August.

But in the meantime, all was not well in Selma and surrounding counties for those who tried to register. Blacks were being beaten, jailed, and made to walk for miles in biting cold weather after being released from prison. Jimmy Lee Jackson of Marion, thirty miles from Selma, Alabama, had been shot to death by one of Governor Wallace's state troopers after a mass meeting. The officers had gone into the church and ordered the people to disperse. The people left peacefully, but they were hounded and harassed. A trooper followed Jimmy Lee and his mother into a neighboring cafe, began to beat the woman, and Jimmy Lee, who stayed with her, was killed in cold blood.

I can never do justice to the great feeling of amazement and encouragement I felt when, perhaps for the first time in American history, white citizens of a Southern state banded themselves together to come to Selma and show their indignation about the injustices against the Blacks. On March 6, 1965, seventy-two concerned white citizens of Alabama came to Selma in protest. They had everything to lose while we, the Blacks, who were deprived and on the bottom rung of the salary scale, had nothing to lose and everything to gain.

The white group included business and professional men and women, ministers and laymen. Before they came they asked to use one of the public buildings for assembly and were refused. The white churches were afraid to open their doors to them, and finally they gathered in a black church, the Reformed Presbyterian. A plan was worked out to keep any of them from coming in bodily contact with the law.

The Reverend Joseph Ellwanger, pastor of an integrated Lutheran congregation in Birmingham, was the group's spokesman. (He was the son of Dr. Walter H. Ellwanger of Selma, president of the Alabama Lutheran Academy and College for twenty years.) Two by two these people marched to the courthouse. As they assembled, other people were already gathered, the whites to jeer and the Blacks to cheer. While the Concerned White Citizens of Alabama (CWCA) sang "My Country, 'Tis of Thee," a group of white hecklers began to scream, yell, and whistle. Even when the minister offered prayers, they showed all kinds of disrespect. The CWCA ignored their irreverence and prayed for them.

During Pastor Ellwanger's reading of the Purpose of the Concerned Citizens, a gang of white men raced down the street in an old car with no exhaust pipe. The noise was horrendous. Suddenly the car stopped in front of the minister, and the gang yelled at him. One of the men held up the hood of the car from which came some type of chemical that made a smoke screen and gave off a repellent odor. The sheriff, who with his deputies were surrounding the CWCA, paid no attention to them, but neither did the CWCA people. The annoying group finally left.

With all our conferences, pleadings, confrontations, and demonstrations, the registration board and the Black Belt officials were determined to beat the Negroes down physically and mentally. Each time the Negroes came up fighting nonviolently.

We knew that the crux of the trouble in Alabama lay in our governor, George Wallace, and we decided to march the fifty miles to the state capital and hand our grievances to him. The march would begin the next day, Sunday, March 7, 1965.

The city knew of our plans for the march but did not know how to stop it. Meetings were held day and night to map out strategy by which we could appeal to the conscience of the diehards. People had begun to come in from all over the country to lend assistance in the registration and voting drive. The county board of registrars refused to permit Negroes to vote, the county officials kicked them about for asking to register, the governor of the state gave them mountains of legal questions that were impossible to answer, and the Congress in Washington was still filibustering and allowing the Southern bigots to twist their arms. We were left no alternative but to walk fifty miles to the capital not to ask, not to plead, but to demand the right to register and vote.

The night before the march we gathered at the church and talked with the citizens, asking them to walk with us regardless of the cost, even if it meant "your life." I was afraid of being killed, and I said to myself, "I cannot pay the supreme price, because I have given too much already." But I also then thought, "Other mothers have given their lives for less in this struggle, and I am determined to go through with it even if it does cost my life." At that moment a heavy burden fell from my mind, and I was ready to suffer if need be.

The next morning I rose early, cooked breakfast, and fed the fifteen guests staying with me. I went to Brown's Chapel to offer my assistance needed before the march. Little did I know that that day would mark one of the greatest struggles for freedom in modern times. Little did I visualize what would really take place and what effect it would have on the nation at large. That day I met such people as the former governor of Florida, LeRoy Collins; Walter Reuther, labor leader; and other dignitaries, and I began to realize more deeply than before that we were not alone.

As we passed a line of well-wishers and little tots who wished they could join the group, a woman said to me, "Honey, I can't walk but I sure will pray for you all." Another said, "Thank God he done sent his disciples to he'p us." Still another said, "I prayed so hard for you all. It might be stormy, but God will bring you through!" All of these sayings I kept in my heart, and I, too, uttered a prayer to be saved from the evil to come.

As we left the church we saw scores of officers of the city, and county and state troopers huddled in groups, smiling and looking somewhat human. I did not have a hat but was otherwise prepared for the cold weather. My friend Margaret Moore said, "Here is my raincap, put it on. You'll be needing it." Then Marie Foster and I fell in line third from the front.

We marched from Brown's Chapel AME Church in the black section toward town. The officers had us close ranks and walk faster and by larger groups. This was different from previous marches, where we had to walk two by two and ten feet apart regardless of our large numbers.

The marchers were accompanied by portable latrines, first-aid buses, water, and food. Like the children of Israel leaving Egypt, we marched toward the Red Sea and we were on our way, not knowing what was before us.

As we approached the Edmund Pettus Bridge which spans the

Alabama River, we saw the sheriff, his posse, deputies, and men plucked out of the fields and stills to help "keep the niggers in their place." As we crossed the bridge, I saw in front of us a solid wall of state troopers standing shoulder to shoulder. I said to Marie, "Those men are standing so close together an ant would get mashed to death if it crawled between them. They are as lifeless as wooden soldiers." Marie pointed to the troopers on the sides of our marching lines and said, "It doesn't take all of them to escort us." But a second look convinced us that trouble was brewing for nearly one thousand marchers.

Each officer was equipped with cans of gas, guns, sticks, or cattle prods as well as his regular paraphernalia. Beyond them men on horses sat at attention. I remembered the words of a little girl who wanted to go with us because she wanted to be free, and the prayers that were being offered on our behalf, and the old lady who said she would stay on her knees while we were away. I knew we would need all those prayers as I looked on the faces of these men who were just waiting for a chance to shed human blood.

When we were less than fifty yards from the human wall, the commander of the troops, on a sound truck, spoke through a bullhorn and commanded us to "stop where you are!" Hosea Williams of SCLC, John Lewis, and all the line behind them halted. Hosea said, "May I say something?" Major Cloud retorted, "No, you may not. Charge on them, men!" The troopers, gas masks on and gas guns drawn, then began to shoot gas on us, and the troopers in front jumped off the trucks. Those standing at attention began to club us. The horses were brought on the scene and were more humane than the troopers; they stepped over the fallen victims!

As I stepped aside from the trooper's club, I felt a blow on my arm that could have injured me permanently had it been on my head. Another blow by a trooper as I was gasping for breath knocked me to the ground, and there I lay unconscious. Others told me that my attacker had called to another that he had the "damn leader." One of them shot tear gas all over me. The plastic rain cap that Margaret Moore gave me may have saved my life; it had slipped down over my face and protected my nose somewhat from the worst of the fumes. Pictures in the paper and those in the possession of the Justice Department show the trooper standing over me with a club. Some of the marchers said to the trooper, "She is dead," and they were told to drag me to the side of the road.

There were screams, cries, groans, and moans as people were bru-
tally beaten from the front of the line all the way back to the church
—a distance of more than a mile. State troopers and the sheriff and
his men beat and clubbed to the ground almost everyone on the
march. The cry went out for ambulances to come over the bridge and
pick up the wounded and those thought to be dead, but Sheriff Clark
dared one of them to cross the bridge. At last a white minister and a
black citizen told him, "If you don't let the ambulance over the
bridge, these people are going to retaliate by killing some of you, and
you may be the first one." The ambulance was then permitted to pick
us up. I also heard that I was taken to the church after being given
first aid on the way, but when I did not respond, I was taken to the
Good Samaritan Hospital.

When I regained consciousness I wondered where I was, but then
I remembered the voice through the bullhorn, the gas being shot,
and the men with gas masks. From the looks of the other patients
around me, highway 80 across Edmund Pettus Bridge must have had
a blood bath.

It was months before I recovered completely from the experience,
but my spirit soared as I realized what it meant to sing and really feel
"Oh freedom, over me; and before I'll be a slave, I'll be buried in my
grave, and go home to my Lord and be free."

What happened to the good white folks of Selma on Bloody Sunday? What happened to the law and order Governor Wallace
screamed about when he illegally sent troops in to exterminate the
marchers? What happened to America's democracy when Congress
and President Johnson cried out against the Hitler-like atrocities only
after many deaths had occurred in the struggle? What is wrong with
America when so many laws have to be placed on the books to protect her 20 million citizens of color? Unless there is equal protection
as well as opportunity for all Americans, she will erupt like a volcano,
and no hurriedly written bill passed in Congress can stop it.

No law passed in Washington is strong enough to protect the
Negro against the lawlessness in the South. There has to be imple-
mentation of the legislation by federal officials, and if this is not done
there will be no justice for the Negro.

LOOKING BACK AT MY TEXAS HERITAGE

ADA DEBLANC SIMOND,
as told to MARIAN E. BARNES

When I was born in 1903, my father was a farmer in Louisiana. But when bad weather caused him to lose all of his crops, the family moved to Austin, Texas, which was a land of opportunity at that time. In Austin my father worked for a man who owned a drugstore and catered wedding receptions and anniversary parties. My mother was a seamstress. She could design clothes from a picture or a thought. There were six of us children, and we were a family of survivors.

Sometimes my mother would close up the house, and somebody would come and get us in a truck or a wagon, and we'd go to a town miles away to pick cotton. We would stay there in a cabin for about a month or as long as it took us to pick the field.

We learned to make what we needed from what we had. For example, the stores bought flour, sugar, bran, and chicken feed in thirty-six-inch-square muslin bags. We'd buy those bags for twenty-five cents, or the store owner would give them to us, and we'd use them to make clothes, sheets, towels, and curtains. First, we'd soak the bags in cold water to take the writing off, then we would wash them in ash water that we made by putting ashes in water. After the ashes settled, the water would be like lye, and it would bleach the muslin white and pretty. One bag would make a pillow case, a skirt, a shirt, or a blouse. We sewed four together to make a sheet, and we briar-stitched the seams and embroidered the hems to make it pretty. A bag was cut in half to make a towel or curtain, and in four pieces to make washcloths. We added embroidery, briar-stitching, and crochet for decoration. The things we made were beautiful. Later, merchants began to use printed cloths for these bags, and instead of writing on the material, they glued on paper labels.

There wasn't much playing for me as a child. I had lots of responsibilities but also lots of fun. Whatever we had to do for life was fun. Of course, my brothers played marbles. That was a popular game with boys. We made up games that helped with our work. I used to make up songs and games that helped to get my little sister to eat or go to bed or bathe. We used lye, old fat from meat drippings, or the crackling dregs left from killing a pig to make our own soap. It wasn't Camay, but it was good soap that we used for everything, including bathing. We bathed in a big number ten tin tub. We used a smaller foot tub for washing our face and hands and feet, which we always washed last. Then we used the sudsy water left from bathing to wash a few clothes or water the garden or scrub the floors.

The floors were made of wide pine boards, and we were very protective of them. We powdered every red brick we found, and we used a baking powder can with holes punched in the top to sprinkle brick powder on the floor. We would brush it in and polish the floor until it was pink and shiny.

On wash days we boiled clothes in a huge, black, iron pot with legs that we set over a fire built in a hole in the ground. Sometimes we used the same fire to cook our food. There might not be a big dinner in the house, but cooking outside while the clothes were boiling made the meal fun.

By the time I was raising my children in the 1920s, we had long-handled hamburger holders for them to stick in the fire and cook their hamburgers. Sometimes we cooked hot water corn bread or patty cakes in these hamburger holders. You made hot water corn bread by pouring boiling hot water into salted cornmeal. When it was the right consistency, it was baked as corn bread or patted with your hands into a patty cake or rolled into balls to make hush puppies, or it was cooked inside the hamburger holders over a fire.

I miss the love, affection, and companionship that families and communities had in those days. We were all together. If one neighbor was sick, we made soup for the person, washed nightgowns and bedclothes, and went to sit with the sick neighbor for a while.

But I do not dwell on those days that have gone. There is so much of life that I have to live *now*. I want to live in the "today." For example, I've just read *Evidence of Things Not Seen,* by James Baldwin, about the Atlanta murders. Baldwin does not believe that Williams committed those crimes. I've never believed it either. I'm glad they didn't electrocute him. There are probably people still working on that, and someday they may prove his innocence. *That* is my life now. I am involved with *today.* Last night I went to hear Dr. John Hope Franklin speak. I read him in *Ebony;* I buy his books. You see, I live *now,* and I fill my life with now.

Of course, if you don't remember where you came from or how you got from there to here, you have a very hard time moving on. And you have to have goals to move from where you are. But progress isn't made by grieving about the way things were when you were little or by longing for the days when you had to go to the cotton patch every year to make the money to pay the note on the mortgage. I wouldn't like to be doing that now. I wouldn't like to have to be going to pick cotton now. There are lots of things I remember about those times, but I do not miss them because I would not like to be living in that time now. I prefer to be living in this age. All those things that I have done, I am resting from them now. I am resting from them.

SOLITARY CONFINEMENT

WINNIE MANDELA

Winnie Mandela and her husband, Nelson, have become living symbols of protest against the apartheid government of South Africa. She has been separated for over twenty years from her husband because of his imprisonment during most of their marriage.

In 1969, Winnie Mandela and twenty-one women and men were arrested under the Terrorism Act. Mrs. Mandela was held in solitary confinement for sixteen months.

When they detained me, I just had been to a heart specialist. I have a heart condition, and the security branch knew that. They knew I had been to the doctor. They knew I had been to a heart specialist. And I think they particularly arrested me then because of that knowledge, with the hope that perhaps the condition would worsen in prison, and that whatever happened to me would then be attributed to natural causes.

The cell in which I was held at the beginning was so small that if I stretched my hands I touched both walls. I could barely exercise. In this cell, all I had was a plastic bottle with about five glasses of water, a homemade sanitary bucket, and three blankets and a sisal mat. That is all, besides what I was wearing.

Being held incommunicado is one of the cruelest things any human being can do to another. About a week after I was held, I was transferred to the condemned cell. A condemned cell means a cell that usually holds prisoners who are going to be executed. In this condemned cell, there were two grille doors besides the prison door.

To this day, the memory of that bunch of keys clicking, the noise that they would deliberately make in the stillness and solitude of a prison life, you actually felt they were hitting the inner core of your soul.

They never switched off the light. I had this floodlight night and day. I lost track of time. This particular wardress always brought my food. She would open the cell door, and I could hear someone outside putting the food down. And she would stand right at the entrance to the cell. They would then take the sanitary bucket and turn the lid upside down, and put your plate of food on that. And she would stand right at the cell door and kick the food in, kick it into the cell.

The mind finds it very difficult to adjust to such solitude. It is such utter torture that I could feel that my mind was so tortured with lack of doing something and not communicating with anyone, that I would find myself talking to the children. I would think I am thinking about them and actually find myself in the end conducting conversations with my children as if they are with me in the cell.

It becomes so difficult to keep sane, with absolutely nothing to do, that I would actually hunt for ants. If I had an ant in the cell or a fly, then I would regard myself as having company for the day.

When I was given anything, anything at all, it was the Bible. One day this Swanipole stood at the cell door and flung the Bible at my face. And he threw it and said, "There you are. Pray. Pray so that your God can get you out of this cell."

He was the one who murdered a lot of my people behind bars. He was actually the horror of Pretoria Central. I was interrogated right through day and night for seven days and seven nights. As they changed the teams, Swanipole would rub his hands and say he was waiting for that moment when they shall break me completely.

By the time they interrogated me, they knew everything. They knew all about my political activities at the time. And the African National Congress of course was a banned organization, which meant that whatever political activities I was involved in at that time were underground political activities. There was nothing they didn't know. They had managed to break a few of those they had interrogated before me.

The body devises its own defensive mechanisms. I didn't know it was such relief to faint, for instance. And during—the only moment I ever had any rest from intensive interrogation and intensive questioning where your mind just loses track of everything was during those fainting spells. They were so relieving. I could recover from each fainting spell. When I came around, I felt a little refreshed to face more and more interrogation.

On the seventh day I started urinating blood, and the body was swollen like a balloon. I don't know the medical explanation for that, whether it was from sitting in one position for days and nights right through. But my legs, for instance, were as if they were just poles that were not part of my body. I could actually feel the weight, so swollen, so edematous they were, that I found it difficult to stand.

And that didn't stop my interrogators in any way. I don't remember how I was brought back to the cell. I found myself just there one Sunday.

In the end, the fainting spells were much more acute, I think as the body was beginning to give in to that type of brutality.

Prior to my detention, I knew that as a mother and as a social worker, life—the human being—was so sacrosanct that I could never, on my own, lift up a finger against any human being, for ideological reasons. But what I went through, that personal experience, hardened me so much that at the end of my interrogation, looking at my interrogators and what I had gone through, I knew that as I sat in that cell—in that cell—if my own father or my brother walked in dangling a gun, and he was on the other side, and I had a gun too, in my hand, in defense of the ideals for which I was being tortured, then I would fire.

The security branch had made me the soldier at heart I am today. There is no way that you could talk any language of peace to vicious men who treated defenseless women and children in that manner. I realized then that the Afrikaner had closed the chapter of negotiation and that the decision taken by my leaders in 1962 was arrived at with difficulty, but that there was no other way: the decision to defend our honor, the decision to stop turning the biblical other cheek. The white man had hit us for too long. Our patience had been tested and had endured for too long. I knew then that somehow there had to be a political crisis in this country for us to reach the ultimate goal. That is what I emerged as in 1969–1970, during my months of solitary confinement.

VIETNAM BLUES

SPECIALIST 4 HAYWOOD T. "THE KID" KIRKLAND (ARI SESU MERRETAZON)

Recoilless Rifleman
25th Infantry Division
U.S. Army
Duc Pho
May 1967–April 1968

I was basically a C-type student in high school. I guess I didn't care much about anything except pool. By the time I was sixteen, I had won a lot of championships at the Boys' Club. But the real competition was at the poolroom.

They only allowed me in the poolroom 'cause I could play so good. A lot of the older brothers used to bet on me. Basically nine-ball, and a little straight pool. One time I made about $300 in one of those type of six-hour sessions. I beat the owner of the poolroom. And then they started calling me the Kid.

My parents came from South Carolina to Washington. My father was a chef in the restaurant at George Washington University, and my mother worked in basically the same type of thing in the cafeteria at the Department of Transportation. They didn't have much money, because they was 11 of us children.

I got drafted on November 22, 1966. I had been working for a book distributor and as a stock boy in some stores coming out of high school. A lot of dudes were trying to do things to get deferments. One of my brothers put some kind of liquid in his eye and said he had an eye problem at the physical. He never went.

I didn't try anything. I knew when I got drafted I was going to Vietnam, no matter what I did.

As soon as I hit boot camp in Fort Jackson, South Carolina, they tried to change your total personality. Transform you out of that civilian mentality to a military mind.

Right away they told us not to call them Vietnamese. Call everybody gooks, dinks.

Then they told us when you go over in Vietnam, you gonna be face to face with Charlie, the Viet Cong. They were like animals, or something other than human. They ain't have no regard for life. They'd blow up little babies just to kill one GI. They wouldn't allow you to talk about them as if they were people. They told us they're not to be treated with any type of mercy or apprehension. That's what they engraved into you. That killer instinct. Just go away and do destruction.

Even the chaplains would turn the thing around in the Ten Commandments. They'd say, "Thou shall not murder," instead of "Thou shall not kill." Basically, you had a right to kill, to take and seize territory, or to protect lives of each other. Our conscience was not to bother us once we engaged in that kind of killing. As long as we didn't murder, it was like the chaplain would give you his blessings. But you knew all of that was murder anyway.

On May 15, 1967, I came into Vietnam as a replacement in the 3rd Brigade of the 25th Division. The Cacti Green. It was the task-force brigade that went anywhere there was trouble. The division was down in Cu Chi, but we operated all over II Corps and Eye Corps.

At the time I basically had a gung ho attitude about being a soldier. But could I get in the best situation and not get hurt was a legitimate concern of mine. So I checked out that the line companies —ones making all the heavy contact—are the ones who are getting overran. I thought maybe I should avoid that and volunteer for one of these long-range recon patrols. It was a smaller group, and I had an opportunity to share my ideas and help make some decisions. With a line company, you're really just a pin on the map for sure.

The recon unit was basically to search out the enemy and call in air strikes or a larger military force to engage the enemy. Most of our activities was at night. We was hide by day, and out by night.

The politics of the war just had not set in when I got there. They told us not to fire unless fired upon. But once we enter into a village, we literally did anything that we wanted to do. There was no rules at all. I began to see a lot of the politics.

When I had just got into my squad, Tango squad, I said, "Anybody here from D.C.?"

There was one brother, Richard Streeter, from D.C., who I used to go with his wife in high school. I mean they weren't married when I was in high school.

Then this white brother said, "Say, hey. I'm from D.C."

I said, "Okay. Just soon as I set up we'll get together."

He began to set up, too. He went down to the water hole to fill up his canteen. On his way back, he stepped on a 500-pound bomb that was laid in a tank track.

You don't walk in no tank tracks, because that's where the bombs are usually. Charlie would use the rationale that most tanks would follow their tracks, and they would booby-trap tank tracks.

We didn't see that white brother anymore. All we saw was a big crater, maybe 6 feet deep. And some remains. You know, guts and stuff. And the dirt had just enveloped the stuff. It looked like batter on fish and batter on chicken pieces. His body looked like that.

That freaked me out, but I wasn't scared yet.

It was those times when information was gotten to us that we were in a bad spot and there's no way you can get out—those were the times that was the most fearful times. Times when I began to understand what fear was all about. It's just that anticipation of something happening as opposed to being in the heat of the battle. In the heat of the battle I don't think people think about getting hurt. In the fire fight, the thought of getting hurt never dawned upon me. You think about doing a blow to the person you're fighting.

The most fearful moment was when we got choppered into the wrong area, right on the perimeter of an NVA camp. It was a pretty huge complex. And there was only about 22 of us. You could smell the food and even feel the heat coming up out of the ground where they was cooking right under us. We could hear them, the muffled sounds. We felt their presence. We was ordered not to make a move in no direction. Everything was 100 percent alert. We just couldn't get out till the morning. They said no way in the world they'd come in there with a chopper at night. Everybody felt the pressure. Everybody felt the stress. Only 22 men. We was gonna get overran. That's the fear of any recon platoon.

The choppers came in bright and early.

Another time we heard there was a NVA battalion coming our way. And our directions was not to move, just hold up and wait till morning again. It was near LZ Montezuma. One of our LURP teams had got wiped out, five of them. We was out there to find they bodies. During the monsoon season. And it was raining sheets and sheets of rain. You couldn't even see the next peron past up from you. And we was in the rice paddies in the lowlands, and the water just rose and rose. Next thing I know I was sleeping in water up to my chest. Weapons were basically submerged in water. Nothing happened, but the fear, the fear, man.

I remember night movement in that monsoon. I'm trying to grab hold of the man in front of me, trying to find him, 'cause you have to do that in the monsoon at night. I just fell. I fell into a well about 8 feet deep. My heart just fell. It hit rock bottom. And I couldn't signal anyone real loud. All I could say was "Hey," in a little breath-type thing. And when the lightning came on, the E-6, my platoon sergeant, he spotted me. And he pulled me right out with my weapon.

The other thing we mainly did was search and destroy mission. On a search and destroy mission you just clear the village and burn the hootches because the village is suspected of a Viet Cong stronghold or Viet Cong sympathizers. We did not have the capacity as a platoon to take them and hold them. We just cleared them, because we wanted them secure.

If we were doing this combat assault of the village, the CP would set up in the center of the village. The CP would have the platoon leader, the medics, and the air observers. The squads would pass the CP, and we would throw off our big heavy gear and keep our weapons. Then the squads would set up a perimeter around the command post. So the lieutenant really didn't have any idea what was going on in the rest of the village itself.

One time, in a village near Danang, we was making a perimeter. We passed these two black guys raping this woman at the door of the hootch. She was down on her back on this porchlike thing. Nothing more than a little mud slab. They had stripped off her top. She was struggling. They was from another squad. And the protocol of the folks in my squad was just keep moving, not to interfere, everything was all right.

Most of the time we just rounded the women and children up, and they were literally ran out of the village. Then we start putting fire in the holes, throwing grenades inside that hootches, inside of little bunkers, down the wells. Hoping that we could ferret out a couple of VC. Then we burn the village. That was like a standard operation procedure when we went into a village.

My platoon did that to 50 to 75 villages. Like being in Vietnam, there are little villages all over the place.

If we use the figure 50 villages, we found suspects in 12 of them.

Maybe 30 suspects in all of them. We very rarely found a real VC.

When a squad caught a suspect, they would put a rope around they neck, kick them in the butt, and knock them out with they fist. Anything short of killing them, 'specially when the lieutenant was aware of the fact that we found someone. Really, it was the squad leader, the E-5, who makes a lot of the decisions about the lives, because most often we were operating about 2 kilometers away from the lieutenant. We would call the CP and say we ran across a dink or two. If it looks like he has no weapons, we would decide to move on. Never telling that we kicked him, knocked him out, or searched him down for drugs.

One time, the VC we found in the village we was going to take back, because we found him with a .50-caliber machine gun—an antiaircraft-type gun—and a lot of ammo. We felt that this man knows something.

This brother and the squad leader, a white dude, for some reason they felt they could interrogate this man. This man wasn't speaking any English. They did not speak any Vietnamese. I could not understand that at all. But they hollerin', "Where you come from? How many you?" And they callin' him everything. Dink. Gook. Motherfucker. He couldn't say anything. He was scared.

The next thing I knew, the man was out of the helicopter.

I turned around and I asked the folks what happened to him.

They told me he jumped out.

I said, "Naw, man. The man ain't jumped out."

The brother said, "Yes, he did. He one of those tough VC."

I didn't believe it. The brother was lying to me, really.

I turned around, and the man was gone. I didn't actually see him pushed, but he was gone. It took a long time for me to believe it. I just kept looking where he sat at. And I couldn't deal with it.

There was two white guys I will never forget. This very young lieutenant, straight out of West Point. He had been out in the field a week and already was doin' things that could get you killed. And Studs Armstrong, this gung ho squad leader. He was the first person that I ran into that I now know as a mercenary-type soldier in Vietnam.

One time we were chasing a VC, and the VC run into this hole. The lieutenant wanted one of our men to crawl into the hole after him. In fact, he was telling this little brother, Bobby Williams from Philadelphia, because Bobby was the smallest one.

That was ridiculous. Because those tunnels may look like to be a little hole but may end up to be a total complex. Many times the holes are dug in off the entrance. VC go in and crawl into this little slot. If a man crawled in behind them, he were subject to get his head blown off.

I said, "Bobby, don't go in there. You crazy?"

So I said let's throw some fire in the hole as opposed to sending one of our men in that hole. Do that, and we'll pull Bobby out by his ankles and he won't have a head.

Bobby did not go in. And we put fire in the hole. And the VC did not come out.

Studs Armstrong. I'll never forget him. It was the first time I was introduced to what Philadelphia is all about. He always used to talk about South Philly this. South Philly that. I'm livin' in Philadelphia now, and I see how racist it is.

Armstrong was ruthless, man, really ruthless. If there was an ambush to be set, he wanted his squad to be the ones to lead the ambush. At the time I was in his squad, it was because his men had got injured and we had to balance off the squad. I dreaded being there, because he was always going to volunteer me for something, and me and him would have to get into some type of altercation.

Armstrong had reenlisted three time to stay in Vietnam.

One night we set up near Quang Tri, and two VC walked down the trail right upon us. We didn't bury them. We just left them out there in full display with a little card on them showing the cactus. The name of our unit.

Armstrong immediately started cutting ears off and put them in his rucksack. Then he cut one man's neck off, and stuck the whole head inside.

It got so funky the lieutenant told Armstrong to get rid of it.

Armstrong said, "Listen. I do what I want. This is my war."

Like he ran his own show. Three tours in Vietnam. He wasn't going to let any young lieutenant tell him what to do.

The lieutenant had to threaten him with court-martial to make him give up that head, but Armstrong kept his ears. Those was his souvenirs.

I didn't lose a close, close friend towards being killed in Vietnam. But I lost a very close friend in terms of his mental functioning.

His name was Richard Streeter. Like I said, I knew his wife in high school. I had known him then, too. We used to play football on opposite teams. He used to play for the Stonewalls, and I used to play for the Romans. We were like rivalry.

Streeter was in Vietnam about I think sixty days before I got there. He received me in the squad. He was a very gung ho individual. Very gung ho. He used to lead fire fights, lead ambushes. That was one of the most impacting things on me. Studs was ruthless. Streeter was brave. Until that particular night at 2 A.M.

We saw two Viet Cong running across the rice paddy through our starlight scopes. So the lieutenant calls in illumination. The VC runs into this village, so the lieutenant tells Whiskey squad to chase them.

They ran right in behind them and got ambushed. The first three men got hit with grenades.

So then the lieutenant hollered Tango squad move in. We dashed into the village and got ambushed, too. We were trapped. They had machine gun fire on us, and we didn't know where it was coming from. All we could feel was it hitting up around us. And they were shooting M-79 grenade launchers at us they got off Whiskey squad. We could tell that they were our weapons, because we know the sound of them. Poop. And then the blast. We could not raise our heads.

Bobby was behind me. A Spanish brother named Martinez was behind Bobby. Streeter, our fire team leader, was in front. Lloyd, the squad leader, and two white dudes was on the side.

Then Bobby screamed, "I got hit." He was shot in the butt.

I moves back for Bobby and said, "Bobby, go up and grab hold of Streeter. Hold Streeter's leg and let him pull you through the hedgerow. Then we can get down behind the dike."

Then they shot Martinez.

So I pushed Bobby up towards Streeter, and Streeter shakes Bobby off. Wouldn't let him grab his leg. Wouldn't help Bobby, right. So I pushed Bobby on up through the hedgerow and went back for Martinez. I was just a pushin' him. But at the time I had an M-72 LAW, which is like an antitank weapon. Very light. You shoot it one time, you discard it. The firing pin is like a cord loop that you just pull out. This cord loop got caught onto one of the bushes. I couldn't raise up because of the machine guns. I feared if I pressed on it, I would blow me and Martinez up. So I had to like squirm out of my web gear and leave that thing hanging.

I finally gets Martinez down behind the dikes, and Streeter is already down there. But he wasn't firing his weapon.

I said, "Return fire, Streeter!"

He said, "I can't fire my weapon. I can't fire my weapon. I can't shoot."

He said, "I'm scared, Kirk. I can't do it. I can't fight."

He was crying down behind the dikes.

Then the squad leader kept telling Streeter to return fire. And he would not fire. So the squad leader said, "Streeter, I'm gon' kill you if you don't fire your weapon."

I said, "No, Lloyd. If you kill him, I'm gon' shoot you. So you gonna have to kill the both of us."

I said, "The man is gone. Let him be."

Then I turned to Streeter.

"We in big trouble, man. Bobby's hurt. Martinez's hurt. Dan just got it. It ain't nothin' but three of us left in this squad. We need to return some fire."

Then this brother in Whiskey squad hollered out his weapon was jammed. Streeter told him, "Here. Take mine."

I said, "No, Streeter. If you don't do a damn thing, don't give up your weapon. I promise you. You're going with the first medevac that we can get in here."

The gunships came in and raked the whole area. Then the medevacs. And they came through a hell of a fire. And we got all the wounded on. Eight of them seriously wounded. A lost eye. A chest shot open. And Streeter. It took a toll on our squad.

We did not seize control of that village until about noon. We found six VC bodies.

Streeter never came back to the field again. He went back to Pleiku to be a supply sergeant and went from E-4 to E-6. Based on him bein' a real top soldier and what have you in the field, it really did something to me. It said any person can go at any moment.

At the time I initially came over to Vietnam they did not have 106 recoilless rifles where I was at. When I was getting short, like three months short, they began to bring them in to secure perimeters. And that was my MOS. So they brought a brother named Sutton from Orlando, Florida, and me into LZ Baldy. We were securing the command post for the entire battalion.

It was the time of Tet. And the VC were making major onslaught.

Me and Sutton were laying around up on the CP, just relaxing, smoking herb, talking, and what have you. Then we heard incoming rounds.

Sutton said, "Kirk, that was incoming rounds."

I said, "No, man. That's something outgoing."

Another came in. Shhhhh, boom!

Johnson said, "That's incoming."

I said, "I think you're right. We better get to the guns."

So we grabbed our steel pots, our weapons, and ran to the jeep where the gun was mounted. And this mortar round hit this big 10-foot rock where the jeep was parked. We had to move from bunker to bunker, because the VC was walking the mortars, from side to side, back and forth, making sure they covered the whole perimeter. They knew where our mortar tubes were, where the command post was. They just had us zeroed in. Oh, yes.

We finally pulled the jeep into position and started returning fire. Sutton spotted the flash of their mortar tubes. I was locking and loading. We must have fired 28 rounds that night. We almost burned the barrel off that thing. And it was no one else returning fire in the whole camp but us. They was about 700 of them taking cover in the bunkers.

Reports came in that our rounds was hitting 100 yards away from the mortar tubes. That's very close at nighttime. We was hitting on the money.

That morning me and Sutton rode down in our jeep to the base of the perimeter and saw all that destruction the mortars had done. Well, we was cheered. The men just raved for us and jumped up in the air. 'Cause they knew the only thing they could hear from our perimeter was that 106 with that back blast. Blast from the front. Boom boom from the back.

Sutton got the Bronze Star for being the person who's firing the 106. I got the Army Commendation Medal with V for valor.

We was heroes, but I didn't feel like it for long. You would see the racialism in the base-camp area. Like rednecks flying rebel flags from their jeeps. I would feel insulated, intimidated. The brothers they was calling quote unquote troublemakers, they would send to the fields. A lot of brothers who had supply clerk or cook MOS when they came over ended up in the field. And when the brothers who was shot came out of the field, most of them got the jobs burning shit in these 50-gallon drums. Most of the white dudes got jobs as supply clerks or in the mess hall.

So we began to talk to each other, close our ranks, and be more organized amongst ourselfs to deal with some of this stuff. The ones like me from the field would tell the brothers in base camp, "Look man, you know how to use grenades. If you run into any problems, throw a grenade in their hootch."

When I came home, I really got upset about the way my peers would relate to me. They called me a crazy nigger for going to the war. And I was still dealing with Vietnam in my head.

Well, they sent me to Fort Carson in Colorado to do the six months I had left. I really didn't want to give no more of myself to the Army. So I played crazy.

I told people I ain't know what rank I was. I told them I was busted in Vietnam. I didn't wear no emblems. I was a buck private. I don't know where the papers at.

They made me cut my bush. What I did, I did not get another size hat. So my hat was falling all over my eyes.

Then I convinced the doctor that my feet was bad. I had jungle rot. I couldn't run, couldn't stand for a long time. I couldn't wear boots. All I could do was wear these Ho Chi Minh sandals I had.

And I would fall out in formation in my sandals, my big hat, and my shades.

I rode them right to the point they was about ready to kick me out of the military.

Then on my twenty-first birthday they said they was going to the Democratic convention. Our unit was going to Chicago to be the riot squadron. I told them I'm not going there holding no weapon in front of my brothers and sisters. The captain said, "Kirkland, you going to Chicago if I have to carry you myself." But I went to the doctor and told him I had a relapse of malaria. He said he couldn't really tell me anything. I would have to stay in the hospital for the weekend. He thought he was getting me. I said, "That's fine."

I was successful playing crazy. I got an honorable discharge.

Because I was a veteran with medals and an honorable discharge, Washington city had a job offer for me. The police force or the post office. The police force had too much military connected to it. My whole thing was to get the military out of my system. I chose the post office. Basically I was sitting on a stool sorting mail. Stuffing mail, sorting mail, do it faster. The supervisors were like first sergeants. Six months later I resigned. I just got tired of it.

I was also enrolled in a computer-operations school. They fulfilled out none of their promises. It was a $2,200 rip-off of the VA money I got for school. They folded at the graduation of my class.

COMMENTARY

THE ROLE OF THE GRIOT

D'JIMO KOUYATE, SENEGALESE GRIOT

It is important that people understand the roles and the power that the griot (known as "jali" and prefixed before the given family name) has been endowed with since the beginning. One of the roles the griot in African society had before the Europeans came was maintaining a cultural and historical past with that of the present. He informed, even to this day, man and woman of the roles they must play in traditional African society. The griot was the oral historian and educator in any given society. The griot was well respected and was very close to kings—in fact, closer to the king than the king's own wife.

The griot served as the king's confidant and personal advisor. The griot would interpret things, such as different facts, for the king. It was also the responsibility of the griot to make sure that the people received all the information about their ancestors—what the father, the grandparents, and their lineages had done and how they had done it. What the griot gave to African society in oral history, cultural information, and ancestral wisdom and knowledge is the key with which all people of African descent can progress and maintain a high level of understanding of their true heritage.

All people of African descent—the Latin, the Jamaican, the Haitian, the Brazilian, the Caribbean, and the African American—all must realize that, although they were not born in Africa, they are still African people and *all* of us have been through the experience of slavery. Most of us have lost our original language and traditions because of having been born outside of the African homeland. When you are away from your ancestral land and lack the necessary cultural information, you become "lost" by concept. The color of the skin remains the same but the concept, the knowledge of Africa, is gone. The traditional names and roles in society, everything that belonged to us by birthright, was taken away from most of us.

This is known as "the painful period." In order to get back what was ours, information and knowledge about African society and culture must be learned now. This the griot gives to all who need it. Our children need to have the facts about their ancestral homeland. This destiny will take a while, however. Everyone has a transition period. When a black person understands his or her African past, accepts being African, he is different from one who does not know these things. Those of us who know, know our value.

The reason I begin with this kind of conversation is that I want people to have the right idea about Africa and the role of the griot in the past and in today's time, so that everyone can understand the "capacity" and potential power that we still have today. This power must be used in a good way so that we can help one another. We are still a proud people and know the significant role we have and the part we must play in our humanity.

So the young man and woman, everybody who stays in the village, get a chance to listen, to live and learn about their culture and such things as I have been saying. In West African society there are various types of stories to communicate these principles. In the evening, after dinner, the stories that are usually told by the griot are called *tahlió* (tah-lee-OH), which means it is not the reality but an imagined event between humans and animals and some kind of spirit. These are the stories that are told for entertainment. A griot has special ways of telling these stories so that they are very entertaining, even though the griot's main intention is not to entertain but to teach the people to know themselves. When *tahlió* takes place, everybody participates. Know, too, that music is not always used and that the stringed harp-like instrument, the kora, for which griots are noted, is new in comparison to other African instruments.

We have to be all that we can be to get our art and all true information about the griot and our rich cultural folklore "out of the closet" in modern society. Most of us know all about the white man's education, his schools, history, and culture, but we lack the necessary information about our own.

I hope that someday we will have the young generation follow you

and me and each of us who is working hard at keeping African culture and tradition alive. Yes, we need our stories; without stories in
an oral tradition, there is no history, no reference. As the song says:
Sy-*yáh Cáh*-pee-sah ma *loo* dee. Death is natural but I won't take
humiliation; which means, if you don't know, you have to learn.
Knowledge is learned. When one does not learn, that is humiliation.

SECTION III
PREACHING THE WORD: Sermons

Let the Church say, "Amen"

SERMONS

THE CREATION

JAMES WELDON JOHNSON

And God stepped out on space,
And He looked around and said:
I'm lonely—
I'll make me a world.

And far as the eye of God could see
Darkness covered everything,
Blacker than a hundred midnights
Down in a cypress swamp.

Then God smiled,
And the light broke,
And the darkness rolled up on one side,
And the light stood shining on the other,
And God said: That's good!

Then God reached out and took the light in His hands,
And God rolled the light around in His hands
Until He made the sun;

And He set that sun a-blazing in the heavens.
And the light that was left from making the sun
God gathered it up in a shining ball
And flung it against the darkness,
Spangling the night with the moon and stars.
Then down between
The darkness and the light

He hurled the world;
And God said: That's good!

Then God himself stepped down—
And the sun was on His right hand,
And the moon was on His left;
The stars were clustered about His head,
And the earth was under His feet.
And God walked, and where He trod
His footsteps hollowed the valleys out
And bulged the mountains up.

Then He stopped and looked and saw
That the earth was hot and barren.
So God stepped over to the edge of the world
And He spat out the seven seas—
He batted His eyes, and the lightnings flashed—
He clapped His hands, and the thunders rolled—
And the waters above the earth came down,
The cooling waters came down.

Then the green grass sprouted,
And the little red flowers blossomed,
The pine tree pointed his finger to the sky,
And the oak spread out his arms,
The lakes cuddled down in the hollows of the ground,
And the rivers ran down to the sea;
And God smiled again,
And the rainbow appeared,
And curled itself around His shoulder.

Then God raised His arm and He waved His hand
Over the sea and over the land,
And He said: Bring forth! Bring forth!
And quicker than God could drop His hand,
Fishes and fowls
And beasts and birds
Swam the rivers and the seas,
Roamed the forests and the woods,
And split the air with their wings.
And God said: That's good!

Then God walked around,
And God looked around
On all that He had made.
He looked at His sun,
And He looked at His moon,
And He looked at His little stars;
He looked on His world
With all its living things,
And God said: I'm lonely still.

Then God sat down —
On the side of a hill where He could think;
By a deep, wide river He sat down;
With His head in His hands,
God thought and thought,
Till He thought: I'll make me a man!

Up from the bed of the river
God scooped the clay;
And by the bank of the river
He kneeled Him down;
And there the great God Almighty
Who lit the sun and fixed it in the sky,
Who flung the stars to the most far corner of the night,
Who rounded the earth in the middle of His hand;
This Great God,
Like a mammy bending over her baby,
Kneeled down in the dust
Toiling over a lump of clay
Till He shaped it in His own image;
Then into it He blew the breath of life,
And man became a living soul.
Amen. Amen.

THE PRODIGAL SON

C. L. FRANKLIN

Reverend Franklin probably began by reading Luke 15:11–32.

I don't believe that there is a greater love story in all of the Bible or in any literature printed, be it secular or sacred, there isn't a greater love story than the story of the prodigal son. Jesus dramatically tells of God's love and God's patience and God's long-suffering and God's concern about man in this passage.

He intended to show, first of all, the danger of self-righteousness in the characterization of the son that stayed at home. Although he stayed at home, although he did not go astray, although he did not engage in wild and riotous living, when his brother was redeemed and was regained, he was too selfish to come in and join in the banquet and celebrate the recovery of his lost brother. So that Jesus intends for us to learn in this that it is as dangerous to stay in the Church and be selfish as it is to go out but finally come back.

Now the theme of this passage is loss. And Jesus intended to show us that God is a God of the lost. Now Jesus also said that God was not the God of the living—or, rather, of the dead—but a God of the living. By that he did not mean that he turned his back on you when you die, but he really meant that no man is dead with God. And David had us to know that we cannot escape to any land where God is not. If he went into the heavens, if he went to the utmost parts of the earth, if he made his bed in hell, behold, God is there. So God is a God of the lost. If you do not believe that he's the God of the lost, make up in your mind to come back to God, and like the father of the

190

prodigal, his arms will be wide open, and a robe will be waiting, you understand, in his wardrobe of blessings.

Now I said the theme of this story is loss. Jesus in this chapter tells of three things that were lost. First he tells of lost sheep. Second he tells of lost money. Third he tells of a lost son. In the case of the lost sheep, the shepherd went back over his steps and over his traveling, the day, the previous day, and searched in every ravine and every mountainside and every valley until he had regained the sheep that was lost. The woman who lost one of her coins of ten swept in every corner and under every bed and behind every door until she had found her lost coin. But then there's no word of anybody having gone out to look for this lost son.

You see, in the case of the sheep we have the loss of property. In the case of the lost coin we have financial loss. In the case of the son we have human loss. People go out looking to regain lost property. People work double shifts in order to regain lost money. But very few people bother themselves about trying to regain lost sons, lost daughters, lost husbands or lost wives, or even lost friends.

This young man, in the case of the prodigal son, why, became restless, according to the story, and became a little impatient with the discipline and order and regulation of his home. Possibly his brother led a life that was too dull. Possibly the loving rule of his father was a little irritating. Yes, he was young, and the blood of youth was dancing for anxiety and excitement in his veins. You understand, his heart had grown alien, alien to his home, alien to the traditional situation among his people, alien to the things that were native to him. The far country of excitement beckoned to him. And he went to his father and petitioned him: "Father, give me all of the goods that fall to me."

His father did not hesitate. He immediately divided his living, you understand, and gave the young man his share. And not many days hence he took his journey into that far country. (Listen if you please.) He didn't go off looking for the young man, for the young man wasn't lost. Yes, he was lost. I don't mean only so far as morals, or so far as that which is spiritual is concerned. I mean he was lost from himself. So the record is that when he found himself in the pigpen, he came to himself, which means that he was not at himself when he left home. (I wished I had somebody here to pray with me.)

You see, there are situations in life— Let me put it this way: I think sometimes that adversity helps us to find ourselves. Some of the folk, some of the folk who are sitting here, listening at me, have gone through experiences and know that there are times in your life when you thought you knew it all, when you thought that you could impose your way and your will upon everybody, when you thought that it was right to be selfish. For you see, the first law of Nature may be self first, but the first law of Grace is others first. (I wish I had somebody here praying with me tonight. Listen if you please.) And it took a little adversity, it took a little sickness, or it took a little misfortune, or it took a little shake-up in your life, to help you to find yourself.

You see, this young man didn't find himself until he had gone all the way from a palace to a pigpen. (Pray with me if you please.) Took his journey into a far country where he was alien: alien from God, alien from his friends, alien from his surroundings and from his native home. The wild blue yonder called and there was nothing at home that could satisfy him. Hence he took his journey into a far country, and the record is that he there wasted his living or his substance in riotous living. Wasted.

Loss always follows waste. If you waste your money, one day you'll want it. (Did you hear what I said?) If you waste your influence, if you abuse your influence, one day you'll wish you had it. If you waste your health, one day you'll want it. For in every instance, loss always follows waste.

The record is that when this young man wasted his substance in riotous living, when he wasted that which had been given to him, then a mighty famine arose and he began to be in want. A mighty famine arose. For you see, famines are still rising. It might not have been an economic famine or it might not be an economic famine in all instances. Sometimes it is the famine of health. A famine may be going on with you in your home and in your community and not necessarily going on with anybody else.

This young man had gone to this far country and no doubt had received a warm reception. When he came in as a prince of an Eastern rich man, with his diamond necklaces, with his gold bracelets, with his servants, with his camels, and with all of his flock, why, no doubt the far country of his desire received him with open arms. For when you don't need anything you always can get anything you want. If you have a car, anybody will let you ride. If you have money, anybody will lend you some money. But if it gets around that you are broke, the story is different. (I wish somebody would pray with me.)

This young man dissipated not only his body, and listen if you please, he dissipated everything else that he had. And, you know, there are a lot of people who think and who talk about how expensive it is to be a member of the church. I want to serve notice on you tonight, it's far more expensive to follow after the ways of the world than it is to be a child of God. For when you get with the crowd out yonder, you're all right as long as you can help bear the load. You're all right as long as you can contribute to the pot. You're all right as long as you can order everybody to sit up. But when it gets to the place where you can't do that, the world is through with you.

If you don't believe I'm telling you the truth, go with me to one of the tuberculosis sanitariums tonight. And talk with, walk with me around with many a young man, and many a young woman, and they will tell you as long as things were going well, they could not sleep for the telephone. They had to be at every party. But when they had wasted all, when the famine of health rose in their lives, the telephone doesn't ring any more. And on visiting day, that crowd of slaves that they used to run with are conspicuously missing. (I wish I had somebody here to pray with me.)

Yes, but listen, brothers and sisters. This young man was reduced to a very shameful level for a man of his nationality. Only a Jew could tell you how he felt about tying himself to a Gentile master in these far-off days and having to work among swine. The young man sat there, you understand, in the hogpen. [Whooping in chant-like rhythm:]

> He sat there
>   hungry
> and set there
>   you understand
> full of experience and wisdom that he'd gained
>   from all of his trials.
> And as he sat there
>   thinking about it,
> hungry
> and realizing
> that he'd come from
>   a palace
>   down to a pigpen,
> and in this situation,
> the record is
>   he came to himself.

I wish somebody tonight
   that's listening to me
would sit right where you are
   and come to yourself.
O Lord.
   You know Jesus told
      this story
in order to let men know
that he had faith
   in men,
that he did not believe that man
   was ultimately
   sinful
   and wicked,
but the ultimate end
   of man was
   to come to God.
For you see, my brothers
   and my sisters,
to do wrong
   is alien with man.
One of these days
   wrongness
   will disappear.
One of these days
   selfishness
will be wiped out on this globe.
One of these days
   wars
   will end,
and
   one of these days peace
   will prevail.
   (I don't believe you know what I'm talking about.)
And this young man
   sat there,
realizing
   that he had ended up there
   and was paying for his folly.
O Lord.

He sat there,
  there among swines,
with hogs
  all around him.
O Lord.
  Realizing,
great God,
  that he'd sought a freedom
    without laws,
O Lord,
  that he wanted a freedom
    at the expense
    of law and order
    and discipline,
O Lord,
  and he'd given up a
    happy home.
  You ought to be able
    to see him sitting there
    thinking to himself:
  Here I am
    in rags,
    in tattered rags,
  but at home my father
    has a wardrobe
    full of robes.
  Here I am
    with the last bracelet gone,
and
    in my father's jewelry box
    there's another bracelet there.
O Lord.
  Here I am
    with no necklace
    about my neck,
  and at my father's house
    there are many necklaces,
O Lord.
  And here I am hungry,
    yeah,

and at home
there's bread
and enough to spare.
O Lord.
I know
that I've done wrong,
yes,
I know,
yes,
yes I know,
I know
I disobeyed my father,
I know
that I'm a violator,
I know
that I've been wild
and then I've been reckless,
yes I have,
but I'm going
back home today.
O Lord.
I've done wrong
but I'm going home,
yes I am.
I'm a rioter
but I'm going home,
yes I am.
I'm hungry
but I'm going home,
yes I am.
I'm outdoors
but I'm going home,
yes.
Yes!
(I wish somebody would pray with me.)
Yes.
Yes.
I'm going to tell my father,
yes,
that Lord, Father,

Father,
Father!
yes,
        Father!
yes,
        I've been wrong,
            yes I have,
        Father!
            I know I disobeyed you,
yes I did,
        I left home talking about
            give me,
        I left home telling you,
            to give me,
        but I've come back home today,
        telling you to make me,
        make me
            one of your servants,
O Lord.
        And that's what I'm telling them now.
        Lord!
        Lord.
        Lord!
        Lord!
        You just make me,
        you just make me,
        as one of your highest servants.
        Lord!
        Lord.
        Lord!
        Lord!
        Lord.
        Lord!
        Just use me,
        anything you want me to do,
        here is my life,
        here is my heart,
        here are my hands,
        here are my eyes,
        Lord!

Lord.
Lord!
O Lord.
Ohh!
Ohh yes!
Yes!
Just make me
one of your highest servants,
yes.

EZEKIEL AND THE VISION OF DRY BONES

CARL J. ANDERSON, collected and transcribed by GERALD DAVIS

If you have your Bibles ready
You may turn with me
To the thirty-seventh chapter of the book of Ezekiel
And we're going to read
The first, second, and third verse
"The hand of the Lord
Was upon me
And carried me out in the Spirit of the Lord
And set me down
In the midst of the valley which was full of bones"
You understand that
"And cause me to pass by them round about
And behold there was very many in the open valley
And lo, they were very dry"
You understand me
I want to use as my theme tonight
Ezekiel and the Vision of Dry Bones
You understand
Not dry bones in the valley
But Ezekiel and the Vision of Dry Bones
And this is one message from the Lord that you cannot run away from it
Yes sir
He that is led by the Spirit
They are the sons of God

And I feel sorry for that individual
That only loves sin
And runs from the Gospel
For it will take the Gospel to save your soul
Now this new Ezekiel signifies God's way of thinking
Ezekiel is known as one of the most mysterious Hebrew prophets
Yes sir
And he began, well, as a boy
He grew up under the influence of Jeremiah
And he began to prophesy at the age of thirty
And for twenty-two years preached by the River of Shafar
At Talabinth
And history says he died at the age of fifty-two
Now this man Ezekiel styles himself
The son of man
Several times he uses this expression
"Thus sayeth the Lord"
You understand me
And you'll find one hundred and seventeen times
Yes sir
The times of his prophesy was stormy and traditional
Ezekiel had two audiences
One real and present, the exiled about him
And the other the whole house of Israel
You understand me
Yes sir
And you'll find many dry Christians in church
As I oftentimes say
I wouldn't have a religion I can't feel
Ezekiel used allegories or parables such as those of Israel as a founding
    child
Representing one with a sound body but unable to walk
Do you understand me
And second as a lioness
Third a stately figure
And fourth a vine doomed
Yes sir
He employed symbolic actions depicting the siege of Jerusalem
By dividing his hair into three parts
Do you understand me

First part to be burned
Second part to be smitten
And the third part to be scattered representing
Do you understand me
Israel and Jerusalem when one-third of the city was smitten
With the sword and the gates were set on fire
Help me Lord
Another third representing the scattered Jews all over the world today
Now by way of parenthesis
I sometimes wonder why
The Lord chose that the hair from Ezekiel's head would be divided three
*   times*
Yes sir
And then as I began to search
I find that one is Heaven's unity number
And seven is Heaven's sacred number
You understand me
But three is Heaven's complete number
Whatever God does He does completely
Am I right about it?
I want the world to know
That there are three heavenly bodies
Yes sir
The sun
Moon
And the planets
Guide me Lord
The earth is constituted of three great elements
They are land, water, and air
And these have three different forms
You understand me
And they are solid, liquid, and vapor
Help me Holy Spirit
Yes sir
Three kinds of animal life
Animals that inhabit the earth
Fish inhabit the waters
And fowls the air
Am I right about it?
Well, I turn to the Bible

And I read where Noah had three sons
Sham, Ham, and Jephtha
Yes sir
You know it's difficult
To preach to people who do not read their Bible
Yes sir
And I read where Moses was hidden for three months
Can I get a witness?
Yeah, his life was divided into three periods
Forty years in Pharaoh's house
Forty years in the wilderness
And forty years in leadership
You understand me
And the workmen of Solomon's temple
Were divided into three classes
Seventy thousand entered apprentices
Eighty thousand fellow craftsmen
And three thousand six hundred master masons
Help me Holy Spirit
And not only that, Daniel prayed three times a day
Yes sir
So you see three is important
The Hebrew children
Shadrack, Meshack, and Abednego
Composed Heaven's fireproof unit
Yes sir
And when Jesus was born
Three wise men came from the East
And presented three kinds of gifts
Am I right about it?
When the Master wanted to confirm his divine nature
And mission in the minds of disciples
He took three of them
Peter, James, and John
Am I right about it?
Yeah, and He took them into a high mountain
Apart and was transfigured before them
And Peter got happy there
And said
Let us build three tabernacles

Am I right about it?
Yes sir
One for Thee
One for Moses
And one for Elijah
So the Lord told Ezekiel to divide his hair
After having shaved his head with a barber's razor
In three parts
Ezekiel used other symbols
He stood out on the street and ate bread with feminine hands
Representing the failing of the stall of life
He set his furniture out of his house
In the broad daylight
Representing the holy vessels and the furniture of the temple
Would be moved out before their eyes
Not only did he speak by parables and symbols
But he saw, he saw visions of the glory of God
Am I right about it?
Yes sir
Of the restored sanctuary and of our discourse this evening
Of the valley of dry bones
My brothers and sisters
In the Lord there are many valleys
Am I right about it?
Now the children of Israel were pictured as in bondage
While in Babylon, Ezekiel was with them in servitude
He heard their cry as is recorded in the one hundred thirty-seventh
*   number of the Psalms*
Judah had lost her political existence as a nation
And their temple was destroyed
And the beautiful service of Jehovah was abolished
I'll hook this train up in a minute
And the walls of Jerusalem was torn down
And the gates had been set on fire
All because the nations had been unfaithful to God
And prepared that their very name was going to be wiped out
From the remembrance of God
In their sorrow they cried
Our bones are dry
You understand me

Our hopes is lost
And we are cut off from our parts
They looked upon themselves, children
As dead in the sight of God
You know it's a bad thing to walk around with the name Christian and
　　do not have no spirit
Am I right about it?
They would find that they resemble the body in the grave
Which nothing remains
And I see Ezekiel he was true to his calling
Yes sir
And he was wearied over the plight of Judah
And the Lord set him down in the valley that was full of bones
Yeah, he saw
You understand me
He saw the flesh
Had been devoured
So to speak
By animals and vultures
He saw bones had been bleached by the chilly winds and parching sun
Yeah, he saw bones scattered by the rolling chariots and the clattering of
　　the horses
And these bones were dry
Do you understand me
They were so dry no footsteps could be heard anywhere
Yeah, it's a sad thing
Yeah, to go to church and find Christians all dry
Yeah, and when the Lord said
Yes sir, when the Lord said make a joyful noise
Am I right about it?
Make it unto the Lord all ye lambs
And right now the world is making their noise
The nightclubs are dancing by the tune of the band
Yeah, and the blues and rock and roll singers
Yeah, those who set around are clapping their hands and they're saying
　　to their favorite singer "Come on!"
You understand me
And I think that you shouldn't mind me crying about Jesus
Yeah, I want to make a noise about the Lord Jesus Christ
I'm so glad

That I'm able to make a noise
And He's been so good to me
Yeah, has He been good to you
Somebody said that the Lord was so good to them
But they never make any noise about what the Lord has said
A woman met Jesus down at the well
You understand me
And He told her everything that she had done
She dropped the water pot and ran downtown saying
"Come and see a man that told me all that I did!"
Oh Lord
Yeah, now this woman can tell what Jesus done for her
Yeah, I think the church ought to witness what the Lord has done for
   you
Yeah, early one morning
Yeah, I found the Lord
Yes I did
I was in the valley of dry bones
Yeah, I had no God on my side
Yeah, I didn't have no spirit
To make me shout
But when I found the Lord
I found joy
Yeah, joy
Yeah, joy was found
I found joy
Peace to my dying soul

COMMENTARIES

THE BLACK PREACHER
AS STORYTELLER

WILLIAM H. WIGGINS, JR.

T he black preacher is the master storyteller in Afro-American culture. His verbal artistry covers Afro-American communal life like the brier patch did Brer Rabbit. And, like Brer Rabbit, their favorite trickster hero, Afro-Americans have instinctively sought protection and reassurance from a hostile world and an uncertain life in the myriad stories told by their ministers. The black preacher comforts bereaved families with a pleasant anecdote about the deceased family member; he affirms those same families' happiness and pride at weddings, anniversaries, baptisms, picnics, and countless other occasions of celebration with a few "remarks" that invariably include a well-told joke; and he inspires his congregation to challenge the racial prejudice that they encounter every day with a series of dramatically retold biblical stories. This verbal thicket is the first line of cultural defense against the racial and the human problems of life for many Afro-Americans.

The black preacher continually sows three types of narrative seeds in order to keep his oral hedge robust and impenetrable. First, there are personal narratives; these are stories that the black preacher fashions out of his own life. In many ways these stories are a variant of the testimonies that members of his flock give during Wednesday night prayer meeting. Dr. Martin Luther King, Jr., and the Reverend Jesse Jackson have been two skillful sowers of this narrative seed. For example, Dr. King referred on several occasions to the frustration he experienced while attempting to explain to his daughter the reasons why she could not attend Atlanta's Fun Town amusement park. By the same token, Reverend Jackson cast some of these narrative seeds during his address to the 1988 Democratic National Convention. In an attempt to inspire poor Blacks to vote, Reverend Jackson returned again and again to the refrain: "I understand when..." Between each repetition he would tell his audience of his own personal encounters with hunger, poverty, despair, and so forth.

Biblical stories are the second type of narrative seed sown by black preachers. Just as lawyers must learn the legal statutes of the states in which they practice and actors must memorize their scripts before stepping on stage or going before a movie or television camera, so, too, must black preachers master the Bible "from cover to cover" or "from Genesis to Revelation," as his church members would say. The more familiar they become with the word, the better able they are to improvise, weaving a biblical character, familiar verse, and/or story into their sermons. James Weldon Johnson captured the poetic eloquence of these stories in *God's Trombones: Seven Negro Sermons in Verse* (1927), a collection of seven poems based on the black preacher's dramatic retelling of such well-known biblical stories as "The Prodigal Son" and "The Creation." The Reverend C. L. Franklin, the father of soul singer Aretha Franklin, was a master teller of these tales. His recordings of these and other biblical stories are still being sold.

Jokes are the third type of narrative sown by black preachers. Humor has always been a major cultural element in the Afro-American religious experience. Young black preachers are reminded of this fact by their elders who occasionally admonish them that "it is just as important to make the people laugh as it is to make them cry." Playwright Ossie Davis harvested some of the fruit from this verbal bush in order to write his popular Broadway musical, *Purlie Victorious* (1963). The Reverend Ralph D. Abernathy is a master teller of these tales. During the civil rights era he consistently demonstrated that rare narrative gift of being able to select and tell a joke that would lower the fears or raise the courage of the nonviolent demonstrators. Reverend Abernathy's humorous depictions of "Miss Ann" and "Mr. Charlie," Afro-American folk designations of white women and white men respectively, energized countless mass meetings and marches of the civil rights movement.

The continuing fascination and enjoyment that many Afro-Americans derive from listening to their pastors tell these three types of stories is an irrefutable affirmation of the fact that the masses of black people are stuck as tightly to their storytelling black preachers as Brer Rabbit was to the Tar Baby.

HISTORICAL ARENAS OF AFRICAN AMERICAN STORYTELLING*

BEVERLY ROBINSON

T here is an old story that the great comedian and mime artist Bert Williams used to tell about his uncle. It seems his uncle had an incredible memory. He could remember who said what, when they said it, how they said it, to whom it was said, and whatever the response was to what was said. His uncle's name was Sam, and he was enslaved by a plantation owner who did not have a good memory. So whenever the owner conducted any business or attended meetings, he always took Sam because he knew Sam could remember who said what, when they said it, to whom it was said, and whatever the response was to what was said. When Sam was not remembering things for the plantation owner, whom the early African Americans called "Massa," he worked in the fields. Everyone was very proud of Sam—particularly his own people because he was a source of pride and had an ability that even the Massa could not match.

One day the devil suddenly appeared out of nowhere before Massa. The devil said, "Massa?" and Massa replied, "Yep." "I got so many folks down below," the devil said, "that I can't remember who's there, why they're there, and what all I'm suppose to do with them. Massa, I need Sam!"* Massa looked sharply at the devil, shook his head, and said, "Nope, you can't have Sam. His memory is better than anybody I know." The devil bargained with Massa that if it

---

*Parts of this paper were presented at the 1988 National Black Storytellers Festival in Oakland, California. This paper is dedicated to the memory of my mother, Mrs. Mildred L. Maiden, who was my first storyteller.

could be proven that Sam's memory was failing, then Massa would agree to let Sam go below. Massa was so assured of Sam's ability to remember that he boastfully replied, "Devil, if *you* prove to me that Sam's memory is failing, I'll not only let you have Sam but a few other slaves to go along with him." As quick as Massa finished the word "him," the devil disappeared.

The day the devil appeared before Massa, Sam was working in the field. He always worked in the field when he was not remembering who said what, when they said it, how they said it, to whom it was said, and whatever the response was to what was said. Sam was singing a tune while plowing land with a mule. Suddenly the devil appeared before him and said, "Sam," to which Sam replied, "Yes, sir." The devil asked him, "Do you like eggs?" and Sam replied, "Yes, sir." Then suddenly the devil disappeared.

Years later there was talk about a possible war in the South, where Sam lived, whereby Southerners would have to abolish slavery because of Northern politics. Massa was constantly going to town for meetings about what was happening between the North and the South. Naturally he took Sam so he could be reminded of who said what, when they said it, how they said it, to whom it was said, and whatever the response was to what was said. By the time the war occurred, known as the Civil War, and the Emancipation Proclamation was passed proclaiming the freedom of enslaved Africans, many years had gone by. In fact, most folks had forgotten about Sam and his incredible memory, while others had moved away and some had died. However, Sam survived and had merely gotten older. After the war he and many others who had been formerly enslaved were promised forty acres and a mule. But Sam had only one acre that he would slowly plow with what was described as a broken-down mule. One day while Sam softly hummed with his back bent from age in an effort to plow his land, the devil appeared. "Sam," the devil said, to which Sam replied, "Yes?" The devil asked, "How?" and Sam said, "Fried."

The story of Sam is part of the oral tradition repertoire of African Americans that Bert Williams and his first partner and tutor, George Walker, introduced to America's stage in the 1890s to 1900s. The story was presented as a theatrical offering when blackface makeup was required as part of the stage arena of minstrelry. An integral element in African-American oral tradition, the tale recounts one form of storytelling that emphasizes how the wit of survival among an enslaved people fostered a sense of pride and undoubted heroism. Seventy-nine-year-old Albert S. Johnson heard the story of Sam from his father who was born in Lexington, Virginia. In the early 1900s, Johnson, Sr., worked one short season as a straight man (the one who took the butt of all the jokes) for Bert Williams:

> So my Dad told a story about this one slave who was working in the cotton field picking cotton. The devil came up him and said, "Sam, what do you like for breakfast?" "Oh, I like ham and eggs," said Sam, and that was the end of the conversation. About twenty years later the devil came again to the cotton fields, and Sam was still picking cotton. The devil said, "How?" Sam said, "Sunnyside up."
>
> There is a moral to that story. They had wonderful memories—they depended on their memories. . . . The slaves in those days had remarkable memories. They had to because they couldn't read, they couldn't write, and whatever they heard they remembered.[1]

Coupled with pride and heroism, the story captures a cultural style that is apparent in the first version collected in 1978, wherein words are consciously placed within rhythmic patterns. These patterns are operable in oral tradition but difficult to capture in writing:

Who said what
When they said it
How they said it
To whom it was said, and
Whatever the response was to what was said.

Storytelling among African Americans can be historically examined relative to four performance arenas. The stage is actually the youngest of these arenas, and for African Americans it has served as a showcase for various structured repertoires stemming from oral tradition. Other performance arenas include the plantation, where many stories later appeared on stage such as the above told by Williams. However, storytelling on plantations was often concealed as games. For example, the Georgia Sea Island Singers (see page 139) formerly led by Mrs. Bessie Jones, often relate how games offered an outlet for resentment and a statement of pride by people for whom indignities were a daily experience.

Mrs. Jones was born in 1902, and one of the games learned from her grandfather was the *Buzzard Lope* which requires mimicked movement of a buzzard and powerful call-and-response singing: "Throw me anywhere, Lord, in an old field. Just so Jesus hold me, in an old field." Interpreting this game, Mrs. Jones explained the soliloquy for her ancestors that allows the soul to rest regardless of where the body is thrown (that is, dies).

> We'll act just like those buzzards and those white people will think we learnt it in Africa. But we are telling them that we don't care if you put our bodies down in the woods just like you did them horses, them dogs that was dead. Just might as well let the buzzards picks the meat off my bones because it doesn't make no difference, you not burying me right nohow. You see, I'm throwed out anyway.

The game was a protest against the "unadorned boxes or naked holes in which the enslaved were buried. The players declared they were equals with whites before the Lord after death."[2] The stories on plantations were rhythmically complex and a primal force to sustaining a physical and cultural existence.

A performance arena simply represents the actual site or location of a performance or the display of theatrical events. For African Americans, a reference to time and/or space may be inferred in most cases from the name of the arena. Storytelling within these arenas was not always the recorded words of early Africans in America. In the case of slave ships, the decks of the ships themselves made up the arena, and the name refers to the Colonial period when Africans were transported across the Atlantic. Hence it was the movement of an enslaved people—their dances—that was recorded. The dancing of African slaves was not only a form of entertainment for the ship crews but also a forced exercise for economic reasons. Richard Drake wrote:

> We had tambourines on board, which some of the younger darkies fought for regularly, and every evening we enjoyed the novelty of African war songs and ring dances, fore and aft, with the satisfaction of feeling that these pleasant exercises were keeping our stock in fine condition and, of course, enhancing our prospect of a profitable voyage.[3]

A fourth arena, the pulpit, witnessed the transformation of religion into something more than what was given to African Americans. The pulpit allowed for the oratory and dramatic skills of a people who were:

> ... uprooted from a culture in which religion applied to all aspects of life, were objects of intensive proselytizing efforts on the part of their masters. They did not so much adapt to Christianity (at least not to the selective Christianity evangelized to them by their masters) as adapt Christianity to themselves. Just as the masters converted Christianity to their own culture, so the slaves converted Christianity to theirs. It was not God the judge of behavior—God the master or overseer—who was the object of worship in Afro-christianity, but a God more like African deities: God the transcendent spirit. They worshiped this new Christian deity in traditional African ways and made European religious forms serve African religious functions.[4]

For many, Jesus became a name that was more representative of the attributes of their former African deities and deceased ancestors, as well as a new tool for psychological strength against slavery when African names could not be safely spoken. In addition, early preachers often used mime to illustrate biblical stories. This was an important dramatic device since most of these preachers were illiterate. One man, Matthew Ewing, was known for reading out of his hand. According to an ex-slave, Elizabeth Ross Hite, "he never learned no real readin' and writin,' but he sure knowed his Bible and would hold his hand out and make like he was readin' and preach de purest preachin' you ever heard."[5]

The early preacher not only had the phenomenal ability to memorize and recite vast amounts of biblical text but also was able to translate text into something understandable. Most of the texts were too cryptic to follow: "Brothers and sisters, this morning I intend to explain the unexplainable, find out the undefinable, ponder the imponderable, and unscrew the inscrutable." Then he became the master storyteller utilizing metaphors and similes to enrich his sermons with imagery, dramatizing every phrase of life that was part of his preserved cultural heritage. The pulpit, whether in an open-air arena on in a building, was an educational place where its members not only learned spiritual truths but also how to apply them to everyday life. It functioned in a system of cooperation where the preacher performed and the congregation responded.

Cooperation and response have been key operatives in traditional African-American storytelling. These two major elements have been instrumental in holding a community of people of African heritage together when so many opposing elements challenged their physical, spiritual, and intellectual survival. Stories taught African Americans how to respond to their abilities (that is, responsibilities), even if this was no more than utilizing their gift for memory and an innate understanding of the situations that confronted them as exemplified in the story of Sam or in the narrative game of Buzzard Lope.

NOTES

1. Collected from Albert Johnson, Jr. (January 1989) at the Mind Builder's Folk Arts Program, Bronx, New York.

2. Beverly J. Robinson and Kate Rinzler, "All Things in My Remembrance (Interpretations of African American Games from Enslaved and Post-Slavery Tradition)," unpublished paper written for the Smithsonian Folklife Program with accompanying videotapes prepared during the 1976 Bicentennial Celebration, Washington, D. C.

3. Charles Joyner, *Down by the Riverside: A South Carolina Slave Community.* Champaign, Illinois: University of Illinois Press, 1984, p. 141.

4. Mechal Sobel, *Travelin' On: The Slave Journey to an Afro-Baptist Faith.* Westport, Connecticut: Greenwood Press, 1979, p. 171.

5. Lynne Fauley Emery, *Black Dance in the United States from 1690 to 1970.* Palo Alto, California: National Press Books, 1972, p. 10.

LOVE WHO LOVES YOU: Traditional and Contemporary Stories of Family and Home

The tree of love gives shade to all.
—*traditional African-American saying*

STORIES

THE CASE OF
THE MISSING STRAWBERRY PIE

JACKIE TORRENCE as told to MARIAN E. BARNES

I was born in Chicago, and shortly afterward the family moved back to Salisbury, North Carolina, where my mother had grown up. My grandfather and my grandmother were my storytellers. He was African American, and his father had been enslaved. He told me Afro-American tales. Grandmother's mother was a Cherokee Indian, and she told me Cherokee legends that her mother had told her. Monday mornings when grandmother did her weekly baking was storytelling time at our house. I think it developed in response to my incessant habit of asking questions about everything, everything, *everything!* The result is a wealth of Afro-Cherokee stories that I now tell all over the world.

When my mother was a little girl, her mother was president of the Willing Workers Club of their church, and just about every other Sunday the pastor of Grandmother's church ate dinner at my grandmother's house. She always had chicken for him, and homemade pie. She would bake the pie early and put it in a pie safe* until Sunday. Grandmother also kept sugar cakes for her children in the pie safe.

One week when the minister was expected for Sunday dinner, Grandmother baked a strawberry pie and put it on the top shelf of the pie safe. My mother went in the pie safe looking for sugar cakes. She ate them; then she tiptoed and stuck her fingers into something gooey on the top shelf, tasted it—*strawberry pie!* Her favorite! She

---

*A large, aerated, wooden box, once used to store pies.

ate as much of the pie as her fingers could reach, then, to get the rest of it, she lifted her baby brother above her head, and together, they finished it off!

Come Sunday, to Grandma's horror, there was no strawberry pie for the pastor's dessert. Grandmother apologized to him and quietly asked the children to leave the table. When the preacher had gone, Grandma lined all of the children up. (There were fourteen of them.) Then she reached up over the mantel and took down an old double-barreled shotgun which hadn't been used in years. "I want each of you to blow your breath into the barrel of this shotgun," she said. "When it smells strawberries on your breath, it will go off, and blow your head off." Stoically she positioned the handle of the gun in her lap. Then, one by one, the children stepped to the gun and diffidently blew into its barrels. My mother and the guilty brother kept working their way to the back of the line. But when it was finally my mother's turn, she confessed to eating the strawberry pie, and everything she had ever done in her life!

"Ain't you going to punish them young uns?" her father asked.

"No," Grandma said. "They *just* punished themselves!"

I CANNOT TELL A LIE
PEACH COBBLER PIE

LINDA GOSS

Momma was a school teacher. Daddy worked at the aluminum plant. He got off from work at 2 o'clock. She got off from work at 3 o'clock. Therefore, Daddy would be anxiously waiting for her to come home and cook dinner. Because she was so tired she would open up some canned goods, thaw out some frozen foods, and whip up something quick. She would cook her big meals and yummy desserts on Saturdays and Sundays. One day when Momma came home, Daddy gave her a sack of peaches and demanded that she bake him a peach pie with "fresh peaches and lots of juice." He also said, "And I don't want to wait until Saturday to eat it."

Momma didn't protest. She just replied, "If you want lots of juice, you want a cobbler, not a pie."

Here's how she made it:

1 package pie crust mix (Jiffy will do)	1 cup of sugar
	1 cup cold water
2 cans of sliced peaches in heavy syrup	Dash of nutmeg
	Butter

Prepare 2-crust pie as directed on package. (Use ½ package of crust for a small pie.)

Stir peaches, sugar, and water together. Add a dash of nutmeg. Pour filling in a medium-size Corning Ware pie container or Pyrex. Cover with strips of pie dough vertically and horizontally (similar to lattice.) Dot with butter. Bake in oven 350° for 30 minutes or until crust is brown. Cool, serve, and eat. Yum-yummy.

After dinner Momma served us the best-tasting homemade peach cobbler. Daddy really loved it.

Later that evening as we sat in the living room, peaches began to roll across the floor one by one.

"Those are my peaches," shouted Daddy.

Amazed by what she saw, Momma confessed, "I cannot tell a lie; I used a can of peaches."

Momma had hidden the fresh peaches, but my little brother Barry had found them in the kitchen and was using them for baseballs.

ANNIE, THE BULLY

LAWANDA RANDALL

Not too long ago in a small town in Ohio, when your grandparents or maybe even your great grandparents were children, there lived a little girl named Annie. She had an older sister named Bertha, four younger sisters named Bernice, Clara, Emma, and Amanda, and a younger brother named Columbus. Annie had quite a large family, and since she was one of the older children, she had quite a lot to do to help care for the younger ones. She had to help change diapers for the babies and watch to see that the toddlers didn't play in the street and see that the ones just a bit older didn't start fires or anything like that. She took all her responsibilities very seriously and always made sure she did everything just right.

Annie was well liked by grown-ups. She was a very well behaved, polite child. She never interrupted grown-up conversations, never made a nuisance of herself, and always did as she was told. Usually children who get along so well with adults don't get along too well with other children (they're goody-goodies, you know), but that wasn't the case with Annie. She was good at keeping secrets, good at playing games—especially mumblety-peg—and she was cute, too. All the other kids in the neighborhood liked her. That is, all the kids except one, a little girl named Pecola. Pecola did not like Annie. More than that, Pecola hated Annie. More than that, she was afraid of Annie.

You see, every time Annie would meet Pecola on the street, she would take Pecola's candy if she had any. Or she would take Pecola's money if she had any. Or she would make Pecola carry her packages if she had any. And when she couldn't do any of those things, she would beat Pecola! That Annie was a terrible bully to Pecola. It got so bad that Pecola would go far out of her way to avoid meeting Annie. If she saw Annie first, Pecola would duck into a doorway to hide or run in the opposite direction to take a different route home. Pecola was very afraid of Annie.

Avoiding Annie worked for a long time until one day when Pecola was helping her mother with the laundry. In those days there were a lot of steps to doing laundry. You had to sort the clothes, putting all the white clothes in one pile and the dark ones in another. You had to wheel the washing machine to a water source to fill the tub with water. While the clothes washed, you had to watch carefully to make sure small articles like socks or underwear didn't get caught in the agitator and that the strong action of the agitator didn't tear up the clothes. Then you had to wring the clothes out either by hand or, if you were lucky, with the wringer attachment that came with the machine. The clothes were put into tin tubs to wait while the water was changed so the clothes could be rinsed. Once rinsed, the clothes had to be hung to dry—outside if the weather was good and inside if it was not. Pecola had helped her mother as far as the step of hanging up the clothes. Her mother said, "Pecola, take the clothes to the backyard and hang them up." Pecola picked up the basket to do so, but when she reached the back porch and looked out into the yard, you know who she saw. Annie! What was she going to do? She *had* to hang up the clothes. But there was Annie, standing in the back-yard, shaking her fist, daring Pecola to come out. What was she going to do? What would you do?

Well, what Pecola finally did was to march out to Annie and beat her up! And that was the last time Annie tried to pick on Pecola. To this day, Pecola and my mother, Annie the bully, are the best of friends.

DADDY

YOLANDA D. KING in collaboration with
HILDA R. TOMPKINS

It still tickles me to think about the excitement two little words brought to our household. Anytime we heard the words "Daddy's home," all previous activity stopped and all eight of our feet scurried toward the door. "Daddy, Daddy," we all yelled at the top of our voices, each of us hoping to be the first he would answer.

Although the routine was the same, each time felt like the very first time. Daddy picked us up one by one so we could kiss him on our "sugar spot." My brothers Dexter and Marty both had their sugar spots on Daddy's cheeks. Bunny, who was the youngest, had hers on the very top of his forehead. Mine was the same as Mommy's— Daddy's lips.

Showing off his baby girl, Daddy often asked Bunny to identify everybody's sugar spot with a kiss. "Where's Marty's sugar spot?" he would ask, and she would kiss Daddy's right cheek. "Where's Yoki's sugar spot?" he would continue, until he went through the entire family. Bunny was always eager to answer Daddy, knowing she would get them all right. But we also knew that she really just enjoyed kissing Daddy on everybody else's sugar spot.

The kissing went on a couple of minutes or until there was an interruption such as a phone call for Daddy. But as soon as we were able to get Daddy's attention again, the fun and games continued. "Martin, don't," Mother would admonish as we all gathered in the kitchen around the refrigerator. "Martin, *please,*" she would continue. But in spite of all her concern and protest, the game went on as

227

usual—Daddy putting us on top of the refrigerator and shouting, "Jump!"

What a feeling, soaring through the air and landing in Daddy's arms. And each time I jumped, Daddy's arms were right where they were supposed to be, strong, safe, and secure. This was one of the best feelings I experienced as a child. I had no idea at the time that these moments with Daddy would become so precious to me.

Daddy was always a lot of fun, and he seemed to enjoy being with me as much as I enjoyed being with him. Of all the things that Daddy and I did together, traveling with him was one of my favorites. The two of us on a big plane in the sky headed for who-knows-where. I don't remember all of the places we traveled to or all of the things we did once we got there, but one thing was always the same: No matter where we were, what we were doing, or who we were with, crowds of people always tried to get close to my daddy.

"Dr. King, Dr. King, can I just shake your hand?" "Dr. King, please, may I just have a picture with you?" And some of the ladies wouldn't even ask, they would just push their way through the crowd and kiss Daddy without ever saying a word. But why? I knew why Daddy was special to me; he was my daddy, and I loved him and he loved me. But what made him so special to other people?

Mother explained that Daddy's work was important to everybody because he was working for freedom and equality. People wanted to touch him and be in his presence because they appreciated so much the things he was trying to do. He wanted to make the world better for everyone.

I understood what Mother was saying. It made me proud to have a father that was so devoted to the cause of human rights. People believed in Daddy. They trusted him and learned from his example. I know I did.

One of the most important lessons I learned happened while I was traveling with Daddy. I remember it like it was yesterday, although I was only seven years old. Daddy and I were strolling through the airport hand in hand. Still having a few minutes before takeoff, Daddy decided to stop in one of the airport gift shops to buy a newspaper and some other reading material. While waiting for Daddy to make his choices, I started to look around for something for me.

Browsing the different counters led me to a delectable row of candy and gum. Just as I picked up the candy bar I wanted, Daddy called, "Come on, Yoki." He took my hand and hurried me to the gate. The candy bar that had been in my hand was now in my purse.

We were settled on the plane when I remembered the treat I had for myself. Without giving it much thought, I reached in my purse and took out the candy bar. Before I could get the wrapper off, Daddy asked, "Where did you get that candy?"

"From the gift shop," I answered.

"You had money?" he asked.

"No," I replied.

"Then how did you pay for it?" he asked.

"Well," I said, "there was no time, so I just put it in my purse."

Calmly, Daddy took the candy bar out of my hand and put it back in my purse. Daddy looked at me with his serious eyes and slowly said, "You will take this back to the store when we return and apologize for taking it. Do you understand me?"

"Yes, sir," I replied, as I sank down in my seat and turned my face to the window.

What Daddy told me I had to do stayed with me the entire time we were away. As the time approached for us to make our return trip, I was hoping that he had either forgotten or changed his mind about returning the candy. But no such luck. When the plane landed, Daddy took my hand and escorted me to the gift shop.

Nervous, embarrassed, and humble, I approached the cashier. "Excuse me, ma'am," I said politely. "I took this candy bar without paying for it, and now I want to return it. I'm sorry." As I handed her the still-wrapped chocolate bar, she extended her hand with a smile and said, "Thank you. Your apology is accepted."

This part of the ordeal had been relatively easy, but I still had to face Daddy. As I turned from the cashier, I expected him to have an angry or disappointed look on his face. To my surprise, he, too, was smiling.

I waved good-bye to the lady, and Daddy took my hand. He looked at me with a real sense of pride. As we walked away, I remember thinking how good it felt to do something right.

DEATH OF A BOY

CHINUA ACHEBE

The dilemma tales are the most powerful traditional stories told in West Africa. The protagonist in such a story is caught in a difficult situation and has to make a quick decision which either way, right or wrong, will cause him emotional grief. Usually there is no ending to these tales and the audience is left to guess the decision. Chinua Achebe, master storyteller, uses elements of the dilemma tale in his writings, causing the reader to ponder conflicting values. When a woman of Okonkwo's clan was killed in a neighboring town, the elders demanded as compensation and as hostages a virgin and a young boy of fifteen. The virgin was given to the man whose wife was killed; the boy Ikemefuna into the charge of Okonkwo, who brought him up together with his own son Nwoye.

So Okonkwo encouraged the boys to sit with him in his *obi*, and he told them stories of the land—masculine stories of violence and bloodshed. Nwoye knew that it was right to be masculine and to be violent, but somehow he still preferred the stories that his mother used to tell, and which she no doubt still told to her younger children—stories of the tortoise and his wily ways, and of the bird *eneke-nti-oba* who challenged the whole world to a wrestling contest and was finally thrown by the cat. He remembered the story she often told of the quarrel between Earth and Sky long ago, and how Sky withheld rain for seven years, until crops withered and the dead could not be buried because the hoes broke on the stony Earth. At last Vulture was sent to plead with Sky, and to soften his heart with a song of the suffering of the sons of men. Whenever Nwoye's mother sang this song he felt carried away to the distant scene in the sky where Vulture, Earth's emissary, sang for mercy. At last Sky was moved to pity and he gave to Vulture rain wrapped in leaves of cocoyam. But as he flew home his long talon pierced the leaves and the rain fell as it had never fallen before. And so heavily did it rain on Vulture that he did not return to deliver his message but flew to a distant land, from where he had espied a fire. And when he got there he found it was a man making a sacrifice. He warmed himself in the fire and ate the entrails.

That was the kind of story that Nwoye loved. But he now knew that they were for foolish women and children, and he knew that his father wanted him to be a man. And so he feigned that he no longer cared for women's stories. And when he did this he saw that his father was pleased and no longer rebuked him or beat him. So Nwoye and Ikemefuna would listen to Okonkwo's stories about tribal wars or how, years ago, he had stalked his victim, overpowered him and obtained his first human head. And as he told them of the past, they sat in darkness or the dim glow of logs, waiting for the women to finish their cooking. When they finished, each brought her bowl of foo-foo and bowl of soup to her husband. An oil lamp was lit and Okonkwo tasted from each bowl and then passed two shares to Nwoye and Ikemefuna.

In this way the moons and the seasons passed. And then the locusts came. It had not happened for many a long year. The elders said locusts came once in a generation, reappeared every year for seven years and then disappeared for another lifetime. They went back to their caves in a distant land where they were guarded by a race of stunted men. And then after another lifetime these men opened the caves again and the locusts came to Umuofia.

They came in the cold harmattan season after the harvests had been gathered and ate up all the wild grass in the fields.

Okonkwo and the two boys were working on the red outer walls of the compound. This was one of the lighter tasks of the after-harvest season. A new cover of thick palm branches and palm leaves was set on the walls to protect them from the next rainy season. Okonkwo worked on the outside of the wall, and the boys worked from within. There were little holes from one side to the other in the upper levels of the wall, and through these Okonkwo passed the rope, or *tie-tie,* to the boys and they passed it around the wooden stays and then back to him; and in this way the cover was strengthened on the wall.

The women had gone to the bush to collect firewood and the little children to visit their playmates in the neighboring compounds. The harmattan was in the air and seemed to distill a hazy feeling of sleep on the world. Okonkwo and the boys worked in complete silence, which was only broken when a new palm frond was lifted on to the wall or when a busy hen moved dry leaves about in her ceaseless search for food.

And then quite suddenly a shadow fell on the world, and the sun seemed hidden behind a thick cloud. Okonkwo looked up from his work and wondered if it was going to rain at such an unlikely time of the year. But almost immediately a shout of joy broke out in all directions and Umuofia, which had dozed in the noonday haze, broke into life and activity.

"Locusts are descending," was joyfully chanted everywhere, and men, women, and children left their work or their play and ran into the open to see the unfamiliar sight. The locusts had not come for many, many years, and only the old people had seen them before.

At first, a fairly small swarm came. They were the harbingers sent to survey the land. And then appeared on the horizon a slowly moving mass like a boundless sheet of black cloud drifting toward Umuofia. Soon it covered half the sky, and the solid mass was now broken by tiny eyes of light like shining stardust. It was a tremendous sight, full of power and beauty.

Everyone was now about, talking excitedly and praying that the locusts should camp in Umuofia for the night. For although locusts had not visited Umuofia for many years, everybody knew by instinct that they were very good to eat. And at last the locusts did descend. They settled on every tree and on every blade of grass; they settled on the roofs and covered the bare ground. Mighty tree branches broke away under them, and the whole country became the brown-earth color of the vast, hungry swarm.

Many people went out with baskets trying to catch them, but elders counseled patience till nightfall. And they were right. The locusts settled in the bushes for the night, and their wings became wet with dew. Then all Umuofia turned out in spite of the cold harmattan, and everyone filled his bags and pots with locusts. The next morning they were roasted in clay pots and then spread in the sun until they became dry and brittle. And for many days this rare food was eaten with solid palm oil.

Okonkwo sat in his *obi* crunching happily with Ikemefuna and Nwoye, and drinking palm wine copiously, when Ogbuefi Ezeudu came in. Ezeudu was the oldest man in this quarter of Umuofia. He had been a great and fearless warrior in his time and was now accorded great respect in all the clan. He refused to join in the meal and asked Okonkwo to have a word with him outside. And so they walked out together, the old man supporting himself with his stick. When they were out of earshot, he said to Okonkwo:

"That boy calls you Father. Do not bear a hand in his death." Okonkwo was surprised and was about to say something when the old man continued:

"Yes, Umuofia has decided to kill him. The Oracle of the Hills and the Caves has pronounced it. They will take him outside Umuofia as is the custom and kill him there. But I want you to have nothing to do with it. He calls you his father."

The next day a group of elders from all the nine villages of Umuofia came to Okonkwo's house early in the morning and, before they began to speak in low tones, Nwoye and Ikemefuna were sent out. They did not stay very long but when they went away Okonkwo sat still for a very long time supporting his chin in his palms. Later in the day he called Ikemefuna and told him that he was to be taken home the next day. Nwoye overheard it and burst into tears, whereupon his father beat him heavily. As for Ikemefuna, he was at a loss. His own home had gradually become very faint and distant. He still missed his mother and his sister and would be very glad to see them. But somehow he knew he was not going to see them. He remembered once when men had talked in low tones with his father, and it seemed now as if it was happening all over again.

Later, Nwoye went to his mother's hut and told her that Ikemefuna was going home. She immediately dropped the pestle with which she was grinding pepper, folded her arms across her breast, and sighed, "Poor child."

The next day, the men returned with a pot of wine. They were all fully dressed as if they were going to a big clan meeting or to pay a visit to a neighboring village. They passed their cloths under the right armpit and hung their goatskin bags and sheathed matchets over their left shoulders. Okonkwo got ready quickly, and the party set out with Ikemefuna carrying the pot of wine. A deathly silence descended on Okonkwo's compound. Even the very little children seemed to know. Throughout the day Nwoye sat in his mother's hut and tears stood in his eyes.

At the beginning of their journey the men of Umuofia talked and laughed about the locusts, about their women, and about some effeminate men who had refused to come with them. But as they drew near to the outskirts of Umuofia silence fell upon them, too.

The sun rose slowly to the center of the sky, and the dry, sandy footway began to throw up the heat that lay buried in it. Some birds chirruped in the forests around. The men trod dry leaves on the sand. All else was silent. Then from the distance came the faint beating of the *ekwe*. It rose and faded with the wind—a peaceful dance from a distant clan.

"It is an *ozo* dance," the men said among themselves. But no one was sure where it was coming from. Some said Ezimili, others Abame or Aninta. They argued for a short while and fell into silence again, and the elusive dance rose and fell with the wind. Somewhere a man was taking one of the titles of his clan, with music and dancing and a great feast.

The footway had now become a narrow line in the heart of the forest. The short trees and sparse undergrowth that surrounded the men's village began to give way to giant trees and climbers which perhaps had stood from the beginning of things, untouched by the ax and the bush fire. The sun breaking through their leaves and branches threw a pattern of light and shade on the sandy footway.

Ikemefuna heard a whisper close behind him and turned around sharply. The man who had whispered now called out aloud, urging the others to hurry up.

"We still have a long way to go," he said. Then he and another man went before Ikemefuna and set a faster pace.

Thus the men of Umuofia pursued their way, armed with sheathed matchets, and Ikemefuna, carrying a pot of palm wine on his head, walked in their midst. Although he had felt uneasy at first, he was not afraid now. Okonkwo walked behind him. He could hardly imagine that Okonkwo was not his real father. He had never been fond of his real father and, at the end of three years, he had become very distant indeed. But his mother and his three-year-old sister ... of course she would not be three now, but six. Would he recognize her now? She must have grown quite big. How his mother would weep for joy and thank Okonkwo for having looked after him so well and for bringing him back. She would want to hear everything that had happened to him in all these years. Could he remember them all? He would tell her about Nwoye and his mother, and about the locusts....Then quite suddenly a thought came upon him. His mother might be dead. He tried in vain to force the thought out of his mind. Then he tried to settle the matter the way he used to settle such matters when he was a little boy. He still remembered the song:

> *Eze elina, elina!*
> > *Sala*
> *Eze ilikwa ya*
> *Ikwaba akwa oligholi*
> *Ebe Danda nechi eze*
> *Ebe Uzuzu nete egwu*
> > *Sala*

He sang it in his mind and walked to its beat. If the song ended on his right foot, his mother was alive. If it ended on his left, she was dead. No, not dead, but ill. It ended on the right. She was alive and well. He sang the song again and it ended on the left. But the second time did not count. The first voice gets to Chukwu, or God's house. That was a favorite saying of children. Ikemefuna felt like a child once more. It must be the thought of going home to his mother.

One of the men behind him cleared his throat. Ikemefuna looked back and the man growled at him to go on and not stand looking back. The way he said it sent cold fear down Ikemefuna's back. His hands trembled vaguely on the black pot he carried. Why had Okonkwo withdrawn to the rear? Ikemefuna felt his legs melting under him. And he was afraid to look back.

As the man who had cleared his throat drew up and raised his matchet, Okonkwo looked away. He heard the blow. The pot fell and broke in the sand. He heard Ikemefuna cry, "My Father, they have killed me!" as he ran toward him. Dazed with fear, Okonkwo drew his matchet and cut him down. He was afraid of being thought weak.

SIKHAMBA-NGE-NYANGA, A TALE FROM SOUTHERN AFRICA

A.C. JORDAN

The beauty of *Sikhamba-nge-nyanga*, "She-who-walks-by-moonlight," involves her whole community. She becomes identified with nature and becomes abstracted as the people see the similarities between the beauty of nature and the beauty of the human female. She is a blessing for all of society, and all may delight in her loveliness. Such beauty must therefore be protected. To abuse it is to negate it, and the happiness engendered by that beauty is thereby lost. It is a man's privilege to gaze on *Sikhamba-nge-nyanga*, but the people are punished when they attempt to consign the wrong function to the girl, i.e., to beauty; when they violate the customs that protect and nourish her. She returns to nature, whence she came, and she cannot be restored until a sacrifice is offered, until the people recognize their guilt and make reparations. Nature does not destroy her, it merely reclaims her from those who have treated her in an uncustomary fashion, who have attempted to force upon her an unwanted function. Beauty is fragile, elusive, evanescent, and it fulfills its own function; when made to serve another function, beauty dies. That which created it (nature and a love of beauty—in this narrative, represented respectively by the doves and the pool on the one hand and the mother on the other) is alone able to restore it.

It came about, according to some tale, that there was a wealthy man who had many wives. Among these women was one very beautiful one. At the beginning, she was her husband's favorite, and this made the co-wives very jealous of her. Unfortunately, she did not bear any children, and this disappointed her husband greatly, and

236

after some time he neglected her altogether, despising her. Then she became the laughing stock of the co-wives. Hardly any of them spoke to her, and even the children were told never to set foot in her house or run any errands for her. The co-wives were in the habit of forming themselves into groups and working together, hoeing their fields together, cutting grass together, weaving mats together, and so on. But none of them would work with her. So she used to do all her work by herself. She could be seen hoeing her field alone, cutting grass alone, sitting on her stoop and weaving her own mats alone. Moons used to roll by without her ever seeing her husband, and when he did come, he used to spend just a day or two with her and then go back to the houses of the wives who bore him children. This made her so sad that she was nearly always in tears.

One day she picked up her hoe and went to hoe her field as usual. She hoed and hoed and hoed until she was tired. Then she went to sit in the shade of a tree in the middle of the field. There her sorrows overcame her, tears flowed down her cheeks, and she wept silently.

"Why are you crying, *nkosikazi* (madam)? What makes you so sad?"

The speaker was one of two doves that had come unnoticed and perched on one of the boughs of the tree under which she was sitting.

"I'm crying because I am sad. I am sad because my husband doesn't love me anymore. He doesn't love me anymore because I don't bear him any children. I don't bear him any children because I cannot."

The doves flew away but soon returned, each of them with a pellet in its beak.

"Take these pellets and swallow them immediately, and very soon you will be heavy with child," they said.

The woman took the pellets eagerly and swallowed them at once. She felt so grateful to the doves that she offered them some corn, but the doves would not accept this.

"No," they said, "we don't want any reward for what we've done for you. We'll be satisfied if you give us a pebble each."

So the woman picked up two pebbles from the ground and gave them to the doves.

True enough, after a few moons she discovered that she was heavy. She was delighted at this, but she made up her mind that she would tell neither her husband nor any of her co-wives about this. And she knew that they cared so little about her that none of them would notice anything until the child was born.

When her time came, she gave birth to a girl of exceptional beauty. This brought her great joy. She gave the child the name Thanga-limlibo (Budding Little Pumpkin), and she felt so bitter against her husband that she could not persuade herself to let him know. If he ever came, he would make the discovery then, but as for her, she would never go out of her house to seek him in the houses of her co-wives. She was so determined about this that she would not take her child into the light of day, lest someone might see it and carry the news to her husband. So she kept the child indoors during the day and only after nightfall would she allow her to come out to drink the evening air. This went on for years until Thanga-limlibo sprouted (reached the age of puberty). It was only at that age that her mother occasionally made her do something or other in the courtyard during the daytime. They were very happy together, and the mother's former beauty was restored.

One morning Thanga-limlibo came out into the courtyard and began to tidy the clearing in front of the huts. For the first time the people saw her. Her beauty was so amazing that they all stood there gazing at her. The men would not go hunting; the women would not go to hoe the fields; the girls would not go and draw water from the spring; the herd boys would not drive the cattle and goats to the pastures; the animals, too, would not go grazing. All living things flocked around the courtyard of her home and gazed at her, feasting their eyes on her beauty. It was not until her mother noticed this and ordered her to come in, that the people and the animals could move away.

The head of the family was not present at this gathering, but the news of the girl of extraordinary beauty reached his ears that same morning. He set out immediately to find out what it meant. He found his neglected wife in the courtyard and was amazed to see her so happy and beautiful. Embracing her warmly, he asked her what had restored her beauty. She smiled and invited him to come in. There for the first time he came face to face with his daughter and with such beauty as he had never seen even in his dreams. With joy he embraced his daughter and then his wife and then his daughter again and then his wife again, begging forgiveness, and making a solemn vow that he would more than make up for his cruelty to her.

Then he set about making preparations for a great feast in honor of his daughter.

Now that Thanga-limlibo had been seen by her father, the mother felt that it was not necessary to keep her indoors anymore. But as soon as Thanga-limlibo stepped into the light of day, all living things flocked where she was. If she went to draw water from the spring, they all followed her. If she was working about the house, they stood there gazing at her and would not move until she went indoors. So the community decided that she was not to come out during the daytime: she was to come out by moonlight, go to the fields by moonlight, go to draw water from the spring or river by moonlight, when the people had finished their day's work and could gaze at her beauty. She therefore became known to the community as Sikhamba-nge-nyanga (She-Who-Walks-by-Moonlight).

By the time the great feast came, the fame of the beauty of the girl who walked by moonlight had spread to all the neighboring villages, and all the people, young and old, made up their minds that they would come. The feast was going to take place in the moonlight, and this unusual arrangement made the occasion even more attractive. It was not surprising therefore that when the day came, the village saw the greatest gathering that had ever been seen even by the oldest men and women in that community. When Sikhamba-nge-nyanga came out, the people were so amazed at her beauty that they all stood there gazing at her. The young people who were seeing her for the first time flocked round her, and the grown-ups who should have left her to those of her own age group and gone about their feasting found it difficult to tear themselves away from the young people. In any case the celebrations went on until daybreak, when Sikhamba-nge-nyanga had to go indoors to make it possible for the people to go.

Soon after this, it was known that Sikhamba-nge-nyanga was going to be married to a handsome young man who had met her at the great feast. All the young men had, of course, fallen in love with her, but she had fallen in love with this particular one, the son of a wealthy man whose home was three days' journey from her home village. When the day came, she was accompanied by the largest bridal party that had ever been seen, and among the cattle given as her *nqakhwe* (dowry) was a beautiful dun-colored ox, the most beautiful ox over a very large area. The wedding took place in the moonlight, and before leaving Sikhamba-nge-nyanga at her new home, her people warned the in-laws that this young woman was not to go out during the daytime, and they stressed that this custom must be observed very strictly.

The in-laws observed the custom. Sikhamba-nge-nyanga stayed indoors during the daytime and came out at moonrise to hoe the fields or draw water from the river. The people knew this and would come out and gaze at her as she passed by. Everything went well until a baby was born, and her parents immediately sent her a *mpelesi* (young girl sent especially to nurse the baby).

One day all the people of the house went out to work in the fields, leaving the young mother with her baby and the *mpelesi*. The only other person in the house was a withered old woman, the mother of Sikhamba-ngenyanga's father-in-law. She was so worn out with old age that she could not help herself in any way, and whoever remained in the house with her had to help her with everything. In the middle of the day, the old woman felt very thirsty. Sikhamba-ngenyanga brought her some water, but the old woman complained that it was sour and she demanded fresh water at once. In vain Sikhamba-ngenyanga tried to coax her to drink the stale water, reminding her that there was no one to bring fresh water as the river was rather far and the *mpelesi* too young to go there alone.

"I can't die of thirst when there is a grown-up woman in the house," said the old woman. "Go and fetch me fresh water at once!"

So She-Who-Walks-by-Moonlight was forced to pick up her water pot and ladle, step into the light of day, and go to draw water from the river. She knew her way very well in the moonlight, but as she had never gone to the river during the day, the light was too strong for her eyes. As she tried to pick her way down the slope, through the bushes and reeds, she stumbled several times and fell. She scratched her arms, her face, her legs. But at last she reached the deep pool where she had drawn water many times in the moonlight. She tired to draw water with the calabash ladle, but this was pulled out of her hand by some unseen power, and it disappeared under the water. She tried to draw with the water pot, but this, too, was pulled out of her hands and disappeared. She took off her leather mantle and tried to draw water with it, but this was also pulled out of her hands and disappeared. She took off her head cover and dipped it in the water so that she could run back home and let the thirsty old woman suck the water from it, but this too disappeared. In despair, she cupped her hands in order to draw just sufficient water to wet the throat of the old woman. Then the unseen power drew her under the water.

When her husband and in-laws returned from the fields and found that she had been away for some time, they sent the *mpelesi* to look for her. The little girl went to the pool, looked around, called out, but received no reply. Then she went back to report. The grown-ups went to the pool, saw her footmarks at the water's edge, and concluded that she was drowned. They did all they could to recover her body, but they could not find it. Meanwhile the baby was hungry and crying for its mother.

At moonrise the *mpelesi* picked up the baby, put it on her back and, without saying a word to the in-laws, she walked quietly to the edge of the pool where the mother had disappeared. There she sang sadly, calling on the mother to come out and suckle her baby:

Uyalila, uyalila, Sikhamba- ngenyanga	It is crying, it is crying, Sikhamba-ngenyanga
Uyalila umntan'akho. Uyalila.	It is crying. Your baby is crying.
Kha uphume umanyise, *Sikhamba-ngenyanga.*	Do come out and suckle it, Sikhamba-ngenyanga

Thereupon there was a disturbance on the surface of the deep pool, and the mother's head and face appeared. Standing breast high in the water, Sikhamba-ngenyanga sang:

Yinto yangabom! Yinto *yangabom,*	It was intentional! It was intentional
Yenziwe ngabagama *ndingalibiziyo,*	On the part of those whose name I may not utter;
Ukuthi ma ndikhe amanzi emini;	To send me to draw water during the daytime;
Ndaba kukha ngomcephe, *watshona;*	I tried to draw with the ladle, and it sank;
Ndaba kukha *ngomphanda, watshona;*	I tried the pot, and it sank;
Ndaba kukha nge ngubo, *yatshona;*	I tried the mantle, and it sank;
Ndaba kukha ngeqhiya, yatshona;	I tried the head cover, and it sank;
Ndathi ndakukha ngezandla, *ndatshona.*	And when I drew with my hands, I sank.

After singing her song, Sikhamba-nge-nyanga came out of the water, took her baby into her arms, suckled and fondled it, and without saying a word, she handed it back to the *mpelesi* and disappeared under the water. The *mpelesi* carried the baby home and put it to bed. She did this again the following night and the night after. Then the in-laws discovered it and questioned her. When she told them what had been happening, the men decided to waylay the mother. They hid themselves in the reeds near the pool sometime before moonrise. They saw the *mpelesi* coming with the baby on her back. They heard her sing her sad song. They saw the mother standing breast-high in the water. They heard her song and saw her come out, suckle and fondle the baby. And just as she was handing the baby back to the *mpelesi,* they sprang upon her, seized her, and would carry her home. But the river followed them, followed them beyond the reeds, followed them through the woods, beyond the woods, up the slope, right up to the village, and there the water turned bloodred! Then the in-laws were seized with fear, and they put her down. The river immediately received her, resumed its normal color, and receded to its place.

When the people were at a loss what to do, two doves appeared and offered to fly immediately to Sikhamba-nge-nyanga's own people, report what had happened, and seek advice. On reaching the village, the doves perched in the gate posts of the cattlefold. The herd boys saw them and were just about to throw sticks at them and kill and roast them when the doves sang:

Asingo mahotyazan' okubethwa,	We are not doves that may be killed,
Size kubika Sikhamba-ngenyanga;	For we come to tell of Sikhamba-ngenyanga;
Ube kukha ngomcephe, watshona,	She dipped the ladle, and it sank,
Waba kukha ngompanda, watshona,	She dipped the pot, and it sank,
Waba kukha ngengubo, yatshona,	She dipped the mantle, and it sank,
Waba kukha ngeqhiya, yatshona,	She dipped the head cover, and it sank,
Waba kukha ngezandla, watshona.	She dipped her hands, and she sank.

Sikhamba-nge-nyanga's parents gave the doves some corn to eat and then asked them to fly back swiftly and tell her in-laws to slaughter and flay the dun-colored ox and throw its carcass into the pool after nightfall. The doves flew back swiftly, delivered their message, and the order was carried out immediately.

At moonrise that night, when the *mpelesi* carried the baby to the water's edge, all the people of the village followed her. They heard her sing her sad song, they saw Sikhamba-nge-nyanga stand breast-high in the water, and heard her sing her song. They saw her come out of the pool and suckle and fondle her baby. But this time, after the baby had been fed, the mother did not hand it back to the *mpelesi*. Instead, she carried it lovingly in her own arms. And as she walked quietly back to village, the people gazed and gazed and gazed at her beauty in the moonlight.

THE LION
AND THE ASHIKO DRUM,
A FABLE
FROM SOUTH CAROLINA

JAMAL KORAM THE STORY MAN

Tsara came from a large family which lived in the village of Sahesis. Her family was very close and shared with one another in many ways. Loaat, her husband, came from the northland coast. He loved his wife very much.

When they were first married, Tsara and Loaat had much fun. Tsara was a dancer, and even though Loaat was a healer, he enjoyed drumming. He would drum on his Ashiko drum and Tsara would dance and dance and dance. She would dance the dance of the griot, the harvest dances, the praise dances, and the dance of love. Deep into the night Tsara and Loaat would dance and drum.

There came a time when the husband and wife moved to the country to farm and to raise the children they hoped to have. At first the work kept them very busy. The dancing and drumming became much less, until, finally, there was none. Well, there was no dancing, but late into the night you could hear the Ashiko drum that Loaat would always carry.

By and by, Tsara became very lonely for her family, and she would visit them quite often. Loaat questioned her: "Why must you visit your family so much? There is a lot of work here, and I cannot do it all by myself."

Tsara would answer, "You are the one who wanted to come out here. You are the one who spent all of our savings to come out here to farm. And look at my front," she said. "Do you see children coming from there?"

Loaat would shake his head and tell her to go ahead.

One day Tsara told Loaat that she was going home, and started off. "Tsara," he called, "be sure you take the Wasdi road, a ferocious lion has been seen on the Alani road! Do you hear me?" he yelled.

His wife called back, "I've been home before!" But she really wasn't listening.

The husband watched as she walked off. "I love you," he said to himself, "and I miss you. Will we ever dance again," he mused as he looked down at his Ashiko drum.

Loaat started back to work. After a short while he had a funny feeling inside. "Something is wrong," he thought. Quickly he dropped what he was doing and headed for the Alani road where the lion had been seen. With the speed of a cheetah, Loaat ran down the road, until he came to a huge baobab tree on a curve in the road.

As he rounded the tree he caught his breath. There was Tsara, and in front of her was a huge lion about to leap on her! Without thinking, Loaat reached for his Ashiko drum and began to play. He beat out the rhythms to the dance of the hunter.

"Boom baat. Boom baat. Boom baat baat boom baat."

Simba, the lion, stopped in his tracks and turned toward the drummer. Loaat kept drumming.

"Boom baat. Boom baat baat boom baat."

The lion tilted his head, first to one side, then to the other side, as if he were moving to the drum beats.

"Boom baat. Boom baat baat boom baat."

The husband yelled, "Run Tsara! Kimbia! Don't look back!" The wife ran, and she did not look back.

"Boom baat. Boom baat baat boom baat." Loaat continued to play the drum. Then the lion lifted his left paw and then his right paw, as if dancing to the drum rhythms. Loaat said, "I must find a way out of this. Simba seems to like the sound of the Ashiko drum." Loaat thought if he could step back around the baobab tree, he had a good chance to get away.

"Boom baat. Boom baat baat boom baat."

He hit the Ashiko and took three steps backward, thinking that he could ease away from the lion. But the lion followed the healer's movements. Simba was actually dancing to the rhythms of the drum!

"Boom baat. Boom baat baat boom baat."

"Maybe if I move a little quicker, I will lose him," thought Loaat. He took three long, quick strides backward around the curve and was about to turn and run when the lion ran up just as close as he was before. Then a most surprising thing happened. The lion spoke!

"Healer, why are you trying to escape me? Do you not know who I am?"

Loaat could not believe his ears, so he kept on playing—louder and faster.

"BOOM BAAT. BOOM BAAT BAAT BOOM BAAT!"

"Healer!" shouted the Lion. "I am your guardian and your muse. I am here to protect you!"

The drumming stopped.

"But you were going to kill my wife!" cried Loaat.

The lion protested. "No, no, no," he said. "I was only talking to her." Cautiously, Loaat asked what they were talking about.

"About both of you," explained Simba. "There is no reason why the two of you cannot be happier together. You both love each other. You both care for each other."

Sometimes when we are afraid of the future, we cling to the past.

The lion continued to speak.

"You want the Tsara of yesterday," he explained, "but yesterday is gone. Look at your wife as she is today. Give her what she wants and needs. Concentrate on her. Have patience, and you will see that the crops will grow, the laughter will flow, the harvest will come, and there will be little dancers for your drum rhythms."

"He is right, my strong one," said a voice from behind the baobab. It was Tsara. As she stepped from behind the tree, she said, "I do love and respect you. I want to make you happy, too."

The husband and wife hugged and kissed each other, as sparks of love jumped from their eyes. The lion began to flick his tail, and Loaat suddenly had an urge to play the Ashiko drum.

"Boom boom baat do baat. Boom boom boom. Baat do baat. Boom boom boom. Baat do baat.

And there, under the wide limbs of the baobab tree, the dancer, the healer, and the lion danced the dance of peace.

Change your mind, and you will change your life. Most times, what we travel miles to see is closer than we think.

WARUGUNGA, BASED ON TRADITIONAL KENYAN STORIES

WACIRA GETHAIGA

This is an original tale based on traditional stories from the Kikuyu people of Kenya.

In one section of the land there lived a most beautiful girl called Waciuma. Her name fitted her perfectly because every time she expectorated, her saliva turned into the most beautiful beads. Her perfect form was a delight to all who saw her. They admired and loved her immensely. Her father had grown so exceedingly rich from selling the beads that he did not require the usual dowry from Waciuma's suitors. Every time a young man won Waciuma's favor, he would go to her father and ask what was required for her hand.

"Son," the father would reply, "you know that my daughter is very precious. I am as rich as I care to be. No amount of cows and sheep and goats would make me part with my daughter. But if you are desirous of marrying my daughter, I'll tell you what you must do. Come outside."

Waciuma and her family lived on a plain overlooking a very expansive almost waveless lake. By straining one's eyes, one could see a very beautiful feather protruding from the exact center of the lake. Its multicolored barbs gave a shimmery, mesmerizing hue to the whole lake, and many a man had desired to put it on his cap. If Waciuma's father could get it, it would give him the last thing he wanted: prestige among his peers.

"You see that feather at the center of the lake?" he would inquire.

"Yes, I see it."

"I am old. I cannot swim that far. Yet I want that feather. That will be Waciuma's dowry. Just bring it to me, and she is all yours."

This sounded silly to most suitors. Why would he ask such a simple thing for the hand of one of the most beautiful women in the land? Princes offered him half their kingdoms instead. But he would not take their money or their thrones. His heart was set on that feather.

Many a young man shed his garment and entered the swim. But few got halfway; and even fewer managed to swim back to the shore. After every failure, the father would send any surviving young man away and tell him not to return. But the fame of Waciuma spread across the country, and suitors came from near and far.

A young man called Kiumbani decided that he would try his hand. It seemed a perfect opportunity to get a wife because although he was very handsome, hence his name, he was poor and could not afford the traditional dowry, which Waciuma's father did not need. He asked his friend Warugunga to accompany him to that far distant land. Warugunga may not have been as handsome, but he was very brave, and his fame had spread far and wide.

They set off and traveled for a long time. They arrived at Waciuma's home. As was customary, they entered Waciuma's hut. Warugunga, the friend of the would-be suitor, began the conversation thus:

"We are seeking adoption in your home."

This was the traditional way of stating the basic purpose: the reason for coming was to woo and to ask for her hand.

"Who is seeking adoption?" Waciuma asked.

Warugunga pointed at his friend. The girl also had certain set responses. At this juncture the girl would look at the man indicated. She could either like or dislike him. If she disliked him, she would answer that her home was not big enough to adopt another person. If on the other hand she liked the man but did not feel ready to get married, she would say that her home was not ready to adopt anybody now but will be at such and such future date.

As it happened, Waciuma was so goodhearted she hardly disliked anybody. In this case she was attracted to the two men, the suitor and his friend, so it did not make any difference which one wanted to marry her. They were both handsome.

"I'll go talk to my mother," she answered. This basic reply communicated to the suitor that, barring any objections that girl's parents might have, the girl was ready and willing.

The final say always rested with the parents. The parents, after investigation into the boy's family, might discover that they are kin and too closely related and would tell the daughter that such a man was not a fitting husband. Also, if they found that the man was irresponsible or too poor, the father might object on the grounds that the man was not able to take care of her properly or to pay the dowry that is required. If none of these existed, then there would be no objections and the girl would be married shortly.

"While I'm gone, I'll leave you something to eat," she said.

She set a big dish of sweet potatoes in front of them and gave each a plate in which to put his peels as he ate. The men did not know that this was a test.

After she had gone out, the men began to eat. The suitor had excellent table manners: Every time he peeled a potato, he put half his peels on his friend's plate. This was an attempt to impress the girl because some girls do not like a man who eats too much. His friend Warugunga was unconcerned as to the height of the pile on his plate. He continued to enjoy the food. That was his function as a friend of a suitor: to comment on the girl's cooking ability and general behavior.

Waciuma returned after they had their fill. She looked at the very small pile of peels in front of her suitor and the very big one in Warugunga's plate.

"Didn't you like my food?" she asked Kiumbani.

"It was delicious. I enjoyed it tremendously. It is only that I do not eat very much," he lied. As a matter of fact, he had eaten just as much as, if not more than, Warugunga.

"I think I'll marry you," she said, turning to Warugunga. "Since you eat a lot, I know I will never go hungry, because when you are working, you will work hard to provide enough food for me and yourself," she joked.

Warugunga was so surprised.

"It is not proper!" he exclaimed. "I cannot do this to my friend."

"I see you are also very loyal. That's good. However, my father will decide. In the meantime I want you to be my suitor, too. But come. He is waiting." She led the way to where her father was waiting for them.

"So you want to marry my daughter?" he said, addressing Kiumbani.

"Yes, I do."

"Are you a rich man?"

"Yes, I am comfortably well off and will pay whatever you ask for your daughter," Kiumbani replied. This again was an untruth, though he was still shaken by Waciuma's comments!

"What about you, Warugunga?"

"I am not well off. That is why I was not the one who came to woo your daughter. Although I had heard of her beauty, now that I have seen her, I love her. If wealth were no problem, I would be very glad to be adopted."

"That is secondary," said the old man. "My daughter and I have agreed that she will be married by the man who brings me that feather sticking out of the lake. I don't require any additional wealth. Just the feather."

The swim seemed deceptive to the original suitor. He requested that all the relatives and the clan of the old man be called. They were to assemble by the lake the following morning, when he would prove his bravery and love for Waciuma. This request was granted.

Early next morning all the people assembled. The suitor Kiumbani shed his clothes. He entered the swim. He swam and swam and swam. At intervals he would take a look at the distance he was yet to cover. It almost seemed that he had not been going anywhere. He tried and tried and tried. Yet his objective seemed to be receding farther and farther. He got very tired and knew that he could not go on. He turned on his back and slowly made his way back to shore, a very disappointed man.

The people who had come to witness this feat were furious. They were angry, not so much at the failure of Kiumbani to reach his objective but at Waciumi's father for being so brutal as to ask the impossible. They seemed to lose interest in the great amount of food that had been prepared for them. They were on the point of leaving, threatening never to return, when Warugunga begged for their patience.

Though Warugunga was not an excellent swimmer, he could not, while life remained in him, let the father of this most unusual girl whom he had come to love so much, be humiliated. Warugunga talked to the people and pleaded with them to be patient with the old man, because as the saying goes, "the heart 'eats' what it desires." And since the old man was so set on that feather, he would die a very unhappy man if no man was found to bring him his desire.

They agreed to give him a chance, albeit he would fail. They had seen too many of these attempts. They had all ended in failure. But since he was set on killing himself, it was no skin off their noses.

Warugunga requested of them that once he entered the water, they should wait patiently until either he pulled himself to shore or they saw his drowned body. In his heart he had no desire to return empty-handed. If he could not reach the feather, he would die trying.

He got in the water. What could he do? He could only swim a few yards! The best way, he thought, was to tread water until it covered his head. Then he would start to swim until he drowned. He couldn't live with failure. Surprisingly, the water remained just below his shoulders for quite a distance. He had been pushing this way when suddenly, to the observers by the shore, he seemed to just drop out of sight. It seemed to them as if he had just fallen into a hole. The lake surface looked so calm. They could not detect any air bubbles nor any signs that Warugunga was trying to come up to the surface. They told each other that it was to be expected. The man was a fool. He knew he would die, yet he had insisted on trying. However, they continued to wait.

Things didn't seem to be going well for Warugunga, but he had decided not to return to shore alive. He expected every step he took on the muddy bottom of the lake to be his last. As long as he could see the feather, he had made a beeline toward it. He knew it was foolhardy, but what choice did he have?

Then all of a sudden the bottom of the lake just dropped. Before he could start swimming, he was engulfed by the waters of the lake. He tasted the slightly salty water, felt himself choke, but continued to fall. He was helpless. After what seemed to him like hours, he touched a solid floor.

Imagine his surprise! He was on solid ground! To add to his surprise, there was no water where he stood. Instead it was dry. And he could breathe once again. He took a deep breath and thanked *Mwenenyaga* (God) that he was still alive. He did not know where he was, but he knew how he had gotten into this mess. He was going for a feather that was in the center of the lake. He had not turned his body, as far as he could remember, and therefore, he concluded, he must be facing the right direction.

He started walking, now, on this new-found road. It was not pitch dark; some light penetrated the water far above him. He could not see how wide the road was, but he could see where he was stepping. He put one foot in front of the other, tested the foothold, and did the same with the other. He traveled this way for a long time. He did not know what time it was. He began to have doubts. Where am I? Which direction am I going? What am I going to find when I reach the end of this path? Should I turn around and go the other way? He started to turn. It was impossible. On either side of where he was standing, his feet could not find a foothold. It seemed to him that the only safe place was where his feet were stepping. I shall walk backward, he decided. But to no avail. The moment he tried to move one foot backward, he found that the solid ground he had been treading in was no longer there. It seemed to him that he was like a man standing on a very high flagpole: nothing on either side of him but air.

All right, he thought; as long as I kept walking, there seemed to be solid ground. I'll try to walk forward. He tried. To his surprise he could move. He gave up all thoughts of ever going back as long as he had any strength left. He would die trying. On and on he walked. Time passed. Still he kept going.

Suddenly there seemed to be an increase in light. He saw in front of him a flight of stairs. He took the steps one at a time. He climbed and climbed and climbed. At the top of the stairs, and just at arm's reach, he saw the base of the feather. He had reached his objective! It looked smaller than he had envisioned it from a distance, but it was so very beautiful. Tentatively he reached for it. Yank! It came off easily. Brave! Now, if he could climb to the top of the stairs, he could push above the water and float back to shore. But no. The whole staircase that he was on collapsed! Down he went, clutching the feather with one hand and trying to grasp at anything. Unfortunately there was nothing to hold on to.

Soon he came to a standstill. He looked about him, and there in front of him was a straight and narrow road. Now he could see it. He resigned himself to his fate and started walking in the one direction that the road seemed to go. He kept the beautiful feather in front of him, admiring it as he went. Now that he had it in his hand he could see why the old man was so set on it. It was the most beautiful feather he had ever seen.

At the shore, the people waited. Since he had gone underwater hours before, they had been scanning the surface of the water for his body. They were puzzled. To anybody's knowledge, there was no man-eating animal in the lake. People had been swimming in it for a long time. All the bodies of those who did not make it back to shore after they had gone in search of the feather had washed back to shore. What happened to that crazy fool? Even those who wanted to leave after giving up on him seemed to be rooted where they were. They were fascinated by this unusual disappearance which had never happened before to their knowledge. They waited. And they waited. And they waited.

It was exactly high noon when Warugunga reached the feather. At the same instant that he yanked it, the whole lake turned red. People started screaming in fear. Yet they could not run. They had no idea that Warugunga had uprooted the feather; they could not see anything beyond a few hundred yards.

"We always felt there was an evil omen on this lake. We have told you time and time again not to test fate too far! Now see what you have done? We shall all be killed! Woe is us!" some screamed at the old man.

He had nothing to say. It was all his fault that this had come to pass. No matter. Whatever will be will be.

At about the eighth hour, Waciuma glanced toward her hut. She wanted to run and lock herself in to mourn her lost lover. Of all the men that had come to marry her, she had come to love this one. He had been charming, handsome, and very interesting. How she wished her father's crazy craving had not sent him to his doom! As she gazed longingly at her hut, she thought she saw the ground in front of it start to move—something like a localized wave. She forced herself to stand up and run. Whatever force had been holding her seemed to break. She jumped up and ran and got to the yard of her hut just as it opened into a wide but limited crevice. She stopped and gaped at it in wonder.

Presently she saw a very beautiful feather. It grew brighter and brighter as it came closer and closer. First the hand, then the head and shoulders. And Warugunga was standing there. She ran to him, embraced him. They had never known such joy.

The people by the shore became aware that something was happening and came running. When they arrived, out of the hole in the ground issued bulls, heifers, and calves. They came out one after the other until they seemed to fill the whole homestead. Then followed a stream of sheep and goats. It took two full hours before all the sheep and goats had come out. There were more animals there than all the animals possessed by fifty of the richest men in the land combined.

Everybody was overcome with awe. What kind of a man was Warugunga? Was he a spirit, or was he the same man they saw entering and disappearing in the lake? Many were overcome with fear and they fainted. To most it was a hundred-year wonder. Some of them ran to their homes to check and see whether all their animals were there. Some believed that some form of magic had been performed and all those animals were their own which had been given to this man while they were watching the lake. But no. Each found his home as he had left it. Then what? None was so brave as to ask Warugunga how he had done it.

Warugunga was very happy to be back where his heart belonged. To tell the truth, he was just as surprised as they were to see all that wealth issuing from the hole. For that matter, he thought it was all a very bad dream, that he was asleep next to his friend waiting for the ordeal in the morning. If so, how come he was holding the feather that had been craved for so long? He shifted his gaze to the lake and was amazed to see how calm the lake looked. It was clear, like glass. But it had lost its central adornment. He was holding it in his hand! He must have done it. He is alive! And this is no dream. But how had he succeeded where so many had failed? He was to puzzle over this thought for the rest of his life.

When the crowd had quieted down, he walked over to Waciuma's father and offered him the feather of his dream.

But the old man would not accept.

"Son," he said, "the wonders that we have seen this day are beyond belief. I know not what happened nor how you managed a feat so great. I'll not ask you what happened, and I'll not ask you how you did it. You are a very exceptional man. Keep the feather and take my daughter with you. I give you my blessings."

"*Aaca, ithe wa Waciuma,*" Warugunga replied. "This feather is yours. I have no desire to possess it. The time for me to wear such finery is too far in the future. We struck a bargain. You wanted a feather, I wanted your daughter. We both got what we wanted. And much besides. All these domestic animals, since they followed one from wherever they came, are mine. They are ours! Now I am rich enough to afford any dowry for Waciuma, my first love." With that he handed the feather to Waciuma's father, who accepted it with trembling hands.

"It is late in the day," Waciuma's father announced. "We all have seen great things today. Let's eat and then go to our homes and rest. Tomorrow we shall assemble here and do what must be done."

Kiumbani could not get over his shame nor the fact that his companion had managed to get Waciuma rather than him. When they went to the cottage assigned to them, he pressed Warugunga to relate how he had managed to accomplish what so many had failed to do.

Warugunga loved his friend very much. However, he could not relate what he did not know. How could he begin to explain what to him was a mystery? He would be called a liar. Whoever heard of a road at the bottom of a body of water? It was too fantastic.

"I can only tell you what I remember. I entered into the lake and started walking on the floor of the lake. Then the bottom just disappeared. The next thing I knew I was standing there embracing the beautiful Waciuma. That's all."

"But what is going to happen to me?" Kiumbani persisted. "I came here to marry Waciuma. I go back as I came. I have lost both my love and my honor."

"Oh, no. That is no way to speak. You go back a very rich man. As for your honor, many an honorable prince has lost his on the waters of yonder lake. As for your love, there is nothing I can do. There is only one Waciuma, and she loves me. Nothing can change that now. You will find a fitting girl to be your wife in time."

They slept. Next morning the people gathered. The men slaughtered a number of cows and sheep and roasted a lot of meat. The rest was handed over to the women to prepare soup. Some women went and brought loads of sugarcane and started to grind them to make extra beer. Other women were involved in preparing foods that were fitting to such a festive occasion. A big feast was had by all. It lasted for a whole week.

The time came for Warugunga, his new bride, and his friend to return home. The elders divided the great herd that came from the lake into four portions. One portion was distributed to the gathered crowd. Another part was given to Kiumbani. A third part was given to Waciuma's father for dowry amid strenuous protests from him. The fourth part was Warugunga's. In each case the portion was too large. The gift from the lake was indeed vast. Waciuma's father gave Warugunga a very beautiful spear and a long sharp sword in an exquisitely decorated scabbard with many of Waciuma's beads, which were exceedingly beautiful.

Waciuma was decked with rings of great value. Each finger and toe was covered with golden rings. Her earrings were made of the best material available. She was indeed a fitting bride.

• • •

The journey from Waciuma's home to Warugunga's was a long one, through hills and valleys and winding paths. A strategy was devised to ensure that they all arrived home safely with their great herd. It was decided that since the herd would follow Warugunga anywhere, he should be at the head of the column. All his cows, sheep, and goats would follow him. In between his herd and that of Kiumbani would be Waciuma, who would act as a natural division between the two herds.

The strategy, in which Kiumbani would bring up the rear, was also a protective move. Warugunga was very brave and would fight anyone who tried to cause trouble. If such trouble did develop, Waciuma would be very far away and would not be hurt. This arrangement was acceptable to the three of them.

Warugunga hugged his bride, donned his sword, took a spear in his right hand and a club in his left hand, said his good-byes to Waciuma's father and mother and the other assembled guests, and started on the journey. The herd filed behind him two by two. First came the bulls, then the cows, then the goats, and finally the sheep: all in double file. He walked half a day's march before his herd could leave the plain by the seashore. Waciuma then started, and Kiumbani's herd followed her.

The first day's march was uneventful but also tiring. The moon was in the first phase so it set early. Warugunga, who was leading the column, came to an open field and determined it was time to rest. He planted his magnificent spear in the center of the field. All the animals circled the spear until they had filled the whole field. He collected some firewood and lit a fire using stone flints. Eventually Waciuma and Kiumbani joined him. They prepared an evening meal and talked far into the night. The next day they repeated the procedure of the day before and continued on their march. This went on every day.

They were about one day's march from home when the unexpected happened. Warugunga was happy that so far they had not been threatened or attacked by anyone. He was becoming mentally relaxed because they had not encountered any of the bad thugs or ogres. He hoped that this final day would be without incident.

But early in the day he passed a female ogre or jinni and her daughter. He did not see them because they were crouching among some low bushes. Ogres or jinnis were not good creatures. They ate domestic animals and humans, too. This particular jinni would have attacked Warugunga but for his already widely known bravery. Also, since Warugunga had such a big herd which the jinni could see stretching for miles, it was not necessary to assault him. The jinni decided it was better to wait until most of the herd had passed, and then she would take a few from the end of the column. Warugunga would never know the difference. So it waited.

By and by Warugunga's flock came to an end, and with it came Waciuma. Immediately the jinni had other ideas. Why should Warugunga have such a beautiful wife while her own daughter was not married? She would exchange Waciuma for her daughter, take everything she had, eat her, and Warugunga would never be any wiser. She magically transformed her daughter into an almost duplicate of Waciuma. Nobody who had never known Waciuma before would be able to tell she was the jinni's daughter. This accomplished, she put her daughter in place of Waciuma and then got ready to eat Waciuma.

Waciuma now realized that something was terribly wrong. She had to have help. But how? Kiumbani was many miles behind and her husband was as many miles in front. Somehow she had to communicate to him that he was being cheated and that she was in danger.

Luckily for Waciuma, she had another quality that had been overlooked due to her other qualities of beauty and ability to spit beads: her voice. She had a most beautiful voice that was well modulated. Whenever she sang, the trees, the birds, the bees, even the wind picked up her singing, repeated it, and passed it along. It was so melodic. This was the only weapon she now had against this unexpected menace.

Then, too, jinni was overwhelmed by all the jewelry on Waciuma, and since she thought she had all the time in the world, she decided that before eating her, she would extend her pleasure, at Waciuma's expense, by asking Waciuma for each and every trinket she had. She made a game. She would say to Waciuma, "Give me this or I'll eat you," pointing to an earring. She was having the time of her life as she repeated this phrase to Waciuma.

Waciuma knew that after all the trinkets were gone, she would eventually be eaten. So she started a song that went like this:

Warugunga-i
Waiikirie itimu rugunga rua iguru,

Waangerekania na mwaari wa irimu
Ria nyakuria!

which means:

Warugunga,
You who braved great dangers to win me,
* I have been exchanged with a jinni's daughter.*
Her mother is going to eat me.

She kept up this song against the barrage of the jinni's "give me this or else." The trees, the birds, the bees, and the wind picked up the song and sang with her.

At length, when all the jewels on her ears, her hair, her hands, and her fingers were gone, Warugunga heard the song. Could that be my beloved? He listened again, and this time was convinced that his wife was in danger. He quickly planted his spear to stop the herd, drew his long shiny sword, and ran back toward the rear of the column. He ran as he had never run before. He came abreast of the jinni's daughter, hesitated, thinking it was Waciuma, noticed that she was not adorned as he had last seen her, remembered the third phrase of the song, and kept on running.

Now soon he could see where the jinni was holding his wife by the roadside. Coincidentally Waciuma was down to the last ring of her last toe. She bent down to remove it, having given up all hope of rescue. It was then they heard the voice of Warugunga.

"By the time I get there, I don't want to find one ring, one trinket, or one bracelet out of place!" he commanded the evil jinni.

The jinni looked to where the voice was coming from, saw Warugunga with his uplifted sword bearing down on her, and was sore afraid. She summoned up all her powers and finger dexterity and started putting everything back that she had taken from Waciuma. She quickly changed herself into human form and fell down on her knees, pleading for her life.

"Please do not hurt me. I was not going to harm your wife. But she had such beautiful decorations. I just wanted to borrow them for a while. Please spare me. Please do not kill me, please." She kept on crying.

Warugunga stood by his shaken wife and regarded the jinni at his feet. "I ought to kill you!"

"Please spare me. Apart from your bravery, it is also known that you are a kind and merciful man. If you kill me, what will become of my daughter? She is so sweet and would never harm a living creature."

"She is an ogre just like her mother. I'll kill you both for putting my wife in jeopardy and trying to deceive me."

"No, my dear husband," Waciuma interceded. "Since I am alive, spare them."

"I beg of you, Warugunga," the ogre pleaded. "Please spare me, and I'll make you a promise that from now on I'll always remain in my human form. I'll never hurt anybody or anything. I will also be your slave; my daughter, too."

"That's an interesting turn of events. First, you want to eat my wife, and now, you offer yourself to be my slave and live in the same homestead. Be off with you and take your daughter with you!"

"Please hear me out, I beg of you," pleaded the ogre. "I was not always an ogre. My daughter is a genuine human being. She is of marrying age. I don't ask for any dowry; just take her to be a companion for your wife. You will need an extra hand with all your flock, and my daughter is very hardworking. You don't want to kill your wife with too much work, seeing she is so beautiful. And since I have taken an oath, I cannot go back on my word. I will be your faithful servant, just so I am close to my daughter...." She went on this way until her former actions seemed insignificant.

Warugunga decided that since the jinni's daughter was just as beautiful as Waciuma, maybe Kiumbani might accept her as a substitute. The idea of having two wives this early was very appealing. At the same time, he did not want to be too selfish. Fate had certainly interceded in his affairs recently.

The three of them waited until Kiumbani, bringing up the rear of the column and without any knowledge of what had transpired, came to them. He stopped and inquired about the state of affairs. He was told the whole story from beginning to end, and then was offered the ogre's daughter.

"I do not doubt that this gesture is made in a friendly spirit, nor do I doubt that this daughter you speak of is very beautiful. Nevertheless, I must pass up this offer. I am a coward. Fate has been very unkind to me recently, and I do not want to test it. You, Warugunga, have been through hell or wherever you went, and you survived. I think you are up to this new challenge. Me, I am satisfied with what I have and my broken heart."

There was no more to say.

Warugunga took Waciuma with him to the head of the column; the mother and daughter were in the center; Kiumbani brought up the rear as usual. They arrived home late that night with no further trouble. There were celebrations and feasting and dancing and all kinds of merrymaking. The identity of the ogre and her daughter was never discussed. Kiumbani went to his home and started the search for a wife all over again. Now that he was very rich, he had little difficulty finding a bride.

In time, and against his better judgment, Warugunga accepted the jinni's daughter as his second wife. He built her and her mother a house below the one he was living in with his beloved Waciuma. A year later his two wives each had a son. Both of the boys were named Ng'ondu.

Life was wonderful. Warugunga and his family prospered. The two boys grew and loved each other's company. It became a practice that they would sleep in one house today and in the other tomorrow. For a long time there was no repetition or reference to what had happened on the road home that long time gone.

RIVER AND THE FOOLISH ONE, A FOLKTALE FROM GHANA

KWASI ASARE

Three children decided to go snail hunting. They decided on the day to go, and when the day came, they chose to go into the forest where they had seen snails before. They packed their bags and went on their way. On the way they came to a river, a very big river, which they had to cross.

The first girl said to the river, "Hello, Mr. River, good morning. I am going looking for snails. Will you let me go through? When I come back, I will bring you some snails."

"Are you sure?" asked the river, and she said, "Yes," and the river said, "Okay. Come on." And she went.

The second girl said to the river, "Hello, Mr. River, how are you? I am going looking for snails with my friends, and if you will let me go through, on the way back I will bring you some snails."

He said, "Okay. Go through."

And she went through.

The third girl was very cocky and thought she knew everything. She could not be told anything. She had been told what to say to the river, but when she came to the river, she said, "Hello, Mr. River. I am going looking for snails, and on my way back I shall bring you some yams, chicken, and eggs if you will let me go through."

He said, "Okay. You may go."

Now this girl knew very well that she did not have these things which she had promised the river. But the river let them go through, and they were gone for many hours until they had enough snails. They all arrived back at the river, and the river was flooding.

"Oh, Mr. River!" said the first girl. "You know, when I came here last, I promised to bring you some snails. Here are your snails."

The river took the snails and said, "Come through, my friend." And off she went.

The second girl approached and said to the river, "Hello, Mr. River! You know, I promised you this morning to bring you some snails, and here they are."

He said, "Oh, thank you very much."

When the third girl came to the river, she did not want to give the river any snails. She tried to get out of it. She knew that she had no yams, chickens, or eggs. She was making a fool of the river. She gave the river some hot argument about it and so disturbed the river that he swelled into a mighty flood and told her to "get lost!" As soon as she put in her right foot, the river grabbed it and said, "Don't mess with me!" and carried her downstream.

"Help! Help! Help!" she screamed and cried. This girl had to fight for her life. She saw some birds flying overhead and cried out, "Hey, birds! Please, please! Would you like to take a message to my parents for me?"

The birds answered, "Wheeaw, heeaw, wheeaw, heeaw."

She said, "Please, when you go, tell my mother to bring me yams, chicken, and eggs. I have promised the river, and I don't have them! Please get them for me, please. I am drowning, I am drowning."

She was fighting wildly for her life in the river and crying out over and over again for help. Finally, they brought her the eggs, chicken, and yams. The river let her go.

And that is why they say that every child must listen in the home and never act as if she knows everything. He or she must not be rude to the parents or to any elders either in the home or outside the home because there is a lot that the child doesn't know. The child must listen carefully and not be cocky because you never know; one day the child might get himself into trouble.

DON'T HAVE A BABY TILL YOU READ THIS

NIKKI GIOVANNI

Well, you see, I hadn't talked with you, that is, you weren't born and I wasn't expecting you to be. So I decided to spend Labor Day with my parents in Cincinnati. Now, when I told my doctor, because you didn't have a doctor yet, that I was going, he thought that I was going to fly, he told me later, though he couldn't have really thought that because airlines won't let you fly in the last month. But anyway he wasn't thinking and neither to tell the truth was I. So I started out in Auntie Barb's new convertible Volkswagen, and we all know how comfortable they are when you plan to drive eight hundred miles. But that's really not important.

We actually got started about 7 A.M. so that we could beat the morning traffic. When we hit the Pennsylvania Turnpike, I thought that was the turning point. We had stopped for lunch before the long stretch into West Virginia when this big black car went zoooooming past us and this thing fell out. I thought, how awful that those white people in the *passing lane* would be throwing out garbage. Then it became obvious that it wasn't, and I said God, I'm gonna hit that dog that fell out of that car, and just as I was adjusting to that Barb said, "IT'S A CHILD!" and I hit the brakes and luckily so did the truck driver in the middle lane and I hopped out of the car while the truck stopped. And the father ran back saying, "Oh, my God! Oh, my God!" but the mother just sat in the car and didn't even turn around and the other small child, another little girl, just looked back to see and maybe there was a glint in her eye, but it's hard to tell under excited circumstances. And Barb said, "What cha doing getting out of the car? What if that truck hit you?" And I thought it would be a terrible thing for an evil militant like me to be hit on the turnpike because some white people threw their child out the window the way they throw their cats in the lake, and I vowed it would never happen to me again. But you were inside and you stirred and I said, "Emma," because I called you Emma, thinking that you were going to be a girl, and I was naming you after your great-grandmother, "I'll never throw you out the car 'cause we don't treat our children that way."

And Barb was so upset by the whole thing that she asked me if I wanted her to drive. Barb was always that way. She figures if she's upset, then everybody is more upset than she is because she thinks she's so cool and all. But knowing that about her I drove until we hit Athens, Ohio, and she brought us into Cincy.

When we walked into the house my mother—since you weren't born she was still just my mother—said, "When you gonna have that thing? You look like you're gonna have it any minute!" And being modern and efficient and knowing she doesn't know anything about having children, I said, "Oh, Mother, the baby isn't due until the middle of September. And I don't look like that." She was walking around the house all bent over backward with her flat tummy poking out and laughing at me. Your Aunt Gary laughed at me also, but I reminded her she hadn't had a baby in ten years and things had changed since then. Plus I was tired so I said I was going to bed, and Gary said, "Why not spend the night with us since we'll have to go to the store tomorrow for the weekend?" And I said the way Mommy was treating me I should go somewhere because it was obvious she wasn't going to let up, so I said, "Emma and I will spend the night with Gary."

At which Gary said, "You're having a boy and we ought to decide on a name for him." You know how group-oriented Gary is. So she called everyone and said, "*We* have to name Nikki's baby." I said, "Her name is Emma. But I don't have a middle name for her." And we kicked that around. Then Gus came upstairs—he always goes downstairs when all his women come home for some reason—and said, "You know, my father's name was Thomas." And I said, "Well, if it's a boy we'll name him Thomas." And the reason I could be so easy about saying I'd name a black child in 1969 Thomas was that I knew you'd be a girl. So we settled the name thing and I went and had an extended B.M., and I thought, that junk on the turnpike really shaped my constipation up. And really, which you may remember, I thought you were constipation all through the first four months, so it wasn't unusual that I still thought that. Your very first foods were milk of magnesia and Epsom salts because I kept thinking I was a little stopped up. And when I didn't get regular I started the sitting-up exercises because I thought I was in bad shape and getting too fat for the laxatives to work. And to tell the truth I didn't think of being pregnant until we were in Barbados and the bikini suit stretched under my tummy and I told Barb, "I think I'm going to have a baby, Barb." And she said she had suspected as much.

So we went out to Gary's to spend the night, and Barb went to Grandma Kate's, and Mommy and Gus had to stay all by themselves. And the next morning I was tired, but I had been tired so long I hopped out of bed with Chris, who offered to fix me one of those good cheese, dried ham, and turkey sandwiches that he fixes for breakfast, and I had to turn the little guy down and settle for tea. Chris asked, "Are you really gonna have a baby?" and I said, "It looks like that." And he said, "Is it hard?" And I said, "I don't know much about it, but Emma probably knows what to do." And he said, "Well, I'm glad to have my own first cousin 'cause everybody else has first cousins. But I wish you'd have a boy." And I said, "It's really out of my hands, Chris." And he smiled that Chris smile that says you-really-could-do-it-if-you-wanted-to-but-you-don't and said, "If you have a boy I can give him all my old clothes and teach him how to swim and give him my football helmet." And I said, "I think it's going to be a girl. But we don't have to worry about that now." So he went to wake his mother up so we could go to the grocery store. Gary came to breakfast saying, "Chris really wants you to have a boy 'cause most of his friends have brothers and since he doesn't he's got nobody to fight with him." And I said, "Gary, why don't you have a baby or talk to Barb or Mommy? Because I'm going to have a girl." And she gave me that Gary smile and says you-really-could-do-it-if-you-wanted-to-but-you-don't and said, "Well, I don't see why Chris never gets anything he wants from this family. He's part of it like anyone else." And we went to the store.

You know Gary's sense of organization, so all her friends and Mommy and Gus came over that night to fix the food for Labor Day. And we were up late playing bid whist because I love bid whist and since most of my friends are ideologists we rarely have time for fun. But I was winning when I told A.J., my brother-in-law, "I think I'll call it a day." And I went to lie down. Gary came back and said, "Are you in labor?" And I said, "Of course not. The baby isn't coming until the middle of September." And I stretched out. Then Barb came back and said, "Are you having pains?" And I said, "No, I'm not, 'cause the baby isn't coming until the middle of September and that's two weeks away and I'm just tired and a little constipated. Maybe I should take a laxative." And she said, "Just stretch out." Then I heard Gus tell Mommy, "You'd better go see about Nikki. Those children don't know anything about babies." And Mommy, who usually prefers not to be involved, said, "They know what they're doing." But he prodded her with *"What kind of mother are you? The baby's back there in pain and all you care about is your bid!"* So she came back and tenderly said, "Your father thinks you're going to have the baby. Are you all right?" And I said, "Of course. I'm just a little constipated." And she asked if I wanted a beer. "When I was pregnant with Gary I drank beer a lot and it helped." So I said yes to pacify her and I heard Gus say, "You're giving the baby a *BEER?* Lord, Yolande! You're gonna *kill* the child!" And she said something real soft and everybody laughed and Mommy didn't come back.

Then the house was quiet and I still didn't feel well and I kept thinking if I could just use the bathroom it would all be okay, but I couldn't use the bathroom. So I was pacing back and forth and Chris came out and said, "Are you having the baby?" and I said no. And Gary came out and said, "It may have been ten years, but I think you're having the baby." And I said, "Don't be ridiculous. I paid my hospital bill in New York, and I'm not having the baby here." And she said, "Okay, but I'm going to call Barb 'cause you've been up all night." And I said, "It's only 3 A.M. and don't wake anybody up. I'm not having the baby. It's the junk I ate on the turnpike." But she called Barb, who said, "Maybe we'd better call Dr. Burch in New York because he would know." And I said, "Don't call him and wake him up. I'm not having any baby." But she did. Dr. Burch said I wasn't having the baby until the first of October according to his calculations but to take me to the hospital anyway to be sure and to let him know no matter what time. And that was when I first realized that he really cared and he said to tell me not to worry because it's a simple thing and I thought, uh-huh. And poor A.J. was awakened to take me. They said I wouldn't be in labor until the water broke but to keep an eye on it. So everybody went back home to bed, and Barb slept on the couch.

Around six I noticed I was still up and I was really tired and I started crying and saying, "If I just understood what's wrong I would feel better!" And Barb said, "You're probably going to have the baby." And I said, "No, Barb. You know I'm not until the middle of September." And she said, "Burch says the first of October so you both may be off." "Emma," I said, "you wouldn't do this to me." But you didn't move. I had started to the toilet for the umpteenth time when I wet on myself, and I was so embarrassed that I felt like a fudgecicle on a hot day or a leaf in autumn. I just wanted to get it over with. So Barb whispered something to Gary who told A.J., and the next thing I knew I was on my way to the hospital again. This time they said, "Take her right on in." And the doctor came to check me and said, "Take her right on upstairs." Then he smiled at me: "You're going to have a baby."

"A BABY? BUT I DON'T KNOW ANYTHING ABOUT HAVING A BABY! I'VE NEVER HAD A BABY BEFORE." And I started crying and crying and crying. What if I messed up? You were probably counting on me to do the right thing and what did I know? I was an intellectual. I thought things through. I didn't know shit about action. I mean, I could follow through in group activities, I could maybe even motivate people, but this was something I had to do all by myself and you were counting on me to do it right. Damn, damn, damn. Why me?

When in doubt, I've always told myself, be cool and positive. Like when they said God was dead and Forman asked for his money back, I said, "God was a good fellow when he was around." You know what I mean—the moderate statement. When L.B.J. decided not to run for president again I said, "That's good." You know? There's something positive in everything. We've got to keep things balanced. So when they wheeled us upstairs and I immediately understood it was you and me and I wasn't going to be much good crying, I stopped and went to sleep.

"SHE WENT TO SLEEP? IN THE MIDDLE OF LABOR?" my mother said. And she came right out to the hospital. But there wasn't anything she could do so she just sat down and had a beer with one of the ambulatory patients. The nurse woke me up and asked how I felt and I said fine because I didn't want to upset her with my troubles. And I tried to go to sleep again. I had been up all night and was quite tired. Then the doctor came and said, "Bear down when you have pain." So I grunted. And he said, "Are you in pain now?" And I said I didn't want him to think I was being negative but I wasn't in pain until he stuck his hand up there. And he told the nurse, "Maybe we'd better take the baby. Get her doctor on the phone." So they called Burch and he said, "You'd better take the baby if she's sleeping because that is a bad sign." And they told me what he'd said. Then this cherubic woman came in and said, "I'm your anesthesiologist, and I'm going to give you a spinal." Then she began explaining all the various things about it, and I said, "Under more normal circumstances I'm sure this would be very interesting. But right now if you'd just like to go ahead and do it, it would be fine with me. I mean, I really trust the hospital a lot right now, and I'm sure you're more than qualified." She looked at me rather perplexedly, and I was going to suggest we meet in the cafeteria the next day when I don't remember anything more. Then there was this blinding light, and the doctor said, "We'll have to give you a Caesarean," and I said I knew that when I realized I was pregnant or at least I wanted to. And he said, "We'll give you a bikini cut," and I tried to explain that I didn't GIVE A DAMN what they gave me, just get the baby. And the bikini cut didn't work because then I heard, "Nurse, he won't come out this way. We'll have to give her..." I decided: when in doubt... Then he said, "I think we've got him," and I opened my eyes because I wanted to know what you looked like in case they misplaced you or something and there you were, butt naked and really quite messy, and they said, "Mother"—why do they call people that?—"you've got a boy." And I thought, but I was having a girl. Then I went to sleep for a good rest.

When I woke up I thought it was the next day, only it was the day after that. And people kept coming around saying, "She looks much better." I thought, God, I must be really fine, so I asked the floor nurse for a mirror and she said, "Be right back," but she wasn't. Then I noticed a line running into my arm and one out of my leg, and it dawned on me I must look like hell on a stick. And I thought it behooved me to ask about my condition. The nurses all said, "You're fine now, Mother," and I said, "My name is Nikki," and they said, "Yes, Mother." So when Gary came I was interested in how I had done. And she, typical of hospital personnel, said, "You're much better now." So I said, "How was I then?" "A good patient." And I said, "Gary, when I get up I'm gonna kill you if you don't tell me." "Well, you would have come through with flying colors if your heart hadn't stopped. That gave the doctors some concern for a while. Then the baby—he's cute; did you know he was sucking his thumb in the incubator? The smartest little guy back there. Well, he was lying on your bladder and a piece of it came out. But other than that you're fine. Mommy and Gus and Barb and I were with you all the time." And I thought, uh-huh. "And Chris is really glad you had a boy. He said he knew you could do it if you wanted." And I thought, uh-huh.

Then she had to leave the floor because the babies were coming. I pulled my gown straight and worked my way into a sitting position and smiled warmly like mothers are supposed to do. And the girl next to me got her baby. Then all the people on my side. Then all the people on the other side. And I started to cry. The floor nurse said, "What's the matter, Mother?" and I cried, "Something has happened to my baby and nobody will tell me about it." And she said, "No. Nursery didn't know you were well. I'll go get it for you." And I said, "Him. It's a boy." So she brought you to me and Gary was right. Undoubtedly the most beautiful, intelligent, everything baby in the world. You had just finished eating so we sat, you in your bassinet and me in my bed, side by side. Then the nurse said, "Don't you want to hold him?" And I started to say, bitch, holding is to mothers what sucking is to babies what corners are to prostitutes what evasion is to politicians. But I just looked at her and she looked at the lines into and out of me so she put you in the bed, and you were very quiet because you knew I didn't feel too swell and if you did anything I wouldn't be able to help you.

The next morning my doctor came by and said his usual and I said, "I guess so I'm alive," and he said, "If you'll eat, I'll take the tube out of your arm." Remembering what hospital food had been like when I'd had my hemorrhoidectomy a couple of years back, I hesitated, but he reminded me that I could feed you so I was suckered. And I was glad because I met the dietitian, who was really a wonderful woman. But I made the mistake of saying I liked oatmeal and she made the mistake of giving me a lot and I didn't eat it, and they said, "Mother, if you don't eat we'll have to put the tube back in." So I had to tell her to keep my diet thing together. Institutions make it hard for you to make friends. Then someone asked if I wanted you circumcised and I said yes and they brought you back and you were maaaad. And I loved it because you showed a lot of spirit. And I snuck you under the covers and we went to sleep because we'd both had a long, hard day. They said you wouldn't let the nurse in white touch you for a good long time after that, which is what I dig about you—you carry grudges. And that was a turning point. I decided to get you out of there before they got your heart.

It's a funny thing about hospitals. The first day I was really up and around they were having demonstrations on how to avoid unwanted pregnancies, and I really was quite interested but since I was from New York and in their opinion didn't belong on the ward, they called everyone who was ambulatory together and left me in the bed. Then they privately visited the catheterized patients, of whom I was still one, and they passed me by with one of those smiles nurses give you. And the aides came over and one said, "I understand you teach school. What are you doing on the ward?" And I said, "I teach school and I'm here to have the baby." "But you're from New York." And failing to see the connection I said, "I'm Gary's little sister," and they said, "Oh." But since they never thought of me as being a poor black unwed mother I didn't get any birth control lessons. Hospitals carry the same inclinations as the other institutions.

That Wednesday they brought you to me for the morning feeding and you, being impatient and hungry, were crying all the way. When I heard the wail, I knew it was you and it was. You cried and cried and I was struggling to get you up in the bed and you didn't care anything at all about the problems Mommy was having. Finally I got you in and fed you and you smiled. I swear you did, just before I put the bottle in. Well, I had pulled the curtain so we could be alone and I guess they forgot about us because when they came to get the babies they left you. And I sat and watched you sleeping. Then I started crying and crying, and Gary came in and caught me. "What's the matter with you?" she sympathetically asked and I said, "He's so beautiful," and I cried a little longer and she said, "You sure are silly," looked at you and then said, "He really is beautiful, almost as pretty as Chris," and I thought, uh-huh.

She left to get me some cigarettes and I decided to sit all the way up so I could cuddle you, and for some reason I started feeling real full but I knew I didn't have to use the bathroom because I was catheterized, so I paid it no mind. Gary brought the cigs back and I lit up my first cigarette since coming to the hospital. Then it happened. The bed was flooded with urine. And I with great exactitude said, "NURRRSE," and she came running. "What's the matter, Mother? What are you doing with the baby still here?" "Never mind that! I've wet the bed." And she laughed and laughed. "You're the only catheterized patient in my knowledge who ever wet the bed." Then she called someone to change it. The aide laughed too and said,

"What's the baby doing still in here?" And I made up my mind to ask the doctor as soon as he came.

"What do I have to do to get out of here?" "What's the rush? You can take your time." "I wanna go home." "To New York? That'll be a long time." "To my mother's." "Well, if you can walk and use the bathroom, we'll let you out Sunday. But I don't think you should worry about that." "I'll be ready."

So the first thing I had to do was get out of bed. I hadn't been out of bed since I got in because I had peeped a couple of days before that the position I was in was the critical position. The woman on the other side in number 1 had been moved but I had stayed. People had moved into number 2 but I was still in 1. And I guess if they had told me how sick I was when I was that sick, I would have died. So in the interest of not upsetting God I just lay back and did what they told me to. Now I had to get up so I could get you home.

First I got the bag and flung my legs over the side. Then I smoked a cigarette to congratulate myself. Then I stood up. And I must say the world had changed considerably since I had lain. Everything was spinning. But you know me. If there's a challenge, I'll overcome. So I moved on to the chair. I was huffing and puffing like I had just felled a tree or climbed a mountain, and I was scared. What if I fell and they decided to keep me there for another week or so? But I made it into the chair and sat up. My timing was perfect. The nurse who messed with stitches came by and smiled. "Oh, you're sitting up?" And I said sure with a smile, hoping she wouldn't see the sweat I was working up. "Maybe I'd better get back in bed so you can examine me" (rather hopefully put out), and she said it would be better. Well, at least I had done the first thing.

That evening I sat up for a delicious dinner of warm milk (just to room temperature), gray goo, and green goo. They smiled and said, "It'll make you strong," and I thought about my mother saying the same thing about Father John's medicine and I thought, uh-huh.

You can tell a lot about a woman from the way she masturbates. Some go at it for a need thing, some because their hand just happened to hit it, some to remember their childhood. Some women turn on their backs, some their stomachs, some their sides. You can peep a whole game from that one set. So in the interest of finding what was left and what wasn't I reached down to this skinned chicken and said to myself, yeah, it's still there but good and tired. And it wasn't in the mood for any games. I felt the necessity to check since every stranger in the world it seemed had looked up my legs. Institutions still haven't found a way to give service and leave the ego intact. Realizing for one that I hadn't needed to be shaved and for two never having been very hairy, I got nervous and wanted my mother. "Will it grow back?" I asked and she said sure, it always does. But it had taken me a good nineteen years of brushing and combing and high-protein diet to get the little I had and maybe it'd take that long to grow back. "Certainly not. It'll be there before you know it," but I still worried. I wanted to get out of there before they shaved my head and took my kidney.

The next thing, since I had so easily mastered sitting up, was walking down to the nursery and back. I made that my goal since I would have you as a reward at the end and the bed at the return. As I stepped lightly from my bed and grabbed my bag, flung my pink robe in grand style over my shoulders, and started from position 1 to the nursery, I heard a collective gasp go up in the ward—"Ooooooo" —and I smiled, waved my hand a little, and then proceeded. Visions of the old house flew before my face. We lived now in an all-black city called Lincoln Heights. It wasn't our first real home but it was our first house. When we'd gotten that house we'd all been very excited because I would have a yard to play kickball in, Gary would have a basement to give parties in, Mommy would have a real living room, and Gus would have peace and quiet. It was ideal. And we all could make all the noise we wanted to. I have always thought it's very important for people to have their own piece of land so that they can argue in peace and quiet. Like when we had rented an apartment, we hadn't really been able to have arguments, and Mommy and Daddy had had to curse each other out on Saturday afternoons so that the landlady wouldn't complain. But now they could fight all day long and well into the night without disturbing anyone. And Gus could throw things and Mommy could call him a motherfucker without appearing to be crude. People need something all to themselves.

I was halfway down the aisle. I passed the fifteen-year-old who had cried, "Help me," because she hadn't known how to feed her baby. I was quickly approaching the thirty-five-year-old who had had the twelve-pound baby. I was going past the girl who listened to "I Can't Get Next to You" all day long on her godawful radio.

We had lived in the old house until I was seventeen; Mommy and I had decided that she and Gus made enough money to have a new house. "I ain't moving" was Gus's reply to our loving suggestion. "I'm happy where I am. A man gets comfortable in his house and the next thing you know they want him to move." And we began looking for houses in Lincoln Heights because we didn't want to lay too much on him at one time. I mean, my father is an old man and it's been proved that old people die earlier when they are uprooted. Like my grandmother would probably have lived another ten or twenty years, but urban renewal took her home that she had lived in for forty-three years, and she was disjointed and lost her will to live. Like a lot of other old folks. I guess nobody likes to see memories paved over into a parking lot. It just doesn't show respect.

So we found a nice little home on the other side of Lincoln Heights and mentioned to my father how we were closing the deal and would be moving in a month. "Nikki, you and your mother can do what you want. She never did listen to me anyway. But I'm staying here." "But you'll be all alone." "Nope. I'll have my radio and I can listen to the ball games. I don't need any of you." "But we need you, Gus. What's a family without you? Who will fuss at us and curse and make us get off the grass? Who will say we can't take the car? Who will promise to build a barbecue pit if you don't come?" "Well, that's different. If you all really need me, I guess I'll go. I thought you didn't want me to." "God, we'd have a dull damn house without you."

So we all prepared to move.

Now, my mother is a very efficient woman, in her mind. And she has a lot to do. So moving day when the movers came we had only packed up the bathroom. But typical of the communal spirit, they all just packed us up and we moved.

The new house was a dream from the git. We were the first and only people to live in it. Gus planted a garden and began to fix up a den and library in the basement. Mommy had a big kitchen and a real living room. We all had a separate bedroom. It was going to be great.

I moved on down to the nursery. You were asleep so I couldn't see you and I headed back.

Yep, I would be good and glad to get home.

The nurse wheeled me down to Gary's waiting car. The nurse carried you and I carried your things. It was the first time you had on clothes and you looked really funny all dolled up and I thought: no doubt about it, the most beautiful baby in the world.

We hightailed it, though I didn't want to go quite that fast, out to

Mom and Gus's. I asked Gary to slow down a couple of times but she said the air was polluted and she didn't want you exposed any more than was absolutely necessary. And I thought, that's good logic, so we hit a cruising altitude and before we knew it we were breaking like crazy for exit 19. Your sweet little hand gripped my sweaty big one and we went to sleep for the last half mile.

When we drove up Gus ran out to grab you but Flora, Mommy's friend, was there and when he set foot in the house she grabbed you. Gary and Chris had run ahead to see if they could hold you and I struggled with your things and my things to get out of the car. Then I had to knock on the door because my hands were full and Gus said, "Come on in, Nikki. Can't I hold the baby? After all, I did name him." And I said, "Can somebody open the door?" and Chris came since he knew he was on the tail end of holding you. Then Flora who is definitely noted for being proper and Christian and ladylike, said, "I have the baby, Gus, so you may as well go sit down because I'm going to hold him," and she put a double clutch on you and I knew there was nothing I could say. I sat down to smile benevolently at you and then Mommy said, "Why don't you go lie down?" and Gary said, "Yeah, go lie down," and Flora, who is almost always reticent, said, "You may as well go lie down because I'm holding the baby till I leave," and she drew you closer, and I decided there was nothing I could say so I went to lie down.

They had fixed up my old room and had very bright colors on the bed and all kinds of jingle toys for you. They had bought a bassinet, which was of course blue with white lace, and three pairs of jeans. Chris later told me that was his idea since he knew little boys preferred jeans to most other clothes. I felt relatively secure when I lay down because your bassinet and diapers were in my room.

Then I noticed that it was dark and no one had been back in my room for anything. Dogs! I said to myself. They have diapers out front, I'll bet cha. So I struggled into a robe and hobbled outside. "Hi, lady," Gary said. "What cha doing outa bed?" "Yeah, Nikki, go on back to bed," Gus said. "We got everything under control." "Nik, can I hold the baby?" Chris asked and Mommy said, "Would you like a beer? I drank a lot of beer when I had Gary." So I decided to go back to bed.

The next couple of days I spent just getting oriented to being in someone else's home after having had my own for so long. Then I made the grand discovery. THE GRAND DISCOVERY. *Finnegans Wake* is true. You have got to overthrow your parents but good or you'll live to regret it. Which is not that some parents aren't hip. Or nice. Or loving. But no matter how old you are or what you do you're a baby to your parents. I'll bet you even when Candy Stripe, the famous striptease dancer, goes home she's a baby to her mother. My grandmother wouldn't give my mother a key to the house when we visited her, and I was old enough to remember that! Even Agnew's mother probably thinks he's still a child. If he ever was. Parents are just like that. So I decided I would have to take complete control of you if I was ever going to get back to my own house again.

First the bath. "Mommy, I think I'll bathe the baby today." "I can do it. I took off from work so I could look after you two." "Yeah, but they taught me a new way to bathe him in the hospital. And you probably aren't familiar with that."

She ambled rather hysterically over to the phone to call Gary. "I think she's still under the anaesthesia because she said I don't know how to wash the baby," and Gary said something and she hung up and called Gus. "I don't know who she thinks bathed her all that time," and Gus said something and she hung up and said, "Why don't you bathe the baby and I'll just watch?" I smiled a sly, sly smile and thought, hurrah for me! But it wore me out so I went back to bed while Gram got to play with a clean baby.

Tuesday after the bath, I sat down with my mother, whom we should hereafter refer to as Gram, for a cup of coffee. "Nikki," she said slowly, like she always does when she has true information to impart, "I don't want you to think I'm meddling in your business. I know you're grown and able to take care of yourself. But don't you think it's time you learned to bake? I didn't learn to bake until after you were born, and it's a terrible burden on your child when everyone else has cakes and cookies homemade and your child is the only one with sweets from the bakery."

I immediately understood the importance of what she was saying. It's true, I thought, only I remembered what it was like having her make lumpy cakes with soggy icing. Maybe she, being a grandmother and all, could help out now. I didn't know a single grandmother who couldn't bake. And after all, who was I to scorn her offer? We younger people should recognize that the older generation didn't survive all these years without some knowledge. So I got up to face the blackberries. Then I understood her sneaky grandmother psychology. If I baked the cobbler I would be too tired to feed the baby. The hurrieder I went the behinder I got, and I accepted my defeat for the day.

By Wednesday I was worn out. She had won. They—because Gus was definitely a part of it all—started coming in in the morning to get you and I would see you at lunch; then I had to go back to bed and wouldn't see you until it was your bedtime. I somehow felt neglected. Now, it's true that I was tired and it's true that they loved me but I sat all day in my old bedroom and I couldn't play with you and I failed to see going through all that mothers go through to have grandparents take over. I decided I would have to go against my history and my ancestors' way of doing things: "I WANT MY BABY NOW, DO YOU HEAR ME? NOW!" And Gus came in to say I'd wake you up if I kept up that noise. "IF I DON'T GET MY BABY RIGHT AWAY, I WILL ROUSE THIS WHOLE NEIGHBORHOOD AGAINST YOU TWO GRAND-PARENTS, DO YOU HEAR ME?" And Gus told Mommy maybe they'd better bring you to me and Mommy said real low, "Or put Nikki in the basement," and I sprang at her: "AHA! I KNOW YOUR SNEAKY PLANS. ALL YOU CARE ABOUT IS TOMMY, AND I WON'T STAND FOR THAT. I'M YOUR BABY AND DON'T YOU FORGET IT." Then she cuddled me on her lap and said real soothing things and walked me back to my room. I had almost gotten you and I would be more successful at dinner, I vowed. Then I had to admit that they still loved me and that did make it a lot better. Or harder. But anyway, I needed a lot of love and that's what I knew.

Friday I went back to the hospital. I was doing fine. I could go home next week and you could too. They gave me a prescription for something and I asked Gus if he'd stop on the way home and get it filled. "Gary can do it. We'd better get the boy home," he said, and I said all right. Then I realized Gary didn't know what it was and I couldn't get it until she and Chris and A. J. came out, but I thought that'll be all right, so we went on home. Then when Gary came out she took pictures of you and I took pictures of you and Gary and I forgot about it. The next morning I asked again and Gus said, "What's the rush? You'll be here another week or so." And I said, "I'll be here longer than that if I don't get it filled." And he said, "Well, there's always plenty to eat in this house and you know you're welcome to stay," and I dug it. So I said, "Tommy needs alcohol, and while you're there get this filled," and he said, "Why didn't you tell me the boy needed something?" and he flew. I called New York and said Sunday I'd be home. Because I had to come to grips with a very important thing—as I said, *Finnegans Wake* is true.

So everyone began adjusting to the fact that we were leaving. Mommy said, "I'll be glad because I have things to do and I haven't been doing them. Besides, I'm a busy woman and I work and I have a lot to do and won't hardly miss you at all. You know I'm a supervisor and I'm..." And I said, "We'll be back Christmas," and she felt better. Gus said, "Well, it's good that you're going, Nikki, 'cause the boy cries in the middle of the night and sometimes when the ball game is on I can't even hear it, and your mother and I kinda like the peace and quiet when nobody is around," and I said, "We'll be coming in on the twenty-first so you'll have to meet us." And Gary just cried and cried, and Chris said, "You shouldn't leave—you should stay and Mommy will go get your things and I'll teach Tommy how to swim," and I said, "You can come visit us, Chris, as soon as school is out, and we'll be home for Christmas." And we began packing and piling into the car and Gus said he wanted to go to the airport but it was going to be frost tomorrow so he had better look after the tomato plants and everybody else just openly cried all the way to the airport but you just peacefully slept while the plane took off and we came home.

AUNT ZURLETHA

RUBY DEE

Dedicated to the memories of Ida, Mrs. Adkins, Pearl, Kitty, Miss Kitts, Mrs. Hovington, Hazel, Yolene, and to all the women who work "sleep-in service" and whose day-to-day family is the people they work for.

Aunt Zurletha had pretty red hair, gray eyes, and blue-black skin. A circle of rouge was on each cheek. The shiny red lipstick on her full mouth matched the fingernail polish which matched the toenail polish. Usually, she wore earrings that looked like diamonds that matched the three rings she always wore.

My brother William said she looked like a witch, which made me wonder when and where he had ever seen a witch. My other brother Curtis said she looked pathetic. "Pathetic" was his new word that year. Everything was "pathetic." My father Hosea said she looked like a hustler. Zurletha the Zero, he used to say. I thought she was pretty, especially when she smiled. Her teeth were even and so white.

Mama used to say, "You can just quit so much talk about Zurletha. She's the only roomer that pays her rent in advance."

I heard her say to Hosea one night, "Who could we turn to when we had that fire in the shop and folks suing you for their clothes and the insurance company practically blaming you for starting your own fire and all the fires in Harlem for the last ten years? Who in this world could we turn to? Tell me. We would have starved to death but for Zurletha. No, I will not let you put her out."

"Now hold on, Mat. Gratitude is a thing you have got to under-

278

stand. I am grateful—grateful to God who made it possible for me
not to go under. That woman was just God's instrument. God's way
of showing me—"

"You just mad because you can't get her to that church of yours."

"Mat, the woman needs a church home. She needs something
more in her life besides those white folks she works for. She needs to
find God."

"Not in that raggedy little broken-down storefront, Hosea. You
know how she likes pretty things."

"That is precisely what worries me, Mat. That is precisely why I
want her out of here. Take Baby—she practically worships her. And
if I catch her one more time messing around in that woman's
room—"

"Zurletha doesn't mind. She told me Baby's just having a little
fun," Mama said.

"A little fun can leave you dragging a lifetime load. I've seen too
much, Mat. I know what I'm talking about."

"All right, Hosea—that's how you feel we can keep Baby out of
there."

"Playing with them beads and that glass junk she calls jewelry.
Rubbing up against those rabbits she's got hanging up on the
door—"

"They are not rabbits, and you know it. Mink, that's what it is. A
mink coat, and she's also got a fox stole."

"Don't care if it's dog. I want Baby's mind steady on her books and
her grades and on what she is going to do with her life."

"All right, all right, Hosea. Stop preaching at me. Put that light
out now. Go on to sleep."

"Keep that door locked when Zurletha's not in there, y'hear."

I didn't understand my father sometimes. Aunt Zurletha—and he
made us call her "aunt"—had been living with us on her days off for
as long as I can remember. She didn't want us to call her Miss Battles.
And Hosea wouldn't let us say just "Zurletha." The people she
worked for just called her "Zurlie." I think that's the only thing she
didn't like—"Zurlie" this and "Zurlie" that for forty years.

She was always giving us something. Gave Curtis his own radio.
Gave William a microscope. My last birthday, last August, she gave
me a guitar. You should've heard her play the guitar. We'd come
home from Sunday school and hear her singing and stomping her
foot. Made us want to dance. Soon after though, she'd stop—espe-

cially if Hosea came home to eat before going back to church. Then she'd open her door, and we'd all go in, me first.

She had so many beautiful things. Real crystal glasses that she could tap with her fingernail and make sounds like music. There wasn't too much room to walk, so mostly I sat on her big brass bed. And she'd let me play with the silver candlesticks or try on the jewelry and hats. She had such pretty suitcases, too. Since the guitar, though, whenever she came home, she'd show me how to play different chords. We'd practice very quietly.

One time she took us to the beach on the subway. Hosea was in Washington, and Mama had promised us we could go. It was still dark when I heard her in the kitchen. I got up and she let me help her pack this big straw basket with all kinds of food she had brought with her the night before. William and Curtis carried the blankets. She carried the basket. I had Curtis's radio. It was a beautiful day, and we had such a good time, too, even Curtis with his smart-alecky self.

Aunt Zurletha had on a silky blue and green bathing suit and some kind of rubber sandals that had lots of straps and curved heels with big holes through them and her pretty red hair was tied in a ponytail, and as always, she had on her jewelry. William and Curtis were whispering behind her back and making fun, saying she looked like a cow-pig. I think she must have heard them talking about her bunion sticking out of her strappy shoes, even though she was laughing and shaking her shoulders to the music on Curtis's radio as she set up the umbrella and opened the blankets. Later, when me and Curtis and William came out of the water, she had the lunch all set out and was stretched out reading *True Love* magazine. The sun was bouncing off her bracelet as I reached over and started twisting it around her arm. She took it off and said, "Here, you can wear it for a while." I put it on my arm and ran out from under the umbrella and started pretending I was a rich lady. William said, "You think you something, huh? She probably stole it." This time I know she heard because just before we started to eat, she took the bracelet off my arm.

"You always have such pretty things, Aunt Zurletha," I said.

And she said, "Ought to. I've been working mighty hard for a lotta years. Then, too, my people buy me—or give me—a lot of stuff. Especially when the children were small. We traveled all over then."

"They must be some rich people, man," Curtis said.

"Rich? They got money's mama," Aunt Zurletha said.

"What does money's mama look like, and who's the daddy?" William asked.

Zurletha laughed and took a dainty little bite of one of the sandwiches.

"They probably stole all that money," William said. "Hosea says that rich folks are thieves."

"Not my people," said Zurletha. "My people are just plain smart. And white, too, you know?"

I thought William sounded jealous and mean, too.

"And how come they didn't give you some of that money instead of all that other junk?"

Aunt Zurletha didn't even seem mad.

"It's not junk, William. They give me expensive things. Years ago, too, when I wanted to bake pies to sell, they were going to set me up a place."

"What happened, Aunt Zurletha?" I asked.

Then she told us how her lady got pregnant again and didn't want her to leave, and how they kept promising to set up the pie place but never did what with all the traveling and more babies coming; then, being in charge of opening all the different houses; and with her people getting sick and dying one right after the other; and how the children not wanting her to leave, she just finally got out of the notion of a pie place.

"Why you never got married, Aunt Zurletha?" Curtis asked.

"One time I was gonna get married—this was before you children were even thought of. But again, something came up with my people, and we stayed in Europe. I should say we stayed all over Europe for a year. And when I came back, lo and behold he had married somebody else. Never will forget. Said it came to him that I was already married—married to a damn job was the way he put it."

Sometimes I could just ball up my fist and hit William in the mouth.

"O-o-o, you should have quit that job, Aunt Zurletha, and married what's-his-name."

"Frank. His name was Frank." Aunt Zurletha looked sad for a second. Then she leaned over and started cutting the cake. "Then I wouldn't have you for my kids," she said.

Curtis nudged William and pointed at the kinky gray hair sticking out from under the red wig. Aunt Zurletha must have eyes all around her head, just like Mama. She fixed the wig, so the gray didn't show. And I thought it was strange—just at that moment that song, "Darling I Am Growing Old" came on the radio. Then Aunt Zurletha started singing and doing a little dance on her tiptoes as she passed out the cake.

I wish I could remember more about Aunt Zurletha, but she was never really home that much. I think often about that last summer, though. Our for-real Aunt Marie was a nurse, and she had arranged for us to go to a summer camp for two weeks. Hosea and Mama just had to get our clothes ready—that's all. We didn't have to pay. We didn't even think about Aunt Zurletha we were having such a good time. And Mama and Hosea didn't tell us in their letter that she had been in the hospital. We didn't find out until they picked us up at the bus terminal on the way home. I was so ashamed that we hadn't thought about her. I could have drawn her a funny get-well card.

After camp, first thing. I knocked on her door and went in before she said come in. Even though she had the biggest of the three rented rooms, it looked so small and crowded. All her beautiful stuff was packed in boxes and piled on top of the radiator, and beside the window, under the bed—everywhere. It looked like she was planning to move. Everything looked gray, except for the afternoon sun against the window shade. A sweet smelling spray mingled with the odor of—something like when Hosea found a dead mouse that had gotten caught in the little space between the stove and the sink. I had never seen Aunt Zurletha without the wig and without the red lipstick and the beautiful earrings. Her black, black face was lying on the white, white pillow. It looked smooth like wax. Her hair was cornrowed, ending in two thin braids, and almost gone in the front and on the sides where the wig used to be. It seemed like she stayed that way for the rest of the summer.

She didn't want us children to come into her room, so I would sit on the little rug outside her door and play some of the things she had showed me on the guitar. Mama would bring food. Hosea used to say, "It's a shame. Why didn't she tell somebody she was so sick?"

Mama said, "Guess she didn't want to worry us. She complained one or two times, but she told me she just didn't have the time to go sit in some doctor's office."

That fall they took her away to the hospital again. And one day while I was in school, Aunt Zurletha died. When I came home, the room was empty. All the boxes, the brass bed, the furs, the lamps, and the glasses, the china ornaments—everything, gone.

"It just so happened, Baby," Mama said, "the people she sold all her things to came today to pick them up."

A bottle of fingernail polish was on the windowsill. It was hard to open. I don't know why, but I started painting my thumbnail. Then I found myself kneeling on the floor, with my head on the windowsill, crying. Crying like I couldn't stop. And the polish spilled all over my middyblouse. Luckily I didn't spill it all. There was a little left, and I promised myself not to ever use it, because it was all I had to remember Aunt Zurletha by.

"Nail polish? That's not what she left you, Baby," Mama said. "She left us all her cash money. She left a will. Enough for each of you to go one year in college."

"I'm hoping they will get scholarships," Hosea said.

"Well, we can see to that when the time comes." Mama started crying.

"Aw, come on now, Mat, sweetheart," Hosea said. "You know Zurletha wanted to go. See how she planned everything. Too bad, though, she never planned time to get with God."

What Hosea said made me scream at him, "Yeah, but she will. And when she does, I hope she'll have on her red wig and her rouge and her fingernail polish with toes to match and all her jewelry, and kiss God with her greasy lipstick on. I bet he'll just hug and kiss her back, and tell her how beautiful she is."

Daddy just looked at me a long time after that. Then he walked across the room and put his arms around me. I couldn't remember the last time he did that. He said, "Come on now. Crying won't bring her back, Baby. If crying would bring her back, maybe I'd cry along with you. Won't find another roomer who—" He went over to Mama, took her by the shoulders, and shook her a little bit before he hugged her and said, "She got to be part of this family, Mat. She really did. We're going to miss her all right. All of us."

That day I felt something that I'd been afraid of all my life tumble down inside my father, and he became a gentler man. From that day whenever I think about Aunt Zurletha I hear the music of crystal glasses as they touch tingling around me and I feel happy.

JUST DON'T NEVER
GIVE UP ON LOVE

SONIA SANCHEZ

Feeling tired that day, I came to the park with the children. I saw her as I rounded the corner, sitting old as stale beer on the bench, ruminating on some uneventful past. And I thought, "Hell. No rap from the roots today. I need the present. On this day. This Monday. This July day buckling me under her summer wings. I need more than old words for my body to squeeze into."

I sat down at the far end of the bench, draping my legs over the edge, baring my back to time and time unwell spent. I screamed to the children to watch those curves threatening their youth as they rode their ten-speed bikes against midwestern rhythms.

I opened my book and began to write. They were coming again, those words insistent as his hands had been, pounding inside me, demanding their time and place. I relaxed as my hands moved across the paper like one possessed.

I wasn't sure just what it was I heard. At first I thought it was one of the boys calling me so I kept on writing. They knew the routine by now. Emergencies demanded a presence. A facial confrontation. No long-distance screams across trees and space and other children's screams. But the sound pierced the pages and I looked around, and there she was inching her bamboo-creased body toward my back, coughing a beaded sentence off her tongue.

"Guess you think I ain't never loved, huh, girl? Hee. Hee. Guess that what you be thinking, huh?"

I turned. Startled by her closeness and impropriety, I stuttered, "I,-I,-I, whhhaat dooooo you mean?"

"Hee. Hee. Guess you think I been old like this fo'ever, huh?" She leaned toward me. "Huh? I was so pretty that mens brought me breakfast in bed. Wouldn't let me hardly do no work at all."

"That's nice, ma'am. I'm glad to hear that." I returned to my book. I didn't want to hear about some ancient love that she carried inside her. I had to finish a review for the journal. I was already late. I hoped she would get the hint and just sit still. I looked at her out of the corner of my eyes.

"He could barely keep hisself in changing clothes. But he was pretty. My first husband looked like the sun. I used to say his name over and over again till it hung from my ears like diamonds. Has you ever loved a pretty man, girl?"

I raised my eyes, determined to keep a distance from this woman disturbing my day.

"No, ma'am. But I've seen many a pretty man. I don't like them though cuz they keep their love up high in a linen closet and I'm too short to reach it."

Her skin shook with laughter.

"Girl, you gots some spunk about you after all. C'mon over here next to me. I wants to see yo' eyes up close. You looks so uneven sittin' over there."

Did she say uneven? Did this old buddah splintering death say uneven? Couldn't she see that I had one eye shorter than the other; that my breath was painted on porcelain; that one breast crocheted keloids under this white blouse?

I moved toward her though. I scooped up the years that had stripped me to the waist and moved toward her. And she called to me to come out, come out wherever you are, young woman, playing hide and go seek with scarecrow men. I gathered myself up at the gateway of her confessionals.

"Do you know what it mean to love a pretty man, girl?" she crooned in my ear. "You always running behind a man like that, girl, while he cradles his privates. Ain't no joy in a pretty yellow man, cuz he always out pleasurin' and givin' pleasure."

I nodded my head as her words sailed in my ears. Here was the pulse of a woman whose black ass shook the world once.

She continued. "A woman crying all the time is pitiful. Pitiful, I says. I wuz pitiful sitting by the window every night like a cow in the fields chewin' on cud. I wanted to cry out, but not even God hisself could hear me. I tried to cry out till my mouth wuz split open at the throat. I 'spoze there is a time all womens has to visit the slaughter-house. My visit lasted five years."

Touching her hands, I felt the summer splintering in prayer; touching her hands, I felt my bones migrating in red noise. I asked, "When did you see the butterflies again?"

Her eyes wandered like quicksand over my face. Then she smiled. "Girl, don't you know yet that you don't never give up on love? Don't you know you has in you the pulse of winds? The noise of dragonflies?" Her eyes squinted close, and she said, "One of them mornings he woke up callin' me and I wuz gone. I wuz gone running with the moon over my shoulders. I looked no which way at all. I had inside me 'nough knives and spoons to cut/scoop out the night. I wuz atremblin' as I met the mornin'."

She stirred in her eighty-four-year-old memory. She stirred up her body as she talked. "They's men and mens. Some good. Some bad. Some breathing death. Some breathing life. William wuz my beginnin'. I come to my second husband spittin' metal, and he just pick me up and fold me inside him. I wuz christen' with his love."

She began to hum. I didn't recognize the song; it was a prayer. I leaned back and listened to her voice rustling like silk. I heard cathedrals and sonnets; I heard tents and revivals and a black woman spilling black juice among her ruins.

"We all gotta salute death one time or 'nother, girl. Death be waitin' outdoors trying to get inside. William died at his job. Death just turned 'round and snatched him right off the street."

Her humming became the only sound in the park. Her voice moved across the bench like a mutilated child. And I cried. For myself. For this woman talkin' about love. For all the women who have ever stretched their bodies out anticipating civilization and finding ruins.

The crashing of the bikes was anticlimactic. I jumped up, rushed toward the accident. Man. Little man. Where you bicycling to so very fast? Man. Second little man. Take it slow. It all passes so fast anyhow.

As I walked the boys and their bikes toward the bench, I smiled at this old woman waiting for our return.

"I want you to meet a great lady, boys."

"Is she a writer, too, Ma?"

"No, honey. She's a lady who has lived life instead of writing about it."

"After we say hello can we ride a little while longer? Please!"

"Okay. But watch your manners now and your bones afterwards."

"These are my sons, ma'am."

"How you do, sons? I'm Mrs. Rosalie Johnson. Glad to meet you."

The boys shook her hand and listened for a minute to her words. Then they rode off, spinning their wheels on a city neutral with pain.

As I stood watching them race the morning, Mrs. Johnson got up.

"Don't go," I cried. "You didn't finish your story."

"We'll talk by and by. I comes out here almost every day. I sits here on the same bench every day. I'll probably die sittin' here one day. As good a place as any, I 'magine."

"May I hug you, ma'am? You've helped me so much today. You've given me strength to keep on looking."

"No. Don't never go looking for love, girl. Just wait. It'll come. Like the rain fallin' from the heaven, it'll come. Just don't never give up on love."

We hugged; then she walked her eighty-four-year-old walk down the street. A black woman. Echoing gold. Carrying couplets from the sky to crease the ground.

SONG FOR MY MOTHER, PRAYER FOR MY FATHER
(A Praise Song)

LINDA GOSS

My mother was no Harriet Tubman.
My father was no Martin Luther King.

She was a mother to ten sisters and brothers.
She was a mother to my brother and me.
She was a wife and friend to my father.
She was a teacher for the whole community.

My mother was no Harriet Tubman.
My father was no Martin Luther King.

He had no time for fun and foolishness.
He had no time, sometimes, to take a rest.
He had no time to complain or weep.
He was a storyteller who rock me to sleep.

My mother was no Harriet Tubman.
My father was no Martin Luther King.

Yet she was a midwife to my aunt Sally.
He was a preacher to Little Willie Jones.

She was a mother who cared and who suffered.
He was a father, Black and strong.
She was a mother who kept the lights burning
So her lost children could find the way home.

He was a father who kept the fires warming
So his little children would never be cold.

You won't find them in the history pages.
Yet they have lived down through the ages.
There will be no "TV Special."
There is no Mother's Day card. There is no Father's Day card.
About the people I'm speaking of.
About the people who've been through it all.

They've lost babies in the womb.
They've lost babies to the hanging tree.
They've lost babies to the battlefields.
They've lost babies to drugs and pills.

Yet they gave birth to the Harriet Tubmans.
Yet they gave birth to the Martin Luther Kings.
Yes, they gave birth to the Langston Hugheses.
Yes, they gave birth to kings and queens.

THIS IS A SONG FOR MY MOTHER.
THIS IS A SONG FOR MY FATHER.

Oh, Black women of Ethiopia.
Black father of Nelson Mandela.
Black mother of Emmett Till.
Black men down in Brazil —
We hear your story, we feel your pain.
We see the blood pouring like rain.
And if thy will be done
To South Africa, FREEDOM WILL COME!

THIS IS A PRAYER FOR MY MOTHER.
THIS IS A PRAYER FOR MY FATHER.

Calling all people in North America.
Calling all people in Northern Ireland.
Calling all people in the Himalayas.
Calling all people down under in Australia.

Calling all people in the Soviet Union.
Calling all people in the People's Republic.

Calling all people in the Middle East.
Let's come together for World Peace.

ALL SHALL NOT BE LOST
IF WE SAVE OURSELVES FROM NUCLEAR HOLOCAUST.

THIS IS A PRAYER FOR MY MOTHER.
THIS IS A PRAYER FOR MY FATHER.
AND FOR ALL LIVING CREATURES
AROUND THE WORLD.

AUNT SUE'S STORIES

LANGSTON HUGHES

Aunt Sue has a head full of stories.
Aunt Sue has a whole heart full of stories.
Summer nights on the front porch
Aunt Sue cuddles a brown-faced child to her bosom
And tells him stories.

Black slaves
Working in the hot sun,
And black slaves
Walking in the dewy night,
And black slaves
Singing sorrow songs on the banks of a mighty river
Mingle themselves softly
In the flow of old Aunt Sue's voice,
Mingle themselves softly
In the dark shadows that cross and recross
Aunt Sue's stories.

And the dark-faced child, listening,
Knows that Aunt Sue's stories are real stories.
He knows that Aunt Sue never got her stories
Out of any book at all,
But that they came
Right out of her own life.

The dark-faced child is quiet
Of a summer night
Listening to Aunt Sue's stories.

COMMENTARY

CADDY BUFFERS: LEGENDS OF A MIDDLE CLASS BLACK FAMILY IN PHILADELPHIA

KATHRYN L. MORGAN

W henever my mother was exasperated with me she would say I was "just like Caddy." I never let her know that as far as I was concerned this was a most desired compliment. For us, as black American children, family legends centered around my great-grandmother, affectionately known to us as "Caddy." Caddy legends have served as "buffers" for the children in our family for four generations. From time immemorial, slaves and members of seriously oppressed groups have used such buffers to overcome fear, anxiety, and anger. Although there are many similar narratives in folk histories dealing with the ordeals of slavery, they did not belong to us, as did the legends of Caddy. The other narratives finally belonged to the world, but Caddy was ours.

Caddy was among the first generation of freed mulatto slaves who, when emancipated, were decidedly underprivileged people. The struggle for survival in the remnants of a slave economy was difficult for her as she was the offspring of a master-slave relationship, illiterate and unskilled. She also had two very young children to care for who had been conceived by former masters. One of the children, Adeline, died at a very early age, but Albert, my grandfather, worked along with Caddy in Lynchburg, Virginia, until he met and married Kate, my grandmother, also the product of a master-slave relationship. Both Kate and Albert were unskilled and could not read, but they worked along with Caddy to help buy property and save money so to enable the third generation to go to school. One of their seven children was my mother Marjorie.

My mother is the major tradition bearer in our family. She told me the legends before I was old enough to go to school. I have kept them alive by telling them to my daughter Susan, who in turn has told several of them to her younger cousins.

This was our folklore and it was functional. It was the antidote used by our parents and our grandparents and our great-grandparents to help counteract the poison of self-hate stirred up by contradictions found in the home of the brave and the land of the free.

I cannot truthfully say that I remember the exact circumstances surrounding the first telling of the legends. I know they were often repeated. They were usually told in the kitchen while my mother was performing some other chore. She never sat to tell them, and sometimes we would have to follow her from room to room to hear the end of a story. They were never told as a series. I was the most avid listener, as I was the only girl. It was my life's ambition to be like Caddy when I was a little girl, as Caddy did all the daring things I secretly wanted to do. Frankly, Caddy comes to my rescue even now when some obstacle seems insurmountable to me. I cannot remember the first time I was told about Caddy being sold on the block when she was eight years old, but all during my childhood I remember having a sense of well-being in the knowledge that nobody could sell me.

CADDY

Caddy was only eight years old when she was sold on the block. After that she was always being sold. She was sent from plantation to plantation, but she would always run away. She grew to be a beautiful young girl, and that made the white women hate her. The white men loved her, and sometimes she was taken to live in the big houses. Big houses or not, Caddy didn't want to be a slave. She would run away. When she was caught, she was usually hung in the barn and whipped across the back with a cat-o'-nine-tails. This didn't stop Caddy from running. She would run and she would be caught and she would be whipped. Do you think she'd cry when they whipped her with a cat-o'-nine-tails? Not Caddy. It would take more than a cat-o'-nine-tails to make Caddy cry.

Despite severe financial hardship brought about by the long illness of one of my brothers, my mother always managed to put "good shoes on our feet and good food in our stomachs," and tell us how Caddy made her money and bought property in spite of adverse conditions.

HOW CADDY MADE HER MONEY AND BOUGHT HER PROPERTY

Caddy couldn't read or write, but she sure could count money. She was never one penny short. Albert and Kate couldn't read or write either, but Caddy taught them how to work hard and count money too. She said that there was only one way children could learn how to read and write. The grown-ups had to work hard and save the money. Caddy had all kinds of ways to make money. She was a midwife for the poor whites and the Negroes. She would go around to all the restaurants and good houses on the other side of the tracks, pick out the spotted fruit that had been thrown in the garbage. Then she would come home, cut the spots off and make preserves and pies, and go back and sell them to the same folks who had thrown the fruit away!

The next legend stresses the need for respectability and character:

WHY CADDY GOT MR. GORDON OUT OF JAIL

Caddy got married to a Mr. Gordon. Getting married in those days wasn't like getting married today. Caddy never bothered to go to a preacher or anything. It was enough for two people to want to be married. Anyway, Caddy wanted a last name for her children, and Mr. Gordon was willing to give them his. It's important for children to have an honest last name. Now Mr. Gordon was not a very good man, but he did have an honest last name and he let Caddy have it for the children. So Caddy put up with his laziness and didn't say too much. Finally, though, he left Caddy and got himself another wife. Caddy got married to a Mr. Rucker. Now Mr. Rucker was a good man, hardworking and all, but he died early. Caddy worked hard and saved her money. One day she heard that Mr. Gordon had gotten himself in some kind of trouble and was going to be sent to jail. Caddy went to the bank. She marched herself right up to the courthouse, marched right up the middle aisle. Stood before that judge. She reached down under her skirt and put the money on the table. She said, "Judge, I don't want no man with my children's name to go to jail so I'm here to bail him out." Now everybody respected Caddy, even the judge, so he let Mr. Gordon go. Caddy was that kind of woman. Respectable. Caddy told Mr. Gordon that as long as he had *her* children's name she didn't want him laying around in jail. Then she gave him money and sent him home to his wife. Caddy was like that. Respected.

The last time Marjorie saw Caddy she was running for the trolley trying to make a train home. She was ninety-six and she said she "was a little bit tired." She wasn't sick a day in her life, and she had a very easy death. Before she died she took time to tell Kate to get her in the ground quick. "Kate, don't let a lot of folks pray and speak in the 'unknown tongue' over me." Kate never talked much and she never cried, not even when Caddy died. But nobody questioned Kate. She just buried Caddy with no praying and that was that.

If we ask what is most distinctive in this small contribution to the study of folklore, we must first make clear that there cannot be anything absolutely unique in the experience of any race, any country, or any individual. I am sure that Caddy had many counterparts throughout the land and, although I have attempted to relate the essence of the incidents as I remember them, I know that there is much implied wisdom learned and transmitted by the enslaved to their descendants which is missing. Further, to say that internal conflict, race hatred, and contempt were destroyed by these accounts would be untrue. They served the purpose of diminishing feelings of racial inferiority imposed on us as children. Analysis of this family lore reveals that it is on the whole essentially impersonal, and it reflects emotion and experience which is deeper, wider, and older than the emotion and wisdom of one individual. It is passionate without any loss of serenity, and it is, in the deepest sense, human.

S·E·C·T·I·O·N V

THE BOGEY MAN'S GONNA GIT YOU: Tales of Ghosts and Witches

Don't trouble trouble till trouble troubles you.
—*Traditional African-American saying*

STORIES

THE BOOGAH MAN

PAUL LAURENCE DUNBAR

W'en de evenin' shadders
Come a-glidin' down,
Fallin' black an' heavy
Ovah hill an' town,
Ef you listen keerful,
Keerful ez you kin,
So's you boun' to notice
Des a drappin' pin;
Den you'll hyeah a funny
Soun' ercross de lan';
Lay low; dat's de callin'
Of de Boogah Man!

Woo-oo, woo-oo!
Hyeah him ez he go erlong de way;
Woo-oo, woo-oo!
Don' you wish de night 'ud tu'n to day?
Woo-oo, woo-oo!
Hide yo' little peepers 'hind yo' han';
Woo-oo, woo-oo!
Callin' of de Boogah Man.

W'en de win's a-shiverin'
Thoo de gloomy lane,
An' dey comes de patterin'
Of de evenin' rain,

W'en de owl's a-hootin',
Out daih in de wood,
Don' you wish, my honey,
Dat you had been good?
'T ain't no use to try to
Snuggle up to Dan;
Bless you, dat's de callin'
Of de Boogah Man!

Ef you loves yo' mammy,
An' you min's yo' pap,
Ef you nevah wriggles
Outen Sukey's lap;
Ef you says yo' "Lay me"
Evah single night
'Fo' dey tucks de kivers
An' puts out de light,
Den de rain kin pattah
Win' blow lak a fan,
But you need n' bothah
'Bout de Boogah Man!

THE MONKEY-WOMAN, AN AFRO-CUBAN FOLKTALE

Retold by CONSTANCE GARCÍA-BARRIO

The monkey-woman had rare powers. From her treetop perch she could speak through time, talk with the dead between bites of banana. Her chatter, some say, could call down rain. But what she liked best was wrapping her monkey self in a human form so she could make love with men.

Once chance put her in bed with a man so sweet that she wanted to stay with him. If he was honey to her, she was sugar to him, and they got married. The man thought he'd lucked up with this honey-hipped cocoa-skinned woman. He did not know she was a monkey.

As will happen when there is so much sweetness about, they had a child. When alone with her baby, the monkey-woman would wriggle out of her human skin and scamper about making monkey sounds. She did this daily when her husband was out tending his yams and yuccas. She liked the lightness of her monkey self but always assumed human form before her man got home. He remained deeply in love with her.

Many the day the baby saw his mother tuck her tail into the woman form, and finally he understood. But he couldn't talk yet. He could tell no one.

The husband worked hard raising his crops. Once he did so much that his foot got sore, and he had to rest at home several days. He wasn't too troubled since he knew it would give him time to get in plenty of good loving. He sat contentedly playing his fiddle.

The baby, older now, saw his chance. He had been busy rehearsing sentences in his head. While his mother kept her eye on the plantains

305

she was frying, he went quietly to his father and said, "Mama is a monkey."

A chill swept over the monkey-woman like unbeckoned murmurs from the dead. The man went on fiddling, watching her from the corner of his eye. Unable to keep still, the monkey-woman picked up a gourd and said, "I'm going to fetch water." She left the house, the murmurs of the dead still in her ears.

She took a long drink at the creek. The water cooled her thoughts. But as she approached the house, the man began playing his fiddle and singing a song with monkey sounds.

Then and there she turned into a monkey. Then and there he cut off her head.

THE WAYS OF A WITCH

retold by WILLIAM J. FAULKNER

Although Simon Brown believed in ghosts and spirits, he never talked much about witches and conjuring, or casting spells. He had an old friend, named Calvin Easterling, however, who knew a lot about witches. In fact, he took pleasure in telling small boys just how witches behaved at night. So Simon promised to take me up into Chesterfield County one day to meet Mr. Easterling, who had been a slave in South Carolina. When I shivered at the prospect, Simon told me not to be afraid of the old fellow, because he wasn't a witch himself and didn't have the power to cast spells on anybody.

"Calvin Easterling couldn't even put a hand on you (hypnotize you) if he tried," said Simon. "The Devil never showed him how."

Nevertheless, I felt more and more uneasy the closer we got to the Easterling place up in the sand hills.

"Calvin's got a heap of scuppernongs (brown grapes) on his farm, Willie, and if you act nice and mannersable when you meet him, he might give you a bucketful."

This good news made me feel better.

Calvin Easterling's farm was fenced with rails, Abraham Lincoln style. I smelled the grapes before we reached his house on the top of a hill. It was a one-room log cabin, with a wide mud-and-sticks chimney at one end. Smoke curled up out of it. Mr. Easterling lived alone.

"Howdy, folks," he called as we neared his door. "Glad to see you, Simon, and the young-un you got with you. What's his name?"

"He's Mrs. Faulkner's youngest boy, Willie," answered Simon. "He pestered me until I just had to fetch him up here to meet you. Somebody at his mother's store told him how bad the witches have been treating you, and he wanted to hear whether it's true or not."

"Sure for certain it's true, son. Just you-all come in the house for a spell, and I'll tell you how bad that old Hessian, Liz Freda, has been a-treating me. She lives down on Joy Hewitt's place near Society Hill. But it's no trouble for that old witch to fly over here at night and devil my milk cow and my old mule. You just look out the door at my cow. Look at the cockleburs in her tail and at how her bag's all shrunk up. She used to give two gallons of milk a day. But since that old witch has been a-riding her at night, the poor creature gives less'n a pint at milking."

I saw something boiling in a tin can in Mr. Easterling's fireplace, and ventured to ask what it was.

He replied angrily, "Why, I'm melting a silver bullet for my musket. That old witch comes to my spring every morning, and she looks like a rabbit, a-sitting there looking at my drinking water. Yesterday I leveled down at that rabbit with my gun and shot a hole plumb through its hide, but when I went to pick it up, it wasn't there. It ain't nothing but a haunt from old Liz Freda. But I'm a-going to get it in the morning. I'm going to shoot it with my silver bullet. Lead can't kill a haunt, but silver can."

I asked Calvin Easterling how a person could become a witch. "I understand a witch has the power to become invisible so nobody can see him move around. I hear he can change himself into anything he wants to."

"Yes, that's so," said the old man. "But if you ever decide you want to be one, you'll have to sell your soul to the Devil first."

"How can you do that if you don't know where the Devil is or how to talk to him?" I asked.

Mr. Easterling cocked his head and looked hard at me.

"Well, let me tell you how to become a witch first, and then you can make up your mind."

I sat on the floor by the hearth and listened—fearful but fascinated.

Now, there was an old woman who lived up in these hills who wanted to be a witch. She lived in a two-room log house with her brother. She stayed in one room, and he stayed in the other. One day she went down to the woods and looked around until she found a hollow stump with water in the middle of it. That's the first thing you must do—find a stump with water in it.

Then the old woman went down to the cornfield and found an ear of Indian corn—the kind with different colored grains on the cob, red and blue and yellow and so forth. Then, every Friday after that, she shelled off one grain of Indian corn and carried it down to the woods and put it on the edge of the hollow stump. Pretty soon a jaybird came down and picked up that grain of corn and flew away to the Devil to give it to him. The jaybird told the Devil the old woman's name and where her house was. In this way the Devil knew she wanted to see him. But nobody except that old jaybird knew where the Devil lived. And he wouldn't tell nobody!

It took the old woman seven weeks to send for the Devil—one grain of corn every Friday for seven weeks. When the jaybird carried him that last grain of corn on that last Friday, poof!—the Devil appeared in the old woman's room! He was dressed in red from head to foot, and two little horns stuck out of the front of his head.

"You sent for me?" the Devil asked with his forked tongue. "What do you want? What do you want?"

"I-I-I want to be a witch, Mr. Devil," the old woman answered, almost scared to death.

"All right," said the Devil. "But you will have to sell me your soul first."

"Yes, sir, I will, if you will give me the power to change myself into a bird or beast and fix me so nobody can see me when I move around."

"I'll do that and more," promised the Devil. "But remember, your soul belongs to me, and I can come for you anytime I take a notion. Good-bye!" And poof!—he was gone.

Late that same night, when her brother was sound asleep, the old woman stood in the middle of her room and took off her nightgown. Then she said, "Skin, skin, drop off me!" and her skin dropped off. She picked it up and hung it on a peg. Then she said, "Skeeter, skeeter, come here to me," and before you could wink your eyes, the old woman had turned into a skeeter (mosquito). And she flew through the keyhole, zing!—just like that.

When the old woman flew around the yard, she said, "Hootin' owl, hootin' owl, come here to me." And the next minute there she was, a great big hootin' owl. Then she flew away over the fields and houses and into sleeping people's cow lots and barns. And all through the night that old Hessian meddled with the horses and mules and cows, putting cockleburs in their tails and manes and tying them in knots.

Then, just before daybreak, the old woman came back home and changed herself from an owl to a skeeter, flew through the keyhole into her room and changed to herself again. She took down her skin from the peg and said, "Skin, skin, come here to me." Then she jumped in her skin, put on her nightgown, and crawled in her bed.

Now, this went on for many a week until one night the old woman's brother peeped through a crack and saw and heard all the curious things going on. He knew then that his sister was a witch. So, when she was gone, he went in her room and sprinkled salt and pepper inside her skin.

When the old woman returned from her mischief, she took down her skin and said, "Skin, skin, come here to me," and she jumped in it. But the skin burned her, and she jumped out again. "Skin, skin, don't you know me?" she cried.

Just then, a great ball of fire came a-roaring through the window and caught the old woman up and roared out the door with her, poof!—and the Devil's voice was heard to say, "Old woman, I have come for your soul!"

No one in the cabin stirred for a moment.

Then Mr. Easterling whispered, "Now, Willie, would you like to become a witch?"

"No, siree," I gasped. "I'd be happy if I could just have a few of your scuppernongs, Mr. Easterling."

THE TWO SONS

ALICE MCGILL

O nce, in a little community near Dismal Swamp, there lived a pretty young woman who had two little boys to raise by herself. Her husband sickened and died during the Big War. He fought bravely and in many battles, too. But somehow or another a terrible sickness came over him, and he was sent home from over the seas to die.

Just before death claimed him he called his sons to his bedside. His dear wife held his hand as he instructed each son in kind:

"Mind your manners, work hard, pay respect to all old folks, don't ever sass your mama, stay away from the swamp, and no matter what happens to me . . . if you listen to what I have told you, you will never have to worry about—"

The poor man died before he could utter his last words. Oh, what a pitiful sight he made. The grieving widow did the best she could to comfort her two sons.

After the burial, friends and neighbors brought comfort to the small family by way of fine food and lively talk. Just at sunset the friends and neighbors departed to their homes through the woods and around the swamp. Then the two sons helped their mother. One lit the oil lamp and the other kindled a fire in the wood stove to chase off the cool of the evening. Their mother seemed to be at peace and she was smiling as the three of them chatted around the fire. At last, one of them ventured to ask his mother if she knew what their father's last words might have been if he had been able to say them before he passed on.

The woman paced the floor as she answered, "Oh, my sons, just do as your father said. Mind your manners, work hard, pay respect to all old folk, don't ever sass your mama, stay away from the swamp, and you will never have to worry." But worry and grief beat at her chest. She did not tell them that their father's meager pension would not pay for the cost of keeping the house, let alone put food on the table and clothes on their backs. Before long she found a job weaving large reed baskets for a storekeeper.

The sons thought about their father's last words many nights after their mother had fallen into exhausted sleep. Over and over they repeated the last sentence to each other. They filled in the missing words from their deepest thoughts.

"You will never have to worry about paying bills." "You will never have to worry about finding a job, making a fortune, ruling the world...." They could not think of suitable words. Some years passed, and as the sons grew taller and stronger the memory of their father grew dimmer and dimmer. Finally they could not remember his face at all, and his last words to them left their restless minds. Their mother, however, worked hard to keep food on the table. Time after time she reminded the sons to feed the chickens, water the garden, and to keep the yard clean. Dutifully the sons obeyed, for a while.

One summer day while they were sprinkling the garden an old man appeared at the garden gate.

"How 'bout givin' me two of them cucumbers," he begged, "I'm so hungry I can eat 'em right off the vine."

The sons screamed, one after the other, "Why don't you plant your own garden." One son sprinkled the old man so that he hobbled away dripping wet. The other son threw his watering can. The can bounced off the old man's back. When he whimpered away in pain the sons laughed.

Just before sundown their mother returned from her basket weaving. Thinking she would be pleased, the sons eagerly told her what they had done to protect the family garden. She was not pleased.

"Shame on you for treatin' a poor old man so. We have a gracious plenty in our garden. Why didn't you give him two cucumbers?"

"He didn't have no rights on our cucumbers!" one of the sons screamed at his mother. "If you think I'm goin' to give away good food to any ol' beggar, you must be silly. Tired of waterin' this ol' garden anyhow."

The other son bragged, "Glad I did hit him with my can. I'll hit him again if I want to, and you can't stop me."

Their mother was so shocked over the change in her sons she could barely speak. "Go in the house," she muttered over and over. "I will talk to you in a little while." She turned and walked toward the chinaberry tree.

The two sons stormed through the front door, thinking that she was going to switch them. Then they eased through the back door and ran to the swamp to hide among the marsh reeds.

The muddy green water sloshed against their knees when they stumbled about, trying to find solid ground. When at last they thought they were safe, their feet began to sink into quicksand. The more they struggled, the deeper they sank, until a rope was thrown around the upper part of their bodies. They felt themselves being pulled out of the mire and along the rough ground. The holder of the other end of the rope was hidden in darkness, but they heard a deep gruff voice grow louder and louder as the tug of the rope pulled them nearer and nearer.

The voice was saying, "Mind your manners, work hard, pay respect to all old folks, don't ever sass your mama, stay away from the swamp, and you will never have to worry about the... BOGEYMAN!" The two sons were never heard of or seen again.

MISS VENORA

ALICE MCGILL

They said Miss Venora was a witch woman.

Bro' Sam heard folks whisperin' 'round 'bout her being a witch woman on his first day on the job in the fall of 1946. He didn't pay much mind to all the talk 'cause he was too busy thinkin' 'bout his boss man and whether or not his boss man would like him. Bro' Sam's crops had failed two years in a row so he let his land lay out, and he had to find a job in town at the peanut factory. The menfolk had gathered at the bottom of the steps to wait for the boss who was always late, so he was told.

Anyhow, he saw a bunch of women walkin' 'cross the yard to the peanut factory. They wasn't wastin' no time neither. Some of them lived right there in the little town of Lee's Meadow, but some had to walk from as far away as Grabball, Hill's Crossroads, Gallberry, and all. Them women had to climb up 'bout twenty steps to the second floor of that big ol', gray buildin', then turn the bend and keep on walkin' down a long hall, and be sittin' in front of grated pulley belts 'fore the seven o'clock whistle bellowed out. The women stepped high and wide, tryin' to get there on time. Their bandannas curved tightly to their heads to keep the peanut dust from their hair. Dinner buckets tucked in the crook of each pair of arms. They knew that the women's boss, Mr. Geeter, was waitin' at the belts to send anybody right back home if the whistle bellowed 'fore they could sit down. Bro' Sam heard 'bout him, too.

After the footsteps of the women died away, Fat John eased up behind Bro' Sam and whispered in his ear, "Look, here she come!"

Bro' Sam whirled 'round to see who he was talkin' 'bout, and sure 'nough he saw Miss Venora for the first time to know who she was. Her bowed legs made her small, humped body rock from side to side. As she made her way toward the steps, Bro' Sam could not help but meet her eyes as she looked the men over and cackled a "good mornin'" so loud some of the men jumped. Then she turned her wrinkled face and streaked eyes away from the men. Her big hand grabbed at the railin' with every step she took. When she reached the fourth step the seven o'clock whistle broke the air.

"The boss gon' send her back home," Bro' Sam spoke sort of low. He didn't want her to hear him.

Fat John shifted his weight and strained his pudgy neck against his tight shirt. He looked at Bro' Sam, but he wanted all of the men to hear his speech. "She ain't gon' be sent back. She a witch woman, and she got a fix on the boss. He can't do nothin' to her. She come in here as late as she pleases, and she leave when she pleases. You a new man on the job, Bro' Sam, but I'm here to tell you, that's a witch woman goin' up dem steps."

The other men looked up the steps just like Fat John was tellin' the natural truth, too. They all kept lookin' till Miss Venora turned the bend.

"Well, I don't know 'bout that," Bro' Sam told them all. "Folks been sayin' things like that 'bout old women since the beginnin' of time, I reckon." Before he could tell them that he didn't believe in witches, the men's boss was standin' there lookin' at them.

Bro' Sam's long, lanky body was first in line behind the boss. Being a new man he felt like he had to show that he was more than ready to work.

When the "quittin' time" whistle told them it was six o'clock, folks was gettin' 'way from there as fast as they could. Some of them was half runnin'. Bro' Sam had just picked up his dinner bucket when the men's boss asked him, Fat John, and Joe Bill to stay on a little longer 'cause the belts was jammed up. 'Bout a half hour passed before they could get that thing fixed. Then all the machines turned off. The whole place was as quiet as a funeral home. Seem like the sun was sinkin' a mile a minute. The three men headed on 'round the front of the factory. Somebody's footsteps stopped them dead in their tracks.

It was Miss Venora. She was slowly clumpin' down the stairway.

Fat John snuck back in the shadows and picked up a stumpy broom the men used to sweep the hulls from the grates. "Come on,

I'm gon' show you somethin'." The men followed him into the shadows, and Miss Venora clumped on down to the twelfth step. She hung on to the railin' with each step.

"They tell me," Fat John heaved out, "you can tell if a person is a witch or not if you put a broom like this one under the steps. If she is a witch, she can't step over a broom. What say we try this out on Miss Venora?"

Bro' Sam and Joe Bill didn't have much say so 'fore Fat John poked the broom under the bottom step. Then he called out, "Come on, y'all, let's stand here and wait for the boss to tell us we can knock off work."

Miss Venora was still clumpin' real slow like she was scared of missin' a step. She got close 'nough to the bottom for the men to make out her white scruffy hair hangin' from under a blue scarf that turbaned her head.

The men stood there like they was waitin' for the boss. They talked 'bout the weather and how fast the sun went down. All the while they was tryin' not to look straight at Miss Venora. But when she put her left foot down on the third step from the bottom, they had to look at her. Seem like her body reeled and rocked when she went to lift her right foot. She saw the men lookin' at her. She smiled up at them and said to herself, "I forgot somethin'." She turned 'round and clumped back up the steps much faster than she had come down.

Even Fat John was scared to speak 'fore the shadow of her body turned the bend. The words came hissin' out of his mouth: "Didn't I tell y'all? I told y'all. That woman is a witch!"

Joe Bill tugged at his mustache and nodded in agreement. He was also tremblin' and sweatin'. Big drops of water ran like little pools down his stout back. He was glad that darkness hid his short frame from the two other men.

Bro' Sam held out that Fat John was wrong. "She's just an old woman with a hump on her back, that's all," he tried to convince both men.

Fat John could not be convinced. He argued long and loud. "Well, why didn't she step over the broom, then? And why ain't she comin' down the steps? Answer me that!"

Bro' Sam didn't have to answer. Miss Venora was clumpin' down the steps in a big hurry. They never seen the old woman move so fast. When she got to the sixth or seventh step, a great noise exploded from underneath the steps. It sounded like bobcats screamin' and cows lowin' and dogs howlin'.

Dinner buckets flew one way, and the men flew the other. Fat John was one of heaviest men in town, but you couldn't tell it that night . . . he left the others far behind.

After that, word spread like brushfire from one and then the other. The whole county believed Miss Venora was a witch woman.

Pretty soon the womenfolk didn't want to sit by her at the factory. Many of them claimed sickness and stayed home. Of course they blamed all their misfortunes on Miss Venora, but Miss Venora never said a word to fend for herself.

Ol' Mister Geeter knew he was losin' control of the women when so many started losin' time on the job. One day he called Miss Venora into his office and told her, "Venora, you know you been at this factory ever since I was a little biddy boy, and I ain't no young man. My daddy said you was here long 'fore he got too old to work. Now I think you ought to go on back home and rest out a spell. Don't worry, I'll slip you a piece of money every week just the same."

So Miss Venora spent the rest of the warm days sittin' on her porch in an ol' rockin' chair. She just rocked back and forth from sunup to sundown. Folks was too scared to walk on the same side of the road as her two-room cabin.

By the end of October that same year Miss Venora wasn't seen for almost a week. Smoke didn't come out the chimney, and the front door was shut tight.

Somebody sent for the high sheriff. He went there and broke the door in. They say he backed out and sent for the sick wagon. The sick wagon rolled up to her front porch. When they brought her out she had left this world.

The undertaker in Lee's Meadow County refused to handle her body. They sent her body to the next county in Richland where folks didn't know about her.

. Fat John kept givin' himself credit for provin' that she was a witch. He stood on the corner of Main Street and grabbed at anybody who had the time to listen 'bout the night he put the broom under the steps. After a while folks shunned him. He didn't tell 'bout how fast he ran that night.

Miss Venora's house just sat there on the side of the road, the same way the high sheriff left it. Several months later the yard grew up in tall grasses and bushes. Somebody threw clods of dirt and broke out some of the windows, too. The rockin' chair was left alone.

One calm spring day durin' the next year, Henry Johnson was takin' a shortcut 'cross the field near the old house. He saw the chair rockin' back and forth, back and forth. He took off, runnin' and hollerin', scared to death. When somebody caught up with him he managed to cry out that Miss Venora was back.

Some of the men at the sawmill said they would give any man, woman, or child $5 to sit in Miss Venora's rockin' chair. Bro' Sam said he would take the money 'cause he needed it so badly. Fat John tried to talk him out of it, but Bro' Sam held on.

On the appointed day the men from the sawmill and the peanut factory met on the other side of the road from Miss Venora's house. Twenty or more townfolks showed.

Bro' Sam kicked his way through the yard. That Saturday mornin' was warm and sunny. The quietness made the buzzin' flies sound as loud as airplanes. His eyes took in the gapin' door and raggedy curtains swingin' through the broken windowpanes. Bro' Sam kept on walkin' till he got to the porch. He put his foot on the porch. That rockin' chair commenced tremblin'. That's when all the men took off. Bro' Sam was all by himself now.

He walked over to the chair and *kicked it over!*

The house moaned and groaned and reeled and rocked. First the roof flew away, then the sides. The bricks of the chimney shot away like bullets. Bro' Sam just stood there on the porch, not knowin' if he was livin' or dead. When the porch melted under his feet he stood on dry ground with the terrible sounds of a dyin' house splittin' his ears. He locked his eyes shut and fell to his knees. There he stayed till the quietness forced his eyes open.

Right in front of his knee-bent and bowed body was a black pot filled with a flowered Purina drawstring feed bag. The house was gone! The ol' rockin' chair was layin' on its side like a wounded animal. Bro' Sam moaned softly, pulled himself to his feet, and slowly opened the bulgin' feed bag. It was packed with paper money.

Bro' Sam lugged the money home. He and his family quietly moved away that very day.

If you go to Lee's Meadow today, no doubt you will hear at least a hundred and fifty different stories 'bout Miss Venora, the witch woman. If you want to find out for sure if she was a witch woman, all you have to do is go to Richland County's cemetery, find her grave, and dig. Folks in Lee's Meadow say ain't nothin' there but an empty hole. Witches don't lie down too long, you know.

THE WHITE DOG

WANDA GIGETTES

E ffie paused uncertainly at the junction where the road to Crumpler crossed the railroad tracks. Which way should she go? Either way could be dangerous.

She could stay on the road. Several colored families lived along the way, but it meant passing "the Greenfields." That beautiful valley was now used for Klan rallies and lynchings. (Or worse, Effie thought. They caught poor Bertha there last summer, God rest her.)

Or she could follow the tracks which cut straight through the dark and desolate foothills of Cherokee Mountain. She'd be saved thirty minutes of walking time—lots of rattlesnakes, though.

Effie sighed. She was desperately tired. She'd been working since dawn for a lady over on the "white folks' side" of Cherokee. "I'm getting too old for this," she mused. Glancing ruefully at her swollen feet, and squaring her little shoulders, she set off down the tracks.

Deep into the mountains, she heard them. Glancing up, she saw the lanterns descending rapidly through the trees. Too late, Effie remembered. This was the Ku Klux Klan's shortcut to the Greenfields. Terror swept over her! Where could she hide? She'd be spotted in this white uniform. Silently she screamed: *What to do, Lord?*

Sinking to her knees, she prayed: My Lord, my Lord, please help me! A crackling sound caused her to spin around. There, on the tracks, was a huge white dog—the biggest dog Effie had ever seen. His shining dark eyes held hers in his gaze.

The Klansmen were near, but Effie couldn't move. As she stared at the dog, a soothing warmth enveloped her, shutting off all sound.

From within the silence came "Effie, keep walking." As she obeyed, the Klansmen emerged from the trees all around her, laughing, shouting, but without sound. She glanced back in wonder at the dog and felt the thought, "Walk, Effie, I am with you."

Effie passed within inches of the white-shrouded figures, between them, in front of them. They did not see her.

When she reached her gate, Effie turned and watched the white dog rise into the sky and melt away. Effie slowly smiled and whispered, "Thank you, dear Lord," and went into her house.

BARNEY MCKAY

JANIE HUNTER as told to MARIAN BARNES

Janie Hunter has been a professional storyteller for twenty-six years. She was born on Johns Island, one of the South Carolina Sea Islands, where the lyrical Gullah language, a combination of English and African languages, is spoken. In great demand throughout the United States for performances from her huge repertoire, this mother of fourteen and grandmother of over one hundred fifty says she learned her first stories at the age of six or seven. "My parents would sit with the family by an old chimney fire and tell stories and folktales, and sing old songs from the life of our people in Africa and during slavery. My mother and father asked me to keep the stories and songs and pass them on as I travel through the world." The story "Barney McKay," a longtime favorite of Ms. Hunter's audiences, has been passed down since the era of the slavocracy in America. Conversant in English, French, and Gullah, Ms. Hunter uses a combination of English, Gullah, and rhythmic chants and wails—sometimes to the beat of a spoon on a washboard—to enchant her listeners.

Once upon a time there was a lady and her husband, and both of them were up in age, and they were very, very poor. They had nothing to give their ch'ren on holidays. But they worked hard on the farm, and every year they saved up their little pennies. They had two children which were twins. The daughter's name was Mary, and her brother's name was Jack. The children were so sad at Christmas because they couldn't get no Sandy Claus. So the mother and the father wanted to make the children surprised; and this special Christmas they saved up enough money to buy them three dogs. They gave the dogs the names Barney McKay, Doodle-Dee-Do, and Sue-Boy. They gave their children these dogs on

Christmas Day, and they bought Jack a bow-and-arrow gun. The children were very happy.

Jack and Mary said, "Mama, could we take a walk?"

So the mother said, "Yes, Jack and Mary. Y'all can go for a walk but y'all be careful. And be back here before dark."

Jack was a very wise boy. He went to the barn and got four grains of corn and put them in his pocket. Then Jack and Mary began to travel. They were so happy to go out, so happy to have some dogs for presents.

They traveled, and it get real dark. The children get so frightened and scared! When they looked through the woods, they saw a little house up in the woods and a little light shine through the window, which was a slambo light.* And the ch'ren gone and knock on the door, and an old lady run to the door and said, "Who are there? My grandch'ren?"

And they said, "Yes, Grandma. We are far from home and we are scared. Could we spend the night here?"

The children didn't know that was an old witchcraft, and what she had in mind was to let the chilren stay there. She was going to cook them and eat them for breakfast, dinner, and supper. So the old lady opened the door, and when the chilren come in, she said, "Are y'all hungry?"

They said, "Yes, ma'am. Very hungry."

She said, "Sit down and let me feed you then!" And she cooked and she fed the children.

She had two bedrooms. One bedroom she kept pumpkins in, and the other bedroom was *she* bedroom. But Jack was *so* wise. Before Jack gone to bed, Jack get two pumpkins and put *them* in the bed to pretend it was him and Mary in the bed.

That old lady had a big, old, huge dishpan and a butcher knife, and she was in that kitchen after she done feed the children, singing (the storyteller sings and keeps time to the chant by strumming on a washboard with a spoon):

Penny get your knife
Penny get your knife
Sharkum, Sharkum
Hump back-a-Josie back

---

*A light made by inserting the end of a cloth into a bottle of kerosene and lighting the end of the cloth outside the bottle.

See Aunt Tooney
Mommy and my Daddy tell me so
See so, I t'ink so
Timer ram aroun'.

Then the children said, "What's all that noise? We can't sleep."

And old witchcraft say, "Aw, that ain't nothin' but your grandma's frock tail switchin' to keep your supper hot!" and she keeps sharpening the knife.

Then Jack dropped one grain of corn through the window and that grain of corn turned to a ladder. Jack and Mary been long gone down that ladder while the old lady keep sharpening she knife. She didn't hear the children. She thought they were sound asleep.

She went and get the big dishpan and butcher knife. She gone in Jack and Mary's room and pulled back the covers. She chopped in the bed. She thought she was chopping Jack and Mary, but she chopped the pumpkin. She get so mad and angry, she gone in the kitchen and grabbed the old ax called a Tommy Hawk. She run down, run down Jack and Mary.

And where Jack is, he drop another corn, and that corn turn into a tall pine tree. Jack and Mary climbed up that tree. Then Jack take his bow-and-arrow gun and shoot exactly to his house, shoot in that dining room, knocked the glass of milk over on the dining room table.

When Jack and Mary's mother saw the arrow knock over the glass of milk, she run to the turned-over glass and see the arrow, and she say, "Lord Jesus, my ch'ren in trouble. Let me go and turn them three dogs loose. Those three dogs get away to find Jack.

Then Jack begin to call the dogs (the storyteller wails):

Barney McKayeeee, an' Doodle-Dee-Doooooo, an' Sue-Boyeee . . .
Your massa's almost gone.

Then the dogs say:

Massa, massa, comin' all the time.
Massa, massa, comin' all the time.

Old witchcraft say (the storyteller chants, strumming on a washbowl with a spoon):

Chip on the old block
Chip on the new block
Chip on the old block
Chip on the new block.

She was chopping on the tree Jack and Mary climbed. That old pine tree was waving to fall, then waving to fall! One more call! And if those dogs don't be there by the time that old lady hold that ax up, then Jack and Mary are going to get killed, and that old lady witch-craft is going to carry them back home for to cook.

So this last call Jack made (the storyteller wails):

Barney McKayeeee, an' Doodle-Dee-Doooooo, an' Sue-Boyeee ...
Your massa's almost gone!

Then the dogs say (again the storyteller chants and strums on a washboard with a spoon):

Massa, massa, comin' all the time.

Old witchcraft say:

Chip on the old block
Chip on the new block
Chip on the old block
Chip on the new block.

My sister, when old witchcraft hold that ax up and give that pine tree one more chop, that pine tree bend down to the ground, all right? Then Jack threw one more corn grain, and it turned into a bridge, and the dogs came across and grabbed that old witchcraft. Sue Boy cut her throat, Doodle-Dee-Do sucked her blood, and Barney McKay dragged her to the bridge.

Then Jack threw the last grain of corn, and it made that bridge bend, and that's the way the story end!

DADDY
AND THE PLAT-EYE GHOST

ELEANORA E. TATE

Confrontations with a plat-eye ghost are to be avoided at all costs in the marshes and swamps of the South Carolina low country, particularly around Pawleys Island, Sandy Island, Georgetown, Plantersville, Charleston, and the Sea Islands. Some say that a plat-eye ghost can take the form of a small animal, a vapory cloud, or an apparition with big, red, burning coals for eyes. In DuBose Heyward's short story, "The Half Pint Flask," an unscrupulous man and a plat-eye have an encounter after he steals a flask from a grave. The plat-eye takes the form of the man's lover and tries to drown him in the marsh.

This story about a plat-eye is based on an account told to me by a young Plantersville area woman whose plat-eye haunted a dark road near a cemetery and a marsh.

Hattie, Maizell, Bunny, Sin-Sin, and the rest of the kids standing under the pine tree hollered at me to come over. I knew they were going to work me over about ghosts.

"A plat-eye ghost's gonna get you, Raisin," said Sin-Sin. "Plat-eye ghost's gonna come in your room, hop on your back, and ride you all night long, just like you was an ole mule. You be thinking you're having the horriblest dream, but it'll be that ole plat-eye riding you."

"I ain't scared of nobody's plat-eye," I said. I crossed my toes inside my shoes, just in case. "And I bet you never even seen one, neither."

Ursula hollered that her daddy had. "And it had big red eyes. Daddy saw it on Cypress Swamp Road just about night when he was a little boy. He say he and some other guys were walking back from fishing in the creek—the part that's up around Cypress Swamp Cove where those condos are now. Him and his Uncle Toe and them.

"He had left his knife back at the creek where they'd been fishing. He decided to go back to get it. The others went on. He had a bucket half full of spots, too. But Daddy say he went back through the swamp grass along the edge of the creek and found his knife. It was moonlight out, see, so he didn't have no problem.

"On the way back he kept thinking something was following him, but when he would look around, he wouldn't see a thing. Just as he got onto the bridge over the creek he felt his back start to get real hot right under his shoulder blades. He said it was like two pins were being burned into his back. He said when he jumped to one side, he looked back and saw two huge round eyes red as blood and with steam rising from them hanging in the air not two feet behind him. He started walking backward from those eyes, trying not to look into them, because a plat-eye can suck your breath out if it can catch your eyes and hypnotize you. Still holding on to his knife in one hand and the bucket in the other, he hit across that bridge and didn't stop until he caught up with Toe and them.

"But you know what? All the fish in his bucket was gone. Daddy said that plat-eye got 'em."

KATE, THE BELL WITCH

JACKIE TORRENCE

T he year was 1830. In the mountains of North Carolina there lived a man named John Bell. He had a wife and six children, one daughter and five sons. John Bell was a very wealthy man. He had land holdings that stretched across the state of North Carolina into Tennessee, all the way into Kentucky. John Bell built himself a thirty-seven-room mansion in a small town named Adams, Tennessee. John Bell, along with being a very wealthy man, was also a very greedy man. Just beside his land holdings, in the state of Tennessee, there lived an old woman named Kate. Kate owned about one hundred fifty acres of land. John Bell saw the land and wanted it, but Kate refused to sell it to him. He offered her top dollar for the land. Now back in those days, top dollar was $3.50 a acre. Kate refused. Finally, John Bell would not be outdone. He offered Kate fifteen times the worth of that land in gold. Kate did not turn him down. She sold him her land. Weeks later Kate realized that she had made a mistake. Kate was a widow. She had been without a family for almost twenty-five years. All of those years she had worn an old black dress with an old black bonnet that fell down onto her face. She tried to return the gold to John Bell.

"I have not spent the gold, Mr. Bell. Please, I'd like my land back."

But John Bell refused. Kate tried to keep John Bell as a friend by talking very nice and sweet and kind, but John Bell would not hear it. He slammed doors in her face, rode off when she spoke to him in the fields. One night, as John Bell was returning home from Nashville, he started down the road to his mansion. The moon shone bright, and there in the middle of the road he saw something—some form of some kind or a shadow. He thought it was a bear that had wandered down out of the hills. He opened his saddle bag and placed his hand on his pistol, but just as he rode closer, he saw the form of the shadow take shape. It was a human. It was Kate.

Kate placed her walking cane in the road, stopped John Bell's horse, looked up at John Bell, and said, "Mr. Bell, I promise you that, as long as you and your children and your children's children own my land, you'll never live happy or satisfied."

Kate turned back and walked into the woods toward her cabin. John Bell was quite shaken, but not enough to return her land. Weeks later they found Kate dead. No one knows if she died of natural causes, for, you see, it was John Bell's servants who buried her.

Months after her burial John Bell was seated in his parlor one night, reading. As he held the book far away from his face because of bad eyesight, he noticed that the pages of the book started to turn. He placed his right hand across the top of the book to stop the movement of the pages but they continued to turn and they tore as they turned. He then closed the book, placed it on the table, and looked up toward the fireplace. The fire that had once burned so high and bright was now dying down as if someone or something poured water between the logs. He walked toward the fireplace, lifted an iron, and pushed it down between the logs to start the fire again. At that moment something pulled the iron from his hand, lifted it high into the air, and brought it down toward his back. If John Bell had not moved when he did, the impact of that iron would have killed him.

From that day on, John Bell, his wife, and his family were plagued with this mysterious spirit that had entered their home. Sometimes at night when John Bell tried to sleep, he awakened and felt the covers being pulled from his bed. He pulled the covers back only to find that they would then be pulled from the bed and dropped into the opposite corner. Sometimes when he tried to eat, he got the food just so close to his mouth before something slapped the fork from his hand. The slaves that lived on his land started to whisper about the spirit that had entered John Bell's home. They started to call it "the Bell Witch."

For five years John Bell and his family were plagued with this mysterious spirit. Sometimes John Bell was so weak from not eating or sleeping, he could barely mount the stairs on his own strength.

His children had to carry him to his room. One night after he was carried to his bedroom, his wife tucked him into bed, kissed him lightly on the forehead, picked up the candle on the table beside his bed, and walked toward her bedroom. As she turned she saw that her husband closed his eyes to sleep. She blew the candle out, placed it on the table beside his bed, went into her bedroom, got into bed, and fell asleep. During the night, as she slept, she was awakened by a strange noise coming from her husband's room.

"Hah hah hah hah hah hah haaaaah."

She got up, walked over to the door, lit the candle. As the light flooded the room, there standing beside her husband's bed was the strange form of what looked to be a woman dressed in black. She walked toward that form and said, "Who are you? What do you want?" But it disappeared into thin air. She touched her husband. John Bell was dead. In the bed beside him was a small bottle of poison.

They have not found the formula to the poison that killed John Bell. In a note written by the Bell Witch, she promised to return in a hundred years. A hundred years would have been 1930. But in 1930 the Bell descendants never saw the Bell Witch. But just a few years ago, the people who now own that land heard and saw many strange things, and sometimes at night you can hear, way off in the trees, that same strange sound: "Hah hah hah hah hah hah haaaaah."

They say the Bell Witch still haunts that land, and that's the end of that.

TAILY PO

as told by LOUISE ANDERSON

A long time ago an old man lived all alone in the deep, dark forest. That old man's cabin didn't have but one room, and that room was his living room, dining room, bedroom, parlor, and kitchen, too. At one end of the cabin the old man had a great big old fireplace, and that's where he cooked himself something to eat. Well, one night, the old man getting a little low in his food, he fixed himself some fatback meat and with some cornmeal made hush puppies. He called his dogs, "Hey, doggie! Hey! Hey! Hey!" and fed them. The old man had three dogs. One was called "Youknow," one was called "Iknow," and one was called "Comtiko Callico." He got up that old cornmeal stuff and stirred it around and gave it to the dogs so they'd have something to eat. He ate that fatback meat but didn't have much, so he felt a little hungry, but that was all he could have for that day. The old man built up his fire a little more and then sat by the fireplace.

The wind was blowing around that cabin, and just as the old man was about to doze off, a most curious looking critter crept through a crack in the wall. It was funny looking. It had a great big old bushy tail. The old man picked up a hatchet, crept by that fireplace all quiet, and said, "Wop!" One lick, he cut off that critter's tail. But before he could raise his arm so he could kill that varmint, it had gone back out through one of the cracks in the wall. Now that old man was still hungry, so he took that big long bushy tail, cleaned it, he cooked it, and ate it. Then he went around the cabin and started sticking papers and rags and stuff in the holes so nothing else could get back in. Now

331

his stomach's all full and the cabin's all nice and warm with all the old holes filled in.

The old man went to bed and before he knowed it, he was fast asleep. Hadn't been to sleep very long before he woke up. Something was trying to get in. It was climbing up the wall. It sounded like a cat: scratch, scrat scrat scrat scra, scratch, scrat, scrat, scra.

"Who's there?" asked the old man.

He listened and heard a sort of keen, whiny kind of voice say, "Taily Po. Taily Po, I'm coming to get my Taily Po."

Oooh, that old man so scared, he was just shivering and shaking. Then he remembered his dogs, so he jumped out of the bed, ran to the door, and flung it open. He said, "Hey, doggie! Hey! Hey! Hey!" The dogs came filing out from under that porch with their noses to the ground, and they chased that wild thing way off into the forest. The old man went back in the house, got back in bed, and went back to sleep.

'Long about midnight the old man woke up again, allowed something trying to get in right above the cabin door: scratch scrat scrat scrat scra. Scrat scra scra.

"Who's there?" asked the old man. "And what you mean out here at this time o' night when all decent folks oughta be in bed?'

He listened and he heard that voice say, "Taily Po, Taily Po, I'm coming to get my Taily Po."

Wah hah hah—that old man was so scared! He was trembling. He was too scared to get out of bed, so he just lay there and called his dogs from his bed, saying, "Hey, doggie! Hey! Hey! Hey!"

The dogs came bounding off that porch, and they caught up with that wild thing at the gate, tore that whole fence down trying to get at it. Then they chased it way back through the forest, way, way down to the swamp. The old man went back to sleep.

Along toward morning something from down in that swamp woke up the old man. At first he thought it was the wind blowing a little louder than usual, but he listened and he heard that voice say, "Oooh wo! I know. All I want is my Taily Po."

The old man said, "Leave me alone!" He called the dogs again: "Hey, doggie! Hey! Hey! Hey!"

This time the dogs didn't come.

He said, "Youknow!" He said, "Iknow!" He said, "Coptiko Cal-lico! Here Dog!"

Still no dog. Ooh, the old man was so scared, he was just shaking out of bed and tiptoed across the floor. He eased the door open and peeped out. All he could see was moonlight shining down on the torn-down fence. He could hear the dogs baying lost from way, way back down there at the swamp. That thing had led the dogs down there to the swamp and had lost them.

Now the old man was all alone and didn't know what to do. He went back into the cabin and pulled the door to and locked it. He put that great big old wooden bar back up there by the door. He went and got the old hatchet and put nails in the door. He knew nothing else to do, so he just lay across the bed and closed his eyes. He didn't go to sleep this time, he just closed his eyes.

Just before daybreak the old man opened his eyes—you know, the way you do when you know somebody's in the room with you. Someone or something was stirring among the pots and pans in the corner. Then it started coming to the bed: scratch scrat scrat scra. A ha! The old man picked up the cover and wrapped it around his shoulders real tight, and he started rocking back and forth. The thing started climbing up the cover at the foot of the bed: scratch scratch scrat scra. The old man held on tight to the cover. He peeped over the foot of the bed.

At first he saw two long, pointed ears. Then—scratch scratch scratch—the thing climbed a little bit higher. The old man peeped again and saw two big, red fiery eyes just staring. Aaaah! He pulled the cover over his head; he couldn't bear to look at that thing. It just kept climbing over the bed and climbing. And then it started climb-ing right up beside the old man: scratch scratch scrat scrat. Then it got right beside the old man's head. It whispered in the old man's ear:

"You know and I know, uh, that I'm *here* to get my Taily Po."

Wah hah hah hah hah! The old man was so scared, he tried to get his voice back. He got his voice back and said, "I ain't got your Taily Po!"

"Yes, you have," said that thing. "Yes, you have it!'

He jumped on the old man and scratched everything to pieces. Some folks say that he got his Taily Po.

Now there is nothing left of the old man's cabin in the deep dark forest, except the chimney. Folks who live in the valley say that when the moon shines bright and the wind blows back down in the valley, you can hear that voice say, "Taily Po, Taily Po, now I've got my Taily Po." And the voice dies away in the valley.

JUMBIE, DUPPY, AN' SPIRIT

PAUL KEENS-DOUGLAS

Paul Keens-Douglas tells this original story told in Trinidadian dialect.

Tonight we goin' to talk 'bout Jumbie, Duppy, an' Spirit.
Now ah don't want to frighten allyu,
But dem is part ah we folklore too;
Never mind some people don't believe in dem,
Jus' wait till dey bounce up one,
Den yu go hear ah different story.
Yes, man, in de ole days, on ah moonlight nite,
We used to get together to ole talk in de yard,
An' sooner or later somebody would start up ah ghost story,
An' after dat is story after story.
Everybody frighten but nobody movin',
Because if yu go inside by yuself,
An' everybody else outside in de yard,
Is den self yu frighten,
So you stayin' where de crowd is,
An' is more ghost story in yu tail.
An' when yu hear is time to finish,
Everybody walkin' in ah group,
An' dey always have somebody hidin' somewhere
Who go suddenly bawl out "boo!"
An' nearly give everybody heart attack.
Ah remember me cousin do me sister dat once,
Dress up in ah sheet an' come in de yard spinnin' somersault.
De poor girl fall down wit' fright.

An' he pick she up bawlin', "Is only me!"
Well is den self she nearly dead.
Yes, man, yu can't talk 'bout de West Indies
Without talkin' 'bout Jumbie, Duppy, or Spirit,
Dem is some ah we leadin' citizens.
Yu ever hear de song, "Back to back,
Belly to belly,
Ah don't give ah damn,
Ah done dead already"?
Yes, man, when yu hear we spirit come out,
Dey does come out in full force.
An' is not one spirit ah talkin' 'bout, yu know,
Let me tell allyu 'bout spirit.
In some islands like Jamaica dey call everyting Duppy,
In other islands like Grenada an' Trinidad, dey call dem
    Jumbie.
An' in other islands dey does jus' call everyting Spirit,
But no matter wha' yu call dem,
When it come to dem kind ah ting,
Dey eh have no place in de worl' to touch de West Indies.
Nowadays allyu only talkin' 'bout Spiderman,
An' de Hulk, an' de Bulk an' tings like dat,
But yu ever hear 'bout La Diablesse?
La Diablesse is de Devil Woman,
An' she always wearin' ah big hat to hide she face,
An ah' long dress down to de groun' to hide she foot,
Because La Diablesse have one good foot
An' one cow foot.
Nowadays ah hear dey wearin' pants suit!
So look to yu lef' an' look to yu right,
Yu might be sittin' down nex' to ah La Diablesse.
Yes, man, La Diablesse like to dress up pretty, pretty,
An' stan' up by de side ah de road at night,
An yu know how allyu man like woman already,
As soon as yu stop to talk to she or pick she up,
Is gone she gone with yu.
Nex' day dey findin' yu with yu neck break over some
    precipice.
Once as Granmudder Rosie tell me
How one day rain was fallin' an' she was inside de house,

An' she hear dese people come on de verandah to shelter de rain.
She say she never look out to see who it was,
But later on when she check de verandah
She see one set ah mud an' cow footprint
All over de place.
Was La Diablesse dat was shelterin' rain.
Yes, sah, yu got to watch out for La Diablesse,
Yu might even find dem behin' yu shower curtain,
Or where yu does hang up yu clothes in yu closet.
Dey like dark places,
An' since dey have so much electric light
In de place dese days,
Dey lookin' for any dark place dey could find.
So when allyu goin' home later be careful,
Don't say ah didn't warn allyu.
Den in Trinidad dey have ah ting call Douen.
Ah Douen is de spirit of ah chile dat dead without gettin' baptise,
An' de Douen foot turn before behin',
So you can't tell whether ah Douen comin' or it goin'!
An' dey like to come out roun' six in de evenin',
An' dey does like to play wid children
An' lead de children in de bush an' get dem loss.
An' sometimes is only de children could see dem,
So when yu see yu chile runnin' 'bout
Talkin' to heself an' playin' by heself,
An' yu feel he so smart an' intelligent,
Is not smart he smart or intelligent he intelligent,
Is Douen he playin' wid.
Yu does find Douen in ah lot ah other places by different name,
In Guyana dey have something like Douen call Bush-Dai-Dai.
Sometimes other spirit does play Douen,
An' yu does meet dis little chile who lookin' loss,
An' yu pick he up say yu takin' he home,
Nex' ting yu hear dis big man voice sayin'
"Put me down, put me down!"
Allyu tink dat bad?
Well allyu should go Guyana, now dat is ah place wid plenty Jumbie.
Yu know how Guyana have plenty, plenty bush,
Nothin' Jumbie eh like more dan dat.
Only ting I 'fraid more dan Jumbie in Guyana is Mosquito.

Ah tell yu, Guyana have some Mosquito
When yu meet dem yu does have to say, "Good mornin'!"
Yes, man, yu have to respect dem mosquito.
Ah fella tell me dey don't fly, dey does take taxi.
But he name Lie-o, so yu know what he give.
Any way comin' back to de Jumbie,
Dey have ah ting in Guyana call Baccoo.
Now de Baccoo is ah little man in ah bottle like ah genie,
An' dey say if yu get dis bottle an' leggo de Baccoo,
He go' help yu get anyting yu want,
Woman, money, land, power—anyting.
Dey say politicians does use Baccoo,
But me eh know 'bout dat.
Only trouble is, once yu get ah Baccoo,
It does be hard to get rid ah it,
Because after all, who want to live in ah bottle?
So yu does have to feed de Baccoo banana an' milk,
An' give it all kind ah ting,
Otherwise is youself de Baccoo hauntin',
An' nex' ting yu know,
All kind ah ting startin' to fly roun' yu house,
Furniture movin', picture breakin', big stone fallin' on yu roof.
Is like what dey does call "Dracula" in Grenada,
Yes sah, when ting so happen in Grenada,
People does say "Dracula in de area!"
So if yu ever go to Guyana, an' yu see ah bottle on de groun',
Don't pick it up!
Otherwise you go only hear somebody say,
"Tank yu very much!"
An' after dat is you an' Baccoo to ketch.
If yu really want to meet some saga Jumbie,
Is to go Grenada, St. Lucia or Dominica.
Yu know dem islands so have ah French backgroun',
An some ah dem change hands so much time,
An' de culture mix up so much,
Dat yu does get all kind ah strange spirits walkin' 'bout de place,
Talkin' French an' Spanish an' English an' Dutch,
Like de spirit ah de Dutchman dat does live in Guyana.
Yes, man, Guyana have ah spirit call Dutchman,
Suppose to be some ole Dutch planter who does give people warnin'.

Ah don't know if is one or more dan one,
Dem Guyanese does jus' say "Dutchman!"
In Grenada dey have ah ting call Mama Maladé
An' dat is de spirit of ah woman who dead in childbirt',
An' dey say de spirit always lookin' for de chile.
So on ah dark nite yu does hear dis soun'
Like ah baby cryin' in de wind, like ah moanin',
An' if yu ever look outside to see who cryin',
Is gone yu gone.
Some ah allyu here boun' to get ketch,
Because allyu too macocious.
Allyu don't have chile, but allyu go' still look out,
To see if allyu child outside.
Ah could understan' de men doin' dat,
Because plenty ah dem have outside chile.
But de women is someting else,
Macociousness go ketch ah lot ah allyu.
Is like de Phantom in Trinidad,
Or wha' dey does call Moongazer in Guyana,
Dey does ketch people thru macociousness.
Dey say dis Phantom or Moongazer is ah tall, tall man,
'Bout forty-foot tall,
An' he does stan' up wid he two foot
Spread right across de road,
An' as soon as anybody pass between he foot,
He does jus' close dem, braps!
An' de person mash up fine, fine.
But what I want to know, is who so stupid,
To see ah man forty-foot tall,
In de middle ah de road, on ah dark nite,
Go' pass between he two foot.
But yu know, some ah allyu would do it.
Ah could jus' see some ah dem Trinidadians,
Passin' right between de Phantom foot sayin',
"Who put dat dey, boy? Mus' be ah marse!
Ah wonder if it real?"
Nex' ting, braps! Dey dead!
But yu know de bes' Jumbie to meet?
Is ah Jumbie from St. Kitts.
Because de only Jumbie ah ever hear 'bout in St. Kitts,

Is ah Rum Jumbie.
Ah Rum Jumbie is ah fella who does drink
Ah serious set ah rum.
But I figure it mus' have more to it dan dat,
Because after dem fellas drink all dat amount ah rum,
Dey boun' to see plenty Jumbie.
Ah know ah fella get to look like ah Jumbie
Jus' by drinkin' plenty rum.
Every time he fire one,
He used to make up he face so—like ah monkey,
For de rum to go down.
Well you do dat all day, every day, for forty years,
An' tell me if yu eh go get ugly.
Well he get so ugly, dey call him Uglito.
An' de Vincentians not too far behin' St. Kitts.
When I ask 'bout Jumbie an' Ghost down dey,
Ah fella mumble someting 'bout jack-o'-lantern
An' he take off
Like he see de Barbados army comin'.
Dey say dis jack-o'-lantern is ah set ah lights
People does see floatin' 'bout de place at night.
I sure is firefly dem people see,
Like de UFOs in Grenada.
Yu can't say dat Gairy eh do nutten for Caribbean culture,
He introduce UFOs.
Now we have Jumbie, Duppy, Spirit, an' UFOs.
An' talkin' 'bout UFOs,
Allyu ever hear 'bout Socouyant, Loupgarou, or Ole Higue?
Dat is de ole woman could take off she skin
An' fly like ah ball ah fire cross de sky,
An' come an' suck allyu like Dracula.
An' when allyu wake up an' see ah black mark on yu neck,
Allyu only sayin' is "hicky,"
Well is not "hicky," is Socouyant suck yu.
In Trinidad dey say Socouyant,
In Guyana dey say Ole Higue an' Fire-ras,
In Grenada dey call de man Loupgarou an' de woman Socouyant,
But sometimes I does feel is UFOs dem people see.
As for Jamaicans, well yu know dey have to be different,
Dey have someting call Rolling Calf.

Some spirit dat look like ah calf,
Wit' big, big eyes an' clankin' chain,
An' does run 'bout de place at nite like it haunted.
An' de Bajans not too far behin' neither,
Yu know how Barbados very British already,
Dey have someting call "Steel Donkey!"
Same kind ah ting like de Rolling Calf,
Excep' dis time is ah donkey, an' ah "steel donkey" to boot,
I say mus' be ah industrial Duppy.
Ah fella tell me ah story
How once one take part in ah horse race on de Garrison.
He say de race start wit' nine horses,
But halfway roun' de track people seein' ten,
Was ah Steel Donkey join de race.
Nex' ting all dem horses bolt fus dey frighten.
De Steel Donkey come in fus,
But jus' as it cross de line it disappear.
So he say—but I tink he lie.
An' for dose of yu who like water,
An' like to go by river an' sea at night,
Dey have plenty spirit to ketch yu down dey too.
In Grenada, Trinidad, an' some ah de patois islands,
Yu go' hear people talk 'bout Mama D'leau or Mama Glo, de Goddess of
    de river.
Dey say yu does see dis beautiful woman
On ah stone in de middle ah de river, combin' she long hair, an' singin'!
An' man who try an' talk to she does disappear.
Dey say she does take dem to live wit' she under de water.
But yu know man can't live under water.
So dem days done.
In Guyana dey have someting like Mama D'leau call Fair Maid or
    Water Mooma,
Guyanese say is ah mermaid.
An' dey say it have ah man who livin' in de river too, like de Fair Maid,
Dey does call him de Massacoura Man or Kanaima.
Well, dem Guyanese should know wha' dey talkin' 'bout,
'Cause when it come to river or water, yu can't beat Guyana.
But talkin' 'bout water,
Allyu ever hear 'bout Techen or Cribeau?
Ah hear 'bout dem in Grenada, is two river snake.

Dey say when de Techen hold yu, it does wrap roun' yu foot,
An' try to break it.
De only way to get away
Is to get ah piece ah dry twig an' break it.
When de Techen (tae—shae) hear de twig break,
It go' tink is yu foot an' let yu go.
But wha' I want to know,
Is where yu go' find dry twig in de middle ah de river?
Is like yu go have to break yu finger instead.
Anyway is better ah break finger dan ah break foot.
As for de Cribeau,
Dey say it does come down to de river to bade an' drink water.
Now dey say dis Cribeau does have ah crown on de head,
An' it does take off de crown when it badin',
An' dey say if yu ever get dis crown yu go get rich, rich, rich,
Because de crown make from diamond an' ting.
Dat de Cribeau get in de groun'.
But dey say dat de Cribeau will follow yu to de end of de earth,
To get back de crown.
Some people say Cribeau can't cross sea,
But I don't know.
Ah hear ah man teaf ah Cribeau crown once,
An' twenty years later de Cribeau ketch up wit' him.
Well I don't know 'bout dat,
But dis Cribeau business have too much "dey say!" in it.
In any case I only sellin' it as ah buy it,
Me eh born wid no caul over me eye.
Yu know when yu born wid caul over yu eye,
Yu does "see" ting.
Like dis neighbor ah mine who always seein' ting.
De other day ah hear she tellin' de Washer
How she was goin' to church five in de mornin',
An' she bounce up ah La Gahou.
Ah La Gahou is like ah Werewolf,
But it wus, because it could change to different shape.
So de Washer ask she if she sure it wasn't ah "Chain Beast,"
Dat is another spirit like de Rolling Calf an' de Steel Donkey.
Ah tell yu de amount ah chain
Some ah dem spirit does drag roun',
Dey mus' be own ah hardware store,

An' each one chain have it own special soun',
I sure some ah dem spirit does hire ah tuner to tune up dey chain.
Yu could imagine ah spirit askin' for ah new chain,
"Ah want twenty yard ah chain—three yard in B flat,
Seven yard in F sharp, five yard in G, an' mix up de last five yard!"
One last spirit ah go' tell allyu 'bout is Papa Bois.
Papa Bois is de guardian of de forest,
An' dey say he is half man, half beast,
An' dat he have ah cow-foot like de La Diablesse
An' he does protect de animals.
So yu see how much Jumbie, Duppy, an' Spirit
We have in de West Indies?
Ah not jokin', man, is serious business.
But yu don't have to frighten,
Dey have good an' dey have bad,
An' dey have ting yu could say to protect yu,
Special prayers like de L'Oracion dey does say in Trinidad,
But dat is another story.
Now I not sure dat everyting I tell allyu is true, yu know,
I only tellin' yu what I hear,
So don't go an' say I say.
When ole people tellin' yu ting dey don't tell yu how or why,
Dey does jus' tell.
So I jus' tellin'!
But yu don't have to 'fraid Spirit man,
Jus' learn to pray—or learn to run!

BIG FEAR AND LITTLE FEAR

collected by ARTHUR HUFF FAUSET

Sam has to drive up the cows from the pasture. He always puts it off until late. His master tries to break him of that. The little boy laughs, he is afraid of nothing. "You have no fear now," says his master, but old Fear will get you one of these nights." On his way Sam has to pass a cemetery. His master puts on a white sheet and goes to the cemetery gate. Jocko, the pet monkey, runs into the house also, grabs a tablecloth, follows to the cemetery, and gets on the opposite gatepost. Sam comes along and sees the two white figures. He is not frightened, he only says three times, "Ugh, two fears. Big Fear on one post and Little Fear on t'other." His master hears him and sees the other white figure. He runs away, the monkey after him. Sam yells, "Run, Big Fear, Little Fear'll sho'. catch yo'."

BALLAD OF THE HOPPY-TOAD

MARGARET WALKER

Ain't been on Market Street for nothing
With my regular washing load
When the Saturday crowd went stomping
Down the Johnny jumping road,

Seen Sally Jones come running
With a razor at her throat,
Seen Deacon's daughter lurching
Like a drunken alley goat.

But the biggest for my money
And the saddest for my throw
Was the night I seen the goopher man
Throw dust around my door.

Come sneaking round my doorway
In a stovepipe hat and coat;
Come sneaking round my doorway
To drop the evil note.

I run down to Sis Avery's
And told her what I seen
"Root-worker's out to git me
What you reckon that there mean?"

Sis Avery she done told me,
"Now honey go on back

345

I knows just what will hex him
And that old goopher sack."

Now I done burned the candles
Till I seen the face of Jim
And I done been to church and prayed
But can't git rid of him.

Don't want to burn his picture
Don't want to dig his grave
Just want to have my peace of mind
And make that dog behave.

Was running through the fields one day
Sis Avery's chopping corn
Big horse come stomping after me
I knowed then I was gone.

Sis Avery grabbed that horse's mane
And not one minute late
Cause trembling down behind her
I seen my ugly fate.

She hollered to that horse to "Whoa!
I gotcha hoppy-toad."
And yonder come the goopher man
A-running down the road.

She hollered to that horse to "Whoa"
And what you wanta think?
Great-God-a-mighty, that there horse
Begun to sweat and shrink.

He shrunk up to a teeny horse
He shrunk up to a toad
And yonder come the goopher man
Still running down the road.

She hollered to that horse to "Whoa"
She said, "I'm killing him.
Now you just watch this hoppy-toad
And you'll be rid of Jim."

The goopher man was hollering
"Don't kill that hoppy-toad."

Sis Avery she said, "Honey,
You bout to lose your load."

That hoppy-toad was dying
Right there in the road
And goopher man was screaming
"Don't kill that hoppy-toad."

The hoppy-toad shook one more time
And then he up and died.
Old goopher man fell dying, too.
"O hoppy-toad," he cried.

THE DEVIL'S DULCIMER

JANICE N. HARRINGTON

In some parts of the country there are places where people have lived for well on a hundred years without ever seeing the outside world. They're just off to themselves in the hollers and hills and backwoods. The people in this story that I'm going to tell you are just like that. Most of them ain't seen anyone their whole lives but their own kinfolk and nearby neighbors.

There's two things you need to know about the people in this story. One is that most of them are poor, don't have nothing, and ain't likely to ever see anything, either. The other thing you need to know is that they're superstitious.

There was an old, old road that ran on the outside of their settlement. Folks called it the Lone Bone Road, and that Lone Bone Road ran past two cemeteries. The first cemetery was called just that: the First Cemetery; and the second cemetery, well, that's just what it was called: the Second Cemetery. Nobody went nowhere near either of those cemeteries unless they had to make an unexpected "visit."

Now, folks in those parts say, and I don't know one way or the other, that if you're on that Lone Bone Road and those cemetery gates get a-swingin', well, it meant the dead were walking on that Lone Bone Road. It meant something bad was bound to happen.

I told you that these were all poor folk, but that isn't quite true. There was one among them that did all right, and that was the Master Fiddler. Whenever folks needed someone to play for them at a birthing, a wedding, or what have you, they'd send for the Master Fiddler. They'd pay him what they could and the Master Fiddler always lived a bit better than most, because if there's one thing poor folk need it's music and a good time, and that's just what the Master Fiddler gave them: music and a good time. The Master Fiddler was so important that every ten years they'd hold a contest to choose a new Master Fiddler. At the time of this story it had come time for such a contest: time to choose a new Master Fiddler.

Now, there was a girl named Nell who lived in this settlement. But Nell didn't play no fiddle. She played a dulcimer, and no one and nothing could play a dulcimer better than Nell. She was just that good. Nell wanted to win that fiddling contest. She wanted to win it, she wanted to win it more than anything else. Because if she did win it, it would mean that she'd never be poor again. Nell was poor, but if she was the Master Fiddler she would have enough to get by.

But Nell didn't have herself much of a dulcimer. It wasn't more than an old two by four with some wire running across it, and it wouldn't hold no kind of tune. She was going to need something a whole lot better if she was going to have any chance at all at that contest. So Nell started out looking for a new dulcimer, but nobody could tell her how to come by one. Seemed like most folks, if they had anything at all, it was a fiddle, and if they had a dulcimer, well, it wasn't much better than her own.

Finally she went to an old wise woman in the settlement, and Nell told her how she wanted to be in the fiddling contest but how she needed a dulcimer. The wise woman told Nell that she'd have to think on it, but after a while she told Nell that it could be that she did know how she could come by a dulcimer. She told Nell how folks hadn't always lived in these parts. At one time, a long time ago, back so far that she could just barely remember it, there had been another settlement. Folks had lived there, most of them anyway, till some strange kind of sickness came. No one knew how it come or where it had come from, but it took most folk. Got so bad, so many of them were dying, that finally most folks just up and left. They came then to this settlement.

"Now, if I remember rightly," she said, "there was one fella who stayed behind. Hear tell he made a mighty fine dulcimer. I can't say what come of him and by now, well, he'll rightly be an old man. But if there's anyone who can help you I reckon he's it."

Then the old woman told Nell that if she was really strong about this, if she was really strong-minded about it, she could tell her how to come to that old settlement.

"First," she said, "you get on that Lone Bone Road. You walk past that First Cemetery, past that Second Cemetery, and you keep on walking till you walk that sun down, you keep on walking till you come to the end of that Lone Bone Road, and that's where you'll find that old settlement."

Well, the next day, Nell gathered up what little she had, because she figured she wasn't going to get a dulcimer worth anything for nothing. When she had everything together, she set off down that Lone Bone Road. She walked past that First Cemetery, past that Second Cemetery, and she kept on walking till she walked that sun down and came, at last, to the end of that Lone Bone Road and got to that first settlement.

The houses were old and abandoned. Moss and weeds covered the windows, and there was a strange, strange smell about the place. It was quiet—so very quiet. Nell almost turned back, but she wanted to win that fiddling contest so bad that she went on.

Nell went to the first house and she knocked. No answer. She went to the second house and knocked. No answer. She went to each house in turn, but there was no answer. Finally, Nell came to a cabin just at the very end of that Lone Bone Road. There was something even stranger about this cabin. It made Nell's skin want to crawl. Again she wanted to turn back, but she wanted to win that contest even more. She stepped up to the cabin door and knocked.

"Come in."

Slowly, Nell opened the door and went in. She expected to find an old man just this side of death's door, but when Nell got inside she saw it wasn't an old man at all. Un-huh, it was a young man, and a mighty good looking one, too. Nell was right pleased by this. She started right in and told him how it was, how she needed a dulcimer, and she showed him what she brought to give him if he'd make her one. He didn't say anything at first. He just looked at Nell.

"Your fine things ain't enough. Give me that ring from off your finger, and I'll make you that dulcimer."

Well, Nell, she didn't think once and she didn't think twice. She wanted to win that contest, so she gave him that ring.

"Your ring ain't enough. Give me that petticoat that you're wearing, and I'll make you that dulcimer."

Again, Nell didn't think once and she didn't think twice. She got out of her petticoat and gave it to him.

"Your petticoat's not enough. Give me the head of the one you love best, and I'll make you that dulcimer."

This time Nell did think once and she did think twice, but what she figured was that she had this fella licked. Nell didn't have no kinfolk, leastways none that were alive, and there was no one that she loved. Nell told him that if he'd give her that dulcimer first, he could have the head of the one she loved best.

He made her that dulcimer. He didn't tell her how he'd made it or what he'd made it from. He just brought it to her, and before Nell left he told her again, "Now, remember what you promised."

Nell took that dulcimer and headed back down that Lone Bone Road, but as she was going she kept getting a strange feeling. She kept thinking that she was hearing voices in all those houses that had been empty before. Nell looked back over her shoulder, and standing there on the step of the cabin she had just left was an old, old man. Nell hurried on, but still she kept hearing those voices. She looked back a second time, and it wasn't an old, old man standing there—it was something that looked like it had just crawled up from out of the grave.

Nell didn't look back over her shoulder a third time. She clutched that dulcimer as tight as she could and ran. She ran as quick as she could back down that Lone Bone Road. Nell ran far enough and fast enough till finally she did come back to her own settlement. But as she passed that Second Cemetery, the Second Cemetery gate got to swinging. Nell didn't pay no mind—she just kept on till she reached her own place.

The next day folks started to gather for the fiddling contest. Folks came from miles around, from the backwoods and the hollers and places not even heard tell of: Sumac Creek, Hungry Holler, Broken Back, and River Rill. There was every type of fiddle you can think of: black, shiny fiddles, new fiddles, old fiddles, large ones, small ones. If it had any strings at all, it was there for the fiddling contest.

Folks were eating and laughing, singing and spitting tobacco, and anything else they had a mind to, just waiting for the contest to begin. Well, finally all the fiddlers in the contest began to gather. Nell put her token in with the rest of them. When some of them seen how it was a girl entering the contest, and with a dulcimer at that, they just kind of snickered out of one side of their face. Like everyone knows, no dulcimer can keep up with no fiddle no kind of way. They just weren't built for it. But seeing how she was a girl and it couldn't do no harm, they let her enter. It'd be good for a hoot, anyway.

There were three rounds to the fiddling contest. In the first round you had to play something sad, and those fiddlers played sad, each one in turn—some of the saddest music you ever did hear. Until finally it was Nell's turn. Nell picked up her dulcimer, but before she played she said to it: "Play sad, play sad, my dulcimer, play a sad song for my listeners' ears."

Nell's dulcimer played sad. Babies started wailing. Grown men broke down and started sobbing. Folks got to crying who never cried a day in their lives. Uh, uh, uh, it was miserable. Well, it was generally conceded that Nell won that first round.

For the second round you had to play something fancy, and those fiddlers played fancy. There were fiddlers playing fiddles behind their backs, fiddlers playing fiddles with one leg in the air, fiddlers playing with the other leg in the air, and fiddlers playing fiddles on top of their heads. That's just how fancy it was. But then it was Nell's turn, and Nell picked up her dulcimer and said to it; "Play fancy, play fancy, play fancy, my dulcimer, play a fancy song for my listeners' ears."

Her dulcimer played fancy. Folks just looked and could hardly believe their eyes at what they saw. It was just pure amazing. Nell won the second round.

For the third round you had to play something fast. This time the fiddlers figured that they had Nell beat because, like everyone knows, a dulcimer can't keep up with no fiddle when it comes to playing fast. They were going to prove it, too. They rosined up their bows, tightened their strings, and got down to it, each in turn playing just as fast and furious as he could, fiddlers from every settlement: Sumac Creek, Hungry Holler, Sway, River Rill, Broken Back, and on down the line till it was Nell's turn. Then it was just as quiet as could be.

"Play fast, play fast, play fast, my dulcimer, play fast for my listeners' ears."

That dulcimer played fast. Folks were clapping their hands, stomping their feet, and spinning around in their tracks trying to keep up with her, she was going so fast.

Nell won that fiddling contest. She played on. Folks danced and sang, stopping every now and then to drop a few coins at her feet.

Nell didn't pay no mind to the time so that it was well after sundown before she quit playing, and well on dark before she headed home.

Nell lived fairly close to that Lone Bone Road. When she got near to those cemeteries, she could hear those cemetery gates swinging. It sounded as if they were saying something. It sounded as if they were talking to her:

"The headddddd."

"The headddddd."

"The headddddd."

When Nell heard them gates saying that, she started to run, and it kept feeling like something was snapping up out of the grass at her ankles. Nell clutched that dulcimer as tight as she could and ran like all hell was after her, and maybe it was. She ran till she came to her own place, and as quick as she could she locked up her gate and went on to her cabin. She pulled the shutters and locked up all the doors. Then Nell sat down in her rocker and laughed.

She hadn't heard no cemetery gates. Those gates hadn't said nothing to her. She'd won that contest! She was the Master Fiddler, and she wasn't ever going to be hungry again. She was never going to be poor.

Nell must have fallen asleep in that rocker, because suddenly she woke up. She thought she heard something at her front gate. Who would be visiting the Master Fiddler this time of night?

A voice called, from way off there by her front gate, so soft that she almost didn't hear it: "I've come for the head of the one you love best."

Nell didn't move. She just sat there, so scared she just shook, so afraid that she could hardly speak. Again the voice called: "I've come for the head of the one you love best."

"I ain't got no head to give you. There's no one that I love. I ain't got nothing to give you...."

The voice called again, a little closer this time, a little nearer, from just there in the middle of her yard: "Play sad, play sad, play a sad song for my listeners' ears."

Nell's fingers picked themselves up. She couldn't stop them, and they began playing, so sad, so sad that Nell began to cry.

Again the voice called, a little closer this time, a little nearer, from just at the foot of her porch stair. "Play fancy, play fancy, play fancy, my dulcimer, play a fancy song for my listeners' ears."

Again, Nell's fingers picked themselves up and began playing. They played and played, and she saw them do things she never thought possible. Still the voice called, even closer, even nearer, from just there on the other side of her cabin door: "Play fast, play fast, play fast, my dulcimer, play fast for my listeners' ears."

Nell's fingers played fast. They played fast, they played faster, and they played faster still until the cabin door opened.

The next day some folks came looking for the Master Fiddler, and they found Nell. She was still sitting in the rocker with her dulcimer on her lap. But her fingers were wore off from playing so fast, and on her neck there was no head.

Well, they buried Nell, but they didn't bury her in that First Cemetery or in that Second Cemetery. They buried her off to herself and buried her dulcimer with her. Folks say if you're in those parts and near that old Lone Bone Road, when the wind is blowing a certain way you'll hear that dulcimer. It plays fast, it plays faster, and it plays faster still.

COMMENTARY

CREATURES
THAT HAUNT THE AMERICAS
CONSTANCE GARCÍA-BARRIO

When Africans were forced into slaving ships, the creatures, invisible, slipped in with them. A witch's brew of supernatural beings, these were creatures remembered from stories from the homeland. When Africans reached the New World, the creatures stepped ashore with them.

The supernatural beings made their homes in the mountains, rivers, and forests of the Americas, wherever the Africans went. The Hairy Man, for example, has the run of Georgia's woods, according to a story told by a former slave from that state. The Hairy Man is a fat, ugly little man with more hair all over than hell has devilment. Tricky as he is hairy, he can shrink or swell at will. He's afraid of dogs and is most at home near rivers. The Hairy Man spends his time capturing careless children.

The guije seems to be a Caribbean cousin of the Hairy Man, the way the late Cuban centenarian Esteban Montejo tells it in *The Autobiography of a Runaway Slave*. The guijes, or jigues, are mischievous little black men who wear no clothes and live near rivers. Their heads are like a frog's. Black people have a natural tendency to see them, according to Montejo. Guijes pop out of the river to admire a señorita as she bathes, especially during Holy Week. The guijes are also known to carry off children.

The Tunda looms large in the folklore of Esmeraldas, a predominantly black province on the northern coast of Ecuador, notes Afro-Ecuadorian writer Adalberto Ortiz. Local legend has it that in the

357

1530s a ship whose cargo included twenty-three enslaved blacks was traveling from Panama to Peru. As it skirted Ecuador's northern coast, the ship struck a reef. In the confusion that followed, the Blacks scrambled from the vessel, swam ashore, and fought with Indians occupying the land.

After one especially fierce battle, dying Blacks and Indians moaned so much that the noise reached hell and disturbed the devil. He decided he'd have to exterminate both sides if he wanted peace and quiet. So the devil went to Esmeraldas disguised as an African prince, Macumba. But before he could carry out his plan, a lively, buxom Esmeraldeña caught his fancy. He married her and settled down, as much as the Devil can ever settle.

One of the creatures born from their union is the Tunda, a deformed black woman with huge lips and clubfoot. As a child of the devil, the Tunda can't have children, so she's taken to carrying off those of black folk in Esmeraldas. The Tunda can make herself look like a member of the potential victim's family. She lures people into the forest, then stuns them by breaking wind in their faces. After this they lose their will power and are easily led to her lair, usually a place in or near water.

Adalberto Ortiz mentioned that there are similarities between the Tunda, characters in Afro-Colombian stories and the Quimbungo from Bantu folklore.

If some creatures pursue black children, others stalk adults. The Afro-Dominican Ciguapa is a gorgeous but strange being who lives in the island's forests. She comes out at night to steal food but is never caught since she escapes by jumping from tree to tree. Her beauty has won many hearts, but she uses her magic to destroy men. Wise to her ways, they try to avoid her. But she can fool them. The Ciguapa's feet are on backward, so they think she's going when she's coming.

Tales of the Lobisón, or Wolfman, made many an Afro-Uruguayan peasant cringe. Legend has it that every Friday night at midnight the seventh consecutive son in a family turns into an animal. This animal has a wolf's body and a misshapen pig's head. It commits acts too horrible to tell. It has great supernatural powers, and only by wounding the Lobisón and drawing its blood can it be made to return to human form.

The old and new worlds blend in the Lobisón legend. The story shows the influence of Bantu, European, and certain South American Indian cultures.

Some tales of the supernatural arose from historic events in which Blacks took part. Such was the case with Spanish America's struggle for independence from Spain from 1810 to 1822. One Afro-Uruguayan story tells of a rich but miserly man who treated his slaves cruelly. Emancipated before the wars of independence, the newly freed Blacks demanded money with which to start a new life. They knew their former master had gold nuggets hidden in the house. When he refused to give them anything, they killed him.

The money remained hidden after the murder until a platoon of black soldiers camped near the old house during the wars of independence. The location of the treasure was revealed to them by the ghost of a Black who had remained with the master even after emancipation. The soldiers divided the cache, each receiving a nice sum. The ghost had waited years but finally saw that his black countrymen got the money.

Like the ghost who showed the soldiers the treasure, black folktales bring to light sometimes forgotten cultural treasures Africans brought to the Americas.

SOURCES

Duncan, Quince and Carlos Melendez, *El Negro en Costa Rica*. San Jose: Editorial Costa Rica, 1974.

Montejo, Esteban, *The Autobiography of a Runaway Slave*. Miguel Barnet (ed.). New York: The World Publishing Company, 1968.

Morner, Magnus, *Race Mixture in the History of Latin America*. Boston: Little, Brown and Company, 1967.

Ortiz, Adalberto, "La Negritud en la Cultura Latinoamericana y Ecutoriana," *Revista de la Universidad Catolica*, Ano III, pp. 97–118, 1975.

Pereda Valdes, Ildefonso, *El Negro en el Uruguay, Pasado y Presente*. Montevideo, 1965.

Rout, Leslie B., *The African Experience in Spanish America*. New York: Cambridge University Press, 1976.

"SHUT MY MOUTH WIDE OPEN": Humorous Tales and Anecdotes

Ninety-nine lies may save you,
but the one hundredth one will give you away.

West African proverb

STORIES

JACK AND DE DEVIL

ZORA NEALE HURSTON

"Zora, did yuh ever hear 'bout Jack and de Devil buckin' 'ginst one 'nother to see which one was de strongest?"

"Naw. Ah done heard a lot about de Devil and dat Jack, but not dat tale *you* know. Tell it."

Jack and de Devil wuz settin' down under a tree one day arguin' 'bout who was de strongest. De Devil got tired of talkin' and went and picked up a mule. Jack went and picked up de same mule. De Devil run to a great big old oak tree and pulled it up by de roots. Jack grabbed holt of one jus' as big and pulled it up. De Devil broke an anchor cable. Jack took it and broke it agin.

So de Devil says, "Shucks! Dis ain't no sho 'nuff trial. Dis is chillun foolishness. Meet me out in dat hund'ed acre clearin' tomorrow mornin' at nine o'clock and we'll see who kin throw mah hammer de furtherest. De one do dat is de strongest."

Jack says, "Dat suits me."

So nex' mornin' de Devil wuz dere on time wid his hammer. It wuz bigger'n de white folks church house in Winter Park. A whole heap uh folks had done come out tuh see which one would win.

Jack wuz late. He come gallopin' up on hawseback and reined in de hawse so short till he reared up his hind legs.

Jack jumped off and says: "Wese all heah, le's go. Who goin' first?"

De Devil tole 'im, "Me. Everybody stand back and gimme room."

So he throwed de hammer and it went so high till it went clean

365

outa sight. Devil tole 'em, "Is Tuesday now. Y'all go home and come back Thursday mornin' at nine. It won't fall till then."

Sho 'nuff de hammer fell on Thursday mornin' at nine o'clock and knocked out a hole big as Polk County.

Dey lifted de hammer out de hole and leveled it and it wuz Jack's time to throw.

Jack took his time and walked 'round de hammer to de handle and took holt of it and throwed his head back and looked up at de sky.

"Look out, Rayfield! Move over, Gabriel! You better stand 'way back, Jesus! Ah'm fixin' to throw." He meant Heaven.

Devil run up to 'im, says, "Hold on dere a minute! Don't you throw mah damn hammer up dere! Ah left a whole lot uh mah tools up dere when dey put me out, and ah ain't got 'em back yet. Don't you *throw* mah hammer up dere!"

A LAUGH
THAT MEANT FREEDOM
collected by J. MASON BREWER

"A Laugh That Meant Freedom" is one of the trickster slave tales, also known as the "John cycle." In these stories the protagonist is an African American slave who uses his wit or humor to outsmart the slave master. These stories became popular after the Civil War and appear to romanticize slavery in the "Old South." Houston A. Baker, Jr. points out in his book *Long Black Song* that "the sentimental elements of the trickster tales cannot obscure the fact that they are tales of rebellion—tales of the subversion of the slave system by the jester slaves."

There were some slaves who had a reputation for keeping out of work because of their wit and humor. Theses slaves kept their masters laughing most of the time, and were able, if not to keep from working altogether, at least to draw the lighter tasks.

Nehemiah was a clever slave, and no master who had owned him had ever been able to keep him at work, or succeeded in getting him to do heavy work. He would always have some funny story to tell or some humorous remark to make in response to the master's question, or scolding. Because of this faculty for avoiding work, Nehemiah was constantly being transferred from one master to another. As soon as an owner found out that Nehemiah was outwitting him, he sold Nehemiah to some other slaveholder. One day David Wharton, known as the most cruel slave master in Southwest Texas, heard about him.

"I bet I can make that rascal work," said David Wharton, and he went to Nehemiah's master and bargained to buy him.

The morning of the first day after his purchase, David Wharton walked over to where Nehemiah was standing and said, "Now you are going to work, you understand. You are going to pick four hundred pounds of cotton today."

"Wal, Massa, dat's aw right," answered Nehemiah, "but ef Ah meks yuh laff, won' yuh lemme off fo' terday?"

"Well," said David Wharton, who had never been known to laugh, "if you make me laugh, I won't only let you off for today, but I'll give you your freedom."

"Ah decla', Boss," said Nehemiah, "yuh sho' is uh goodlookin' man."

"I am sorry I can't say the same thing about you," retorted David Wharton.

"Oh, yes, Boss, yuh could," Nehemiah laughed out, "yuh could, ef yuh tole ez big uh lie ez Ah did."

David Wharton could not help laughing at this; he laughed before he thought. Nehemiah got his freedom.

THE LYING BEE

JOHN HENRIK CLARKE

For a long time my uncle Albert held the record as the greatest yarn spinner or the most convincing liar in our town. He was proud of this record in spite of the criticism showered upon him by the church-going branch of our family. Sometimes he used to tell me hair-raising stories of his adventures in foreign lands, and I listened to them with great interest, fully aware that he had never set foot outside the state of Georgia.

One day a stranger came to our town who began to dim the glow of Uncle Albert's lying record. The lies that this stranger told were more farfetched than Uncle Albert's. The stranger told his lies with a unique choice of words that was fascinating to people of a small town. As if this was not enough, his well-tailored clothes and his big-city mannerisms gained him the attention of the crowd and held him aloft from them all at the same time.

All of a sudden Uncle Albert began to lose the enthusiastic flock that formerly gathered around him whenever he sat down to tell a yarn. The invasion by an out-of-town liar so enraged Uncle Albert that his ability as a yarn-spinner was dulled almost to the point of being uninteresting. He spent most of his time moping around the streets of the town, labeling the out-of-town liar as an imposter and reprimanding the people for paying attention to him. Soon he dropped all other activities and devoted all of his time to conceiving a way he could avenge himself upon the other liar and retrieve his former status.

Twice Uncle Albert challenged the stranger to fight, and twice the stranger refused, saying there was nothing to fight about, for he had nothing against Uncle Albert. After this, Uncle Albert was more disturbed than ever. Every avenue for revenge seemed to have been closed, and his reputation as the greatest liar in Columbus, Georgia, had declined pathetically.

Finally one day after Felix Wilkinson, the town's leading grocer, had heard a lengthy discussion about the discord between Uncle Albert and the stranger, he suggested that a "lying bee" should be arranged, to determine once and for all who was the greatest liar.

Some of the church-going people protested, calling the whole affair a sinful outrage. This did not alter anything because most of the people in town were anxious to see the outcome of such a contest.

Three of the town's noted yarn-spinners, Jed Williams, the blacksmith, George Davis, the town's lone milkman, and Wilber Freepoint, the local drunk, who had partially sobered up for the occasion (this event was almost as noteworthy as the contest itself), were selected by Wilkinson to be the judges. Mr. Wilkinson, whose lies merited considerable attention, although they were nothing compared with Uncle Albert's, appointed himself supervisor of the contest, and to give himself more authority, he suggested that the affair be held in his grocery store.

During the three days before the contest a flood of comments and anticipation swept through the town. There were two groups of boosters: one group considered it their civic duty to favor Uncle Albert, and the other was bold enough to favor the stranger. A number of small bets were waged. Two townsmen came to striking blows while boosting the merits of the two liars. This contest was, by far, the most unusual thing that had ever happened in our town. Even some of the church people who had condemned it at first were quietly taking sides.

Finally the evening of the long-awaited lying bee arrived. Long before the time set for the contest an enthusiastic crowd was packed into Mr. Wilkinson's store. Uncle Albert, who had arrived well ahead of the crowd, had gained some attention by saying that the stranger had backed out, but the store was packed before the stranger arrived.

After the impatient crowd had started to whisper among themselves and Mr. Wilkinson had almost chewed up two pencils in near rage, the stranger appeared. He was quite handsome and he carried his tall, erect form in a smooth, effortless manner that always demanded attention. For this occasion he was dressed more stylish than ever. Although he had not said so, everybody took it for granted that he was from a big city. When he was fully inside the door, he removed his hat and fur-collared overcoat. He seated himself before removing his gloves. Everyone had fixed an avid stare upon him.

Gradually the atmosphere became tense. With an air of envy, Mr. Wilkinson observed the stranger's well-tailored outfit and rapped on the glass counter to turn the eyes of the audience in his direction.

"Ladies and gentlemen," he announced, "the much discussed lying bee will now begin. You know as well as I do why this affair has been arranged. For a long time Albert Carrol has held the record as the greatest liar in this town. Since the coming of one Josef Hendrik, there has been some doubt as to Albert's right to claim that title. We have assembled here on this December evening to settle, once and for all, the question of who is the greatest liar in Muskogee County. On my right sit the judges. They are too well-known to be introduced. After the two gentlemen have delivered their lies, the judges will retire to the back room of my store and reach a decision. To add more interest to this contest, I will give the winner a box of my most expensive cigars."

Mr. Wilkinson came from behind the counter and said, "Will the contestants please step forward." The stranger rose promptly and started toward Mr. Wilkinson. Both his expression and his graceful stride mirrored confidence. Albert threw one resentful glance at him, then rose and followed him to the front of the store.

"There is no use introducing you two gentlemen," Mr. Wilkinson said. "I have no doubt you know each other. This contest has been delayed long enough, so without further ado, we will get under way. I will thump a coin. If it lands heads up, the stranger will be the first to tell his lie; if it falls the other way, our Albert Carrol will be first."

Mr. Wilkinson thumped a coin into the air. A slight murmur came from the audience as it fell to the floor. Hesitantly, he bent over and lifted the coin. "It's heads, ladies and gentlemen," he said. "The stranger will tell the first lie."

Mr. Wilkinson climbed upon the high stool in front of the counter. Uncle Albert went back to his seat. The stranger waited until the audience became quiet, then he spoke.

"Friends," he began, "there is a little unfairness attached to my competing in this lying bee..." His voice possessed a cultured clearness that fastened the eyes of the audience upon him at once. "You see," he continued, "I am a professional liar. My opponent is an amateur."

An indignant murmur came from the crowd. With surprising swiftness Uncle Albert was on his feet, his face aflame with resentment.

The stranger stretched his hands forward, pleading for attention. "No offense, ladies and gentlemen," he said. "I only meant to convey that I tell lies for a living. You see, I write gags and jokes for stage comedians."

Uncle Albert sat down as if he had won some sort of victory. This put the audience back at ease. All eyes were again turned toward the stranger. At last he said:

"My favorite lie, the one that I shall now tell, is about Hi-John, the great Magician. Hi-John stopped off in a small southern town, and he was unnoticed and unheard of until one day two fellows, who were once partners, came to him for advice. The one-time partners had bought a mule together for one hundred dollars. One of the partners had paid twenty-five dollars; the other had paid seventy-five. When they broke up partnership, each wanted a share of the mule. The one who owned the greater interest offered to buy the other one out, but he refused to sell.

"Puzzling as this problem was, the great Hi-John encountered no difficulty in finding a solution. With one wave of his wand, he turned the mule into a mare. The two partners were frightened speechless.

"He paused and observed his accomplishment. Then with one more wave of his mighty wand, he gave the mare a beautiful colt. He instructed the partner who had paid the seventy-five dollars to take the mare, and the one who had paid twenty-five dollars to take the colt. The one-time partners were too shocked by this miracle to ask questions or disobey his orders. They thanked him and went away, amazed but satisfied.

"After that the fame of Hi-John, the Great Magician, grew like a potato vine. He performed many more miracles, some of them far greater than the first one.

"One day, in spite of the great throng that flocked around him, the mighty magician found himself getting lonesome. So right then and there he decided to take himself a wife. There wasn't a woman in the town who didn't consider it an honor to be the wife of the great magician. Hi-John exercised his privilege to its fullest extent by choosing the most beautiful woman in the town for his wife. They were married in the finest style.

"For a long time their marriage was the marvel of all the townspeople. Hi-John, who had long been very rich, was now very happy. His happiness lasted until one day he came home from his miracle-performing and found his wife in the arms of another man. On seeing this, the magician flew into an awful rage. His wife and her lover fell at his feet, pleading for mercy. He gave one scornful look and turned away, walking toward the door. He stopped suddenly and spoke in a troubled tone: 'This is a grave situation,' he said. 'The great Hi-John is not accustomed to coping with such problems. I think I'll let the Lord take care of this one.'

"The magician turned his great figure back toward his wife and her lover, scratching his head as if he were expecting to discover a super-thinking machine. He spoke again, the pitch of his voice rising with every word. 'Probably the Lord is too busy with other things,' he said, 'I think I will take over this situation myself.'

"The two betrayers continued to plead for mercy, but Hi-John paid little heed to them. He seemed to be searching for his real self. Then, as if he had suddenly reached a decision, he pulled out his mighty wand and the whole house disappeared. The three of them were now standing in an empty lot. Hi-John's wife fought her way through the veil of astonishment and began to scream. Her lover made an attempt to run. Hi-John spoke just one word; the lover halted in his tracks and stood as if in a trance. The magician paused as if in meditation. When his wife started to plead again, he waved his mighty wand as if guided by a streak of madness and turned both his wife and her lover into mammoth oak trees.

"After this, the great magician walked away, weeping sorrowfully. He loved his wife, and this was one miracle he had hated to perform. Soon he disappeared and since then no one has ever heard any more about Hi-John, the Great Magician."

Josef Hendrick, the stranger, took a slight bow, indicating that he had finished his lie. As he started for his seat, he smiled, reflecting a tinge of victory. The few ladies in the audience gasped in utter amazement. There was some applause from the men. The three judges stared at one another in wonderment. Mr. Wilkinson moved down from his high stool, stroking his chin. At least the stranger had told a good lie. No one seemed to doubt that.

Uncle Albert threw a scornful glance at him as he took his seat. Suddenly a series of whispering debates about the merits and demerits of the stranger's lie spread through the store. Mr. Wilkinson rapped on the counter for silence, and the murmuring died down.

"Ladies and gentlemen," he announced, "we will now hear from our great liar, Albert Carrol." "Hurray for Albert," a local drunk yelled. A slight shower of applause greeted these words, although there were some among the crowd who doubted whether Uncle Albert could tell anything that would surpass the stranger's lie.

Mr. Wilkinson climbed back up on his high stool as Uncle Albert rose and walked to the front of the store. He was the center of attraction now. All eyes were fixed on him, burning with anticipation. He glanced at Mr. Wilkinson and the box of cigars that was to become the property of the winner. He smiled at his audience, then spoke in a thick, uncultured tone, as he always did:

"Folks," he began, "I only know one lie that I haven't tol' roun' this burg, an' that's th' one about Sam Tolbert's jackass. That's th' one I will now tell y' all.

"To begin with, Sam Tolbert's jackass was the kickingest thing that ever put a foot in this worl'. Th' first time Sam took 'im t' town, 'e kicked th' court house two miles outside th' city limit and left the ol' jedge an' all th' members of his court hangin' on midair. On his way back t' th' country th' jackass passed th' court house, an' t' prove that th' first mess of kickin' was no accident, th' durn jackass kicked th' court house all th' way back t' town. After this, Sam had t' keep his jackass in th' country. Hit was against th' law t' let 'im enter a city.

"Very li'l was heard about th' jackass until, finally, one day two beggars came by Sam's farm an' axed fer some food. Sam tol' 'em dat he had no food ready, but dey didn't believe 'im. So dey kept on axin'. Th' jackass was standing nearby, an' after a while 'e became annoyed by th' beggars' pleas. Sam could tell by th' look in th' jackass's eyes that one of his kickin' spells was comin' on. Th' nearest thing t' th' jackass was one of Sam's cows. So, like a streak o' lightnin', th' dern jackass kicked th' cow two miles in th' air. One minute later th' cow fell at th' beggars' feet on a pure gold platter, in the form of nice, fat, juicy steaks wit' onions an' gravy for good measure. I tell ya, ladies an' gennemun, dem steaks was cooked t' please a king.

"Dis struck th' beggars as bein' very funny, so dey began t' laughin', an' never in dis worl' have any two people laughed so much. Ladies an' gennemun, those two beggars laughed until holes split in dere sides big enuf fer a wagon train t' go through. But dey didn't stop laughin'. No sir, not den. Dey was laughin' an' cryin' all at th' same time, and th' water from dere cryin' eyes was floodin' Sam Tolbert's farm. After a while dere eyes began t' shine like th' sun, but dey went right on laughin', ladies an' gennemun. Dey laughed until their eyes was brighter den th' sun. No, dey didn't stop den.

"In a li'l while th' beggars' eyes an' th' sun began t' fight a little battle fer th' right t' shine all over th' worl'. Soon th' sun threw up its hands, admitting defeat. Now th' beggars' eyes took dat of th' sun . . . an' dey was still laughin'.

"As I've said before, their sides had split open wide enuf fer a wagon train t' go through, an' th' water from dere cryin' eyes was floodin' Sam Tolbert's farm, 'n' dere eyes had outshined th' sun. But in spite of all dis, dey went right on laughin', ladies an' gennemun. . . . Fer all I know, dey could still be laughin'."

Upon finishing his lie Uncle Albert glanced again at Mr. Wilkinson and the box of cigars at his elbow. An expression of complete astonishment was on every face in the store. There was a heavy silence, a silence of tribute and approval. Uncle Albert's lie had so affected the audience that no one would dare speak. The judges thought it useless to retire to the back room of the store for their decision. The decision was written plainly across the face of everyone in the store.

Mr. Wilkinson climbed down from his high stool, scanned the audience, and took a deep breath. Without uttering a word, he went over and placed the box of cigars in Uncle Albert's hands.

GOOD AND DRUNK

DANIEL BARNES, as told to MARIAN E. BARNES

One night a minister delayed starting a revival service because a drunk man was in the congregation talking loud and filling the air with the smell of whiskey from his breath. After the scheduled starting time, he began yelling, "What's the hold up? You people are late! God is a on-time God. Let's go!" Finally, usher Watkins went toward him, and he jumped up and ran out the door with Watkins right behind.

The whole church was uneasy—waiting for Watkins...but when the door finally burst open, *the drunk man lurched in,* laughed, and staggered to his seat. "I don't have no faith in none of y'all now," he shouted. "When I first came here I thought y'all were some of the apostles—especially that baldheaded one in the pulpit!"

Elder Jones was insulted! He took a deep breath. "*Well!* I've got too much sense to put in my bald head what you've put in your head!"

The man straightened his shoulders, threw his head up, and took a deep breath, mimicking Jones, and said, *Well!* I've got sense enough in my head to know Jesus wouldn't ha' put me out of church 'cause I'm a little drunk!"

Just then Watkins rushed in all out of breath and said, "I lost him!" He was apologizing.

"Naw you didn't." The drunken man swayed to his feet, waved, and hollered consolingly, "You didn't lose me. I'm still here! Come on in. Let's have church."

By then, some of us felt like rolling on the floor laughing! But we couldn't do that. So we took his advice and had church.

ROCK, CHURCH

LANGSTON HUGHES

Elder William Jones was one of them rock-church preachers who know how to make the spirit rise and the soul get right. Sometimes in the pulpit he used to start talking real slow, and you'd think his sermon warn't gonna be nothing; but by the time he got through, the walls of the temple would be almost rent, the doors busted open, and the benches turned over from pure shouting on the part of the brothers and sisters.

He were a great preacher, was Reverend William Jones. But he warn't satisfied—he wanted to be greater than he was. He wanted to be another Billy Graham or Elmer Gantry or a resurrected Daddy Grace. And that's what brought about his downfall—ambition!

Now, Reverend Jones had been for nearly a year the pastor of one of them little colored churches in the back alleys of St. Louis that are open every night in the week for preaching, singing, and praying, where sisters come to shake tambourines, shout, swing gospel songs, and get happy while the Reverend presents the Word.

Elder Jones always opened his part of the services with "In His Hand," his theme song, and he always closed his services with the same. Now, the rhythm of "In His Hand" was such that once it got to swinging, you couldn't help but move your arms or feet or both, and since the Reverend always took up collection at the beginning and ending of his sermons, the dancing movement of the crowd at such times was always toward the collection table—which was exactly where the Elder wanted it to be.

In His hand!
In His hand!
I'm safe and sound
I'll be bound —
Settin' in Jesus' hand!

"Come one! Come all! Come, my Lambs," Elder Jones would shout, "and put it down for Jesus!"

Poor old washer-ladies, big fat cooks, long, lean truck drivers and heavyset roustabouts would come up and lay their money down two times every evening for Elder Jones.

That minister was getting rich right there in that St. Louis alley.

In His hand!
In His hand!
I'll have you know
I'm white as snow —
Settin' in Jesus' hand!

With the piano just a-going, tambourines a-flying, and people shouting right on up to the altar.

"Rock, church, rock!" Elder Jones would cry at such intensely lucrative moments.

But he were too ambitious. He wouldn't let well enough alone. He wanted to be a big shot and panic Harlem, gas Detroit, sew up Chicago, then move on to Hollywood. He warn't satisfied with just St. Louis.

So he got to thinking, "Now, what can I do to get everybody excited, to get everybody talking about my church, to get the streets outside crowded and my name known all over, even unto the far reaches of the nation? Now, what can I do?"

Billy Sunday had a sawdust trail, so he had heard. Reverend Becton had two valets in the pulpit with him as he cast off garment after garment in the heat of preaching, and used up dozens of white handkerchiefs every evening wiping his brow while calling on the Lord to come. Meanwhile, the Angel of Angelus Temple had just kept on getting married and divorced and making the front pages of everybody's newspapers.

"I got to be news, too, in my day and time," mused Elder Jones. "This town's too small for me! I want the world to hear my name!"

Now, as I've said before, Elder Jones was a good preacher—and a good-looking preacher, too. He could cry real loud and moan real deep, and he could move the sisters as no other black preacher on this side of town had ever moved them before. Besides, in his youth, as a sinner, he had done a little light hustling around Memphis and Vicksburg—so he knew just how to appeal to the feminine nature.

Since his recent sojourn in St. Louis, Elder Jones had been looking for a special female Lamb to shelter in his private fold. Out of all the sisters in his church, he had finally chosen Sister Maggie Bradford. Not that Sister Maggie was pretty. No, far from it. But Sister Maggie was well fed, brown skin, good-natured, fat, and *prosperous*. She owned four two-family houses that she rented out, upstairs and down, so she made a good living. Besides, she had sweet and loving ways as well as the interest of her pastor at heart.

Elder Jones confided his personal ambitions to said Sister Bradford one morning when he woke up to find her by his side.

"I want to branch out, Maggie," he said. "I want to be a really big man! Now, what can I do to get the 'tention of the world on me? I mean, in a religious way?"

They thought and they thought. Since it was a Fourth of July morning, and Sister Maggie didn't have to go collect rents, they just lay there and thought.

Finally, Sister Maggie said, "Bill Jones, you know something I ain't never forgot that I seed as a child? There was a preacher down in Mississippi named old man Eubanks who one time got himself dead and buried and then rose from the dead. Now, I ain't never forgot that. Neither has nobody else in that part of the Delta. That's something mem'rable. Why don't you do something like that?"

"How did he do it, Sister Maggie?"

"He ain't never told nobody how he do it, Brother Bill. He say it were the Grace of God, that's all."

"It mighta been," said Elder Jones. "It mighta been."

He lay there and thought awhile longer. By and by he said, "But honey, I'm gonna do something better'n that. I'm gonna be nailed on a cross."

"Do, Jesus!" said Sister Maggie Bradford. "Jones, you's a mess!"

Now, the Elder, in order to pull off his intended miracle, had, of necessity, to take somebody else into his confidence, so he picked out Brother Hicks, his chief deacon, one of the main pillars of the church long before Jones came as pastor.

It was too bad, though, that Jones never knew that Brother Hicks (more familiarly known as Bulldog) used to be in love with Sister Bradford. Sister Bradford neglected to tell the new reverend about any of her former sweethearts. So how was Elder Jones to know that some of them still coveted her and were envious of him in their hearts?

"Hicks," whispered Elder Jones in telling his chief deacon of his plan to die on the cross and then come back to life, "that miracle will make me the greatest minister in the world. No doubt about it! When I get to be world renowned, Bulldog, and go traveling about the firmament, I'll take you with me as my chief deacon. You shall be my right hand, and Sister Maggie Bradford shall be my left. Amen!"

"I hear you," said Brother Hicks. "I hope it comes true."

But if Elder Jones had looked closely, he would have seen an evil light in his deacon's eyes.

"It will come true," said Elder Jones, "if you keep your mouth shut and follow out my instructions—exactly as I lay 'em down to you. I trust you, so listen! You know and I know that I ain't gonna *really* die. Neither is I *really* gonna be nailed. That's why I wants you to help me. I wants you to have me a great big cross made, higher than the altar—so high I has to have a stepladder to get up to it to be nailed thereon, and you to nail me. The higher the better, so's they won't see the straps—cause I'm gonna be tied on by straps, you hear. The light'll be rose-colored so they can't see the straps. Now, here you come and do the nailin'—nobody else but you. Put them nails *between* my fingers and toes, not through 'em—*between*—and don't nail too deep. Leave the heads kinder stickin' out. You get the jibe?"

"I get the jibe," said Brother Bulldog Hicks.

"Then you and me'll stay right on there in the church all night and all day till the next night when the people come back to see me rise. Ever so often, you can let me down to rest a little bit. But as long as I'm on the cross, I play off like I'm dead, particularly when reporters come around. On Monday night, hallelujah! I will rise, and take up collection!"

"Amen!" said Brother Hicks.

Well, you couldn't get a-near the church on the night that Reverend Jones had had it announced by press, by radio, and by word of mouth that he would be crucified *dead*, stay dead, and rise. Negroes

came from all over St. Louis, East St. Louis, and mighty nigh everywhere else to be present at the witnessing of the miracle. Lots of 'em
didn't believe in Reverend Jones, but lots of 'em *did*. Sometimes false
prophets can bamboozle you so you can't tell yonder from whither—
and that's the way Jones had the crowd.

The church was packed and jammed. Not a seat to be found,
and tears were flowing (from sorrowing sisters' eyes) long before
the Elder even approached the cross which, made out of new
lumber right straight from the sawmill, loomed up behind the pulpit. In the rose-colored lights, with big paper lilies that Sister
Bradford had made decorating its head and foot, the cross looked
mighty pretty.

Elder Jones preached a mighty sermon that night, and hot as it
was, there was plenty of leaping and jumping and shouting in that
crowded church. It looked like the walls would fall. Then when he
got through preaching, Elder Jones made a solemn announcement.
As he termed it, for a night and a day, his last pronouncement.

"Church! Tonight, as I have told the world, I'm gonna die. I'm
gonna be nailed to this cross and let the breath pass from me. But
tomorrow, Monday night, August the twenty-first, at twelve P.M., I
am coming back to life. Amen! After twenty-four hours on the cross,
hallelujah! And all the city of St. Louis can be saved—if they will just
come out to see me. Now, before I mounts the steps to the cross, let
us sing for the last time "In His Hand"—'cause I tell you, that's
where I am! As we sing, let everybody come forward to the collection
table and help this church before I go. Give largely!"

The piano tinkled, the tambourines rang, hands clapped. Elder
Jones and his children sang:

In His hand!
In His hand!
You'll never stray
Down the Devil's way—
Settin' in Jesus' hand!

Oh, in His hand!
In His hand!
Though I may die
I'll mount on high—
Settin' in Jesus' hand!

"Let us pray." And while every back was bowed in prayer, the Elder went up the stepladder to the cross. Brother Hicks followed with the hammer and nails. Sister Bradford wailed at the top of her voice. Woe filled the Amen Corner. Emotion rocked the church.

Folks outside was saying all up and down the street, "Lawd, I wish we could have got in. Listen yonder at that noise! I wonder what *is* going on!"

Elder Jones was about to make himself famous—that's what was going on. And all would have went well had it not been for Brother Hicks—a two-faced rascal. Somehow that night the Devil got into Bulldog Hicks and took full possession.

The truth of the matter is that Hicks got to thinking about Sister Maggie Bradford, and how Reverend Jones had worked up to be her No. 1 Man. That made him mad. The old green snake of jealousy began to coil around his heart, right there in the meeting, right there on the steps of the cross. Lord, have mercy! At the very high point of the ceremonies!

Hicks had the hammer in one hand and his other hand was full of nails as he mounted the ladder behind his pastor. He was going up to nail Elder Jones on that sawmill cross.

"While I'm nailin', I might as well nail him right," Hicks thought. "A low-down klinker—comin' here out of Mississippi to take my woman away from me! He'll never know the pleasure of my help in none o' his schemes to out-Divine Father! No, sir!"

Elder Jones had himself all fixed up with a system of straps round his waist, round his shoulder blades, and round his wrists and ankles, hidden under his long black coat. These straps fastened in hooks on the back of the cross, out of sight of the audience, so he could just hang up there all sad and sorrowful looking, and make out like he was being nailed. Brother Bulldog Hicks was to plant the nails *between* his fingers and toes. Hallelujah! Rock, church, rock!

Excitement was intense.

All went well until the nailing began. Elder Jones removed his shoes and socks and, in his bare black feet, bade farewell to his weeping congregation. As he leaned back against the cross and allowed Brother Hicks to compose him there, the crowd began to moan. But it was when Hicks placed the first nail between Elder Jones's toes that they became hysterical. Sister Bradford outyelled them all.

Hicks placed that first nail between the big toe and the next toe of the left foot and began to hammer. The foot was well strapped down, so the Elder couldn't move it. The closer the head of the nail got to his toes, the harder Hicks struck it. Finally the hammer collided with Elder Jones's foot, *bam* against his big toe.

"Aw-oh!" he moaned under his breath. "Go easy, man!"

"Have mercy," shouted the brothers and sisters of the church. "Have mercy on our Elder!"

Once more the hammer struck his toe. But the all-too-human sound of his surprised and agonized "Ouch!" was lost in the tumult of the shouting church.

"Bulldog, I say, go easy," hissed the Elder. "This *ain't* real."

Brother Hicks desisted, a grim smile on his face. Then he turned his attention to the right foot. There he placed another nail between the toes and began to hammer. Again, as the nail went into the wood, he showed no signs of stopping when the hammer reached the foot. He just kept on landing cruel metallic blows on the Elder's bare toenails until the preacher howled with pain, no longer able to keep back a sudden hair-raising cry. The sweat popped out on his forehead and dripped down on his shirt.

At first the Elder thought, naturally, that it was just a slip of the hammer on the deacon's part. Then he thought the man must have gone crazy—like the rest of the audience. Then it hurt him so bad, he didn't know what he thought—so he just hollered, "Aw-ooo-oo-o!"

It was a good thing the church was full of noise, or they would have heard a strange dialogue.

"My God, Hicks, what are you doing?" the Elder cried, staring wildly at his deacon on the ladder.

"I'm nailin' you to the cross, Jones! And man, I'm *really* nailin'."

"Aw-oow-ow! Don't you know you're hurting me? I told you *not* to nail so hard!"

But the deacon was unruffled.

"Who'd you say's gonna be your right hand when you get down from here and start your travelings?" Hicks asked.

"You, brother," the sweating Elder cried.

"And who'd you say was gonna be your left hand?"

"Sister Maggie Bradford," moaned Elder Jones from the cross.

"Naw she ain't," said Brother Hicks, whereupon he struck the Reverend's toe a really righteous blow.

"Lord, help me!" cried the tortured minister. The weeping congregation echoed his cry. It was certainly real. The Elder *was* being crucified!

Brother Bulldog Hicks took two more steps up the ladder, preparing to nail the hands. With his evil face right in front of Elder Jones, he hissed: "I'll teach you nappy-headed jack-leg ministers to come to St. Louis and think you-all can walk away with any woman you's a mind to. I'm gonna teach you to leave my women alone. Here— here's a nail!"

Brother Hicks placed a great big spike right in the palm of Elder Jones's left hand. He was just about to drive it in when the frightened Reverend let out a scream that could be heard two blocks away. At the same time he began to struggle to get down. Jones tried to bust the straps, but they was too strong for him.

If he could just get one foot loose to kick Brother Bulldog Hicks!

Hicks lifted the hammer to let go when the Reverend's second yell, this time, was loud enough to be heard in East St. Louis. It burst like a bomb above the shouts of the crowd—and it had its effect. Suddenly the congregation was quiet. Everybody knew that was no way for a dying man to yell.

Sister Bradford realized that something had gone wrong, so she began to chant the song her beloved pastor had told her to chant at the propitious moment after the nailing was done. Now, even though the nailing was not done, Sister Bradford thought she had better sing:

> *Elder Jones will rise again,*
> *Elder Jones will rise again,*
> *Rise again, rise again!*
> *Elder Jones will rise again,*
> *Yes, my Lawd!*

But nobody took up the refrain to help her carry it on. Everybody was too interested in what was happening in front of them, so Sister Bradford's voice just died out.

Meanwhile Brother Hicks lifted the hammer again, but Elder Jones spat right in his face. He not only spat but suddenly called his deacon a name unworthy of man or beast. Then he let out another frightful yell and, in mortal anguish, called, "Sister Maggie Bradford, lemme down from here! I say, come and get...me...down...*from here!*"

Those in the church that had not already stopped moaning and shouting did so at once. You could have heard a pin drop. Folks were petrified.

Brother Hicks stood on the ladder, glaring with satisfaction at Reverend Jones, his hammer still raised. Under his breath the panting Elder dared him to nail another nail, and threatened to kill him stone-dead with a forty-four if he did.

"Just lemme get loost from here, and I'll fight you like a natural man," he gasped, twisting and turning like a tree in a storm.

"Come down, then," yelled Hicks, right out loud from the ladder. "Come on down! As sure as water runs, Jones, I'll show you up for what you is—a woman-chasing no-good low-down faker! I'll beat you to a batter with my bare hands!"

"Lawd, have mercy!" cried the church.

Jones almost broke a blood vessel trying to get loose from his cross. "Sister Maggie, come and lemme down," he pleaded, sweat streaming from his face.

But Sister Bradford was covered with confusion. In fact, she was petrified. What could have gone wrong for the Elder to call on her like this in public in the very midst of the thing that was to bring him famous-glory and make them all rich, preaching throughout the land with her at his side? Sister Bradford's head was in a whirl, her heart was in her mouth.

"Elder Jones, you means you really wants to get down?" she asked weakly from her seat in the Amen Corner.

"Yes," cried the Elder, "can't you hear? I done called on you twenty times to let me down!"

At this point Brother Hicks gave the foot nails one more good hammering. The words that came from the cross were not to be found in the Bible.

In a twinkling, Sister Bradford was at Jones's side. Realizing at last that the Devil must've done got into Hicks (like it used to sometimes in the days when she knowed him), she went to the aid of her battered Elder, grabbed the foot of the ladder, and sent Hicks sprawling across the pulpit.

"You'll never crucify my Elder," she cried, "not for real." Energetically she began to cut the straps away that bound the Reverend.

Soon poor Jones slid to the floor, his feet too sore from the hammer's blows to even stand on them without help.

"Just lemme get at Hicks" was all Reverend Jones could gasp. "He knowed I didn't want them nails that close." In the dead silence that took possession of the church, everybody heard him moan, "Lawd, lemme get at Hicks," as he hobbled away on the protecting arm of Sister Maggie.

"Stand back, Bulldog," Sister Maggie said to the deacon, "and let your pastor pass. Soon as he's able, he'll flatten you out like a shadow—but now, I'm in charge. Stand back, I say, and let him pass!"

Hicks stood back. The crowd murmured. The minister made his exit. Thus ended the ambitious career of Elder William Jones. He never did pastor in St. Louis anymore. Neither did he fight Hicks. He just snuck away for parts unknown.

REVOLT OF THE ANGELS

JOHN HENRIK CLARKE

T he two Harlem piano movers who had taken the negative side of the argument were quiet now, waiting for the defender of the affirmative to gather his thoughts. He was a big man; seemingly bigger than his two friendly opponents put together. Because of this, it did not seem unfair that he had no one to assist him in imparting his point of view.

For more than an hour the three men had been standing by their large red truck, waiting between assignments. It was their custom on these occasions to test each other's knowledge of the great subjects and issues that influence the destiny of mankind. The fact that their formal knowledge of these subjects was extremely limited did not deter their discussions in the slightest.

The two small men waited and stole quick glances at their large companion. Their faces were aglow with the signs of assured victory. Finally one turned to the other and said: "We've got 'im at las', Leroy. We've taken King Solomon off of his throne. We've made another wise man bit th' dust."

The speaker's dark face looked as if age had been baked into it. He kept watching the large man who was collecting his thoughts in preparation for stating his side of the argument.

"I knew we'd tame this wise man some day," the other small man said. The note of triumph and mock haughtiness in his voice gave it a distinct play-acting tone. "We got 'im up a creek without a paddle," he went on, laughing a little. "Now, Hawkshaw, lemme see you talk your way out of this trap."

"Don't count your eggs before you buy your chickens," the big man said, straightening up as his loosely hanging stomach spilled over the rim of his belt. "Th' thing to be resolved is whether a man who has been a drunkard most of his life can straighten himself out and become a pillar of respectability an' a credit to his community. You fellas have said this cannot be done an' I disagree.... I know just th' case to prove my point." He exhaled audibly with some of the pompousness of a political orator preparing for a long discourse.

Then he spoke again, slowly, measuring his words very carefully at first.

"During th' last part of th' depression years there was a fella here in Harlem named Luther Jackson who had been drunk so long nobody could remember how he looked when he was sober. Luther wasn't a violent man; he didn't bother nobody unless he wanted some likker and they wouldn't give it to him.

"One day when Luther was near th' end of a three-week stupor, he wandered into one of Father Divine's restaurants and sat down at th' bes' table. He thought th' restaurant was a bar and th' bes' table in th' house meant nothing to him. Now, fellas, when I say this was the bes' table in th' house, I mean it was th' bes' table you'd see anywhere. In those days most of Father Divine's restaurants set up a special table for Father just in case he came in an' wanted to dine in style. This special table had snow white linen, th' bes' of silverware, crystal glasses, th' kind you only see in the homes of millionaires, and a fresh bowl of flowers. A picture of Father Divine was in front of th' flowers with a message under it sayin', *Thank you, Father.* It was some kind of deadly sin for anybody but Father Divine and his invited guests to set at this table.

"A big fat angel saw Luther at th' table an' strutted out of th' kitchen blowin' like a mad bull.

"'Peace, brother,' she said real loud. 'This is Father Divine's table, get up an' get out of here.'

"'I want some likker,' Luther says, 'an' I want some more t' wash it down.'

"'Peace, brother,' th' angel says, puffin' an' trying to keep her temper from explodin'. 'This is Father Divine's table, get up an' get out of here.'

"'I won't go till you give me some likker,' Luther says, 'an' I don't care whose table this is.'

"Th' angel threw her hands in th' air and looked at th' ceilin' like she expected something over her head to come down an' help her.

"'Peace, Father,' she says, 'remove this evil man from your premises.'

"'I want some likker!' Luther shouted at her an' slammed his hand on th' table, knockin' down some of th' fine silverware. 'A drinkin' man is in th' house. Go away, old woman, an' send me a bartender.'

"This made th' angel madder than ever. She went back to th' kitchen holdin' her head like she was scared it was goin' t' fly off.

"'Where's th' bartender in this place?' Luther asked an' stood up lookin' 'round like he was just fixin' to mop up th' place with his madness.

"Th' big angel was standing in th' kitchen door, shoutin', 'Father Divine don't allow no alcohol drinkers in here. No obscenities! No adulteries!'

"Luther slammed his hand on th' table again an' knocked down some more of th' fine silverware. This made th' angel so angry she couldn't speak. She just stood in th' door of th' kitchen swellin' up like a big toad frog.

"'Gimme some likker and let me get outa here,' Luther says.

"Then th' angel hollered out all of a sudden and frightened Luther so much he almost jumped over the table.

"'Peace Father!' th' angel was sayin'. 'Give me console, Father, you are wonderful!'

"Father or someone else must have given her console an' some new strength to go with it, because she threw a pot at Luther's head like he was a long-lost husband who deserted her with a house full of hungry young'uns.

"The pot bounced off of Luther's head an' he hollered like a wild bull. 'What's goin' on in this place?' Luther was sayin'. 'Where's th' bartender?'

"'Father Divine don't 'low no alcohol drinkers in here,' th' angel was sayin' again. 'No obscenities! No adulteries.' Before she finished sayin' this she threw another pot at Luther's head.

"Luther ducked and stood up in a chair as a skillet missed his head by an inch. Then he stepped into the middle of th' table. He had knocked down th' flowers and some of th' fine silverware. Now th' angel was hollerin' like judgment day was at hand. You see, fellas, Luther was standin' on Father Divine's picture. She ran out of pots an' began t' throw big spoons an' ladles.

"'Peace Father, give me strength,' she hollered, 'give me th' strength to move this Satan from your premises.'

"Then she jumped toward Luther like a tiger an' knocked 'im off th' table with a rollin' pin. As Luther fell, he turned th' table over. All of th' snow white table linen was on th' floor. Th' silverware was scattered around th' table and some of it was in Luther's pockets. Most of th' millionaire crystal glasses were broken.

"The fat angel kept screamin', 'Peace! Peace! Peace!' until some more angels joined up with her. They came at Luther with fire in their eyes. They beat him until he got up, then they beat him down again. Still more angels came and joined the war on Luther—black ones, white ones, lean ones, fat ones, an' all th' sizes in between. They kicked him, they scratched him an' spit on him. While all of this was happenin', an angel came up an' started whackin' at Luther with a cleaver.

"Now Luther was screamin' for his life an' tryin' to get to th' door. Th' angels knocked him down again, an' he crawled out of th' door hollerin' for a police to save him. He saw a red box on th' side of a building an' opened it, thinkin' it was a police telephone. He pulled down a lever an' let it stay down. Th' angels had followed him into th' streets. Soon, fire trucks started comin' from every direction—patrol wagons from th' riot squads an' th' emergency squads came. Policemen in cars an' on foot came to th' scene like they were being rained down from th' sky. Still th' angry angels kept chargin' at Luther. The commotion tied up traffic for ten blocks.

"It took more than one hundred policemen to rescue Luther from them angry angels. They had hit him every place including under his feet. The policemen had to take him to th' hospital before they could take him to jail. When he was well enough for his trial, th' judge threw th' book at him an' said he was sorry that he did not have a much bigger book. Life in jail changed Luther. He was, indeed, a new man when he came out. He was upright, law abidin', and he refused to drink anything stronger than coffee.

"So, fellas, I give you the case of Luther Jackson as my proof that a man who has been a drunkard most of his life can straighten himself out and become a pillar of respectability an' a credit to his community.

"Now Luther is a foreman of a stevedore group down on th' docks, an' he's also an officer in th' union. He sent down south for his wife an' children, an' he made a good home for them right here in Harlem. He is a church-goin' man, too, an' a senior deacon. Nowhere in this land would you find a more peaceful an' law abidin' citizen than Luther Jackson. Since th' day of that fracas with those angry angels to this day, he never again touched another drop of likker."

The opposition had conceded defeat long before the fat man finished the story. A rebuttal was unnecessary.

TWO KINDS OF WOMEN

TEJUMOLA F. OLOGBONI

It was a Friday night, about 7:30, and I was *slick*. I had just come from the bathroom, after putting on my daddy's cologne. I said to myself, "Dude! You dressed and ready to 'mess.'" My father leaned back, gave me a long look, and said, "You smellin' mighty sweet."

I said, "Daddy, I ain't smellin' sweet. I'm smellin' mel-low."

"Well, boy, whether you smellin' sweet or mellow, that's my cologne you done bathed in," he said. "Now where you think you goin'?"

"Uh, I'm goin' to a party, Daddy."

"What you gon' do, hmmmm? Gon' party with them little girls?"

"Aw, now, Daddy, I'm fourteen. I'm gon' mess with some women."

"You gon' mess with some women, huh? Boy, now what *you* know 'bout women?"

I puffed out my chest. "Aw, Daddy, I know all I need to know 'bout women."

"Oh, you do, huh?" He rubbed his chin. "Well, then, you tell me, boy, what's the only two kinds of women on earth?"

"Oh, that's easy. The pretty women and the ugly ones."

"No."

"The tall ones and the short ones."

"Nope."

"Oh, I got it. The fat ones and the skinny ones."

"Naw."

"Uh . . . The old ones and the young ones?"

"Shut up, boy. You don't know nothin' 'bout women. Now I'm gon' tell you. See, ain't but two kinds of women on earth. But, first of all, let me tell you, they all treacherous."

"Huh? Treacherous? You mean, even Mama?"

"'Specially Mama, boy. But, hold on, now, boy. Don't you go gettin' all bent out of shape. See, you gotta understand what the word mean. The word 'treachery' got to do with loyalty. Now, I love your mama with all my heart. I love her with all my money, and I trust her with the thing I hold most sacred on earth and that's all you kids. But I'm gon' tell you something, boy. If it get down to somethin' little, not somethin' big, but if it get down to somethin' real little, that both me and your mama want, and we want it the same, you can betcha she gon' do everythin' she can to get her way.

"Now your mama's a good Christian woman. When we first got married she usta argue with me all the time 'bout drinkin'. She said alcohol is the devil's business. And one day she threw away all my liquor and told me I couldn't bring no more in the house. Well suh, I snuck and hid me a bottle of wine way back in the corner behind the tools where I just knew she wouldn't find it. Well, one day when she was gone, I went behind the tools and got my bottle. I had drunk it half the way down before I realized wasn't nothin' in that bottle but grape juice. There was a note written on the bottle sayin', 'You can't hide the devil, honey.'

"Then there was the time I was gon' go play poker with the boys. And she told me I couldn't go. 'A Christian man ain't got no business gamblin',' she say. I told her the other fellas is Christians and they goin' so I'm goin'. She say, 'No, you ain't.' I said, 'Look! I'm the man of *this* house. Ain't nobody tell the man of the house what to do. I goes where I wants and does what I pleases! And I'm gon' play poker.' She speak real quiet and say, 'Well, if you leavin', I may as well go to bed.' While I'm gettin' my shoes on, she go into the bedroom and come back out wearin' that black silk nightgown—the one I bought her for Valentine's Day. She walk over to me, kiss me. Then she wink at me and switch back to the bedroom. Wellsuh, boy, I never did make it to that poker game.

"Son, let me tell ya. Ain't nothin' on God's earth more treacherous than a good woman."

"But, Daddy... what's the only two kinds of women on earth?"

"Well, boy, the first kind of woman is a woman that'll kill you."

"Ooh, that's dangerous, ain't it, Daddy?"

"Naw, boy. You'll know a woman that'll kill you. You can see her coming a mile away. You'll know what she look like. She got her hand on her hip. She got her finger pointed, shakin' it at somebody, and her mouth goin' a mile a minute. Boy, you just step aside and say, 'Excuse me, ma'am' and keep on goin' where you goin'. The woman that'll kill you ain't even dangerous."

"Well, then, Daddy, what...what's the dangerous woman, Daddy?"

"Boy, that's the woman that'll make you kill *yourself.* You'll come home from work, and you've been workin' two jobs, and you drag yourself up on the front porch, as tired as you can be, and right before you can put your hand on the handle of the screen door, she pull the screen door open and she say, 'Hi, baby.' And she put her arms around you, to hold you real tight. She got on that pretty dress, you know; the one you like. And she got on that perfume that you just love. She say, 'Did you work hard today, baby?' You say, 'Uh-huh.' She say, 'Why don't you come on in the kitchen? I got somethin' for you to eat.' So you go in the kitchen, boy, and sittin' right up there on the table is a big old ham with them pineapples and them little bitty black things just like white folks make on TV and in the movies. She cut you a big ol' piece of ham, lay it in your plate. She got some little bitty potatoes that she done peeled off and boiled, but they still whole and she done sit them in the plate, put some gravy over them and everythin' like that, you know. And you just eat and eat and eat and eat until you can't eat no more and you ready to push yourself away from the table. She say, 'Just a minute, baby.' And she go in the cupboard and bring out this big ol' chocolate cake. Big ol' chocolate cake, umph! And got that icin' on it that's hard, not like that white folks' icin' that stay soft all the time. This is some good ol' icin'. And she cut that piece of cake and she lay it on that plate, too. Done cut you a big ol' hunk, and you eat until you know you can't hold no more. You gon' bust. And you stagger off to bed and you fall across it, and before you can go to sleep she put her arms and legs around you and make love to you all night. And right before you fall asleep, the alarm clock go off and you get up and you go back to work.

"You see, boy, you workin' two jobs! And you come home. Come home just as dog tired as can be. You stagger up on the porch and reach for the screen door. Before you can reach the screen door, she open the door and say, 'Hi, baby.' And she put her arms around you and she got on that pretty dress, and you can smell that perfume she wears. She say, 'You work hard today, baby?' You say, 'Yeah, baby, I worked hard today.' She say, 'Well, baby, I don't like you workin' two jobs. You workin' too—' 'Naw, baby,' you say, 'I want to get you a car and a fur and a new house and a—.' She say, 'Come on, I cooked somethin' for you.' And you go in the kitchen. Boy, there's a big ol' turkey sittin' on the stove. And it got that cornbread dressin', not that ol' white bread dressin' like them white folks make. It got that good ol' *cornbread* dressin'. And she cut you some of that turkey and put some of that dressin' in your plate and some of that gravy over it, then she put some of them sweet potatoes beside it. Then, boy, I mean, you just eat until you can't eat no more and you ready to pull yourself back from the table. But she say, 'Just a minute, baby.' And then she go in the oven and get out a sweet potato pie that's so sweet it's soft in the middle. She cut you a big piece and lay it on your plate, and you eat until you know if you swallow one more time you gon' bust. You say, 'Time for *me* to go to bed.' You fall across the bed. Before you can go to sleep, she put her arms and legs around you and make love to you all night and right before you fall asleep, the alarm clock go off. You get up and you go back to work. And, see, pretty soon it gon' tell on you, boy. It gon' tell on you. Yes, you gon' be at work. The boys at work gon' say, 'Ooo-wee! What is wrong with you? You look terrible!' You say, 'Naw, naw, naw, I got it made. I got the best wife on earth. Why, right now she's cookin' me the best dinner...'"

My daddy said, "Now, boy, that's a dangerous woman. That's a woman that'll make you kill yourself."

I said, "But, Daddy, what kind... I mean... what kind should I—"

He said, "Now, boy, don't you even worry 'bout it. I know what kind you gon' get 'cause you got a gentle side like me."

I said, "But Daddy, you ain't dead. You ain't workin' two jobs now."

"Well suh, you see, your mama told me if I didn't stop overworkin' myself that she wasn't gon' give me no more— I mean, she wasn't gon' let me—uh..."

"She wasn't gon' give you no more what, Daddy?"

My daddy looked at me and he raised his eyebrows and said, "You meddlin' now, son, you meddlin'. You better git on out of here an' go to your party."

CINDY ELLIE, A MODERN FAIRY TALE

MARY CARTER SMITH

O nce upon a time, over in East Baltimore, there lived a happy family: Sam Johnson, his wife Lula, and their daughter Ellie. Lula was good and kind; a quiet, church-going woman but mighty puny and sickly. One day Lula called Ellie to her bedside. "Child, Mama ain't feeling so well. One of these days I might leave you." "Oh, Mama, don't say that," Ellie said with tears in her eyes. "Don't cry, child. All of us go sometime, and I'd rather it be me than you. So there are a few things I want to tell you. Always mind your daddy. Stay in church, go to school, and learn that book. Remember what I'm telling you." "All right, Mama, I'll remember."

One day, not long after, the poor woman just up and died; real peaceful-like and quiet.

Honey, let me tell you, they had a beautiful funeral. Sam sure put her away nice. The Senior Choir turned out full force. The Junior Choir was there. And the Gospel Chorus just sung their hearts out! The church was crowded! Folks all on the outside, with loudspeakers going. Lula's lodge sisters was there in their white dresses, and them purple sashes all edged in gold. Ellie was on the front row beside her daddy. Just as cute as she could be in a white dress and her hair in a fine bush. Ellie was one purty young black sister, her skin like black velvet.

Child, let me tell you, that poor woman's body wasn't hardly cold before them church sisters was after Sam Johnson like flies after honey! 'Cause he had a good job down Sparrow's Point, with lots of seniority. And they had just paid for one of them pretty, big houses on Broadway, with them pretty white marble steps. It was a lovely block; won first prize in the AFRO Clean Block three years running!

That poor man, like so many good men, was weak for a pretty face and big legs and big hips. One huzzy, the boldest of 'em all, had a heart as hard as a rock. The milk of human kindness had curdled in her breast. But she did have a pretty face, big legs, and great big hips. Ooh-wee! She could put on! Made like she loved Ellie so, and was always bringing good barbecued ribs, collard greens, cracklin' bread, and jelly-layer cake to Ellie and Sam. Well, that fool man fell right into that woman's trap. She had that man cornered and married before you could say, "Jackie Robinson."

Then bless my soul. You ain't never seen such a change in nobody! First off that woman went down to Souse Car'lina for her two big-footed, ugly gals her Mama'd been keeping. Brought them back to Baltimore, and put poor Ellie out of the pretty room with the canopied bed and let her ugly gals sleep in that pretty room. Made poor little Ellie sleep on a pallet in the cellar.

Now Ellie's mama had been wise. When everybody else was converting they furnaces to oil and gas, she said, "Uh-uh. One day they gone be hard to get." She had kept her coal furnace. Poor little Ellie had to do all the cooking, cleaning, washing, and ironing. She had to scrub them marble steps twice a day and wait on them ugly gals hand and foot. Not only that, but in the winter she had to keep the fire going and clean out the ashes and cinders. So they got to calling her Cindy Ellie.

Tell you the truth, I believe that woman had put some roots on that man! 'Cause no matter how she mistreated Cindy Ellie, he never said a word, just *crazy* 'bout that big-legged woman.

That November, the good white folks, the good Asian folks, and the good black folks all turned out and voted for a good black brother, running for mayor. And he won the election by a landslide! He was having his inauguration ball down at the convention center. So many folks voted for him that they had to hold it for two nights running. The mayor's son had come home from college to go to the ball.

Oh, them stepsisters was primping and buying designer gowns to go to the ball. Poor Cindy Ellie had to give one a perm, the other a jheri curl, and both of them facials; not that it helped much. Honey, them gals was ugly from the inside out!

"Cindy Ellie, don't you wish you could go to the ball?" they asked her.

"Oh, you are making fun of me," Cindy Ellie said.

So Cindy Ellie's daddy, her stepmother, and them two ugly gals all went to the ball and left poor Cindy Ellie home.

Now Cindy Ellie had a godma. She had been her dear mama's best friend, and she still had a key to the house. She came to the house, as she often did, to sneak food to poor Cindy Ellie and found the child lying on her hard pallet, just crying her heart out!

"Why are you crying, child?" she asked her.

"Be-because I want to go to the ball."

Now this godma had been born with a veil over her face, down in New Orleans. She knew a thing or two about voodoo and hoodoo. Besides that, she had a High John the Conqueror Root that she always used for good. The godma told Cindy Ellie, "Go upstairs to the kitchen, child. Look in the kitchen cabinet drawer and bring me the biggest white onion you can find." Cindy Ellie was an obedient child. She didn't ask, "Why?" She just did what her godma told her to do. Cindy Ellie brought her the onion. She gave it to her godma. Then they went out in the backyard. The godma laid that onion on the ground. Then she stepped back and waved that root over that onion! And right before their eyes that onion turned into a long white Cadillac that parked itself in the back alley!

"Cindy Ellie go up on the third floor and bring me that mouse-trap." Cindy Ellie brought it down. There were two little black mice trapped in a little cage. She told Cindy Ellie to open the door and them mice started out. But that godma waved that root over them and they turned into two six-foot-tall black chauffeurs dressed in shining white uniforms with fancy white caps! And they had on long black boots! And they was bowing and scraping. "All right, Cindy Ellie, you can go to the ball now."

"But, godma, look at me. I'm clean but I'm ragged."

"Don't worry 'bout it," her godma said. Then she stepped back and waved that root over Cindy Ellie. Her rags turned into a dazzling dress of pink African laces! Her hair was braided into a hundred shining braids, and on the end of each braid were beads of pure gold! Her eyes were beautifully shaded and her skin was shining like polished ebony! Golden bracelets covered her arms clean up to her elbows! On each ear hung five small diamond earrings. On her tiny feet were dainty golden sandals encrusted with dazzling jewels! Cindy Ellie was laid back!

As one of the chauffeurs helped her into the white Cadillac her godma told her, "Be sure you leave before midnight or you'll be as you was. Your Cadillac will turn back into an onion, your chauffeurs into mice, and your clothes into rags." Cindy Ellie promised her godma that she would leave before midnight. Away she went, as happy as could be.

The mayor's son heard that a beautiful girl had arrived who looked like an African princess. He came out to see and said to himself, "This sure is a fine fox!" He asked her, "May I escort you into the ballroom?" Cindy Ellie replied in tones soft and low, "I don't mind if you do." He helped her out of her limousine and escorted her into the ballroom and to the head table where he was sitting. Every eye was on Cindy Ellie. You could have heard a pin drop. Then voices could be heard, "Gorgeous," "Lovely," "Devastating," "Elegant," etc. Even the mayor himself could not take his eyes off her. His wife agreed that she was indeed a charming young woman. The other ladies were looking at her clothes and wishing they had material in their gowns as beautiful as that in Cindy Ellie's.

Although the table was loaded with sumptuous food, Toussaint, the mayor's son, couldn't eat a bite! Just busy looking at Cindy Ellie. In her honor, the band played the Ghanian High-Life. Cindy Ellie and Toussaint danced it as if they had been dancing together all their lives. Cindy Ellie was friendly and courteous to everyone she met. She even sat beside her stepsisters (who had no idea who she was) and invited them to come back the next night. For Toussaint had begged Cindy Ellie to return for the second night of the ball.

Then Cindy Ellie heard the clock strike forty-five minutes after eleven! She murmered to Toussaint, "Really, I must be getting home." And she rushed out as fast as she could go.

As soon as she was home Cindy Ellie called her godma and thanked her for such a splendid time. The doorbell rang and she heard her stepsisters' voices: "Hurry, stupid! Open the door!" Cindy Ellie came, yawning and rubbing her eyes, as if she'd been asleep. "Did you have a good time?" she asked. "Oh, it was all right, but we didn't get to dance with the mayor's son. He danced only with some new girl. No one had seen her before. She had on some old African clothes. But on her they did look good. She did have the good sense to recognize what quality people we are, and she had the mayor's son invite all of us tomorrow night. "What was her name?" asked Cindy Ellie. "No one knows. The mayor's son is dying to find out who she is." Cindy Ellie said, "You don't mean it. Oh, how I wish I could go to the ball tomorrow night. Lillie, won't you lend me your old blue gown so I can go also?" They almost split their sides laughing. "You, with your ragged self, going to the inauguration ball? Wouldn't that be something else! Of course not. Come and help us get undressed and turn back the covers on the bed so we can go to sleep."

As on the night before, poor little Cindy Ellie was left behind while the rest of them went to the ball again. Her godma came in and heard the child crying again. "Why you crying, child? You want to go to that ball again?" "Yes, ma'am." "I thought so. You've been a good child all your life, and you always respect your elders. So don't worry. You can go to the ball again. Now dry your eyes and get your face together. Look in that kitchen cabinet drawer and bring me the biggest yellow onion you can find." Cindy Ellie came back with the biggest yellow onion you ever laid your eyes on. Then they went out in the backyard. The godma laid that onion on the ground. Then she stepped back and waved that root over that onion! And right before their eyes that onion turned into a solid gold Mercedes-Benz about half a block long! And it parked itself in the back alley.

"Cindy Ellie, go up on the third floor and bring me that rat trap." Cindy Ellie brought it down. There were two big white rats trapped in a big wire cage.

That family lived so close to Johns Hopkins Hospital that mice and rats used to escape from them laboratories up there. They took that cage out in the backyard. She told Cindy Ellie to open the door and them rats started out. But that godma stood back and waved that High John the Conqueror root over them, and they turned into two seven-foot-tall white chauffeurs dressed in shining gold uniforms with fancy gold caps! And they had on shining white boots! And they was bowing and scraping.

"All right, Cindy Ellie, you can go to the ball now."

"But godma, lok at me. I'm clean but I'm ragged."

"Don't worry 'bout it," her godma said. Then she stepped back and waved that root over Cindy Ellie. Her rags turned into a dress made of pure silk kente, that royal cloth from Ghana! Worth thousands of dollars! On her head was a geelee of the rarest of taffeta, standing tall and stiff and just gorgeous! Her big pretty eyes were beautifully shaded, and her skin was shining like polished ebony. Golden bracelets covered her arms clean up to her shoulders! On each ear hung five small diamond earrings. On her tiny feet were dainty golden sandals encrusted with dazzling jewels. She was cool!

As one of the chauffeurs helped her into that gold Mercedes-Benz, her godma told her, "Be sure you leave before midnight or you'll be as you was. That Mercedes-Benz will turn back into an onion, your chauffeurs into rats, and your clothes into rags." Cindy Ellie promised her godma that she would leave before midnight. Away she went, as happy as could be.

As they drove up, Toussaint was waiting for her. She went into the ballroom draped on his arm. Oh, they was having such a good time laughing and talking and cha-cha-chaing and waltzing and boogey-ing! That poor child forgot all about time! Then she heard the clock as it began to strike twelve! She ran out of there as fast as her legs would carry her. She ran so fast, she ran out of one of those sandals. She put the other in her hand and ran on. Toussaint ran behind her, but he couldn't see where she had gone. He picked up the golden sandal.

He asked the security people, "Did you see an African princess run by you?" "No. We did see a girl dressed in rags run out of the door. We thought she had stole something. But that chick was gone!"

That night when the family came home from the ball they told Cindy Ellie, "Something mighty strange happened tonight. As the clock on city hall began to strike twelve that African princess began to run like crazy! She ran so fast, she ran out of one of her golden sandals. The mayor's son found it and kept it. He just kept looking at it. He's really upset over that sister."

Child, the next day the mayor's son came on television, came on the radio, and announced to every paper in Baltimore that he would marry the girl whose foot would fit that sandal he had picked up. Now a lot of folks who had supported the mayor lived in the places surrounding Baltimore. So first all them sorority girls and debutantes and folks like that tried to fit their foot in that sandal. Wouldn't fit none of them girls in Columbia, Cockeysville, Randallstown, and places like that. Then they went to them rich folks' houses up on Cadillac Row and places like that. Wouldn't fit none of them girls neither. Then they went to all them condominiums downtown by The Inner Harbor and them fancy town houses. Wouldn't fit none of them neither. Finally they come to East Baltimore. Length and long they came to Broadway and knocked at the Johnsons' residence. The mayor's men came in with that golden sandal on a red velvet pillow. Them two stepsisters tried their best to put on that shoe! They pushed and they jugged. But their big feet would not get into that shoe. No way, Jose! "May I try?" asked Cindy Ellie. "No, stupid. It's not for the likes of you." "Yes, you may try on the sandal," the mayor's representative said. "For the proclamation issued by the mayor said that any girl in Baltimore and surrounding areas may try. He spoke kindly to Cindy Ellie. "Sit down, miss, and see if it fits you." And do you know, that sandal just slid on Cindy Ellie's little foot as smooth as silk. Then she pulled from the pocket in her clean but ragged dress the other sandal. As soon as she put it on her foot, right there before their very eyes, Cindy Ellie was transformed into the African princess they had seen the nights before! Them two stepsisters had a fit! "Oh, Cindy Ellie, we didn't mean no harm! Oh, Cindy Ellie, please forgive us!" They was on the floor rolling round and carrying on.

Cindy Ellie told them, "Get up off that floor and stop all that whooping and hollering. I forgive you."

Then Cindy Ellie was transported to the mayor's mansion in his private limousine. Toussaint was there waiting to welcome her with open arms. Cindy Ellie was true to her word, for she not only forgave her stepsisters in word but in deed. She found them two ugly councilmen for husbands. Toussaint and Cindy Ellie were married in the biggest Baptist church in East Baltimore, and the reception was held in the convention center. And they lived happily, happily forever after.

SI MARY BIGFOOT,
A FOLKTALE FROM ANTIGUA

ELAINE WARREN-JACOBS

Lang ago certain kinds of ailments were common. Dere was yaws, chigga, cocobay, an' bigfoot. Dere was dis lady, Si[1] Mary, an' she had a bigfoot. Smaddy[2] tell she fuh go see de bacra[3] dactah fram 'merica, but she say nat she. No dactah ago touch she foot—bacra ar no! So she continued to hav de foot. Anoddah smaddy tell she fuh go see de obyah[4] man. She say okay an' she went.

De obyah man tell she dat smaddy geh she de bigfoot, an' he cud cure it. But when she hear de heap a money he plan fuh charge she fuh he work, she tell he "fire he backside" an' left. So she continued to hav' de foot.

Well, if Si Mary had lived on an island by sheself, she cud a keep she bigfoot to sheself! But she lived among oddah people, an' de bigfoot became ebrebady problem. How? Hear dis. Si Mary house where she lived was at de head of de alley. Arl de oddah neighbors had to pass her place to get to an' fram dem house. Si Mary had a habit of pitchin' de water dat she wash she sore bigfoot inna, out in de alley. If you happen to be passin' by at de same time, you get arl dat sore foot water pan you. Dat happen often. Si Mary wash she bigfoot twice a day—marnin' an' afternoon. Man an' woman going to work get doused wit' bigfoot water an' pickinneagah going to

---

1. *Si* is sister
2. *Smaddy* is somebody. This term is common in the dialects spoken in Antigua and Jamaica.
3. *Bacra* is a caucasian or white person. Also *bucra* on the island of St. Croix. Both *bacra* and *bucra* are old terms and are not as frequently used in modern-day vernacular.
4. Obyah (also *obeah*) is witchcraft

school get doused, too. It is de same ting in de afternoon, too, when dem a come back. De neighbors got real fed up an' decide to do someting. Dey made up a song about her. It went like dis.

Si Mary tek she bigfoot water an' pitch um in de alley
Si Mary tek she bigfoot water an' pitch um in de alley
   No walk dey, no walk dey
   Yo ago ketch she bigfoot
   (repeat)

The song ketch on fas', an' young an' ole singing it daily. Si Mary was not singing. She was cussing. Whenever she heard de song, she cus an' cus an' cus till she cud nat cus anymore. It was den dat she decide to tek matters into she own hand.

One day she grabbed she walking stick an' a watwe bucket. She habbled over to de roadside where arl kind a bush grow wild. She pick pissabed bush, manbettaman, yaws bush, and cattle tongue, and carry dem home. Si Mary separated de leaves from de stems. She bruck de leaves up in a bason a sea water. The mixture was so green on top dat it looked lik duck pond.[5] Handful after handful, she took dat mixture an' scrubbed dat foot. She scrubbed it till arl de dry scab cum arf, till de sores turn red. When she finished, de foot was clean an' shining. But it was also a little sore an' tendah with a little rawness here an' dere.

Si Mary went to de druggis' and bought bluestone.[6] She sprinkled it on de sores. De burnin' started. Si Mary bawl out "me poor 'oman!" But Si Mary was tuff an' determined, an' she was not goin' to let any stinging fram de bluestone stop her fram curing dis foot. So she bore de bunnin' till it wore arf.

Si Mary no hav no bigfoot now. But de song is still famous. An' when she hear dem sing it, she join in an' sing an' dance as if de song is about smaddy else.

So de story en' so de nail head ben'.

---

5. *Duck pond* is a water pond located in Urlings village on the island of Antigua
6. *Bluestone* is a powdered preparation used to cure sores

UMU MADU
IN THE GOOD OLD DAYS

T. OBINKARAM ECHEWA

T here was once a village called Umu Madu where the people loved to have feasts. Every chance the villagers had, they called a feast to celebrate one thing or another.

"There is a new moon in the sky," the people of Umu Madu would say sometimes. "Let us have a feast to celebrate it."

"The moon is now full," the villagers might say a few weeks later. "Let us have a feast to celebrate the full moon."

At the beginning of the farming season, after they had planted their crops, the people of Umu Madu had a feast.

In the middle of the farming season, after the rains had started and the farms were green with growing crops, the people of Umu Madu held a feast.

At the end of the farming season, after the crops had been harvested and placed in the barns, the people of Umu Madu had a feast.

Sometimes even when nothing happened, the people of Umu Madu had a feast. If anyone asked them what the feast was for, they replied: "We are having this feast because nothing has happened."

Some of the feasts were small and some were big, but always there was a feast in the village of Umu Madu, and all the feasts were long and happy.

All the feasts were held under the big cottonwood tree in the middle of the market clearing at the center of the village of Umu Madu. The men killed the chickens or the goats or a cow, depending on how big the feast was. They also cut up the meat and cooked it in big iron pots, which they stirred with long sticks. The women cooked the soup and the stew as well as the rice and the fufu. Children fetched water or firewood and darted here and there on errands for the adults.

When everything was ready, the elders of Umu Madu appointed four or five young men to divide the food so that every man, woman and child would get a share. Fufu and rice were piled high on everyone's plate. Big pieces of meat stuck out above the surface of everyone's stew and soup. However, the heart of the feast was the big lumps of meat which were spread out in long rows on banana leaves or raffia mats. From the oldest man to the youngest child, the people of Umu Madu chose their shares of meat according to their ages.

For as long as anyone could remember, the people of Umu Madu had always eaten their feasts on the ground. Some people squatted ont the ground. Some people knelt on the ground. Some people sat on the ground.

Then one day a stranger arrived in the village of Umu Madu.

This was not the first time a stranger had come to Umu Madu. However, this stranger was very strange. No one had ever seen or heard anyone like him before. The villagers nicknamed the stranger No Skin because his skin had no color. No Skin had hair which looked like corn silk and eyes which shone like glass beads. At first everyone thought he had no toes, until he took off his shoes and allowed some of the villagers to count his toes. He had ten of them.

"Urupirisi. Urupirisi. Urupirisi," No Skin said to the villagers of Umu Madu. When someone was found who could understand No Skin's language, what he was saying was: "What have we here? Why are intelligent people like you eating their feast on the ground?"

"We have always eaten our feasts on the ground," the villagers replied. "Where do you want us to eat? On the treetops or in the sky?"

"Haven't you ever heard of tables?" No Skin asked.

"No," the villagers replied, surprised and a little ashamed. "We have never heard of tables. What are tables?"

No Skin began describing a table to the people of Umu Madu. He drew a picture of a table on the ground for them as he said: "My friends, these are modern times. If you want to be modern and up to date, you must stop eating on the ground and start eating on tables."

"Where can we find a table?" the villagers begged. "We do not want to be left behind by progress. We want to be modern and up to date."

"No problem," No Skin replied. "Send along four ablebodied men with me, and they will bring back a table to the village within a week."

Within a week, just as No Skin had promised, there was a table in the village of Umu Madu. It was big and long and heavy, and the villagers spent many hours admiring it, walking around it, rubbing their hands on it, and smiling at their reflections on its shiny top.

"This table is so good," the elders of the village said, "that we cannot wait until the next feast several weeks from now to try it. Let us have a feast at once and try the new table."

Everyone thought that was a good idea.

So a feast was called immediately. Two cows were killed. Fufu and rice were cooked in abundance. Everyone in the village came out to enjoy the big feast on the new table. No one bothered about raffia mats and banana leaves anymore.

However, as the young men who had been appointed by the elders began to divide the meat, they made a disturbing discovery. There was not enough space around the table for everyone.

"We have a problem here," one old man said. "How are we going to solve it?"

"Why don't the elders go into a conference with one another, as is our custom," someone suggested. "Let the elders tell us what to do about this problem."

"Yes, yes," everyone agreed. "Let the elders decide for us."

So the elders went into a conference. After a long time, they came back to the assembly and announced: "We cannot agree on how to satisfy everyone about the table. We cannot agree who should eat at the table and who should not. So we have decided instead to return the table to No Skin, so we can continue our unity and eat our feasts on the ground together, as we have always done. If we cannot find No Skin, we can put the table away, and he can take it back whenever he comes this way again."

"No-o-o-oh!" many members of the assembly shouted. There was a lot of murmuring and grumbling.

Then one young man said: "We now have the table, and everyone agrees it is a good thing. Would it not be foolish to let it sit idle? Would it not be even more foolish to give it back to No Skin? . . . All members of the assembly of Umu Madu who agree with me, please say Hay-ay-ay!"

"Hay-ay-ay!" everyone in the assembly seemed to shout.

The elders were surprised and disappointed. Not often did the community assembly fail to heed their advice. "All right," the elders said, "if that is the will of Umu Madu, then so be it. However, we will choose positions around the table according to age. Old people will choose first. People of Umu Madu, show that you agree with us by saying Hay-ay-ay!"

"Hay-ay-ay!" most voices shouted.

However, there were some voices which said "No!"

The village of Umu Madu liked to do things by having everyone agree. So the elders said, "If we cannot do it by age, how then shall we do it?"

One young man raised his hand and was given permission to speak.

"The times we live in are modern times," the young man said. "Modern times and modern things like the table are for the young. So I say, the young men should eat at the table. The elders can eat on the ground. Everyone who agrees with me say Hay-ay-ay!"

"Hay-ay-ay!" most of the young people shouted.

"No-o-o-oh!" most of the older people shouted.

The village of Umu Madu was faced with one of the sharpest disagreements its community assembly had ever seen. The elders looked at one another, shook their heads and scratched them. Then one elder cleared his throat and said:

"Perhaps we can do it by volunteering. Perhaps some people will volunteer to eat on the ground."

Everyone thought that was a good idea. However, when the elder said, "Who will volunteer to eat on the ground?" people began to answer: "Someone else."

"Who else?" the elders asked.

"Anyone else but me," everyone said.

At this point the elders decided to go into another conference. For a long time and after many debates they still could not agree on what to do. In the end they decided to settle the matter by drawing sticks. Anyone who drew a short stick would eat on the ground. Anyone who drew a long stick would eat at the table.

However, by the time the elders returned from their conference to announce their decision, the people were pushing, shoving, and fighting for places around the table.

"Shame!" the elders cried in dismay. "Shame, Umu Madu, shame!"

When the fighting stopped, the elders said, "All right, all right, if this is what we have been driven to, then let everyone keep the place he now has. Those of you who have occupied places around the table, keep your places. Those of you who are on the ground, stay on the ground. But please stop fighting like hyenas. We came here to feast, not to fight."

That was how the matter was settled for that day. However, it did not end there. Disunity had come to the feasts of Umu Madu, because when there was a feast some people ate at the table and some people on the ground. Envy had come to the feasts of Umu Madu. Those who ate on the ground looked enviously or rolled their eyes at those who ate at the table. Pride had come to the feasts of Umu Madu. Those who ate at the table stuck up their noses in the air and looked down on those who ate on the ground. Unhappiness had come to the feasts of Umu Madu. For the first time ever, everyone was not happy at the feasts.

Every feast that the people of Umu Madu held now ended in a fight. People came to the feasts not just to enjoy themselves but to fight for places around the table. Those who had eaten on the ground during the last feast thought it was their turn to eat at the table this time. However, those who had eaten at the table the last time thought they should do so again.

"Once a person has fought to get a place by the table," some of the villagers said, "he should keep it permanently."

Some villagers even felt that once a person had begun to eat at the table, his wives and children should also eat at the table, and even his children and his children's children, whenever they were born, should have the future right to eat at the table.

Some villagers became so angry at what was going on that they refused to attend any more feasts.

Then one day just before a very big feast, someone secretly sawed more than halfway through one of the table's legs. In the middle of the feast, when the meat and all other goodies had been heaped on the table, the leg broke, the table tipped over, and all the meat fell to the ground.

Various people accused one another of the trick. A big free-for-all fight broke out. Pots were broken. Basins of rice were kicked over. The meat was trampled underfoot.

The day after the big fight, the elders called everyone together in the market clearing. "Umu Madu," the elders said, "the table which No Skin gave us has been nothing but trouble. There is only one way to solve our problem—destroy the table before it destroys us."

"Hay-ay-ay!" the whole assembly responded in unison. "Let us destroy the table before it destroys us!"

The men, women, and children of Umu Madu went home and got their axes, machetes, clubs, and pestles and set upon the table and smashed it to pieces.

"Now we can be one again," one elder said after the task was done.

"Yes," another elder replied. "We can eat our feasts in unity and harmony once again."

"Yes," someone else in the assembly said. "Let us call a feast immediately to celebrate our freedom from the table."

"Yes, yes," everyone agreed.

A date was set for the special feast. Three cows were killed. Banana leaves and clean raffia mats were laid out on the swept ground, as in the old days. This was going to be the biggest and happiest feast Umu Madu had ever had.

However, just as the feast was about to start, someone pointed out that a few villagers had brought their own little, private tables to the feast.

"Why?" the elders asked. "Did we not agree to eat together on the ground as we used to do before No Skin brought us the table?"

"We agreed! Yes, we agreed!" a majority of the assembly replied.

"Why then have some people brought tables?" the elders asked.

"I now like tables," one table owner said. "I found No Skin, and he said I can have my own table if I wish. So, since I enjoy eating at a table, why shouldn't I be able to do so?"

"Me, too," another table owner said. "I not only like tables, but I have become so used to them that I can no longer bear to eat my meals on the ground."

Other table owners gave similar answers.

"You must destroy the tables," the elders commanded, "so that we can have harmony and unity as of old."

"My table is mine to do with as I please," one table owner said in an insulting voice. "It cost me plenty of money. No one can destroy it."

Another table owner agreed with the first one. He said: "If I cannot eat *my* part of the feast on *my* table, then I will not share in the feast at all!"

So the big feast which was supposed to bring back peace and harmony to Umu Madu instead brought disharmony and discord. There was first a long argument and then a big fight, during which many bones were broken. Since that day harmony and unity left the village and have not returned.

LIBERATED

J. CALIFORNIA COOPER

O nce upon a time, not too long ago but long enough, there lived Middy and James who had just celebrated their fortieth wedding anniversary. They had married when James was twenty-three and Middy was sixteen years of age. Middy was a smart young girl raised by solid parents till her daddy died and her mama, being a strong woman, never missed a step. She kept right on working and taking care of her family with an extra job or two . . . tired, toiling, but determined! I always say Middy took after her, except I knew Middy had big dreams for herself; I didn't know about her mama.

Yes, Middy dreamed she would go a long way in life, but when she was sixteen, James came along, back from some war, even way back then. He had looked good, was strong, and had deep healthy laughter. He had been raised by hardworking parents, and he was a solid hard-working man. He continued that way all his life. His mind had one direction . . . work, money, and buying property. He was like a lotta people . . . a little work here, a little love there; these things was his excitement and his living and never changed. Several women were after him, and that's probably what prompted Middy to get him first. She was one of them look-back-again girls, so she got him. She had always said she would be a virgin when she married, so when she lost her virginity, her mind and body followed. Some people said she was being foolish, but people can't tell you nothing for sure. . . . Only time can! Anyway she tucked them dreams of hers back in third or fourth place.

Middy told the white woman she worked for after school that she was gonna get married and was leavin' for good. The woman told her she would never be happy married to a poor black man, being used as a baby carrier and slave-worker woman. Ain't that somethin'! Middy thought a moment about that and knew that she wasn't really liberated anyway, the only difference between James and the white woman was makin' love! Other than the makin' babies, everything else was the same. And makin' babies could be fun! Besides, she loved James. She left!

You know, life proved out that white woman never did find a man to marry her, least not around here. She had a child out of wedlock and left town!

Anyway, Middy married James and closed that part of her life that was her dreams. They had two children, a boy, now thirty-eight years old, and a girl, now thirty-five years old. Several hundred times over the years she would be standin' over a washtub, early in the morning as the sun comes up, stars still out, birds singing and flying through the air, flowers and weeds just opening up to drink the dew, and she would look way off into her own mind and them dreams just stole out, but she push 'em back. They come out again when she be hanging them clothes up, she push 'em back. She be standin' over a hot stove, sweat running down her face, clothes sticking to her back and sides from the sweat of her body...them dreams come out, but she squeeze them back. Because she was lucky! James was a good man, working hard to take care of her and the children.

Work got lighter as the children grew up and moved away to college, but it never did stop. Forty years of washing clothes, cooking, making love, grocery shopping, cleaning, ironing, making love, sewing, mending, making love, looking at TV, making sex and reading books. The first two years were exciting, the next four were good, the next thirty-four were okay! Thank God, it was okay.

Finally, now, James was balding, treasured teeth left at the dentist. Both of them! Just changes! One thing at a time, one hair, one tooth. A piece of skin wrinkles here, another piece loosens there. A piece of brain sets, won't move again. Just things...don't you know?

James kept his wife and home satisfied but with no fringes. After being married twenty-five years he got an extra woman, Sally, who he also kept but gave none of the fringes to. Sally even paid a small rent. He insisted on that, saying his wife Middy would know if she, Sally, didn't pay. But he would give half of it back to her later and she, being a quiet and gentle type woman, thought that was very nice and accepted it and was very nice back to him and remained faithful. She

made him her own life. James always came to the house she rented
from him to make love, and he never took her anywhere, except fishin'
sometimes . . . his wife, you know. So she was very deeply involved in
the church for her social life and the sewing circles, which three or four
times a year went to the county fairs. James really had a nice, even life
and it suited him fine, leaving him time to work on his houses and use
his truck to haul things to the junkyard for the white folks. He got a lot
of clothes and furniture and stuff for his two women that way. He
didn't really need or want another woman besides Middy, but there
was a long-lived rumor still going round that a man had to have an
extra woman on the side or he wasn't a man! So he had one . . . 'cause
he sure was the man . . . in both houses . . . he said!

Now Middy was a small but energetic woman who did her work
but, with the children being grown and gone, her life had been given
over to readin' books and magazines and looking at TV. She could
care less about a sewing circle. She watched all the civil rights action
and had wished she wasn't too old for it. And now, the last few years,
television was full of liberated women and was about men and
women being equal and all! In the talk shows she would shake her
fist and scream and yell and argue with the TV and James would get
less, whatever. She had already told him she wasn't gettin' up cooking
breakfast anymore, only dinner and several other little changes which
didn't really bother James. He just attributed these things to
"womenfolk" and went on over to Sally's for breakfast or whatever.
Middy knew about Sally and at first, years ago, she was mad and
scared but held her own counsel and soon after she had thought
about it enough, she knew she wasn't going nowhere, she had a
home for life. Besides, several times, she got looks at Sally who was a
fairly nice-looking, clean woman, not a flaming Jezebel, so she decided to be quiet and accept the help. Let it be. Middy never thought
of another man for herself, hell, she had one! He took better care of
her than some of the women she knew. Besides, one little wiggling
thing couldn't be too different from another little wiggling thing up
there . . . so what for? Middy had never known another man to make
love to, so she could make no comparisons. She would rather watch
TV, read, or work on her list. Middy kept a list of all the things she
would do if she had money and was free. It was a long list but a few
of the items were: a fur coat, learn to drive, get a car, a diamond ring,
a diamond watch, silk underwear, go to Europe or India, a face lift, a
real hairdresser, and last but not least, clothes made just for her or

bought off the rack just for her! At that time all her clothes, even the dress-up ones, were secondhand from James's truck. Because James complained all the time of being broke she had quit bothering him, and after she checked to see if Sally was ever wearing anything new, and she wasn't ever, she just tried to look the best she could in what she had and did her own hair and shopped at the Five and Dime for her perfumes and creams. She liked to bathe and cream her body all over, put her perfume on over her patched nightgowns, and sip a little cheap wine out of the chipped crystal glass (from the truck) before she went to sleep. Champagne was on her list. That TV really was her window to the world. She was fifty-six and holding on to her living for dear life. James often told her, after some declaration or argument of hers, that she was watching too much TV, but she would laugh and say she "never would see too much TV! TV was a liberator!" Well, that's how the last ten years or so passed. Life goes on, you know, and on and on and on for some.

One day the television broke at the same time the library books were all read. The repair man came and said it was gone for good, they needed a new one. James said, "No, they couldn't afford it"; "Maybe next month, or so." He really should have run down then and got another one but, instead, he laughed to himself as he said, "Not right now, can't afford it!" Well, Middy turned herself to doing things around the house that you really never feel like doing. Cleaning out drawers and closets. Not just hers, but James's also. Now happy accidents are almost only somethin' you read about, but sometimes they really do happen! That's what happened to Middy! As she was throwing James's clothes across the bed to clean his closet a bankbook fell on the floor. She picked it up with no special interest because she knew they had a little money in the bank. James often showed the book to her. But when she took it from its case and opened it, it was not the same book . . . this one was still in both their names, but it had $38,978 listed as balance. Middy thought at first there was some mistake or a joke book, but her hands just kept moving with a life all their own and she went through those clothes and found the other book he had always shared with her. It had $2,000 as balance. She put all the clothes back, struck too dumb to even think about cleaning anything. She was in a daze. She replaced both books in his clothes and went to the kitchen and drank all the rest of her little cheap wine and went to bed, drunk!

It was at least two weeks or a month before Middy had formed her plans. During that time, James would catch her looking at him in wonder (she hadn't told him she knew) and ask, "What's wrong with you?" and she would answer "Nothing wrong with me!" She was thinking now about all them little pieces of property he had rented out and how long he had been doing carpentry work and hauling things in his truck...forty years! More than a thousand dollars a year he had saved! And still sent the kids to college and all! But she also thought of all he had made her do without, so he could save money! It was good...but not so good when she thought she had passed the age to enjoy some things that she would never be of an age to enjoy again! Just passed! Gone! Somehow, she knew, if this bankbook with $38,000 was in her name also, all the property was, too, 'cause if he was going to hold anything back to call his own, it would have been the money! After a few calls, anonymous, to the bank to find out how accounts worked and if she could withdraw any money, she learned about the "and/or" business, and checking the bankbook it said "or," somebody's mistake, the clerk's, not James's. Now when she pulled her list out, and she did that often now, she smiled all through her little body, head to toes. The next fishing trip James planned, he would be gone all day and all night. She was ready. She went to the bank with the book and started to withdraw $18,000 but changed to $20,000 because he would have the other account of $2,000. She wanted cash! The bank said, "What a large amount for cash!" Middy calmly replied James sent her for cash because he was buying another piece of property and the seller wanted cash. They told her to come back in an hour and she did. Then she took a bus to another small town and got a safe deposit box and put $18,000 in it and came home, but not before she signed up for driving lessons and bought herself a large diamond ring and watch, a bottle of champagne and a *new* satin nightgown! All the rest of that day she glittered and sipped and ate a filet mignon steak with all the trimmings and read a stack of the latest *new* fashion magazines. Bought and paid for by herself! Hadn't no rich white woman read or used them first. Everything was put away in the morning.

When James returned, laughing under his brain at how smart he was and how he fooled Middy and had enjoyed his little trip with Sally, they sat over cups of coffee, smiling at each other!

Middy wasn't worried about James finding out...she wasn't scared of him and it was rightfully half hers! But oddly enough, the bank didn't say a word to James. Thought he would know about his own money, I guess. She did think he would take the ring and watch if he knew, so she did not wear them. She learned how to drive while he was busy at work, then went to her safe deposit box and took half the cost of a new car out and put the other half on credit... after all, half was his. She parked it in a safe place and went home.

It was now time to go see a little of the world. She felt some pity for Sally and wanted to go talk to her but decided to leave well enough alone and didn't. She announced she was going to visit the daughter who taught school over in Atlanta. James smiled and said, "That is nice," so after he left for work or wherever, she got in her car and drove to Atlanta, went shopping at the best stores, bought a suitcase, and packed it in the store! The salesgirls laughed at her behind their hands, but she didn't even see them cause she was fulfilling *her* dreams, not theirs! She drove on to her daughter's, whose mouth opened in surprise when her mother drove up and announced she had come to see some City Life, some of the World! The daughter was just a country girl living in the city so the places she took her mother were ordinary places. A restaurant here, a nightclub or two there, very ordinary places. Middy asked her daughter, "This what an education and a good job got you? This kind of life? What's exciting in your life?" But campus parties and drinking and makin' love were what her daughter had been doing since her divorce, and she really did not know what her mother was talkin' about, so her mother left her, sayin,' "Better save your money so you can learn to do somethin' someday 'fore you get too old! It comes a time when it's too late for dreams... makin' 'em or makin' them come true!" Daughter laughed and said, "I don't have to worry, Mama. Daddy told me I'll be well taken care of when he die!" Middy drove off, scarf flying in the wind, saying, "He got to take care me first!" Middy stopped to get "just one more little thing" before leaving that shopping heaven, and right next door was a travel agency. She went in and browsed a minute or two, then pulled a page torn from her fashion magazines from her purse... a trip to Europe. Mostly Paris, France, but including Greece and Switzerland! She left the agency saying the "money will be forthcoming!" She drove home.

James was sitting on the porch... looking as if he had been dragged across fifty miles of hard road. He had even been cryin'. The first thing he said was, "Middy, where my money?" "What money?" Middy asked, deciding to leave her bag in the car. "Where you get that car? Whose car is that?" She started to answer "Ours" but changed to "Mine! You like it?" "No, I don't! Where is my money? That what you doin' with it? Spending it on every foolish thing? Spending it?" Tears in his voice.

Middy took a deep breath and resigned herself to go through whatever was to come with as little trouble as possible.

"That's what money is for, James, to spend if you need to and to save if you don't need it."

James was almost crying again. "I spose you *neeeeeded* that car?"

"You got a car and a truck, James."

"I work . . . I need them . . . 'sides, theys yours, too!"

"I couldn't even drive, James. Wasn't no car mine!"

"Why didn't you tell me what you wanted?"

"Been telling you forty years, James."

"Well . . . gimme the rest of the money and keep the car and all the rest them things you bought up there in Atlanta with our daughter! But gimme the rest! I'll see can I put things back together!" He held out his hand.

"What is that money for, James?" Middy looked up at James.

"Our children, Middy, yours and mine!" Hand still held out.

"We paid for their education, James. They can get their own!" She was still standing at the bottom of the porch steps. Suitcases still in the car, too heavy for her to carry, and she didn't want to ask James to carry them!

James sighed and wiped his brow. He didn't look like the proud owner of two women anymore.

"Gimme that money back, Middy! I worked for that money, Middy! Give it else I'm a hafta keep myself from half killin' you! I mean it!" His nose was runnin' now, and he didn't care.

Middy sighed and wiped her brow under the pretty scarf blowing in the breeze. "Can't, James! Just can't. Done worked for that money right 'long side of you. It's mine, too! And . . . if you almost kill me . . . I'll go to court and take half these houses and that will kill you." She didn't shout, though, she talked soft but firm. James snarled through snot and tears, but he did not move to half-kill Middy.

Middy came up a step. "James," she said softly, "you ain't never gone nowhere in forty years you wasn't wearin' something I washed, ironed, sewed, or hung up or folded. Not in forty years without somethin' I hadn't cooked, cleaned, stirred, and shopped in your body. I made the bed you sleep in every night for forty years!" Her voice almost lost control and shouted, but she caught it. "I am your wife...was your wife before them kids was your kids. I'm the one you spose to work for and with now. We did it for them already! I'm suppose to be more than a maid or a cook or a flat back in your bed! We work for each other!" She lost control, the voice went on up. "The kids have forty or fifty years more to get what we got! We don't! I'm going to live a little before I get on away from this earth! You can come if you want to, but if you don't I'm goin' anyway! Got to go! Been dreamin' about things all my life! If you goin' to make any more dreams come true, James, they sposed to be your own and your woman's!"

James's hand was still out but his head was bowed down to his knees, and he was rockin' back and forth and wasn't in no rockin' chair! Middy kept on coming. "I love my children...but to hell with them kids! They still gonna have plenty when I die! And the most important thing they will have is *breath!* To fill their own dreams and plans!"

James, a truly responsible man, bowed his head lower and cried. He wanted to hit her so hard her head would soar and fly like a bird...but he didn't want to divide his property...so he cried. Middy went on in the house and called the travel agency.

In a few weeks, after many hours of silence, with James dragging around, losing weight and sometimes snapping at her, punishing her by eating dinner out (over at Sally's, who thought he was falling more in love with her and out of love with Middy), Middy drove her car to Atlanta, bought a fur coat, put the car in storage, and boarded a plane bound for Europe. She sat in the seat, her list and plenty money in her purse which she patted unconsciously. She cried. Not from pity for James, not from fear...but for the joy in her heart at being able to live a few of her dreams. She thanked James in her heart for being the kind of man he was...a saving man. As the plane moved out on the runway and gathered speed to lift itself to the skies, Middy looked through the bright window, smiled through her tears...and flew away.

Switzerland first, for a rejuvenation program. Mud packed, mud bathed, massaged, exercised, coiffed, manicured, relaxed, handled gently but body coaxed somehow into looking like she had always wanted to look. Waking to a soft knock on her door, someone bringing fresh juice and fruits and breads ten minutes old, eating beside a window out of which mountains stretched to forever, sparkling white with snow. Tall green trees everywhere dripping icicles while inside her room the fireplace crackled with flames of warmth. Middy snuggled down into her satin-covered bed and thought to herself, "I never even dreamed of this," and slept. On my, she looked good when she left there two weeks later. On to Paris to a splendid hotel. She decided not to spend money on clothes made custom for her, she'd rather travel! There were beautiful clothes everywhere anyway!

The gentlemen in Paris, wealthy and middle class, looked interestedly at the little, healthy, bright-eyed, brown-skinned, well-dressed woman and sent flowers to her room and champagne to her table. She glowed and gleamed and spoke haltingly in French and English, sipped champagne held in the hand of the sparkling diamond ring and watch, to which diamond earrings had been added and one stone at her throat. They smiled in anticipation beneath their mustaches, but she allowed no one in her room after light dancing in the nightclubs was over. She kissed once or twice, her few false teeth firmly glued in place. Ohhh and the French perfume she wore! Her nose was as happy as the rest of her.

The one man she noticed most, sent the most flowers, candy, and champagne, but beyond a nod and smile, never approached her. She began to look for him in the lobby or dining room. One morning near the end of her stay (she had canceled out Greece but still the time was coming to leave Paris) she came down for breakfast and passing him with a smile where he sat with his roll and coffee, she stopped and said, "Bon jour!" He answered, "Good morning." He was French, however. Being the kind of black woman I know, she went directly to the point. "Why are you so generous to me with flowers and candy and champagne, yet you never say anything to me?"

He replied, standing and indicating the seat opposite him, "Will you join me for your breakfast?"

"Yes," she said, laughing softly, "I will, thank you."

She sat and asked again, "Why?"

He answered with a question, "Why?"

"Why do you send so many pleasant thoughts and never speak to me?"

He said, "I was waiting."

She said, "Waiting? For what?"

He smiled. "For you to come to me."

She smiled. "And so I did. Too aggressive!"

He smiled. "Too slow! But you are here."

She said, "Well...now...what were you waiting for?"

He said, "To spend my day with you."

She laughed lightly, pleased and smiling, then she raised the crystal glass of sparkling water to him, with the ice tinkling as she pressed it to her lips.

They spent the day at the Louvre and the sidewalk cafes between the sights he showed to her. Paris! It was a beautiful city. The evening was spent over dinner and wine with many glasses of champagne later at the club he took her to hear soft singing entertainment. The few remaining days were spent in much the same way. All pleasant. The last day before she was to leave, he stayed the night. I cannot describe it to you for I am not a poet. It was different and it was good. Perhaps because of the luxury hotel, the beautiful days spent doing beautiful things with delightful meals in lovely clothes, perhaps the expensive champagne. She had not even known this lovemaking was on her list of dreams, but she thrilled to all his touches and the woman in her who was neither young nor old was passionate, thrilled, and satisfied beyond even her knowledge of her dreams. She left the next day. For home? Where was home? On arriving in Atlanta much later, she cried again...for a different reason.

When she got home Sally was there with James. He said, "This ain't your home no more. You done left it, so go on away somewhere again, you got your money!" She answered, "Going away six weeks don't pay for forty years! Go on to your house, Sally, this one is mine!" James grunted but took Sally home. He came back to argue all night with Middy and even try to make love. She let him, but she stayed aware of how he felt to her. It was good...and comfortable, but there was no feeling except one of familiarity and that was not enough anymore, somehow.

Her thoughts in the next two or three months were so tangled. She drove a lot, going nowhere, walked a lot, going nowhere. Lay awake a lot, saying to herself, "Now listen here, enough is enough!" Herself answered back, "What's enough?"

One day she went back to the bank and got out enough money from James's account and went to the lawyers and paid $3,000 for the house Sally lived in and deeded it to Sally. Then she got a bottle of champagne, went to Sally's house to tell her, and give her a copy of the deed.

She told Sally, "You'd better do something for yourself before it's too late!"

Sally said, "But I'm going on fifty years old!"

Middy answered, "That's what I mean... you still got time... don't waste it! And another thing, I may still want my husband! Now you got your own house, so don't ever move in mine again!"

Sally said, "I sure won't! I'd rather have my own anyway!"

Middy said, "That's smart. Stay that way!" They finished the champagne and Middy left, leaving Sally high as a kite with a smile on her face.

Middy then went to a piece of their property she particularly liked and told the people they had thirty days to move, to keep their last month's rent and find a new place. When they had moved, she went in and had it all redone. New paint, new wallpaper, new stove, just new everything! All out of her own money.

James was fightin' mad and arguing and screaming all the time. Couldn't hardly work, but did. Had his own bank account now, all by himself. But signed the proper deeds for the little house Middy wanted for her own in exchange for her letting all his other future property alone till he died. However, all the property and its income was still half hers. She told him. "Take it and do what you want with it when you buy property, just see that I always have some money." She still takes care of all his home needs... when she is home.

She commenced to take them trips every six months or so. She go to Africa and Greece and France and everywhere. She took up that sculpture and some painting classes. Sometimes she stay for two months or so. Lately she been stayin' six months. House just full of things she bring back to sell. Say she may stay forever one day. Brings me back some material, beautiful, that some woman in Africa makes, 'cause I love to sew and knit.

I'm her friend, that's why I know all about it, and two years ago, when I was forty-seven years old, I got out and got me a job 'cause my husband never did save no money! He just always in the street playin' after he put in his eight hours! Ain't spent no time with me in years and years. The TV says he takes me for granted... say he neglects me! So I been saving my money, ain't spent a dime on nothin' but what I really, really, really need! It all goes in the bank! Made my reservation for that place in Switzerland for the rejuvenation, then I'm going on to Africa. Middy has made me a appointment with that lady who makes the homemade material, and I'm going to learn it and maybe start a little business of my own. Leavin' two days from now! My list ain't long as Middy's, but my money ain't neither and

I'ma have to come back and work again, but I don't care! I'm going where none of the people in my family ever been! I'm going to fly! My mama ain't never had a chance to do that either; now she is dead and never will have a chance! That map I learned in school, when I could go, gonna mean somethin' to me after all these years.

You may not think so, but liberated is somethin'!

Middy is liberated!

I can't hardly wait! I'm gettin' liberated, too!

FEBRUARY

DICK GREGORY

Dick Gregory says he does one-liners, but in between the one-liners he tells a story.

An example of black people's progress in America is that what we used to call Negro History Week is now called Black History Month. Of course, wouldn't you know that when they got around to giving us a month, it would be the month of February, with all them days missing? And when you think about the month of February, I think about the fact that most black folks I know not only don't like February, they don't even understand it.

Like what's a groundhog? On February 2, if the groundhog sees his shadow, there will be six more weeks of winter. Tell that to somebody living in San Diego. I remember the last February 2, I was in New York City. I was on this radio show, and the guy said to me, "You know, today is Groundhog Day. What do you think is going to happen if the groundhog comes out today?"

I said, "Man, you know I don't play that groundhog stuff."

He almost accused me of being un-American. I mean, this is an American tradition.

So then I said, "Okay, if that's the way you feel about it, ask me again."

He said, "Today is February 2. What do you think will happen when the groundhog sees his shadow?"

I said, "When the groundhog sees his shadow, it will be six more weeks of winter."

He said, "That's right."

I said, "Well, wait a minute. Let's don't stop. Suppose the ground-hog comes out today and doesn't see his shadow but sees five black dudes. What does that mean?"

He said, "I don't know."

I said, "Six more weeks of basketball."

Then we move on from February 2 to February 12. That's Abraham Lincoln's birthday, and it was always a big day in my hometown 'cause I lived in St. Louis, Missouri, which was right across the river from East St. Louis, Illinois. The fact that Abraham Lincoln was born in Illinois meant big festivities, and the fact that you were in St. Louis meant you really had big festivities. I never will forget: I was six years old, on my way to school, and I didn't know about Abraham Lincoln. I got to school, school was locked. A white cop came by, thought I was breaking in: "What you doing there at that school, nigger?"

I said, "I'm trying to get in."

"School closed today."

I said, "Closed today? For what?"

He said, "Abraham Lincoln's birthday."

I said, "Who's that?"

He said, "He *freed* you, nigger."

And I got to thinking about that, living in an all-segregated neighborhood, going to an all-black school, telling me I'm free.

The next day of February that we celebrate is February 14, Valentine's Day—not just Valentine's Day, but St. Valentine's Day. That's kind of amusing because that's the one day that people lie that don't lie no other time of the year. How many people do we know get more than one valentine card to send that say the same thing: "I love you, dear. Without you I'd just as soon be dead." One thing about Valentine's Day that I've always felt is that black folks need a greeting card. I mean, Hallmark has some beautiful cards, but it don't tune in to the black vibration. I mean, do you love me or not? That other stuff don't mean nothing to me. So if black folks got together and put their money together and opened up a black greeting card company, they would just have simple phrases:

I ain't gon' do it no more.

Give me another chance, baby.

I know what you're thinking about, but she hit on me first.

After Valentine's Day we get to the big one, the great February 22, which is George Washington's birthday. We know it's George Washington's birthday because they tell all these strange stories: George Washington chopped down the cherry tree, and his father didn't whup him. George just chopped down the cherry tree. It had nothing to do with him telling the truth. He probably walked in the house with that ax in his hand, and as a father of ten children I don't think I'd hit one of my children carrying a big ax in his hand either, especially if he had just finished chopping down a tree.

The interesting thing about February, you know, is Black History Month: black folks and white folks talking to one another and inviting one another by their houses for dinner. I just tell all my white friends that we can be friends but I don't want to come by for dinner, because they basically don't eat what I like. I mean, I don't like mushrooms; hors d'oeuvres is like an insult to me. You take one piece of cheese and cut it up five hundred times and put it on a platter. If we gon' have some cheese, just open up the refrigerator, pull it out, let me cut off a piece, and let's get down.

There is another thing they have, what they call "before-dinner drink, before-dinner wine." I was sitting at a white cat's house, and before I could tell him I didn't care for any, he had already poured me some. I drank one glass. Next thing I knew, I had drunk about eight glasses.

I asked him, "What kind of wine is this?"

He said, "Before-dinner wine. Why?"

I said, "Because I didn't get no buzz."

Well, he wanted to act like I was culturally deprived. He wanted to tell me: "Well, you know, when you drink before-dinner wine, you are not supposed to get a buzz. It's supposed to open the enzymes in your stomach so you have an appetite."

I said, "Man, I was hungry before I left my house. I didn't come over here to work up no appetite."

Later on, when they bring out the meat, it's got all that blood in it. I just tell them, "If you gon' cook it, kill it."

And so I don't go by white folks' houses for dinner. I got a lot of white friends, but we part when it comes to dinner.

Now, it's kind of interesting. I was talking to this cousin of mine, and he is really kind of weird. He has this Harvard-Yale mentality: finished Harvard, got his master's at Yale, and works for a company where he has an office on the second floor of a forty-two-story build-ing, and they got him believing that he's making decisions. We were talking about something one day, and he said, "Why don't you come with me. I got to go by these white folks' house for dinner."

I said, "Well, that's fine, as long as I don't have to eat. I have a lot of white friends, but they don't like what I like."

There's a whole different cultural pattern at work when black folks say, "Why don't you come by my house for dinner?" You going home, and they say, "Where are you going?"

You say, "I'm going to Mary's house."

They say, "Can I go?"

You say, "Come on!" and you just bring a crowd. That's a cultural difference because white folks are locked into a budget, whereas black folks aren't.

You know, white folks made enough money so they have the lux-ury of a budget, but black folks never had big money until recently, so we just spent. When a white person tells you to come by the house for dinner, that means the budget will admit *you*. If he says bring your husband or your wife, budget will admit two. Problems develop because a lot of black folks don't know that. A whole lot of black folks get together and get invited to white folks' houses for dinner, and they show up with fifteen, sixteen people. I remember this hap-pened to this white friend of mine who panicked. He called me and said, "Hey, man, I got a serious problem."

I said, "What?"

He said, "I invited this black couple by my house for dinner, and I'm looking out the window. It looks like about three or four thou-sand."

I said, "Now, just go back to the window and count 'em. It's not that many."

He came back and said, "You're right. It's thirteen. What should I do? I just have enough food for two."

So I said, "Treat them the way you would a white couple you had invited. Open the door, look 'em right in the face, and say, 'I invited two of you. You all can come in, but I'm feeding only two. The rest of you can all watch.'"

He said, "Oh, no, I can't do that! I'm scared!"

I said, "Then trick 'em. You know how to do that."

He said, "Well. What do you want me to do?"

I said, "Just open the door and say, 'Oh, I'm so glad you're here. My wife and I have been cookin' for three weeks. We just hope you can eat it all.'"

He said, "But Greg, I don't have enough food."

"You don't need 'nough food. Trick 'em. Just bring them on in, put them in the living room, and tell 'em, 'Food will be ready in about five minutes. We have enough food, but we don't have enough chairs. You have to stand around the table.'"

"I'm telling you. We don't have enough," he said.

"You don't need the food. Let the minutes pass, and then open up the door. Let your dog and cat run up there, jumpin' on the table, lickin' the plates, and black folks will leave."

Black folks don't play that cat stuff—cat lickin' my food, my plate. The cat can have my dinner. That's why I tell all my friends, my white friends: We can be friends, but I don't want nothing to eat.

COMMENTARY

STORYTELLING
AND COMIC PERFORMANCE

LARRY G. COLEMAN with remarks by
Bill Cosby and Alvin Poussaint

Humorous folktales were shared among the Black captives in the South from the beginning. They joked about the food they had to eat, about the size of their feet, about the unethical nature of some preachers. As poet Langston Hughes said, they were "laughing to keep from crying."

In Janheinz Jahn's *Muntu,* an anthropological study of the traditional world view of African people, words are portrayed as forces with the ability to assist people in their effort to accomplish goals. Words can do things, powerful things.

Black comedians like Bert Williams, Redd Foxx, Moms Mabley, Dusty Fletcher, Slappy White, Bill Cosby, Dick Gregory, Richard Pryor, Eddie Murphy, Whoopi Goldberg, and Sinbad are bearers of the African tradition of the power of words to entertain, to celebrate cultural traditions, to make political statements, and to provide a temporary release from frustration. They developed hilarious and memorable characters like "Moms," "Mudbone," "Fat Albert and Cryin' Charlie," and "Fontaine and the Old Raisin," and they taught us how to make light of our frustrations and how to shake off the terrible effects of situations over which we had very little control.

The following remarks of Bill Cosby and Alvin Poussaint, excerpts from a two-hour audio documentary I co-produced for National Public Radio, illustrate these ideas.

Bill Cosby: My particular philosophy is that, when I plant my feet, I want people to identify with this blackness that stands there. The only difference is that I don't bring the color to them. I want to get

431

the same kind of laughter, present the same kind of image that you get when you're sitting at the table with friends that you know.

As a child, we, the Cosbys, and, on my mother's side, the Hites, lived in Germantown. There were great dinners—Thanksgiving, Easter, Christmas, and then at times just plain everybody's gonna have dinner. And this was held at either of the homes of the grandparents, my grandparents. When I was young—six, seven, eight, nine—all I did was just come to dinner and sit, but the Cosbys, males and females, were all very, very dominant in speaking out and saying funny things. I knew they were funny because everybody would laugh, but I didn't understand what they were saying.

The chief funny person, the person who always just climbed all over everybody, was my grandfather, and the one who was funnier than he was was my grandmother, who would tell him to be quiet or say that that wasn't right, you know, and everybody would say, "That's right."

Because I lived a block and a half away from these grandparents of mine, I had a chance to listen to an awful lot of stories because that's what grandparents do. And whenever I wanted a quarter, I'd go down and wait for my grandfather to get off from work, and he'd come in and he'd go down to the cellar and fix the furnace and put the heat up for the evening, and then he'd reach up and grab one of his cigars, and then he'd begin to tell me some kind of story about life and some kind of philosophy, and I would listen, but mostly the tension that was building was when he was going to give me this quarter.

When I came into the business, it's like '63. Dick Gregory had already started his civil rights work, and I was working in Greenwich Village and doing long, extended stories. I had one extended story, I think it went for about twenty minutes, about Stephen Foster. Essentially, all it was about was lynching and the fact that there was an awful lot of things that black Americans had done that were really stolen from them. There was the story about Stephen Foster and what would happen when people would speak up and say: "This is our song Stephen has stolen," and, you know, the eraser was the rope.

One day I was sitting in the coffee shop, sitting with other comedians, and we were discussing how well we were doing in the Village, in these little coffee shops, and one of the guys jokingly said, "You know, man, if you turned white tomorrow, I don't think you would have any material." And I began to weigh that. I mean, what, essentially, was this guy saying to me? Was he saying to me this is the only note that I can play? Because I think I can play other notes. And is he saying to me his job is more difficult than mine because he has nothing to lean on, and is he saying that the white comedians are more flexible, therefore, more intelligent? So I said, "I accept." I accept this challenge. I began to erase the color, I began to go inside and find myself. Nine thousand is greater than nine, and as we all know, exaggeration is something that is great in comedy but in brain surgery is not too hip.

If I do my job and if I really, really were fantastic, the way I could describe it was I made some people throw up, I made some people's faces hurt, I made some people's stomach muscles hurt so much that they decided they did not like me, I made some people pee on themselves, you dig? I made some people bang on the table. I gave all of them a headache. I made them knock glasses over, made them hit each other, saying, literally saying, "Stop! I don't want to hear anymore. Give me a break."

Alvin Poussaint: Humor does heal, does keep you going so that you can laugh at your hardships, sustain your impacts, the oppression that you're facing. I also feel that you are in some way much wiser than the oppressor may see you, that you have your own thing.

Most good comedians, unless they're really contrived, who have that kind of special impact, the humor is coming from their own life experiences in some way: what they felt, what they experienced— some of the hardships, in fact—what they've been exposed to. Black humor has always taken a slice of life. I'm talking about the black humor that's more honest, that's not playing to white stereotypes.

Sometimes mixed with the humor is the sadness and the pain of the experience. Laughing to keep from crying. I think it served as a coping mechanism for black people in a number of ways. There's at least a number of styles of humor that black people had that they used functionally. For instance, there was the humor dating back to slavery which, essentially, was humor prepared for white people, to entertain them and to play into their stereotypes, because that's what they thought of us. And there was the more subtle kind, psychological humor, that we used for each other. It was a way of sustaining ourselves in situations that were very, very difficult—easing the tension, making the telling comments about the master, understanding their psychology. It's hard to imagine someone white quite like Richard Pryor or even Eddie Murphy or Bill Cosby. There's that special ethnic black tinge to what they do: taking snatches of life and the caricature and exaggeration, picking up on some of the subtle psychological relationships that go on between people and exposing them.

AH-LA-DEE-DA-DEE-BOP-DE-BOP: Raps, Rhythms, and Rhymes in the Storytelling Tradition

Fly like a butterfly, sting like a bee.
We all can't be like Muhammad Ali.

—*Children's jump rope rhyme*

RHYMES

THE PARTY

PAUL LAURENCE DUNBAR

Dey had a gread big pahty down to Tom's de othah night;
Was I dah? You bet! I nevah in my life see sich a sight;
All de folks f'om fou' plantations was invited, an' dey come,
Dey come troopin' thick ez chillun when dey hyeahs a fife an' drum.
Evahbody dressed deir fines'—Heish yo' mouf an' git away,
Ain't seen no sich fancy dressin' sence las' quah'tly meetin' day;
Gals all dressed in silks an' satins, not a wrinkle ner a crease,
Eyes a-battin', teeth a-shinin', haih breshed back ez slick ez grease;
Sku'ts all tucked an' puffed an' ruffled, evah blessed seam an' stitch;
Ef you'd seen 'em wif deir mistus, couldn't swahed to which was which.
Men all dressed up in Prince Alberts, swaller-tails 'u'd tek yo' bref!
I cain't tell you nothin' 'bout it, y' ought to seen it fu' yo'se'f.
Who was dah? Now who you askin'? How you 'spect I gwine to know?
You mus' think I stood an' counted evahbody at de do.'
Ole man Babah's houseboy Isaac, brung dat gal, Malindy Jane,
Huh a-hangin' to his elbow, him a-struttin' wif a cane;
My, but Hahvey Jones was jealous! seemed to stick him lak a tho'n;
But he laughed with Viney Cahteh, tryin' ha'd to not let on,
But a pusson would 'a' noticed f'om de d'rection of his look,
Dat he was watchin' ev'ry step dat Ike an' Lindy took.
Ike he foun' a cheer an' asked huh: "Won't you set down?" wif a smile,
An' she answe'd up a-bowin', "Oh, I reckon 't ain't wuthwhile."
Dat was jes' fu' style, I reckon, 'cause she sot down jes' de same,
An' she stayed dah 'twell he fetched huh fu' to jine some so't o' game;
Den I hyeahd huh sayin' propah, ez she riz to go away,

"Oh, you raly mus' excuse me, fu' I hardly keers to play."
But I seen huh in a minute wif de othahs on de flo',
An' dah wasn't any one o' dem a-playin' any mo';
Comin' down de flo' a-bowin' an' a-swayin' an' a-swingin',
Puttin' on huh high-toned mannahs all de time dat she was singin':
"Oh, swing Johnny up an' down, swing him all aroun',
Swing Johnny up an' down, swing him all aroun',
Oh, swing Johnny up an' down, swing him all aroun'
Fa' you well, my dahlin'."
Had to laff at ole man Johnson, he's a caution now, you bet—
Hittin' clost onto a hundred, but he's spry an' nimble yet;
He 'lowed how a-so't o' gigglin', "I ain't ole, I'll let you see,
D'ain't no use in gittin' feeble, now you youngstahs jes' watch me,"
An' he grabbed ole Aunt Marier—weighs th'ee hunderd mo' er less,
An' he spun huh 'roun' de cabin swingin' Johnny lak de res'.
Evahbody laffed an' hollahed: "Go it! Swing huh, Uncle Jim!"
An' he swung huh too, I reckon, lak a youngstah, who but him.
Dat was bettah'n young Scott Thomas, tryin' to be so awful smaht.
You know when dey gits to singin' an' dey comes to dat ere paht:
>   *"In some lady's new brick house,*
>   *In some lady's gyahden.*
>   *Ef you don't let me out, I will jump out,*
>   *So fa' you well, my dahlin'."*
Den dey's got a circle 'roun' you, an' you's got to break de line;
Well, dat dahky was so anxious, lak to bust hisse'f a-tryin';
Kep' on blund'rin' 'roun' an' foolin' 'twell he giv' one gread big jump,
Broke de line, an lit head-fo'most in de fiah-place right plump;
Hit 'ad fiah in it, mind you; well, I thought my soul I'd bust,
Tried my best to keep f'om laffin', but hit seemed like die I must!
Y'ought to seen dat man a-scramblin' f'om de ashes an' de grime.
Did it bu'n him! Sich a question, why he didn't give it time;
Th'ow'd dem ashes and dem cindahs evah which-a-way I guess,
An' you nevah did, I reckon, clap yo' eyes on sich a mess;
Fu' he sholy made a picter an' a funny one to boot,
Wif his clothes all full o' ashes an' his face all full o' soot.
Well, hit laked to stopped de pahty, an' I reckon lak ez not
Dat it would ef Tom's wife, Mandy, hadn't happened on de spot,
To invite us out to suppah—well, we scrambled to de table,
An' I'd lak to tell you 'bout it—what we had—but I ain't able,
Mention jes' a few things, dough I know I hadn't orter,

Fu' I know 't will staht a hank'rin' an' yo' mouf'll 'mence to worter
We had wheat bread white ez cotton an' a egg pone jes like gol',
Hog hole, bilin' hot an' steamin' roasted shoat an' ham sliced cold—
Look out! What's de mattah wif you? Don't be fallin' on de flo';
Ef it's go'n' to 'fect you dat way, I won't tell you nothin' mo'.
Dah now—well, we had hot chittlin's—now you's tryin' ag'in to fall,
Cain't you stan' to hyeah about it? S'pose you'd been an' seed it all;
Seed dem gread big sweet pertaters, layin' by de possum's side,
Seed dat coon in all his gravy, reckon den you'd up and died!
Mandy 'lowed "you all mus' 'scuse me, d' wa'n't much upon my she'ves,
But I's done my bes' to suit you, so set down an' he'p yo'se'ves."
Tom, he 'lowed: "I don't b'lieve in 'pologisin' an' perfessin',
Let 'em tek it lak dey ketch it. Eldah Thompson, ask de blessin'."
Wish you'd seed dat colo'ed preachah cleah his th'oat an' bow his head;
One eye shet, an' one eye open—dis is evah wud he said:
"Lawd, look down in tendah mussy on sich generous hea'ts ez dese;
Make us truly thankful, amen. Pass dat possum, ef you please!"
Well, we eat and drunk ouah po'tion, 'twell dah was n't nothin' lef,
An' we felt jes' like new sausage, we was mos' nigh stuffed to def!
Tom, he knowed how we'd be feelin', so he had de fiddlah 'roun',
An' he made us cleah de cabin fu' to dance dat suppah down.
Jim, de fiddlah, chuned his fiddle, put some rosum on his bow,
Set a pine box on de table, mounted it an' let huh go!
He's a fiddlah, now I tell you, an' he made dat fiddle ring,
'Twell de ol'est an' de lamest had to give deir feet a fling.
Jigs, cotillions, reels an' breakdowns, cordrills an' a waltz er two;
Bless yo' soul, dat music winged 'em an' dem people lak to flew.
Cripple Joe, de old rheumatic, danced dat flo' f'om side to middle,
*Th'owed away his crutch an' hopped it; what's rheumatics 'ginst a
    fiddle?*
Eldah Thompson got so tickled dat he lak to los' his grace,
Had to tek bofe feet an' hol' dem so 's to keep 'em in deir place.
An' de Christuns an' de sinnahs got so mixed up on dat flo',
Dat I don't see how dey'd pahted ef de trump had chanced to blow.
Well, we danced dat way an' capahed in de mos' redic'lous way,
*'Twell de roostahs in de bahnyard cleahed deir th'oats an' crowed fu'
    day.*
Y' ought to been dah, fu' I tell you evahthing was rich an' prime,
An' dey ain't no use in talkin', we jes had one scrumptious time!

JUMP ROPE RHYMES

TRADITIONAL

Jump rope rhymes are primarily told by girls, but boys have been known to make up a few also. These rhymes and songs are a combination of a game, a song, and a story (the action is centered on a character or a plot). The African-American jump rope rhymes and play-party songs accompany ring games or dancelike movements. Some are very simple, such as "Little Sally Walker sitting in her saucer"; others are more complicated, such as "Foot-hop, limbo rock—take it to the top and down to the bottom and spell your name on one foot," a double-Dutch jump rope chant. Jump rope rhymes and play-party songs reflect the rhythms and events in communities both urban and rural. These childlike chants and tunes tell us what children are listening to, what is influencing them, and how they feel about what is going on around them.

AUNT DINAH DIED
from the backyards of Alcoa, Tennessee

CALL: *Aunt Dinah died.*

RESPONSE: *How she die?*

CALL: *Oh she die like this* (makes facial expression and gestures).

RESPONSE: *Oh, she die like this* (participants imitate expression and gesture).

CALL: *Aunt Dinah died.*

RESPONSE: *How she die?*

CALL: *Oh, she die like this* (does expression and gesture).

RESPONSE: *Oh, she die like this.*

CALL (excited): *Aunt Dinah's living!*

RESPONSE: *Where she living?*

ALL (fast): *Oh, she living in a place called Tennessee.*
She wear short, short dresses up above her knees.
She gon' shake that shimmy wherever she go.
Hands up, tootsie-tootsie-tootsie-too.
Hands down, tootsie-tootsie-tootsie-too.
Turn around, tootsie-tootsie-tootsie-too.
Touch the ground, tootsie-tootsie-tootsie-too.

(Repeat.)

ALL HID
from the backyards of Alcoa, Tennessee

CALL: *Last night*
Night before
Twenty-five blackbirds
At my door.
I got up
Let 'em in
Hit 'em in the head
With a rolling pin.
All hid!

RESPONSE: *All hid!*

CALL: *All hid!*

RESPONSE: *All hid!*

ALL: *5, 10, 15, 20, all hid, all hid.*

CALL: *25, 30, 35, 40, 45, 50, 55, 60, all hid.*

RESPONSE: *All hid!*

CALL: *All hid!*

RESPONSE: *All hid!*

ALL: *5, 10, 15, 20, all hid, all hid.*

CALL: *65, 70, 75, 80, 85, 90, 95, 100, all hid.*

RESPONSE: *All hid!*

CALL: *All hid!*

RESPONSE: *All hid!*

ALL: *5, 10, 15, 20, all hid, all hid.*

CALL: *Jack be nimble, Jack be quick, Jack jump over the candle-*
            stick.
            Little boy blue, come blow your horn, sheep in the
            meadow, cows in the corn.
            Tom, Tom, the piper's son, stole a pig and away he run.
            Peter, Peter, pumpkin eater, had a wife but couldn't keep
            her.
            Juba this and Juba that, Juba stole a yellow cat.
            I spy a pocketful of rye, how many blackbirds in my pie?
            All hid!

RESPONSE: *All hid!*

CALL: *All hid!*

RESPONSE: *All hid!*

ALL: *5, 10, 15, 20, all hid, all hid.*

PIZZA, PIZZA, DADDY-O!
from the Philadelphia School at 25th and Lombard
in South Philadelphia

CALLER: *(Jimmy) is having a birthday party.*

RESPONSE: *Pizza, pizza, daddy-o!*

CALLER: *How you know it?*

RESPONSE: *Pizza, pizza, daddy-o!*

CALLER: *'Cause I saw it!*

RESPONSE: *Pizza, pizza, daddy-o!*

CALLER: *Let's jump it!*

RESPONSE: *Jump it, jump it, daddy-o!*

CALLER: *Let's shake it!*

RESPONSE: *Shake it, shake it, daddy-o!*

CALLER: *Let's hop it!*

RESPONSE: *Hop it, hop it, daddy-o!*

CALLER: *Let's twist it!*

RESPONSE: *Twist it, twist it, daddy-o!*

CALLER: *Let's monkey it!*

RESPONSE: *Monkey it, monkey, it, daddy-o!*

CALLER: *Let's boogie it!*

RESPONSE: *Boogie it, boogie it, daddy-o!*

(Repeat entire chant using a different name. "Monkey it" refers to a rhythm and blues dance.)

MISS SUE
from the schoolyard of Henry Houston Public School in the Germantown section of Philadelphia

Miss Sue (clap, clap),
Miss Sue (clap, clap),
Miss Sue from Alabam.
She got the A-B-C-D-E-F-G
She got the H-I-J-K-L-M-N-O-P
She got the smooth thighs
She got the smooth thighs
She got the freeze —
My name is Black-eyed Peas.

I'M A STAR
from Sharon Wilson Dixon's third-grade class in Winchester, Virginia

LEADER: *My name is (Sarah).*

RESPONSE: *Uh huh.*

LEADER: *And I'm a star.*

RESPONSE: *Uh huh.*

LEADER: *You mess with me*

RESPONSE: *Uh huh.*

LEADER: *I'll take you far.*

RESPONSE: *Uh! She think she bad.*

LEADER: *Correction, baby, I know I'm bad.*

RESPONSE: *Uh! She think she bad, po-leeease leeease.*

LEADER: *Honeey! Po-leease (please).*

(Repeat. Different leader, change name.)

CHITTY CHITTY BANG BANG!
from the Mount Airy neighborhood in Philadelphia

Chitty Chitty Bang Bang!
Sitting on a fence.
Trying to make a dollar
Out of 15¢.
She missed, she missed, she missed like this.
She missed, she missed, she missed like this.
Chitty Chitty Bang Bang!
I can shake my body.
Chitty Chitty Bang Bang!
I can do ka-ra-te.
Chitty Chitty Bang Bang!
I can hurt somebody.
Chitty Chitty Bang Bang!
Oops! I'm sorry.

The first six lines of "Chitty Chitty Bang Bang," are told in the traditional style and can be heard in schoolyards in urban cities. I heard the chant and the other lines from a child in my neighborhood back in 1979.

JOHN HENRY

LEADBELLY (Huddie Ledbetter)

A work song is when you sing—that gives you a feelin' and keeps you from gettin' tired. And when you get hongry, if you sing, you forget about bein' hongry. And when you sing, you swing, *as* you sing; and that's what you call a work song—it's a feelin'. John Henry was a steel-*drivin'* man—well, that's mighty fine—he was a double-jointed man, I don't guess you knew that, did you? That's what made him drive so much steel. He drove steel from Newport—Cincinnati, Ohio, and he drove all that by himself. So I'll tell you a story about it—

John Henry was a newborn baby, settin' down on his mama's knee,
Say that Big Ben toyin' on that Savannah tunnel
It is going to be the death of me, Lord, Lord, it is going to be the death
   of me.
It is going to be the death of me, Lord, Lord, it is going to be the death
   of me.

John Henry had two women, one was named Mary Magdalene.
She would go out on the job and she would sing,
"Can you hear John Henry's hammer ring, Lord, Lord, can you hear
   John Henry's hammer ring?"
Can you hear John Henry's hammer ring, Lord, Lord, can you
   hear, can you hear John Henry's hammer ring?"

John Henry had another little woman, her name was sweet Polly Ann.
John Henry taken sick, boy, had to go to bed,
Polly Ann drove steel like a man, Lord, Lord, Polly Ann drove steel like
a man.
Polly Ann drove steel like a man, Lord, Lord, Polly Ann drove steel like
a man.

John Henry was sick, he called Polly Ann to his bedside, and this is what he asked her:

Baby, who's going to shoe your little feet, baby, who's going to glove your
hand,
Tell me who's going to kiss you sweet little lips,
Tell me who's going to be your man, Lord, Lord, tell me who's going to
be your man.
Tell me who's going to be your man, Lord, Lord, tell me who's going to
be your man.

This is what she told him:

My papa's going to shoe my little feet, my mama's going to glove my
hand,
My sister's going to kiss my sweet little lips,
And you know I don't need no man, Lord, Lord, you know I don't need
no man.
And you know I don't need no man, Lord, Lord, you know I don't need
no man.

Talk to 'em now!

They take John Henry to the White House, and they bury him in the
sand,
And every locomotive comes a-rollin' by sayin'
"There lie that steel-drivin' man, Oh Lord, there lie that steel-drivin'
man.
There lie that steel-drivin' man, Oh Lord, there lie that steel-drivin'
man."

THE TALE OF BOLL WEEVIL

LEADBELLY (Huddie Ledbetter)

A blues is a feelin'—and when you get the blues, it'll make some people wear out their shoes and they got the blues when they wear out their shoes and blues is the sad news. The Boll Weevil—I'll tell you a little story about it—which is a bug long years ago—robbed people of their homes—and ever since the Boll Weevil been gone—the people been singin' this song:

You can talk about the latest, the latest of your home,
These Boll Weevils they will rob you of a home,
They're a-lookin' for a home, they're a-lookin' for a home.

One time I seen a Boll Weevil, he was settin' on a square,
Next time I seen the Boll Weevil, he had his whole family there,
He was lookin' for a home, he was lookin' for a home.

The farmer take the Boll Weevil, put him in the sand,
The Boll Weevil said to the farmer, "You treat me just like a man.
And I'll have a home, and I'll have a home."

I will have a home, I will have a home,
I will have a home, I will have a home

The farmer take the Boll Weevil, put him on the ice,
Boll Weevil said to the farmer, "You's treatin' me mighty nice,
And I'll have a home, and I will have a home."

The old lady said to the old man, "I been tryin' my level best,
To keep these Boll Weevils out of my brand-new cotton dress,
And it's full of holes, and it's full of holes."

The old man said to the old lady, "What do you think of that?
I got one of them Boll Weevils out of my brand-new Stetson hat,
And its full of holes, and it's full of holes."

It is full of holes, it is full of holes,
It is full of holes, it is full of holes.

Now the farmer he said to the merchant, "I never made but one bale,
Before I'll let you have that last one, I will suffer and die in jail,
I will have a home, I will have a home."

Now this last verse is about myself and I want you children to come
in on the chorus—"He's lookin' for a home."

Now, if, anybody should ask you children, who made up this song?
Tell 'em this is Huddie Ledbetter, he's done been here and gone,
He's lookin' for a home, he's lookin' for a home.

Now come with me!

He's lookin' for a home, he's lookin' for a home,
He's lookin' for a home, he's lookin' for a home.

THE LEGEND OF DOLEMITE

Retold by MLANJENI NDUMA

My folks used to say that it was me . . .
That I was the baddest one, the world's ever seen.
But that's not true
For there was one person badder than me or you.
So relax and sit tight
While I tell you about a bad little boy named Dolemite.
Now Dolemite was born in San Antoine
A bold, cold, bad little boy from the day he was born.
From the time he came from the hospital
Till he was a man,
Dolemite put everyone in a horrible jam.
Now why is that, you may say,
Because Dolemite did everything his way.
At the age of one
He was drinking sodas with the men.
At the age of two
He was eating the bottles the sodas came in.
At three
He could throw a stone farther than you could see.
At four
He could throw a tree.
Whenever his mom tried to say grace,
Dolemite said, "Hey, cool out, Mom.
I'm running this place."
When he was supposed to eat

451

Dolemite would be running in the street.
When he was supposed to sleep
Dolemite would be ready to eat.
No matter what his mom would say
Dolemite did everything his way.
His mom said every day,
"Dolemite, you need to get yourself together and do right."
And Dolemite would look and say,
"Mom, you want to fight?"
"Don't talk to your mom that way,"
Aunt Mabel said one day.
"Treat her with love and respect."
"Aunt Mabel," said Dolemite,
"I don't have to listen to you,
And if you don't get quiet,
I'm going to pop you with my shoe."
Well, Aunt Mabel told Dolemite's uncle
'Bout what he'd said.
His uncle's eyes got bloodred.
He said, "Let me go over there and see how he's treating his ma.
Let me go over there before that little guy goes too far."
So Dolemite's Uncle Jim came over.
He said, "Dolemite, you better straighten up and treat your mother
Right,
'Cause if you keep on with your mistreating,
I'm gonna beat you till your heart stop beating."
Now Dolemite had been on the living room floor playing.
He looked at his uncle and said,
"Uncle, I don't hear nothing you're saying."
That made Dolemite's uncle real mad.
He took off his belt and started twirling it in place.
But Dolemite grabbed it and pushed it in his uncle's face.
His uncle ran out and shouted for help.
He now knew Dolemite needed more than a belt.
So all the men of San Antoine came out that night
To see what they could do about that bad little boy called
Dolemite.
It took one hundred of the baddest, the fattest, the ugliest men
In town
To go in there and hold Dolemite down.

They took him to jail
Held him without bail.
The judge said,
"Dolemite, we're gonna hold you here until you say, 'I'm sorry.'
Is that clear?"
Dolemite said, "Hey judge, I'm not saying it tonight.
And if I get out of here, you and me's gonna fight."
The judge said, "Eight years.
Lock him up now, tight."
It was eight long years
Nothing but water and bread,
The average boy would have long been dead,
But not him, not Dolemite.
For it was just as I say
Dolemite did everything his way.
His mom would visit him every other night,
She would say,
"Dolemite, you need to get yourself together and do right."
One day the sheriff came up and said,
"Dolemite, we gonna do you a favor,
We gonna open the door, give you a dollar and one good meal
If you promise to leave us alone
And get out of our city, San Antoine."
Dolemite said, "Okay, Sheriff, I'll take your dollar and
Your one good meal,
And as soon as I fight you, I promise to leave,
Is it a deal?"
So the sheriff opened the door.
Dolemite knocked him out right on the floor,
Took the dollar and the one good meal,
But didn't keep the rest of the deal.
Started beating up everyone in San Antoine,
Beating up everyone till they'd moan.
For it was just as I say
Dolemite did everything his way.
Beat up the bus driver for not saying please,
Kicked a man for trying to sneeze,
Beat up a puppy for trying to bite,
Kicked a lady for saying, "That's not right."
Dolemite would beat up anyone any day.

He wanted everything his way.
One day he said, "I'm going over Tennessee way."
It came on the news that night.
The announcer said, "Watch out. Watch out
For fire, bombs, and that bad boy, Dolemite."
Dolemite started walking,
Came to a stream.
"Hey, move," said Dolemite, "move."
The stream screamed,
"Yes, sir, Mr. Dolemite."
And made the biggest path you've ever seen.
Next Dolemite came to some mountains.
"Mountains," he said, "what yaw'll gonna do?"
They said, "We're gonna part, Mr. Dolemite,
And let you on through."
Roads jumped, rocks rolled, trees moved away.
There was nothing that Dolemite couldn't sway.
Until he came to Kentucky.
There he found right on the street
A boy named Two Gun Pete.
"Move," said Dolemite, "I'm going past."
"You move," said Pete, "and make it fast."
"You want to fight?" said Dolemite.
Pete said, "Hey, you got that right."
Dolemite grabbed Pete, and Pete grabbed Dolemite.
They started twisting, punching, turning around
But for one whole day and night
Neither could punch the other down,
Neither would fall to the ground.
They punched, they kicked, they hit,
But neither could win, even a bit.
Dolemite finally jumped up in the sky.
He said, "Let's see if you can jump this high?"
Pete did.
Jumped on a cloud
And tried to push Dolemite down.
The fight started again,
But those two never came back to the ground.
From that day to this
They're still up in the air

Fighting on clouds just about anywhere.
Pushing, bumping, punching, thumping.
You can hear them,
Especially on warm summer nights,
That thunder you hear
Is Pete
Fighting
That bad little boy
Named Dolemite.

SIGNIFYIN' MONKEY

OSCAR BROWN, JR.

Said the signifyin' monkey to the lion one day:
"Hey, dere's a great big elephant down th' way
Goin' 'roun' talkin', I'm sorry t' say,
About yo' momma in a scandalous way!"

"Yea, he's talkin' 'bout yo' momma an' yo' grandma, too;
And he don' show too much respect fo' you.
Now, you weren't there an' I sho' am glad
'Cause what he said about yo' momma made me mad!"

Signifyin' monkey, stay up in yo' tree
You are always lyin' and signifyin'
But you better not monkey wit' me.

The lion said, "Yea? Well, I'll fix him;
I'll tear that elephant limb from limb."
Then he shook the jungle with a mighty roar
Took off like a shot from a forty-four.

He found the elephant where the tall grass grows
And said, "I come to punch you in your long nose."
The elephant looked at the lion in surprise
And said, "Boy, you better go pick on somebody your size."

But the lion wouldn't listen; he made a pass;
The elephant slapped him down in the grass.

The lion roared and sprung from the ground
And that's when that elephant really went to town.

I mean he whupped that lion for the rest of the day
And I still don't see how the lion got away
But he dragged on off, more dead than alive,
And that's when that monkey started his signifyin' jive.

The monkey looked down and said, "Oooh wee!
What is this beat-up mess I see?
Is that you, Lion? Ha, ha! Do tell!
Man, he whupped yo' head to a fare-thee-well!

"Give you a beatin' that was rough enough;
You' s'pposed to be king of the jungle, ain't dat some stuff?
You big overgrown pussycat! Don' choo roar
Or I'll hop down there an' whip you some more."

The monkey got to laughing and a' jumpin' up an' down,
But his foot missed the limb and he plunged to the ground.
The lion was on him with all four feet
Gonna grind that monkey to hamburger meat.

The monkey looked up with tears in his eyes
And said, "Please, Mr. Lion, I apologize,
I meant no harm, please, let me go
And I'll tell you something you really need to know."

The lion stepped back to hear what he'd say,
And that monkey scampered up the tree and got away.
"What I wanted to tell you," the monkey hollered then,
"Is if you fool with me, I'll sic the elephant on you again!"

The lion just shook his head, and said, "You jive . . .
If you and yo' monkey children wanna stay alive,
Up in them trees is where you better stay"
And that's where they are to this very day.

Signifyin' monkey, stay up in yo' tree
You are always lyin' and signifyin'
But you better not monkey wit' me.

DE WEDDING

PAUL KEENS-DOUGLAS

Paul Keens-Douglas tells this story in rhyme in a Trinidadian dialect.

Yu know someting,
When yu mind tell yu not to do someting,
Is not to do it.
Take ah man like me for instance,
I happy, happy siddown in me wuk,
Enjoyin' meself, mindin' me business,
Not interferin' with nobody,
When dis fella name Errol, come cool, cool so
An' invite me to wedding.
Now I is ah man don't like to go
In any and everybody wedding,
Because my mother always used to tell me
Dat all skin-teet is not grin,
To make sure ah pick me friends,
An' not to hang me hat
Where me hand can't reach.
Plus, every time I go in wedding,
Is ah whole set ah money ah does have to spend
An ah could never ever eat enough to cover it.
But Mr. Errol wukkin in de same office with me,
So ah feel kind ah funny to come out plain, plain so

An' tell him dat me eh feel like goin' in he wedding.
Plus how I figure it out,
De whole office go put together to give he present
So dat bound to cut down on me costs,
So yu boy brains wukkin overtime.
Now Errol is ah fella
Dat me dont lime too much with,
So ah wasn't too sure wha' kinda friends
He would ah have in dis wedding.
An' dat is another ting,
Me don't like to rub shoulder
With any an' everybody,
But he is ah real speaky spokey fella,
So it eh take him long to drop ah hint
'Bout how it go' be one big wedding,
With all kinda big-pappy guests an' ting
An he say to me, "Keith boy, de way I figure it
Is like ah have to spend 'bout ten thou' for sure."
Den he start sayin' how is ah real "treads" fete,
An' how everybody comin' dress up, dress up. An' he carryin' on.
Now I figure he tryin' to give me ah "wire,"
Because everybody know
Dat me don't dress up to go nowhere.
Dis one pair ah slipper ah have on me foot here,
Is dat ah does wear to wuk, church, an' funeral.
Well me eh tell he nutten, ah jus' let him talk.
But like is better ah did tell him someting yes,
Because dat man wedding was someting else.
Fus of all he put me in expense.
I get up early, early to organize me clothes,
An' who tell yu ah eh burn ah big whole in me one good shirt?
An' ah didn't have another clean one to put on,
So is straight in the dutty clothes basket ah had to go,
An' is because ah had to wear dis half-dutty shirt ah did throw dey.
Ah put it in de sun for ah while to air out,
An' den ah give it ah dry-clean with some Old Spice.
So I head for dat wedding smellin' like ah drugstore,
People only lookin' round to see where de smell comin' from,
Ah straight case of dutty-clothes basket an' Old Spice.
Well, when ah reach de place where dis wedding suppose to be —

Me eh go in no church yu know, dat was askin' ah bit much,
I decide ah only goin' by de house for de reception,
Yes, when ah reach de wedding place ah get ah shock.
De way dis man talk 'bout de amount ah guest an' ting
Dat he did expect in dis wedding,
I say ah go see 'bout ah tousand car park up dey
With police directing traffic.
Partner, ah only see 'bout two car park in front de house.
So ah say to meself, ah early.
So I just makin' up me mind to make ah rounds round de block,
When ah spot ah little fella standin' by de gate,
So ah decide to ask he if he see ah wedding pass by dey.
He tell me wedding reception start long days.
Yu know is only two car dey had in dat man wedding?
Is like everybody walk.
Now dey eh have nothing in dat,
Ah mean, not everybody bound to have car in dey wedding,
But after de man boast up
How much big-shot guest an' ting he go have,
Ah feel shame.
If ah did follow me mind,
Ah would ah just go down de road,
Buy ah roti, an' go home.
But after ah take so much time to reach dey,
Ah decide to stay,
Plus ah did really want to see
Who dis man have in he wedding.
So ah traips up to de door an' ring de bell.
Ah little maga-lookin' boy,
Ah find out later was Errol brudder,
Open de door, an' de first ting he say is
"Where yu bottle?"
Well, yu could imagine how ah feel!
Me eh bring no present because ah dependin' on de office,
An' me never hear 'bout no "bring ah bottle" wedding
In all me life.
Well ah did just openin' me mout to cuss he tail
When de granmudder come out an' say,
"Is alright, don't mind he, come inside, but wipe yu foot."
Well ah feel like penny-hapeny, but ah say to meself

"Ten like dem can't stop me, ah go make marse today."
So ah ease inside, back ah stand against de wall,
An' start to survey de scene.
Now, ah stand up just by de kitchen door
To make sure I fus gettin' when de food comin' out,
Because de amount ah rab I see in dat man wedding
Ah tell yu, if yu play gentleman, yu starve.
Boy, dat man had some guests
Dat look like refugee from hurricane Alma.
Some ah dem dress up in suit an' ting.
Dat look as if it just come out from under ah mattress.
Ah mean yu could ah see style from as far back as 1936.
De father-in-law had on ah Zoot suit,
An' de mudder-in-law, well she was someting else,
Was like she did starrin' in de Great Gatsby.
De woman dress up in Kan-Kan an' organdy.
Ah tell yu if ah didn't know dis was Errol wedding,
Ah would ah tought was a j'ouvert band.
Now I is ah fella not no hypocrite, ah mean,
I don't look down on nobody,
So ah decide ah go just carry on as usual an enjoy meself.
So ah make me way to de table where de bride an' groom was sittin',
To say de usual congratulations an' ting.
Well partner, is like de man didn't want me to kiss de bride.
From de time he spot me, he start to wave hello,
Dis time me eh even halfway cross de floor.
Before ah could even reach him de man done meet me on de hall
So me eh even get nowhere near de bride.
An' if yu hear him, talkin' loud and carryin' on,
"Nice of yu to come, thanks for de lovely gift."
Now ah feel he was mamaguying me,
Because me didn't have no gift in me hand.
But ah let dat pass, as ah wasn't too sure
If de office did send de gift with my name on it.
Anyway, me boy start gallerying an' ting, bawlin' out
"Eat, drink, an' be merry, de bar open yu cant miss it
Bat yu liquors like Kanhai, but don't get drunk in me place."
An' if all yu see dis bar? Yu tink is bar?
One bottle ah rum at ah time, an' de father-in-law serving.
Ah eh see no whisky, no champagne, no sherry . . . just puncheon.

Well ah is ah drinker from way back, so dat eh bother me,
Ah just liberate ah paper cup an' join de lineup.
It take me 'bout half-hour to reach dat bar,
An' by de time ah reach up ah so thirsty, all me mout white.
An' if yu see how de father-in-law servin' out de liquor,
Yu would swear was communion.
De man measurin' out drink as if he is ah chemist.
But de strange ting about de whole setup is
Ah keep smellin' whisky, but ah cant see none.
An' everybody drinkin' rum.
Is den ah realise dat is de father-in-law I smellin'.
De man had ah bottle ah whisky under de table,
An' every now an' den when nobody eh lookin',
He bendin' down an' takin' ah small one.
An' when he straighten up is to hear him shoutin'
'Drink up, drink up, all yu chinksin'.
So ah say to meself "watch dat criminal, eh!"
But ah take me puncheon cool, cool an' start lookin' for food.
Well, dat was someting else.
Ah spot ah tray ah someting comin' through de crowd,
Well, yu ever see shark?
If yu see how Errol friend an' dem attack dat tray
Yu would ah dead with shame.
Is like dem never hear 'bout etiquette,
Before de tray could reach two yards from de kitchen door it empty.
Well by dis time hunger busting me belly,
So ah say to meself, Keith boy, is every man for he self,
Who have one foot take in front.
So ah back ah stand by de door again,
An' as de next tray ah sandwich pass,
Is because ah take ten.
Well de girl dat servin' want to dead.
She tell me how ah too damn lickerish
An' start to carry on,
By de time she done talk ah take ten more.
Not dat ah did like de sandwich yu know,
Dey did have ah kind ah stalish taste.
Yu ever see ah tired lookin' sandwich?
Well dem sandwich did look tired an' all squingy, squingy
As if somebody sit down on dem.

Next ting pass round was stuff-egg.
Well when it come to stuff-egg yu self know
I is ah real champ.
But, partner, me never see little stuff-egg so in me life,
It look to me like is pigeon egg dey did use.
Ah had to eat 'bout forty before ah even get de taste.
An' hear nuh, when dem tray pass yu have to make sure
an' take enough,
Because dey eh passin' back again.
Well de cook food take so long to come,
Dat I realize dat dey probably hopin' dat everybody
get tired an' go home
Before dey bring out de chicken an' ting.
Well de way tings been shapin' up I eatin' anyting I get,
Me eh playin' no big shot, is belly-full time.
All dis time fete going on, but de soun' system so bad,
An' so much rab in de place, dat yu could scarcely hear de music.
Only one speaker workin', an' everybody dancin' under
dis one speaker,
So yu could imagine de situation, de wedding lookin'
kind ah lopsided,
Half de place empty, and de other half
pack up with people under dis one speaker.
Well ah decide I not in dat,
An' ah see me chance to move in by de kitchen
An' negotiate ah piece ah chicken from ah little girl ah see dey.
Well who tell me do dat, yu know who ah bounce up?
De granmudder. Yu ever see ah Viking?
Well boy, Errol granmudder look like Eric de Red,
An' he was ah real bad Viking.
But ah didn't even have chance to beg ah chicken leg,
Because de next ting ah know is ah hear "POW," bottle bus' inside.
Somebody hit de father-in-law with ah bottle an' fite start.
Ah find out all dat later, because jus den ah was
only studyin' one ting,
Wha' was de best way to get out ah dat place.
Because de amount ah bottle an' chair dat start to fly,
Yu would ah tink dat de Pele riot was ah joke.
So I head through de kitchen door
To try an' make it through de backyard.

All dis time police siren wailin', an' crowd start to gather.
Well ah make it 'bout halfway cross de yard,
But ah didn't make allowance for de dog.
Yu ever see ah St. James dog? Well Errol an dem have one.
Dat dog starvin' so long, it would ah eat stone
If yu give it ah chance, much less big fat Keith.
Well dat dog nearly eat me.
Ah did read once in ah book dat if yu stan' up an' play brave,
An' watch ah bad dog in de eye, an say "STOP," it go' stop.
Well ah try dat.
Ah watch dat dog as it chargin' an' ah bawl "STOP"!
Partner, like dat dog didn't read de same book with me,
It leggo one bite at me, if it did ever catch me ah dead.
It miss me by an "uh-huh" not ah "uh" yu know, but ah uh huh.
Well yu could imagine de scene, ah take off,
With de dog hangin' on to me pants leg, me good, good, pants leg.
Ah barely make it to de fence, an' as ah jump up,
Is because ah leave half me pants in de dog mout.
Next ting ah know, ah police collar me, ah respectable man like me,
Askin' me if I see wha' happen inside, like he want witness.
So ah look him in de eye, an ah say in me best voice,
"Officer, does I look like de kind ah man dat would get involve
in ah ting like dat?"
All dis time ah tryin' to hide de bite-up pants foot.
De man say, "Yes!" an' look like he was go bus' ah lash on me.
Same time more bachanal start up,
De police was arrestin' everybody dey catch,
An' de granmudder start to get on like ah real Viking.
She was stonin' de police with ah set ah fry chicken,
De same chicken she wouldn't give me,
So de officer let me go, an' take off to help he friends.
Well partner, dat was one wedding ah go never forget,
An' as ah stan up in de crowd watchin' dem hussle Errol in de van,
Ah say to meself, never me again.
Ah lose me best shirt, ah lose me best pants,
An' nearly starve to death, an' dey nearly jail me.
An' yu know nine months later dis same Errol come tellin' me
He havin' christenin?

WEEKEND GLORY

MAYA ANGELOU

Some dichty folks
don't know the facts,
posin' and preenin'
and puttin' on acts,
stretchin' their necks
and strainin' their backs.

They move into condos
up over the ranks,
pawn their souls
to the local banks.
Buying big cars
they can't afford,
ridin' around town
actin' bored.

If they want to learn how to live life right,
they ought to study me on Saturday night.

My job at the plant
ain't the biggest bet,
but I pay my bills
and stay out of debt.

I get my hair done
for my own self's sake,

so I don't have to pick
and I don't have to rake.

Take the church money out
and head cross town
to my friend girl's house
where we plan our round.
We meet our men and go to a joint
where the music is blues
and to the point.

Folks write about me.
They just can't see
how I work all week
at the factory.
Then get spruced up
and laugh and dance
And turn away from worry
with sassy glance.

They accuse me of livin'
from day to day,
but who are they kiddin'?
So are they.

My life ain't heaven
but it sure ain't hell.
I'm not on top
but I call it swell
if I'm able to work
and get paid right
and have the luck to be Black
on a Saturday night.

THE BALLAD OF JOE MEEK

STERLING BROWN

I

You cain't never tell
How far a frog will jump,
When you jes' see him planted
On his big broad rump.

Nor what a monkey's thinking
By the working of his jaws —
You jes' cain't figger;
And I knows, because

Had me a buddy,
Soft as pie
Joe Meek they called him
And they didn't lie.

The good book say
"Turn the other cheek,"
But that warn't no turning
To my boy Joe Meek.

He turned up all parts,
And baigged you to spank,
Pulled down his breeches,
And supplied the plank.

The worm that didn't turn
Was a rattlesnake to Joe:
Wasn't scary—jes' meek, suh,
Was made up so.

II

It was late in August
What dey calls dog days,
Made even beetle hounds
Git bulldog ways.

Would make a pet bunny
Chase a bad bloodhound
Make a newborn baby
Slap his grandpa down.

The air it was muggy
And heavy with heat,
The people all sizzled
Like frying meat.

The icehouse was heaven
The pavements was hell
Even Joe didn't feel
So agreeable.

Strolling down Claiborne
In the wrong end of town
Joe saw two policemen
Knock a po' gal down.

He didn't know her at all,
Never saw her befo',
But that didn't make no difference,
To my ole boy Joe.

Walks up to the cops,
And, very polite,
Ast them ef they thought
They had done just right.

One cracked him with his billy
Above the left eye,

One thugged him with his pistol
And let him lie.   ·

III

When he woke up, and knew
What the cops had done,
Went to a hockshop,
Got hisself a gun.

Felt mo' out of sorts
Than ever befo',
So he went on a rampage
My ole boy Joe.

Shot his way to the station house.
Rushed right in,
Wasn't nothing but space
Where the cops had been.

They called the reserves,
And the national guard,
Joe was in a cell
Overlooking the yard.

The machine guns sputtered,
Didn't faze Joe at all—
But evvytime he fired
A cop would fall.

The teargas made him laugh
When they let it fly,
Laughing gas made him hang
His head an' cry.

He threw the hand grenades back
With a outshoot drop,
An' evvytime he threw
They was one less cop.

The Chief of Police said
"What kinda man is this?"

And held up his shirt
For a armistice.

"Stop gunning, black boy,
And we'll let you go."
"I thank you very kindly,"
Said my ole boy Joe.

"We promise you safety
If you'll leave us be—"
Joe said: "That's agreeable
Sir, by me..."

IV

The sun had gone down
The air it was cool,
Joe stepped out on the pavement
A fighting fool.

Had walked from the jail
About half a square,
When a cop behind a post
Let him have it fair.

Put a bullet in his left side
And one in his thigh,
But Joe didn't lose
His shootin' eye.

Drew a cool bead
On the cop's broad head;
"I returns you yo' favor"
And the cop fell dead.

The next to last words
He was heard to speak,
Was just what you would look for
From my boy Joe Meek.

Spoke real polite
To the folks standing by:

"Would you please do me one kindness,
Fo' I die?

"Won't be here much longer
To bother you so,
Would you bring me a drink of water
Fo' I go?"

The very last words
He was heard to say,
Showed a different Joe talking
In a different way.

"Ef my bullets weren't gone,
An' my strength all spent—
I'd send the chief something
With a compliment.

"And we'd race to hell,
And I'd best him there,
Like I would of done here
Ef he'd played me fair."

V

So you cain't never tell
How fas' a dog can run
When you see him a-sleeping,
In the sun.

HARRIET TUBMAN

ELOISE GREENFIELD

Harriet Tubman didn't take no stuff
Wasn't scared of nothing neither
Didn't come in this world to be no slave
And wasn't going to stay one either

"Farewell!" she sang to her friends one night
She was mighty sad to leave 'em
But she ran away that dark, hot night
Ran looking for her freedom

She ran to the woods and she ran through the woods
With the slave catchers right behind her
And she kept on going till she got to the North
Where those mean men couldn't find her

Nineteen times she went back South
To get three hundred others
She ran for her freedom nineteen times
To save black sisters and brothers
Harriet Tubman didn't take no stuff
Wasn't scared of nothing neither
Didn't come in this world to be no slave
And didn't stay one either

And didn't stay one either

AFRICAN-AMERICAN
HISTORY RAP

SHARON JORDAN HOLLEY

I say A B C D E F G
African-American History
H I J K L M N O P
African-American History
Q R S, T U V
African-American History
W X Y and Z.
This is a story all about me:
A for African-American,
My true identity.
B for Benjamin Banneker,
Surveyor of Washington, D. C.
C for my community,
A place that I call home.
D for all the discoveries
I made just on my own.
E for education
We use from day to day.
F for all the families
And the love that they portray.
G for all the talents and gifts
Of those who entertain.
H for the writers—Hughes and Hurston—
Who wrote about the people plain.
I for rhythm, blues, and jazz

And all our instruments.
J for Jesse Jackson
Who ran for president.
K for Martin Luther King
We honor with a holiday.
L for the cowboy, Nat Love,
"Deadwood Dick" they say.
M for Madam C. J. Walker
A black woman millionaire.
N for the prophet Nat Turner,
A freedom fighter who dared.
O for oppression that we must fight
To keep our struggle alive.
P for the principles some have held
that fill our hearts with pride.
Q for the questions that I ask
about my history.
R for religion
Islam to Christianity.
S for the seven days
Of the Kwanzaa celebration.
T for Harriet Tubman,
Conductor on Freedom's station.
U for the Underground Railroad,
A secret passageway.
V for the values that make me strong
From unity to faith, I pray.
W for Woodson, Carter G.,
A vision he did see
When he proclaimed February
For Black History.
X for the name that Malcolm took
Because it means unknown.
Y for You—to be all you can
From the first day you are born.
Z for zenith, the highest point
In this universe.
You're reaching up
When you learn
An African-American history verse.

I say A B C D E F G
African-American History
H I J K L M N O P
African-American History
Q R S, T U V
African-American History
W X Y and Z.
This is a story all about me.
This is a story all about me.
This is a story all about me.

GET READY, INC.

DOUGLASS "JOCKO" HENDERSON

I am Douglass Henderson, known on radio as Jocko. The name
Jocko came from when I started in radio back in Baltimore,
Maryland. I didn't want to really be like the other disc jockeys; I
wanted to do something a little bit different. I thought of the name
Jocko because it rhymed with so many things: mommy-o, daddy-o,
hottest show on the radio.

There was a tradition of rapping carried from my father, who
talked in rhyme at the piano, to son, to my son, who is now a disc
jockey. Where did rap come from? I know people used to say, "Let's
rap." They said that long before the music came out. I don't know
the origin of the word. It means "let's talk," even with music. When
they're rapping, they're really talking the rhythm.

Jocko, Jocko, where have you been?
I helped bust a pusher.
Now I'm back again.

Don't feel guilty if you turn in a friend.
Let the cops know,
Be a good citizen, save some lives.
That's the way to go.

Now there's a pusher trying to hook you.
His name could be Jim.
Tell the cops he's dealing — drop a dime on him!

476

Don't let anybody know —you made the call.
You did a good deed, now you're standing tall.

You can't cope when it comes to dope.
No way is that being cool.
If you're dumb enough to be a dopey dope,
You're the world's biggest fool.

Now, if you don't want your life blown away,
When it comes to drugs —say, "No way!"

If you're using drugs —hey! You bit.
Your mind's been blown —you're out of it!

You'll rob, you'll steal, you'll even kill
To get those drugs, you need the dollar bill.

There's a tranquilizer called PCP.
It can knock out a horse so easy.
It was made for animals
To stop them in their tracks.
Take it from the Jock
These are cold stone facts.

PCP makes you crazy.
If you use it, how dumb can you be?
The question is, why you want to die?
If that's the way you want to go —bye, bye.

Then there's a deadly drug —ah, Cocaine.
Scientists discovered it to ease a pain.
Doctors prescribe it very carefully.
Without the right prescription, it's deadly.
Don't try Cocaine —take a tip from me.
It's a thrill —that can kill immediately.
It's not OK to light up a "J."
It can blow your mind for the rest of the day.
When you've had a "J" —your eyes are red.
You're half asleep —your brain is dead.

Some students light up before they go to class.
They nod —learn nothing —no way can they pass.
Education that they need has passed them by.
They have missed the boat —they are too high to try.

Now drugs are designed to destroy you.
You'll wake up one morning and you won't know what to do.
Your body is wrecked, your mind confused.
No way can you win—you've got to lose!

That junk can back up and damage the brain.
Many thousands of users have gone insane.
Think about it, just a moment or two.
Is this really, really, really what you want to do?
No way, Jose! Can you throw your life away?
Live the drug free life—it's so great that way!

Speed—could make you think you have wings.
You may try to fly—or do many dumb things.
Do yourself a big favor—pass it by.
You don't have wings—you just can't fly.
Speed confuses the mind,
It'll destroy you—it's just a matter of time.

Quaaludes and alcohol
Is the wrong way to have a ball.
Use them together, they can do you in.
Together they can be like poison.
They can put you in a coma for a long time,
Or take you away long before your time.

I knew a junky—his name was Ted.
Stayed high on drugs and now he's dead.
Mary—Reggie—Janie, and Tom
They thought it was hip to be turned on.
They took pills, shot needles—snorted "Coke" they bought.
They're all gone, I'm sorry to report.

You see, the big drug pushers don't care who they kill.
They're dealing for that dollar bill.
Ashes to ashes, dust to dust.
If drugs kill you—don't blame us.

You're a big fool if you drop out of school.
Don't even be late.
Forget about the drugs.
Hang in there—hang till you graduate.

SPREAD THE WORD: A STORYTELLER'S RAP

LINDA GOSS

In the late 1980's, rappers dominate the music scene. In this rap, the storyteller delivers a message to popular rap groups.

I'm a storyteller
With a story to tell
I can tell 'em loud
I can tell 'em well
I don't need a microphone
When I talk
I don't need a chair
'Cause I'm going to walk
I can strut and stroll
'Cause I'm bad
And I'm bold
Gonna tell it "like it is"
This ain't no show biz
Gonna tell my own story
Tell it to the world
For all the boys
For all the girls
From the mountain top
To the valley low
Gonna "talk dat talk"
Gonna go-go-go

CALL: *Have you heard?*
RESPONSE: *SPREAD THE WORD*
CALL: *Have you heard?*
RESPONSE: *SPREAD THE WORD*
Yeah, storytelling is the thing to do
It's an ancient art
It's also brand new
Medicine for the spirit
Healing for the soul
It's for the young
And it's for the old
It's for the rich
And it's for the poor
For the sick at heart
And what's more
It's for Black people
White people, Brown people too
Red, Yellow, Orange
Green, Purple, and Blue
From the break of day
Till the cool midnight
I can weave a tale
That's outta sight
Yeah, storytelling is what I'm about
I can run my mouth
Till my eyes pop out
CALL: *Have you heard?*
RESPONSE: *Have you heard?*
CALL: *SPREAD THE WORD!*
RESPONSE: *SPREAD THE WORD!*
Listen good people
All over the world
Start telling stories
Start Spreading the Word
In the tradition
Is a natural condition
You just pass it on down
Hand it on around
It's mythical, it's history
It's magical, it's mystery

Use your imagination
Talk about your dreams
Talk about your heroes
Plans and schemes
Talk about your family
Life or love
Talk about the Master
up above
Talk about the birds
Talk about the bees
Talk about zebras
Talk about trees
A little common sense
A little sense of humor
Let it all hang out
But don't drop your bloomers
CALL: *Have you heard?*
RESPONSE: *Have you heard?*
CALL: *SPREAD THE WORD!*
RESPONSE: *SPREAD THE WORD!*
(Improvise)
Tell the truth, snaggle tooth
What's your story, morning glory?
You don't miss your water
Till your well runs dry
Anansi is a trickster
Brother Rabbit is sly
Bocka booka bocka booka bocka bam bam bam
Bocka booka bocka booka bocka bam bam bam
Bocka booka bocka booka bocka bam bam bam
Bocka booka bocka booka bocka bam bam bam
Bocka booka bocka booka bocka bam bam bam
Ah-la-dee-da dee
Dougie Fresh
Ah-la-dee-da dee
You are a mess
L. L. Cool J.
You are a joke
Wash your mouth
Out with soap

Kurtis Blow
Take a seat
Roxanne, Roxanne
I'm tired of your beat
Hey Whodini
You need to be quiet
Fat Boys
Go on a diet
Run —DMC
You better run the other way
Afrika Bam baataa
Here what I say
(Hold nose while saying this part)
"New York is calling
Planet rock is falling.
Sugar Hill gang
You better listen to me
You sound too flat
You can't sweeten my tea
Who? What? Where? Why?
I better not mess
With what five guys?
HOLD IT! STOP THE MUSIC!
Grand Master Flash
And the Furious Five
You're all played out
You sound kind-a-jive
I don't have to scratch records
Storytelling is live!
I know I might look crazy
I might sound strange
I'm a storyteller
I ain't ashame
You can steal my style
You can steal my rhyme
But I'll be back
Just give me time
You've heard my tales
You've heard my rap
And if you don't like it

You can bust on dat!
CALL: *Have you Heard?*
RESPONSE: *Have you Heard?*
CALL: *SPREAD THE WORD*
RESPONSE: *SPREAD THE WORD*

COMMENTARIES

THE GEORGIA SEA ISLAND SINGERS: FRANKIE AND DOUG QUIMBY

MARIAN E. BARNES

Every year Frankie and Doug Quimby travel thousands of miles sharing stories, games, and dances passed down from captives enslaved in the antebellum South. In the tradition of these black captives hampered by laws forbidding them to use the instruments of music and rhythm they had created, the Quimbys employ a few simple percussion instruments, sing a cappella, and use their bodies to make music and rhythm.

"We grew up doing these songs, games, and dances. Then as we got older we listened to the stories behind them," says Frankie Quimby. Born and reared in the Georgia Sea Island area, where much of the original African culture still survives, she traces her family lineage to the Foulah national group in West Africa.

Doug Quimby was born into an Albany, Georgia, sharecropping family that sometimes earned as little as $9.52 a year. He began singing for others at the age of five. Like Frankie, he has performed as an oral historian for some twenty years. The two were married in 1971 and became a professional duo in 1984. Since then they have been featured in national publications and provided musical background for several motion pictures and live theater productions.

For every song, game, or dance they offer, the Quimbys tell a story, explain how their presentation relates to the story, and show how both evolved from the life of the times.

Many performances include the spirituals "Down by the Riverside" and "Wade in the Water." Relating the story behind these songs, Frankie observes, "They were sung in the fields to let people who were escaping know that dogs were in pursuit and they should get in the water to hide their scent."

The Quimbys go into greater detail when they present the history of two popular game chants in their repertoire, "Miss Frog" and "Old Bill Rolling Pin," usually with Frankie as narrator.

Years ago the slaves would get a whipping if they went to visit relatives or friends on another plantation without a written permit. Each slaveowner had a man riding on a horse from one end of the plantation to the other. He was patrolling—like a patrolman does today—to keep slaves from going off the plantation and to keep them from going onto some other plantation.

They always used a big man, and if he caught the slaves, he whipped them. The slaves called him "the Paddy Roller," and they didn't like him because he was mean. When they wanted to warn each other that he was around, they couldn't say, "The Paddy Roller is up the road patrolling" because he would know they were talking about him. So they said, "Okay, we'll name him 'Old Bill Rolling Pin,' and he won't know we're talking about him." They remembered how they rolled dough out back and forth, back and forth with a rolling pin, so they made up the chant:

> *Old Bill Rolling Pin*
> *He's up the road*
> *And back again*
> *With big eyes, big ears*
> *And a double chin.*

They meant that the Paddy Rollers were going back and forth just like you do with rolling dough.

When they sang "Miss Frog," what they were saying was, "Whenever we go over to visit our relatives, we get caught and whipped by the Paddy Rollers—we get caught and swallowed by the Paddy Rollers." So they chanted:

> *Miss Frog went swimming*
> *Down the lake*
> *She got swallowed*
> *By a big black snake.*

Actually, the Paddy Rollers were always big white men, but they said "big black snake" to throw them off. They were talking about them —sometimes they were talking *to* them—but they couldn't walk up and express themselves so they put it in a song.

Before he sings the traditional Gullah chantey, "Peh Me Ma Munie Doun," (which means "Pay me my money now"), Doug Quimby tells the story of the struggle of black men and women to survive after emancipation.

"The song was created by dockworkers in Georgia who were being cheated by ship captains who had them load their ships and then sailed out from the harbor without paying them," he says.

The audience feels the anger of the dockworkers as Doug and Frankie blast the song out, their bodies bent with emotion while Frankie's fist swoops toward the tambourine which she slams with open fingers:

> *Peh me, peh me,*
> *Peh me ma munie doun...HUNH*
> *Peh me or go to jayul,*
> *Peh me ma munie doun...HUNH!*
>
> *Ay trought Ay heard ma cahpt'n seh,*
> *Peh me ma munie doun...HUNH*
> *Tomorra is ma sailin deh,*
> *Peh me ma munie doun...HUNH!*
>
> *Peh me, peh me,*
> *Peh me ma munie doun...HUNH*
> *Peh me or go to jayul,*
> *Peh me ma munie doun...HUNH!*
>
> *If Ay was Mis'a Affa Jones' son,*
> *Peh me ma munie doun...HUNH*
> *Ay steh in th' hoos till breakfas is done,*
> *Peh me ma munie doun...HUNH!*
>
> *Peh me, peh me,*
> *Peh me ma munie doun...HUNH*
> *Peh me or go to jayul,*
> *Peh me ma munie doun...HUNH!*

Games and songs were also used to send messages of love and thanks. As an example of this, the Quimbys showcase the "Sally Walker" game and the story behind it.

"There were restrictions on what an enslaved person could say or do, even if it was complimentary," Frankie observes. Explaining that sometimes a member of the master class might be kind to a captive who would then want to show appreciation, she adds, "You just couldn't walk up and say, 'Thank you.' It was forbidden. So they said it by playing a game."

> *Sally Walker, Sally Walker, Sally Walker, sitting in a saucer,*
> *Crying and weeping for all you have done*
> *Fly to the East and fly to the West*
> *And fly to the very one that you love the best.*

(Here the person playing Sally Walker points to the person he or she selects as best loved.)

Many dances also have interesting histories. The dance "Jump for Joy," featuring jumps with crossed legs that eventually became known as "The Charleston," was created to thwart rules that forbid captives to cross their legs because it was considered presumptuous.

The song and game combination "Hambone, Hambone, Where You Been" is perhaps the performance most requested of Doug Quimby.

> *Hambone, Hambone, where you been?*
> *Round the world and back again.*

The song speaks of the times when the best parts of a slaughtered hog were reserved for whites and the discarded ham bone was circulated among the enslaved people to "season" the cooking of one family after another.

FOLK POETRY IN THE STORYTELLING TRADITION

MOLEFI KETE ASANTE

T here is something musical about the way the storyteller weaves the ups and downs of experience into the fabric of life. We are captured, enamored, by the twist of language, the turn of the phrase, the indirection of the truth. We like to have our knowledge, our information, brought to us on the basis of indirection. A story serves that purpose preeminently.

No art form reflects the tremendous impact of our presence in America more powerfully or eloquently than does folk poetry in the storytelling tradition. Perhaps because it is the earliest poetry we heard in our homes and our churches, folk poetry became for us the fundamental lyrics for folk music and the door to our own appreciation of the stories, tales, proverbs, and raps that came from the ancestors.

Woven together in a pattern of verbal brilliance, because the word is generative and productive, are the most telling folk poetry examples of our culture, arts, crafts, secrets, ceremonies, and rites of passage. At the beginning of the sojourn on this side of the ocean, our ancestors brought forth the most remarkable poetry from Asante, Mandingo, Yoruba, Wolof, Serere, Baule, Hausa, Congo, Angola, and Ibo, poured the essence of this poetry into what Viki Akiwumi has called "the wisdom cup" and created the African American folk tradition. Spoken power has a tradition going back to the ancient Africans of the Nile Valley who saw *Mdu Neter,* the language of the ancient Egyptians, as sacred words. In West Africa the use of word games, stories, and folk poetry became an integral part of all societies. Magic itself was word magic.

Transforming words were placed in the mouths of folk poets from the earliest times in America. Africans in the Americas remembered the storytellers, the *griots,* who stood in the midst of the children and adults at night and told them rhythmic stories that possessed the special quality of moral and verbal resolution. These memories were to be the memories that would guide the rhymes, rhythms, and raps of the African American. The words were to provide transformations, social and moral, to the hearers. The best speakers would surely know how to reach the spirit of the ancestors through language.

There is no mystery in what was presented in the preceding pages from the folk poetry tradition of the African American. These poems, stories, and raps are central to the tradition that has been constant for more than three hundred years in America and goes back to the traditions seen in ancient Africa in the *HuSia,* sacred writings from Egypt. There are many elements that compose this tradition, but there are three principal aspects: (1) rhyming, (2) moralizing, and (3) telling a story. Rhyming must be accompanied by some solution to a human or communal problem. In most instances the author is attempting to resolve a personal or communal conflict, but if it is a personal conflict, its resolution must be made in the interest of harmony in the entire community. Moralizing without the rhyme is preaching, and rhyming without moralizing is mere versification. The African American poet, whether playing the dozens, reciting folk poetry, or rapping, knows precisely the boundaries of the art form. The story is the most salient characteristic of the folk poetry. Without the story there is no folk poetry. Paul Laurence Dunbar, the most able writer in this category, established the standard form of this poetry and made it acceptable to a wide audience. Dunbar's genius was the quick, sharp pun that turned a story on its head and made its point forcefully. But he was always in charge of the rhyme and the moral, despite the fact that he was such a major storyteller.

In this section, "Ah-la-dee-da-dee-bop-de-bop: Raps, Rhythms, and Rhymes in the Storytelling Tradition," the editors have chosen authors from a variety of regions, interests, and specific styles, yet each of the authors shows a particular gift to rap or recite in the tradition. One should not go overboard in trying to make a special place for rap; it is simply the extension of the tradition that has been well established for many years. The poetry of former heavyweight champion Muhammad Ali and the works of Paul Keens-Douglas are within the same folk tradition; Paul Laurence Dunbar and Linda Goss are both in the same school of African American verbal art; they are all singing the same song although in different places and spaces.

BIOGRAPHICAL NOTES

CHINUA ACHEBE is from Eastern Nigeria where he is president of the town council in his village. His first novel, *Things Fall Apart,* sold over three million copies and has been translated into over thirty languages. His other works include *No Longer at Ease, A Man of the People, Arrow of God,* and most recently, *Anthills of the Savannah.*

REV. CARL J. ANDERSON is the pastor of the St. John Missionary Baptist Church in Oakland, California.

LOUISE ANDERSON, who has been telling stories for over forty years, was born in Alabama and is currently living in North Carolina.

MAYA ANGELOU has a lifetime appointment as Reynolds Professor of American Studies at Wake Forest University in Winston-Salem, North Carolina. Ms. Angelou is a poet, actress, activist, producer and storyteller. She is the author of five acclaimed volumes of autobiography including *I Know Why the Caged Bird Sings,* and most recently, *All God's Children Need Traveling Shoes,* and four collections of poetry.

MOLEFI KETE ASANTE, Ph.D., Professor and Chair of the Department of African American Studies at Temple University, is author of several books, the latest of which are *The African Culture: The Rhythms of Unity* and *The Afrocentric Idea.*

KWASI ASARE, a native of Larteh, Ghana, is a master drummer and musician. During the 1950s he collaborated with Duke Ellington, Count Basie, Louis Armstrong, Thelonius Monk and others.

HOUSTON A. BAKER, JR. is the Director of the Center for the Study of Black Literature and Culture and Albert M. Greenfield Professor of Human Relations at the University of Pennsylvania. A critic, poet, and author of five books of criticism including *Long Black Song: Essays in Black American Literature and Culture, The Journey Back: Issues in Black Literature and Criticism,* his most recent work is *Afro-American Poetics: Revisions of Harlem and the Black Aesthetic.*

ELDER DANIEL BARNES, father of storyteller Marian E. Barnes, was a master storyteller during his fifty-year ministry. He was a revered spiritual advisor and teacher of many people of the clergy across the nation.

RAMONA BASS has graduate training in education and anthropology to complement her undergraduate studies in theater and the tradition of storytelling in her family. Her company, Hatful of Dreams Productions, features storytelling shows, workshops and artist-in-residence programs.

LOUISE BENNETT, born in 1919 in Kingston, and known as "Miss Lou," is the leading comedienne, storyteller, and folklorist of Jamaica. She studied at the Royal Academy of Dramatic Art in England. Performed in authentic dialect, her works include *Laugh with Louise,* and *Anancy and Miss Lou.*

J. MASON BREWER, born in Texas in 1896, was one of the few professionally trained African-American folklorists of his time. He was the first African American officer of the American Folklore Society. His books include *Humorous Folktales of the South Carolina Negro, The Word on the Brazos, "Aunt Dicy" Tales, Dog Ghosts and Other Texas Negro Folk Tales,* and *American Negro Folklore.*

ARDIE STUART BROWN who performs with her sister Patricia Stuart Robinson, was born and reared in Philadelphia, Pennsylvania. Founders and directors of the Spring Nursery School of the Arts, the sisters combine rural drama, storytelling, song, and dance.

OSCAR BROWN, JR., writer, producer, singer, director, and composer, has over 450 songs to his credit. Notable titles include: "Signifying Monkey," "Lone Ranger," "Brown Baby," and "Brother Where Are You?" He has collaborated with such jazz masters as Miles Davis, Nat Adderly, and Bobby Timmons.

STERLING BROWN (1901–1989), born in Washington, D.C., was the dean of African American poets. An influential scholar, Dr. Brown joined the faculty of Howard University in 1929, and remained associated with the University for more than half a century. He is the co-editor of the classic anthology, *The Negro Caravan*.

NAOMI CLARKE was born in British Guyana, in 1930. Ms. Clarke became a storyteller "way back there" at the age of four by telling stories about the people and the customs on the estate where she was born.

JOHN HENRIK CLARKE is a professor in the Department of Black and Puerto Rican Studies at Hunter College in New York City. He has published over fifty short stories—his best known short story, "The Boy Who Painted Christ Black," has been translated into more than twelve languages. Professor Clarke has written and edited twenty-one books. The best known are: *American Negro Short Stories, Malcolm X: The Man and His Time, Harlem U.S.A.,* and *Marcus Garvey and the Vision of Africa.*

LARRY G. COLEMAN, Ph.D., is a professor with the department of Communications at Gallaudet College and Howard University. He is an expert on humor and comedy as it relates to storytelling.

J. CALIFORNIA COOPER is the author of seventeen plays. Her books include *A Piece of Mine: A New Short Story Collection, Some Soul to Keep,* and *Homemade Love.* Ms. Cooper currently lives in Texas.

RITA COX brought tales of the Carribean from the West Indies to Canada. A student of Augusta Baker, she is a director of the Storytellers School of Toronto, and Coordinator of Cumbaya, a festival of black heritage and storytelling.

GERALD L. DAVIS, Ph.D., folklorist, is an associate professor of African studies at Rutgers University and visiting professor in the Department of American Studies at the University of New Mexico. He is the author of *I Got the Word In Me and I Can Sing It, You Know: A Study of the Performed African-American Sermon.*

RUBY DEE has had a distinguished career as an actress, writer, and director. In film, she is best remembered in *Purlie Victorious, A Raisin In the Sun,* and *Do the Right Thing.* Ms. Dee won an Obie for *Boesman and Lena,* and most recently on Broadway starred in *Checkmates.* She and her husband Ossie Davis were featured on *A Walk through the 20th Century.* Her published works include *My One Good Nerve,* and *Two Ways to Count to Ten.*

PAUL LAURENCE DUNBAR (1872–1906) was the most successful of the early African-American poets. Born in Dayton, Ohio, where he worked as an elevator operator after graduating from high school, he also worked as a journalist and on the staff of the Congressional Library. His works include *Lyrics of Lowly Life, Lyrics of the Hearthside,* and *Lyrics of Love and Laughter,* four collections of short stories, and four novels.

T. OBINKARAM ECHEWA was born in Nigeria and studied in Paris and at Columbia before becoming an associate professor at Cheyney State University. He has written for *Time* and *The New York Times. The Land's Lord,* his first novel, won the 1976 English Speaking Union Prize. He currently teaches at West Chester State University.

REV. DR. WILLIAM J. FAULKNER, author of *The Days When the Animals Talked: Black American Folktales and How They Came to Be* was born in Society Hills, South Carolina in 1891. He was president of the Nashville Tennesee Branch of the NAACP and Dean of the Chapel at Fisk University from 1934–1953.

ARTHUR HUFF FAUSET, Ph.D., folklorist, educator, and civil rights leader, wrote the landmark commentary "American Negro Folk Literature" for the anthology *The New Negro* which captured the spirit of the Harlem Renaissance. A protegé of Alain Locke, and brother of the writer Jessie Fauset, Dr. Fauset was born in Flemington, New Jersey in 1899.

REV. C. L. FRANKLIN was one of the foremost African-American preachers of his generation. His congregation in Detroit numbered over ten thousand. A civil rights activist, Rev. Franklin was the father of Aretha Franklin, "The Queen of Soul."

CONSTANCE GARCÍA-BARRIO is a writer living in Philadelphia. She is Spanish–English bilingual, has a Ph.D. in Romance languages and speaks Chinese. Her more than one hundred articles have appeared in such publications as *Essence* and *The Philadelphia Inquirer.*

HENRY LOUIS GATES, JR. is W.E.B. DuBois Professor of Literature at Cornell University. He is the author of *Figures in Black: Words, Signs, and the Racial Self,* the editor of *The Slave's Narrative* and *In the House of Osubgo: Critical Essays on Wole Soyinka.* He has been the recipient of a prestigious MacArthur Foundation grant and is general editor of the *Norton Anthology of Afro-American Literature* as well as the editor of *The Schomburg Library of Nineteenth-Century Black Women Writers.* Dr. Gates's most recent book is *The Signifying Monkey.*

WACIRA GETHAIGA, Ph.D., a member of the Kikuyu, the largest ethnic group in Kenya is a professor of African and African-American Studies at California State University in Fullerton. Dr. Gethaiga learned the art of storytelling through traditional competitions between young men (similar to the liars' contest held at the Festival of Black Storytelling). The older men acted as referees and helped to correct any mistakes.

WANDA GIGETTES was born Wanda Smith, in the Appalachian Mountains of southern West Virginia. Many of her stories are based on the lives and experiences of her family in the farming and coal mining regions of West Virginia. A graduate of Temple University she is an elementary school teacher.

NIKKI GIOVANNI is considered by many to be the princess of black poetry. Her books include *Black Feeling, Black Talk, Black Judgment, Re-Creation, Night Comes Softly, Gemini* and *Spin a Soft Black Song.*

ELOISE GREENFIELD is an author of over twenty books including, *Honey, I Love, Under the Sunday Tree,* and most recently *Nathaniel Talking.* Ms. Greenfield has received the American Library Association's Notable Book Award, as well as citations from the Council on Interracial Books for Children. She lives in Washington, D.C.

DICK GREGORY, activist, author, comedian, and businessman, makes over three hundred speaking appearances a year. His latest book, *Dick*

Gregory's Natural Diet, For Folks Who Eat: Cookin' with Mother Nature, is a bestseller on fasting, diet, and nutrition.

JERDINE NOLEN HAROLD writes picture books and folktales for children. Her stories include: *Mountains: The Sleep People* and *Farmer Potter's Balloon Farm*. A native of Chicago, she now resides in Baltimore.

JANICE N. HARRINGTON holds degrees in education and library science, and has worked as a teacher and as a public library director. She currently lives in Louisiana.

DOUGLASS "JOCKO" HENDERSON was one of the most popular radio disc jockeys on the East coast during the rise of Rhythm and Blues. Mr. Henderson has developed the "Get Ready, Inc." program, which uses the "rap" style of talking as a teaching tool for the Philadelphia public schools.

HUGH MORGAN HILL is known throughout the world as Brother Blue and is the father of contemporary storytelling in the United States. His freeflowing improvisational style consists of jazz and calypso rhythms. An ordained minister and graduate of Harvard College and the Yale Drama School, Dr. Hill is the official storyteller of Cambridge, Massachusetts.

SHARON JORDAN HOLLEY is a librarian and storyteller in Buffalo, New York, and performs locally with "Spin-A-Storytellers" of western New York, and with Karima Amin, teacher and storyteller, as "We All Storytellers."

LANGSTON HUGHES, the poet laureate of the African-American people, was born in 1902, in Joplin, Missouri. His first poem to appear in a nationally known publication, "The Negro Speaks of Rivers," which appeared in *Crisis Magizine* in 1921, is still being recited today. In 1925, he was awarded the first prize for poetry by the magazine *Opportunity* for his poem "The Weary Blues." His many books and plays include *The Big Sea, The Sweet Flypaper of Life, I Wonder as I Wander,* and *The Ways of White Folks.*

JANIE HUNTER, a professional storyteller for twenty-six years, was born on the South Carolina Sea Island of Johns Island, where the lyrical Gullah language, a combination of English and African languages, is spoken. Ms. Hunter's work is included in the book *Ain't You Got a Right to the Tree of Life*.

ZORA NEALE HURSTON (1903–1960) was a folklorist, novelist, anthropologist, and celebrated daughter of the Harlem Renaissance. Her works include: *Jonah's Gourd Vine, Mules and Men, Their Eyes Were Watching God, Tell My Horse, Moses: Man of the Mountain Dust Tracks on a Road*, and *Seraph on the Suwanee*.

JAMES WELDON JOHNSON (born in 1871) together with his brother Rosamond composed the African-American anthem "Lift Every Voice and Sing." One of the leading figures in American literature and politics during the early part of the twentieth century, he was the executive secretary of the NAACP. His works include *God's Trombones, The Autobiography of an Ex-Coloured Man, Black Manhattan*, and *The Book of American Negro Spirituals*.

A. C. JORDAN (1906–1968) was an Xhosa novelist, teacher, and scholar. In 1961, he left South Africa and became a professor of African Languages and Literature at the University of Wisconsin. His published works include *Ingqumbo Veminyany (Wrath of the Ancestors), Tales from Southern Africa*, and *Towards an African Literature: The Emergence of Literary Form in Xhosa*.

PAUL KEENS-DOUGLAS, better known as Tim Tim, is one of the leading poets and storytellers of Trinidad. An international performer, Mr. Keens-Douglas's published works include: *Tim Tim, Is Town Say So, When Moon Shie*, and *Tell Me Again*.

DR. MARTIN LUTHER KING, JR. (1929–1968), Baptist minister and slain civil rights activist, transformed American politics and social consciousness. A Nobel Peace Prize winner, Dr. King was the author of *Strength to Love, Why We Can't Wait*, and *Stride Toward Freedom*.

YOLANDA D. KING, daughter of Dr. Martin Luther, Jr., is an actress, producer and director. She, along with Attallah Shabazz, daughter of

Malcolm X, are the founders of Nucleus, a theatrical touring company which performs *Stepping into Tomorrow*.

HAYWOOD T. "THE KID" KIRKLAND (Ari Sesu Merretazon), from Washington, D.C., is a veteran of the Vietnam War. His story was collected by Wallace Terry, a journalist who covered the war in Vietnam for *Time* for two years.

JAMAL KORAM, the Story Man, is the author of *When Lions Could Fly*. He resides in Maryland.

DJIMO KOUYATE, a native of Tambacounda, Senegal, is a member of the Kouyate family of griots (historian-musicians) of the Malinke tradition. He is a founding member of the National Ballet of Senegal, and currently teaches music at the University of Maryland.

LEADBELLY, whose real name was Huddie Ledbetter, was one of America's greatest folksingers. Born in Louisiana in 1888 and raised in Texas, he was once jailed for murder. Folklorist John A. Lomax recorded his singing for the Library of Congress; during the 1940s, he performed in many nightclubs in New York City. His twelve-string guitar playing and singing influenced many contemporary folksingers and rock stars.

JULIUS LESTER is the critically acclaimed author of books for children and adults. He was the first African-American author to receive the Newbery Medal. He was a National Book Award finalist for his book *Long Journey Home: Stories from Black History*. Mr. Lester teaches at the University of Massachusetts in Amherst.

JACK AND ROSA MADDOX were a former slave couple who managed to stay together despite hardships. Their life story was recorded by the Federal Writers' Project between 1934 and 1941.

WINNIE MANDELA is the wife of the jailed South African leader Nelson Mandela. A powerful political figure in her own right, she has been banished, jailed, and publicly silenced. Mrs. Mandela, who was a social worker when she married her husband, has spent only two years of her 28-year marriage together with him.

ALICE McGILL was born in Scotland Neck, North Carolina. Her album "Flying African" won the 1989 ALA Notable award. Currently living in Maryland, Ms. McGill is the co-author of *The Griot's Cookbook*.

KATHRYN L. MORGAN was one of the first African American women to receive her Ph.D. in folklore. She is currently associate professor of history at Swarthmore College. She is the author of *Children of Strangers*.

JERMIAH NABAWI is cofounder of Hola Kumba Ya Cultural Arts Organization in Philadelphia and The William J. Faulkner Friends of Folklore in Miami, Florida of which he is honorary Chairperson.

MLANJENI NDUMA, a native of Philadelphia, is a magician, storyteller, and puppeteer in the African tradition. He is called Africa's unoffical cultural ambassador.

GERALD J. A. NWANKWO of Nigeria is known for his talking turtle tales. Nwankwo means "child born on market day." He is one of 102 children of his father's 31 wives. He was the nineteenth child in his family to attend college. Mr. Nwankwo currently lives in Philadelphia where he teaches at a community college.

TEJUMOLA F. OLOGBONI is one of the "biggest liars" in the country; he won the liar's cup at the 1986 Festival of Black Storytelling in Chicago. Mr. Ologboni, who blends the African tradition of "call and response" with the African American rap beats which make his audience jump up and dance and sing along with him, lives in Milwaukee, Wisconsin.

PEARL E. PRIMUS, anthropologist, folklorist, and pioneer in the field of dance was born in Trinidad, and her African grandfather was a member of the Ashanti people. Three of her celebrated solos from 1943, "The Negro Speaks of Rivers," "Strange Fruit," and "Hard Times Blues," were featured recently at the American Dance Festival. She is a professor in western Massachusetts.

FRANKIE AND DOUG QUIMBY come from the Georgia Sea Islands. This husband-and-wife team performs songs, games, dances, and stories handed down for over two centuries in their isolated communities on the coast of Georgia.

LAWANDA RANDALL is a Washington, D.C. resident and a teller of tales since childhood. She frequently appears at the Smithsonian's National Museum of African Art. Ms. Randall was co-director of the 1985 National Festival of Black Storytelling in Washington, D.C.

ANNIE REED was one of the former slaves whose narrative was recorded by the Federal Writers' Project between 1934 and 1941.

AMELIA PLATTS BOYNTON ROBINSON has been an activist in the civil rights movement for the past fifty-five years, and was in front of the march with others who tried to cross the Edmond Pettus Bridge in Selma, Alabama.

BEVERLY ROBINSON, PH.D., a native Californian, is a specialist in folklore, theater, and ethnic arts. She has taught at the University of California, Los Angeles since 1978.

DR. EDWARD W. ROBINSON, historian, educator, and business administrator, is known for his bestselling historical album, "Black Rhapsody." He has co-authored numerous books, most recently, *The Journey of the Songhay People* with his brother, Redman Battle.

SONIA SANCHEZ is the author of twelve books including *I've Been a woman, New & Selected Poems, homegirls & handgrenades,* and *Under a Soprano Sky.* She is currently associate professor at Temple University in Philadelphia.

ADA DEBLANC SIMOND, a Louisiana Creole by birth, began to write and tell stories in 1979. Her work to keep black heritage alive earned her the NAACP's Arthur B. DeWitty Award. She has been cited by Austin's School District, the Texas state legislature Black Caucus, and in the U.S. Congressional Record.

MARY CARTER SMITH is the "Official Griot" of Baltimore, Maryland. She is cofounder of the "In The Tradition. . . ." National Festival of Black Storytelling, author of *Heart to Heart* and *Town Child,* two collections of poetry, and co-author of *The Griot's Cook Book.*

ELEANORA E. TATE, currently living in South Carolina, has written fifteen books, including *Just an Overnight Guest, The Secret of Gumbo Grove,* and the upcoming *Thank You, Dr. Martin Luther King, Jr. Just an Overnight Guest* was made into an award-winning movie.

JACKIE TORRENCE, the "Story Lady," was born in Chicago and raised in North Carolina. Ms. Torrence has been featured regularly at the National Storytelling Festival in Jonesboro, Tennessee. She is included in the bestselling book *I Dream a World, Portraits of 75 Black Women Who Have Influenced America.* Ms. Torrence knows over three hundred ghost tales.

MARY H. UMOLU, Ph.D., storyteller, broadcaster, and lecturer, is a professor of communications, arts, and sciences at Medgar Evers College of the City of New York. Dr. Umolu lived in Africa for over eleven years where she worked in television and radio. She is the director of the 1989 "In the Tradition..." Festival of Black Storytelling. Her published works include *The Griot Speaks.*

IVAN VAN SERTIMA is an associate professor of African studies at Rutgers University in New Jersey. A literary critic, linguist, and anthropologist, he is editor of the distinguished series *Journal of African Civilizations,* and author of *They Came Before Columbus: The African Presence in Ancient America.*

MARGARET WALKER is the author of nine books. Her work includes the classic *For My People,* and the highly praised novel *Jubilee.* Her current work is *Richard Wright: Daemonic Genius, a Portrait of the Man, a Critical Look at His Work.* She is professor emeritus of English at Jackson State University in Mississippi.

ELAINE WARREN-JACOBS was born on the island of Antigua where her mother would open the family story hour with "Dat Bra Nancy, no ask how he tricksie!" Ms. Warren Jacobs, educator and storyteller, is the editor of *Caribbean Notes, a Newsletter,* and has served as editor for UCLA's folklore journal, *Folklore and Mythology Studies.* She currently lives in California.

WILLIAM H. WIGGINS, JR., PH.D., is an associate professor of African American studies and a fellow of the Folklore Institute at the University of Indiana. He is currently conducting research on Joe Louis as an African American folk hero, under the sponsorship of the John Simon Guggenheim Foundation.

MARILINE J. WILKINS, storyteller, oral historian and lecturer, is the great-grandniece of Harriet Tubman. Ms. Wilkins learned stories about "Aunt Harriet" from her mother, Eva S. Northrup.

FOR FURTHER READING

African and African-American Folklore

Abrahams, Roger. *African Folktales*. New York: Pantheon, 1983.
———. *Afro-American Folktales: Stories from Black Traditions in the New World*. New York: Pantheon, 1985.

Brewer, J. Mason. *American Negro Folktales*. New York: Quadrangle Books/New York Times Book Company, 1968.

Chinweizu. *Voices from Twentieth Century Africa: Griots and Town Criers*. London: Faber & Faber, 1988.

Courlander, Harold. *A Treasury of African Folklore*. New York: Crown, 1976.
———. *A Treasury of Afro-American Folklore*. New York: Crown, 1976.

Dance, Daryl Cumber. *Shuckin' and Jivin': Folklore from Contemporary Black Americans*. Bloomington: Indiana University Press, 1978.

Dorson, Richard M. *African Folklore*. Bloomington: Indiana University Press, 1972.
———. *American Negro Folktales*. Gloucester, MA: Peter Smith, 1970.

Faulkner, William J. *The Days When the Animals Talked*. Chicago: Follett, 1972.

Feldman, Susan, ed. *African Myths and Tales*. New York: Dell, 1970.

Fuja, Abayomi. *Fourteen Hundred Cowries and Other Tales from Africa*. New York: Lothrop, Lee and Shepard, 1971.

Hughes, Langston and Arna Bontemps. *The Book of Negro Folklore*. New York: Dodd, Mead, 1958.

Hurston, Zora Neale. *Mules and Men*. Philadelphia: 1935; New York: Harper and Row, 1970.

Puckett, Newbell Niles. *Folk Beliefs of the Southern Negro*. 1926; New York: Negro Universities Press, 1968.

Caribbean Folklore

Bennett, Louise. *Anancy and Miss Lou*. Jamaica: Sangster's Book Stores, Ltd., 1979.

Dance, Daryl C. *Folklore from Contemporary Jamaicans*. Knoxville, TN: University of Tennessee Press, 1985.

Sherlock, Philip. *West Indian Folk-Tales*. Oxford: Oxford University Press, 1988.

Wolkstein, Diane. *The Magic Orange Tree: and Other Haitian Folktales*. New York: Schocken, 1980.

African-American Folklore and Culture: Criticism

Baker, Houston A., Jr. *Long Black Song: Essays in Black American Literature and Culture*. Charlottesville: University Press of Virginia, 1972.

Dundes, Alan, ed. *Mother Wit from the Laughing Barrel: Readings in the Interpretation of Afro-American Folklore*. 1973; New York: Garland, 1981.

Gates, Henry Louis, Jr. *The Signifying Monkey: A Theory of Afro-American Literary Criticism*. New York: Oxford, 1988.

Levine, Lawrence J. *Black Culture and Black Consciousness: Afro-American Folk Thought from Slavery to Freedom*. New York: Oxford University Press, 1977.

Locke, Alain, ed. The New Negro. New York: Atheneum, 1968.

Roberts, John. *From Badman to Trickster*. Philadelphia: University of Pennsylvania Press, 1989.

Slave Narratives

Bontemps, Arna, ed. *Great Slave Narratives*. Boston: Beacon, 1969.

Botkin, B.A. *Lay My Burden Down, A Folk History of Slavery*. Chicago: University of Chicago Press, 1965.

Douglass, Frederick. *Narrative of the Life of Frederick Douglass, An American Slave*. Houston A. Baker, Jr., ed. 1845; New York: Penguin, 1982.

Gates, Henry Louis Jr., and Charles T. Davis, eds. *The Slave's Narrative*. New York: Oxford University Press, 1985.

Mellon, James. *Bullwhip Days: The Slaves Remember*. New York: Weindenfeld and Nicolson, 1988.

Osofsky, Gilbert. *Puttin On Ole Massa: Three Slave Narratives*. New York: Harper and Row, 1969.

Starling, Marion Wilson. *The Slave Narrative: Its Place in American History*. Washington, D.C.: Howard University Press, 1988.

Family and Personal Narratives

Andreski, Iris. *Old Wives Tales: Life-Stories of African Women*. New York: Schocken, 1970.

Buckley, Gail Lumet. *The Hornes: An American Family*. New York: Knopf, 1986.

Carawan, Guy and Candie. *Ain't You Got a Right to the Tree of Life—The People of Johns Island: Their Faces, Their Words, and Their Songs.* 1966; Atlanta: University of Georgia Press, 1989.

Darden, Norma Jean and Carole Darden. *Spoon Bread and Strawberry Wine: Recipes and Reminiscences of a Family.* New York: Fawcett, 1980.

Gwaltney, John Langston. *Drylongso.* New York: Vintage, 1981.

Morgan, Kathryn L. *Children of Strangers: The Stories of a Black Family.* Philadelphia: Temple University Press, 1980.

Pruett, Jakie L. and Everett B. Cole. *As We Lived: Stories Told by Black Story Tellers.* Burnet, Texas: Eakin Publications, 1982.

Terry, Wallace. *Bloods: An Oral History of the Vietnam War by Black Veterans.* New York: Random House, 1984.

Zeitlin, Steven J., Army J. Kotkin and Holly Cutting Baker. *A Celebration of American Family Folklore: Tales and Traditions from the Smithsonian Collection.* New York: Pantheon, 1982.

Black Preacher as Storyteller

Davis, Gerald L. *I Got the Word in Me and I Can Sing It, You Know: A Study of the Performed African American Sermon.* Philadelphia: University of Pennsylvania Press, 1987.

Johnson, James Weldon. *God's Trombones: Seven Negro Sermons in Verse.* New York: Viking, 1969.

Titon, Jeff T. *Give Me This Mountain: Life, History, and Selected Sermons, Rev. C. L. Franklin.* Champaign, IL: University of Illinois Press, 1989.

African-American Folklore and Humor

Coleman, Larry G., producer. *Funny as a Way of Being Serious* (audio documentary). Washington, D.C.: National Public Radio Satellite Program Development Fund, 1986.

Foxx, Redd and Norma Miller. *The Redd Foxx Encyclopedia of Black Humor.* Pasadena, California: Ward Ritchie Press, 1977.

Spalding, Henry D. *Encyclopedia of Black Folklore and Humor.* Middle Village, New York: Jonathan David Publishers, 1972.

Folk Poetry in the Storytelling Tradition

Abrahams, Roger D. *Deep Down in the Jungle: Negro Narrative Folklore from the Streets of Philadelphia.* Chicago: Aldine, 1970.

Brown, Sterling. *Collected Poems.* Michael Harper, ed. New York: Harper and Row, 1983.

Dunbar, Paul Laurence. *The Complete Poems of Paul Laurence Dunbar.* 1913; New York: Dodd, Mead, 1980.

Henderson, Stephen. *Understanding the New Black Poetry: Black Speech and Black Music as Poetic References* New York: Morrow, 1973.

Keens-Douglas, Paul. *Is Town Say So.* Trinidad: Keensdee Productions, 1981.
———. *Tim Tim.* Trinidad: Keensdee Productions, 1976.

Young Readers—Pre-School

Goss, Linda, and Clay Goss. *The Baby Leopard.* New York: Bantam, 1989. (Pre-School [Ages 3–5])

McDermott, Gerald. *Anansi the Spider: A Tale from the Ashanti.* New York: Holt, 1972.

Young Readers—Folktale Collections

Arkhurst, Joyce Cooper. *The Adventures of Spider.* New York: Scholastic, 1964. (Grades K–4)
———. *More Adventures of Spider.* New York: Scholastic, 1972. (Grades K–4)

Bryan, Ashley. *Beat the Story Drum Pum-Pum.* New York: Atheneum, 1989. (Grades K–4)

Hamilton, Virginia. *The People Could Fly.* New York: Knopf, 1985. (Grades 5–up)

Young Readers—Grades K–12

Lester, Julius. *Black Folktales.* New York: Grove Press, 1970. (Grades 5-up)
———. *The Tales of Uncle Remus: The Adventures of Br'er Rabbit,* Vol. 1 New York: Dial, 1987. (Grades 3–up)
———. *The Knee-High Man and Other Tales.* New York: Dial, 1972. (Grades 2–4)
———. *To Be a Slave.* New York: Dial, 1968. (Grades 7–12)

Woodson, Carter G. *African Myths.* 1948; Washington, D.C.: Associated Publishers, 1964. (Grades 3–4)

Games and Play Songs

Burroughs, Margaret Taylor. *Did You Feed My Cow.* Chicago: Follett, 1969. (Grades 3–5)

Jones, Bessie and Bess Lomax Hawes. *Step It Down Games, Plays, Songs and Stories from the Afro-American Heritage.* New York: Harper and Row, 1972.

Storytellers and Storytelling

Baker, Augusta and Ellin Greene. *Storytelling: Art and Technique.* New York: Bowker, 1977.

Bauer, Caroline. *Handbook For Storytellers.* Chicago: American Library Association, 1977.

Miller, Teresa. *Joining In: An Anthology of Audience Participation Stories and How to Tell Them.* Cambridge, MA: Yellow Moon Press, 1988.

Pellowski, Anne. *The World of Storytelling.* New York: Bowker, 1977.

Schimmel, Nancy. *Just Enough to Make A Story: A Sourcebook for Storytelling.* Berkeley: Sisters Choice Press, 1987.

Smith, Jimmy Neil, ed. *Homespun.* New York: Crown, 1988.

INDEX OF STORIES FOR CHILDREN

AUTHOR AND TITLE INDEX

ABOUT THE EDITORS

LINDA GOSS is one of the leading experts in the field of African-American storytelling. The official storyteller of Philadelphia, she is the founder of "Hola-Cumbaya" and one of the founders of "Patchwork," a storytelling guild in the Delaware Valley, and the co-founder of the "In the Tradition..." National Festival of Black Storytelling. Mrs. Goss has been featured on the cover of *American Visions* and on the *Today* show, as well as in the *New York Times* and in *Essence* magazine. She performs often at the National Association for the Preservation and Perpetuation of Storytelling in Jonesboro, Tennessee. She is co-author with her husband Clay Goss of *Baby Leopard*, and serves as president of the Association of Black Storytellers.

MARIAN E. BARNES, the "Heritage Storyteller," was born in South Carolina and reared in Philadelphia and in Austin, Texas. She has traveled and told stories around the world, most recently in Kenya, France, and Scotland. Ms. Barnes is a past director of "Patchwork," a storytelling guild, and a founding member of Austin's storyteller's guild. She has performed at the National Association for the Preservation and Perpetuation of Storytelling in Jonesboro, Tennessee. Her professional career has spanned many fields including broadcasting, public relations, and higher education. Today, she lectures throughout the country on African and African-American history and is a staff member of the Counseling and Mental Health Center of the University of Texas at Austin.